PENGUIN BOOKS

UMBRIA

Campbell Ross is a Fellow of Trinity College, Dublin, where he
hes English Literature. He writes extensively on eighteenth-century
tish and Irish literature and on the novel. His other publications
lude *Public Virtue, Public Love: The Early Years of the Dublin Lying-in
spital, the Rotunda* and critical editions of Laurence Sterne's *Tristram
ndy* and Henry James's *The Europeans*. He lived in Umbria for a
ar, and now returns there as often as possible.

IAN CAMPBELL ROSS

UMBRIA
A CULTURAL HISTORY

PENGUIN BOOKS

PENGUIN BOOKS

Published by the Penguin Group
Penguin Books Ltd, 27 Wrights Lane, London W8 5TZ, England
Penguin Books USA Inc., 375 Hudson Street, New York, New York 10014, USA
Penguin Books Australia Ltd, Ringwood, Victoria, Australia
Penguin Books Canada Ltd, 10 Alcorn Avenue, Toronto, Ontario, Canada M4V 3B2
Penguin Books (NZ) Ltd, 182–190 Wairau Road, Auckland 10, New Zealand

Penguin Books Ltd, Registered Offices: Harmondsworth, Middlesex, England

First published by Viking 1996
Published in Penguin Books 1996
1 3 5 7 9 10 8 6 4 2

a
Maria Luisa
Anna Laura
e
Daniela Giulia

umbre per adozione

Contents

✳

List of Illustrations

❋

1. Etruscan Arch, or Arch of Augustus, Perugia (3rd c. BC) (*Italian State Tourist Office, E.N.I.T., London*)
2. Etruscan necropolis called the 'Crocifisso del Tufo', Orvieto (6th–3rd c. BC) (*Regione dell'Umbria: Ufficio Promozione Turistica*)
3. Ipogeo dei Volumni, in the Palazzone necropolis, Perugia (2nd–1st c. BC) (*Azienda di Promozione Turistica di Perugia*)
4. Roman theatre, Gubbio (1st c. AD) (*Azienda di Promozione Turistica di Gubbio*)
5. Roman bridge, known as the Bridge of Augustus, on the Via Flaminia, Narni (1st c. BC) (*Regione dell'Umbria: Ufficio Promozione Turistica*)
6. The Springs of Clitumnus, at Campello: a spot sacred in antiquity, described in the 1st c. AD by Pliny and Propertius, where the poet Giosuè Carducci first hailed 'Umbria Verde!' or 'Green Umbria!' (*Azienda di Promozione Turistica di Spoleto*)
7. Church of San Salvatore a Campello, or the Tempietto del Clitunno; perhaps built using materials from Roman temples at the nearby Springs of Clitumnus (4th c.) (*Azienda di Promozione Turistica di Spoleto*)
8. Church of Sant'Angelo, Perugia (5th–6th c.) (*Azienda di Promozione Turistica di Perugia*)
9. Church of San Salvatore, Spoleto (4th–9th c.) (*Azienda di Promozione Turistica di Spoleto; photo Lucarini*)

List of Maps

✳

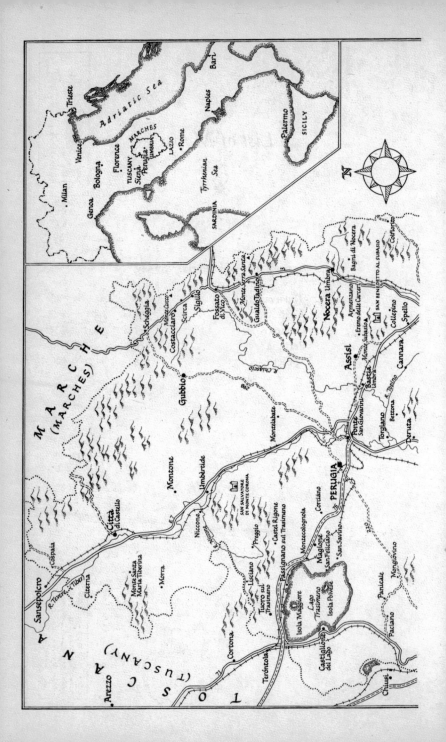

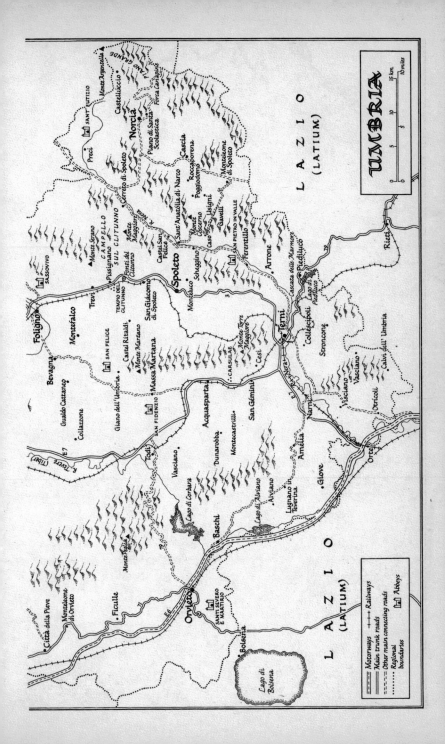

UMBRIA

LAZIO (LATIUM)

| Motorways |
| Main trunk roads |
| Other main connecting roads |
| Railways |
| Regional boundaries |
| Abbeys |

Scale: 0   5   10   15 km.
0   5   10 miles

Città della Pieve
Monteleone di Orvieto
Ficulle
Monte Peglia
Orvieto
SANTI SEVERO E MARTIRIO
Bolsena
Lago di Bolsena
Lago di Corbara
Baschi
Lago di Alviano
Alviano
Lugnano in Teverina
Giove
Amelia
Orte
Otricoli
R. Tevere (Tiber)
Todi
Vasciano
Collazzone
Dunarobba
Montecastrilli
San Gemini
Acquasparta
CARSULI
Vasciano
Orvinio
Calvi dell'Umbria
Otricoli
Stroncone
Collescipoli
Narni
Terni
Cascata delle Marmore
Lago di Piediluco
Piediluco
Rieti
Colfiorito
Gualdo Cattaneo
Bevagna
Foligno
Montefalco
SAN FIDENZIO
Giano dell'Umbria
SAN FELICE
Castel Ritaldi
Massa Martana
Monte Martano
Monte Torre Maggiore
Cesi
San Giacomo di Spoleto
SASSOVIVO
Trevi
Pissignano
TEMPIO DEL CLITUNNO
FONTI DEL CLITUNNO
CAMPELLO SUL CLITUNNO
Monte Serano
Spoleto
Monteluco
Schiggino
Castel San Felice
Monte Maggiore
Monte Coscerno
Sant'Anatòlia di Narco
Eggi
Gavelli
SAN PIETRO IN VALLE
Ferentillo
Arrone
Vallo di Nera
Scheggino
Cerreto di Spoleto
Preci
SANT'EUTIZIO
Castelluccio
PIANO GRANDE
Monte Argentella
Norcia
Piano di Santa Scolastica
Forca Canapine
Cascia
Roccaporena
Poggiodomo
Monteleone di Spoleto
Usigni
PIANO PERDUTO

LAZIO (LATIUM)

Acknowledgements

✳

I wish to thank the following for their assistance in various ways during the writing of this book: Marcello, Daniela and Serena Baffetti, Cav. Danilo Cardinali, Aileen Douglas, Roberto Nini, Virginia Llewellyn Smith, Chiara Sarteanesi, Ian and Janet Small, and Carlo Tirilli; I am particularly grateful to Maria Pia Cozzi Ross who saved me from a number of errors. I was also helped by the staff of the Biblioteca Augusta, Perugia, the Library of Trinity College, Dublin, Father Ruf of the Sacro Convento, Assisi, the Director and staff of the Regione dell'Umbria, and the Aziende di Promozione Turistica di Perugia, del Folignate-Nocera Umbra, di Gubbio, di Spoleto, dell'Orvietano, del Trasimeno, del Tuderte, and dell'Amerino. Among those involved with production, I am especially grateful to Annie Lee for her careful copy-editing, to Penny Daniel, and to Eleo Gordon, who saw the work through from the beginning.

CHAPTER ONE

The Greening of Umbria

✳

Umbria, so many books and more advertisements proclaim, is Italy's Green Heart. Enjoying the view from Perugia's Carducci Gardens the visitor may well agree. All around, the green hills of peninsular Italy's only landlocked region frame a prospect as fine as may easily be seen anywhere – 'the most beautiful garden in all the world', Henry James called it. The hills are green in spring, when freshened by showers, and green in early summer, before the flowering broom turns them yellow. Where, in the distance, they are covered with thick woods of chestnut or turkey-oak, Umbria's hills retain their verdure throughout the summer months. Large areas of the region, indeed, continue green throughout the year, on hills where ilex or Aleppo pine are to be found, or where rows of cypresses watch over the region's scattered farmhouses. Green Umbria is a fertile region and Perugia is surrounded by cultivated hills, its own slopes covered with groves of gnarled olives and rows of leafy vines. In the valleys below, meadows vie for space with fields of wheat or maize, or those splashed, in early summer, with the brilliant yellow of sunflowers. Looking north-west from the heights of Perugia, the eye is caught by the reflected light of Lake Trasimeno, central and southern Italy's largest lake, shimmering under the bright sun. To the south and east, the Tiber snakes around Perugia's hill, as it meanders from the Tuscan mountains to Rome and the Mediterranean. Lake Trasimeno is encircled by hills which, rolling away to the west, rise more steeply to the east. The Tiber, too, flows between green hills, more or less distant, as it traverses the region from north to south-west. From Perugia, the Valle Umbra – the Vale of Umbria – cuts a wide, green swathe from the regional capital down to Spoleto, which lies beneath the green woods of Monteluco. Shortly before Spoleto is reached is found one of the oldest, most sacred sites in Umbria: the Springs of Clitumnus, where pure waters still stream from the rocks to gather in shallow crystal pools beneath poplars and weeping willows. It was here that Green Umbria was born. What is surprising, for such an ancient region, is that it was born so recently – little more than a century ago. It was in the 1870s that Italy's Nobel Prize-winning poet, Giosuè Carducci – from whom Perugia's gardens take their name – first hailed '*Umbria verde!*' or 'Green Umbria!', giving rise to a characterization of the region that has found favour ever since.

It is easy to see the epithet's appeal – and still easier to understand the attraction of one of modern tourism's most successful slogans: '*L'Italia ha un cuore verde: l'Umbria*' – 'Italy has a green heart: Umbria.' The vision it conjures up is at once romantic and vigorous, suggesting both affection and vitality. It also implies that Umbria is as old as Italy itself. And so it is. We do well, however, to remember that Italy – as a political reality, rather than an ideal – goes no further back than 1860. The name 'Umbria' returns us to one of the earliest periods of the peninsula's history and to some of the region's first inhabitants – the Umbri, an Italic people who lived here 1,000 years before the birth of Christ. Umbria, though, took on its modern shape only with Italian unification. In the intervening period it was almost protean in its transformations, and the very name of Umbria itself disappeared from the map for 1,000 years or more. The fact, though, that Umbria is not as old as we had thought, or it appears, should not distress us. The modern region *is* a land marked out by history – an extraordinary history which, as we look backwards, shows us German and French invaders, Grand Tourists of the eighteenth century, Renaissance popes and painters, medieval monks and soldiers of fortune, Longobards, Goths and Vandals, early Christians seeking safety from persecution, Romans, Etruscans and those aboriginal Umbrians who gave this land their name. Umbria is also a region which belies its compact size – it covers less than 3 per cent of the total area of Italy – and a total population of little more than 800,000 people. Indeed, it reveals such cultural and geographical variety as to defy attempts to impose on it a unity it does not possess. Umbria, in fact, is more properly characterized by diversity than uniformity.

Geographically, the celebrated greenness of the Vale of Umbria or the middle Tiber valley, which are at its own heart, gives way at the margins to much more varied landscapes. There, it shares in the characteristics of its neighbours: the pale, rolling hills of Tuscany to the west, the stark, rocky mountains or towering Apennine peaks of the Marches to the east, and the bare, volcanic plateaux of Lazio to the south. Culturally, Umbria reveals the importance of its central position in the Italian peninsula in the influence of all those – hunters, herdsmen, traders, hermits, monks, friars, and soldiers (always soldiers) – who have passed through or who have settled within its borders, helping shape the region we see today. Subject, throughout its entire history, to a bewildering range of influences from all points of the compass, Umbria stands at the crossroads of Italy.

In terms of human history, we need to approach the modern region from the east. The confines of the land the Umbri occupied were very different from Umbria's today, the ancient territory extending from the Adriatic coast as far as the river Tiber, and taking in much of the Marches and parts of Lazio. To the west of the Tiber lay the land occupied by the Etruscans, a people whose advanced culture contributed much to the early history of the region. When the Roman Emperor Augustus (63 BC–AD 14) made an administrative division of his Italian lands he attempted to respect existing ethnic divisions. Umbria was the name given to the Sixth Region, and referred to an area again comprising the territories to the east of the Tiber and extending across the Apennines as far as the Adriatic. That part of modern Umbria lying to the west of the Tiber was incorporated into the Seventh Region, called Etruria, while Norcia and the surrounding countryside became part of Samnium, the Fourth Region. When the Emperor Diocletian (c. 247–313) introduced an administrative reordering of Italy at the end of the third century, the lands of the modern region were again divided. The river Tiber once more formed the boundary. Now, however, Flaminia et Picenum lay to the east, on the Tiber's left bank, while Tuscia et Umbria was to be found to the west, on the right. The name Umbria, in other words, applied to quite different geographical areas in these successive Roman divisions. Nor was it long before the name disappeared entirely, for Tuscia et Umbria became known simply as Tuscia – from which modern Tuscany derives its name. The fall of the Roman Empire in the fifth century, and the successive waves of northern invaders, were to make all such divisions irrelevant. When the Longobards (or Lombards) established the Duchy of Spoleto after 571, the region was divided into two: the Longobard territories to the south and east, and the lands claimed by the popes in Rome – part of 'Peter's Patrimony' – to the north and west.

By this time, the very name Umbria was entirely lost – not just in political or administrative terms but in learned discourse and popular speech. It was not to re-emerge for 1,000 years. Only with the revival of classical learning in the Renaissance did the name reappear – on maps. The long disappearance of the name led, however, to very considerable disagreement among cartographers as to what the region's boundaries actually were. By the sixteenth century, as we shall see, the largely independent city-states of the late Middle Ages had come under the effective control of the papacy and formed part of a Church State. With the continuance of political stability, the pressure for local autonomy weakened and the region's sense of local identity became less sure. Map-makers were now divided as to whether 'Umbria' might describe the old Duchy of Spoleto or whether it should also include Perugia and the surrounding countryside. (On the whole, they opted for the former, so that the Perugino became the preferred geographical term employed to describe the area around Perugia – as numerous prints and maps still testify.) As late as the eighteenth century, major differences of opinion existed. In Vincenzo Coronelli's atlas of 1708, Umbria excludes both the territory around Perugia and the lands around Orvieto.

Just four years later, in 1712, Moroncelli da Fabriano's *Tavola generale . . . dell'Umbria* included both the Perugian and Orvietan territories but left out Città di Castello and Gubbio to the north-east. In the circumstances, it is not altogether surprising that, in the wake of the Congress of Vienna, which established a new geo-political order in Europe, Pope Pius VII, who now ruled much of central Italy, should have been moved to comment, in the bull *Motu proprio* (1816), that the Church State was sadly lacking in any kind of uniformity in its local laws and regulations. It was in the same year of 1816 that Umbria became a province, being divided into two delegations: Perugia and Spoleto.

Only following the unification of Italy in 1860-61, however, was there general agreement as to where the boundaries of the region were. Umbria then became a single province, having Perugia as its capital, reclaiming Gubbio (which, for centuries, had been administratively associated with the Marches) and gaining Rieti to the south. The province continued in this form until 1923, when Rieti was detached and transferred to Lazio. Four years later, the single province of Umbria was divided into two – Perugia and Terni. Today, Umbria is one of Italy's twenty regions, with its regional capital in Perugia; its two provinces remain those of Perugia and Terni.

It should not simply be assumed that the modern regional organization will remain unaltered, however. In the changing political and economic circumstances of modern Italy, two very different proposals have gained currency, either of which would dramatically alter the present situation. The Lega Lombarda (Lombard League), which aspires to virtual autonomy for the prosperous north of Italy, has proposed the splitting of Italy into three macro-regions: the north to be called the Regione Padana, and the south simply Sud, while central Italy would become Etruria. The economically, rather than politically, driven pro-posal of the Fondazione Agnelli argues for the reduction of the number of Italy's regions from the present twenty to just twelve. Under the terms of this proposal, there would be a region called Toscana-Umbria which would, however, include only the province of Perugia, while the second Umbrian province, Terni, would be joined to the region of Lazio, centred on Rome. (A newspaper straw poll, in 1994, suggested this plan to be strongly opposed by those who lived in the province of Perugia, and as strongly welcomed by the inhabitants of Terni.)

Whatever may happen in the future, it is apparent that the appellation 'Green Umbria' had political implications – following so soon on the political unification of Italy in 1860–61, and even sooner after the final removal of Rome from papal control, and its incorporation into the Italian national territory, in 1870. Part of the popularity of the phrase, in fact, derived from its acknowledgement of a distinct regional identity for Umbria, while allowing this identity to contribute to a more all-embracing national identity. Carducci's phrase, though, was soon being used out of context, and even elided with other popular characterizations of the region.

Umbria had long been notable for the number and fame of its saints – St Benedict and St Francis of Assisi are only two of the hundreds Umbria can boast – but by the 1870s, the phrase 'Umbria santa' was being used to imply that the entire region was, in some sense, holy or mystical. Writers sought to trace an essential connection between the land and the people (especially artists) it produced. The artists of the so-called Umbrian school were then considered 'santi pittori', or holy painters, whose art was a response to the landscape in which they worked. The nineteenth-century renewal of scholarly and pious interest in St Francis carried this notion one stage further. The French orientalist Ernest Renan – famous for his La vie de Jésus (1863) – proposed a causal relationship between the saint's life and teaching and the Umbrian countryside in which he spent most of his life. A slightly younger French writer, Paul Sabatier, in an influential biography, La Vie de Saint François d'Assise (1893), went so far as to make the saint and his native region reflections of each other. To know Francis, the most characteristic son of Umbria, Sabatier avowed, it was necessary to live in Umbria. True to this conviction, Sabatier himself settled for many years in Assisi, from where, like the saint, he could see to his left the heights of Monte Subasio and to his right the Vale of Umbria 'with its farms, its villages, its misty hills on whose slopes grow cedars, oaks, vines and olive trees' – a landscape of 'harmonious and wholly human beauty'. Rather as St Francis was considered a second Christ, Umbria was, for Renan and Sabatier, the 'Galilee of Italy'.

So pervasive were these ideas that, by the beginning of the twentieth century, a local politician, Guido Pompili, considered the concept of an Umbria at once 'green and mystical' – '*verde e mistica*' – to be familiar to Italians everywhere. A green and mystical Umbria might be fine for the religiously inclined, but it could not wholly satisfy Pompili – who represented Umbria in parliament between 1886 and 1920 and was anxious to persuade others that modern Umbria was a region of growing industry and improving agriculture, of personal and social transformation. '*Mistica*' was therefore reconceptualized to imply not St Francis's ascetic or contemplative nature but the active spiritual idealism of his evangelical mission. Umbria soon became not only 'green' but '*operosa*' or 'industrious'.

A green, holy and industrious Umbria became a familiar stereotype throughout Italy in the first decades of the twentieth century. Carducci's poem was copied into millions of schoolbooks. Texts specifically designed for school use, such as Carlo Faina's *Umbria verde* (1925), now told their readers that Umbria was to be admired for its glorious past and its infinite beauty. By the 1920s, however, the need to present a particular image of Umbria was no longer dictated by the needs of a new region in a new state but by the requirements of fascist ideology. Since Mussolini's march on Rome in 1922 had actually been planned in Perugia, Umbria might even hope to have a central place in the articulation of a new national identity. While Faina's *Umbria verde* lent itself helpfully to fascism's ruralist ideology, Maurilio Maurizi and Natale Beccafichi quoted Mussolini himself when praising the Umbrians' 'simplicity of spirit and ardour of ideal conquests and, wherever necessary, the virtues of renunciation and sacrifice'. The title of their book – *Umbria cuore d'Italia* (*Umbria: Heart of Italy*; 2nd edn, 1926) – makes the modern tourist slogan all but complete.

For fascist Italy, tourism was not itself the point – though Italy's image abroad, as well as at home, certainly was. Corrado

Ricci, whose *Umbria santa* appeared in 1927 (it was published in English translation in the same year), epitomized the prevailing mood. Ricci asserted that, just as no other nation had done so much for world civilization as Italy, so each region of the country – still united for only just over sixty years – had contributed its particular qualities to the national 'mission'. Umbria's contribution was its holiness – a holiness which Ricci, following the nineteenth century, found in both the region's saints and its painters. Mussolini had taken this line when marking the seven-hundredth anniversary of the death of St Francis – commemorated in 1926 – using the phrase Maurizi and Beccafichi were to cite, in order to praise the saint's Umbrian qualities. For fascist Italy, however, the qualities of Umbria could not be exhausted by sanctity. So writers looked to another period of the region's past, and alighted on the Umbrian *condottieri*, the famous mercenary soldiers of the fifteenth century, such as Braccio Fortebraccio da Montone, Erasmo da Narni, known as Gattamelata, or Niccolò Piccinino. These were men whose military prowess was suited to the Duce's desire for an imperial future to match Italy's much celebrated but very distant past as the centre of the Roman Empire. Umbria now became '*l'Umbria guerriera*' – 'warrior' or 'warlike' Umbria.

Though the notions of a holy, mystical Umbria and a warlike region might seem as much contradictory as complementary, neither Mussolini nor fascism was much perturbed by inconsistency. The ideologues of Umbrian identity could even thrive on it. In 1928 a new monthly journal was founded, under the title *Vita umbra* (*Umbrian Life*), to celebrate the 'glorious and beautiful' region. One propagandizing contributor, the Orvietan aristocrat Maria Luisa Fiumi, entitled one of her essays 'L'Umbria qual è (tra mistici e ribelli)' or 'Umbria as it is (between mystics and rebels)'. The ideal of individual sacrifice lauded by Mussolini could lend itself equally well to saint or warrior, and Fiumi made no secret of the relevance of her view of Umbria's past to its fascist present. It was the fierceness and warlike nature of the Umbrians, she avowed, 'which pushed our young men first into the front line, to make an offering of their spirit and their blood when the fascist formations moved united on the streets of Rome'.

However dubious her motivation, Fiumi was right in one point. No single characterization of Umbria – whether 'holy', 'mystical' or 'warlike' – could (or can) tell the whole story of the region. Umbria continues to thrive, as it always has, on diversity, not uniformity – which is what makes the region so satisfying to explore, both historically and geographically.

As we have already noted, Umbria – despite its compactness – is not a single landscape but many. Throughout the region as a whole there is a notable variation in altitude: from just forty metres above sea level south of Otrícoli, close to Umbria's southern border, to the 2,201 metres of Monte Argentella, in the Sibillini or Sibylline mountains, in the extreme east. Stated so baldly, however, this is a little misleading, for while the plains account for a mere 6 per cent of Umbrian territory, hills make up 43 per cent and mountains – anything above 800 metres – no less than 51 per cent. Today the mountains of Umbria, including the high Apennine peaks above Norcia as well as Monte Cucco (1,566 m.) and Monte Subasio (1,290 m.), are only sparsely populated. Economically they are important, above all, for tourism: four of Umbria's regional parks are in mountain, or high upland, areas – Monte Cucco, Monte Subasio, Valnerina, and Colfiorito (the other two are Trasimeno and the Tiber). These are, at least in part, genuinely wild areas, rich in flora, and home to such animals as wild cats, martens and polecats. Wolves are present in the east – one was even found close to Assisi in 1992, and another above Nocera two years later – while the brown bear has left its stronghold in the Abruzzo and reappeared in the Sibylline mountains. Once, however, as we shall see, Umbria's mountain areas were much more densely settled than they are today, serving as places of refuge for inhabitants of the region anxious to escape the predations of foreign (and native) troops. Though the times when the mountains around Norcia were as prosperous as the hills around Perugia are long past, many isolated villages serve to remind visitors that, for Umbria, the past really was a different country.

The importance of the region's hills as sites of human settlement, now and in the past, is apparent even to the most casual glance. Characteristic hilltop villages, towns, and even cities are to be found everywhere, as they have been since the days of the Etruscans and early Umbrians. The hills were prosperous areas half a millennium or more before the birth of Christ, not only rising above the marshes of the valleys below but ideal locations for the vines and olive trees brought to central Italy by Greek settlers in the seventh and fifth centuries BC respectively. The continuity of cultivation of the olive, for instance, is such that, around Trevi today, there are olive trees believed to be over 1,000 years old. To watch or take part in the still unmechanized olive harvest, which traditionally begins on St Catherine's Day (25 November), is to participate in a rite that has remained essentially unchanged for 2,500 years. These green hills, whether cultivated or wooded, also hold their own fauna and flora: among the animals to be found are wild boar and porcupine, as well as badgers, foxes, red squirrels and hare. Umbria is also a favoured haunt of migrating birds, and hunting retains a popularity here beyond that known in much of modern Italy (with 60,000 shotgun licences issued in a region of just 800,000 inhabitants, Umbria is foremost in density of hunters among the Italian regions).

Understandably, in a region with so little flat land, the valleys have always been much prized. It was a desire to control the southern shores of Lake Trasimeno, suitable for wheat-growing, that persuaded the Etruscans to move eastwards from their stronghold at Chiusi, and which led to the founding of Perugia. Wheat still grows widely throughout Umbria. Today this is mainly common wheat (*Triticum vulgare*), but the wheat the Etruscans planted (spelt, or *Triticum spelta*) is still found – and, as *farro*, is the basis of a popular soup known throughout the region. Other crops have an important role to play, more locally, in the regional economy. Tobacco has long been widely planted in the upper Tiber valley and the valley of the river Niccone, in the north-east; in Italy, tobacco is a state monopoly, and Umbria is the nation's largest supplier of the 'Bright' variety. Today, though, agriculture is able to respond quickly to changing conditions, and a recent European Community subsidy for sunflowers has done nothing to discourage the cultivation of these, wherever they will grow.

The availability of water is, of course, a determining factor for many crops. Water and water courses have assumed a particular importance in shaping the development of Umbria. Now, it is perhaps hard to imagine how much of the region was made up of marsh and swamp until even comparatively recently in human history – and how much effort and ingenuity has been expended over centuries to reclaim land from the waters. It is easy, by contrast, to grasp the significance of rivers and lakes in this landlocked region. For the earliest inhabitants, in Umbria's prehistory, river valleys were used by nomadic populations, constantly on the move. The Umbrians, Etruscans and Romans all knew how crucial rivers and springs were – as the many sacred sites associated with water would indicate. From the time of the Romans to the nineteenth century, rivers played a crucial economic role, at first for transport (the Tiber joining Umbria with Rome itself), and latterly when the waters of the Nera were harnessed to generate the electricity used to power Umbria's own industrial revolution. Similarly, Lake Trasimeno, Italy's fourth largest lake, and the biggest in peninsular Italy, was a valuable and hotly contested resource for fish in the Middle Ages, and today has an economic importance as an attraction for tourists in search of beaches, swimming and water-sports.

Umbria's geology has also encouraged, or forced, it to develop in particular ways. The region is rich in caves, for example, which fostered extremely early habitation. Among the most important caves are those called the Devil's Lair, near Parrano, in the west – where archaeologists have found evidence of human existence dating from as much as 35,000 years ago. The Valcastoriana and Monte Cucco – which has deep limestone caverns a kilometre below ground – were both much favoured in the Middle Ages by hermits, who sought solitude in the many caves they found there. On many occasions, however, Umbria's inhabitants have been dramatically affected by the geology of their region in ways in which they have had no choice. The east of the region, in particular, is noted for continual and sometimes violent seismic activity. In the course of the centuries, towns hit by earthquake have included Città di Castello, Gubbio, Gualdo

Tadino, Spoleto, Cascia, and Norcia (which was badly struck in 1328, 1703, 1730, and 1859); the most serious of recent earth-quakes struck the Valnerina in 1979, and there was another in the north of the region in 1984.

Umbria's diverse geography means that there is also some significant variation in climate. Terni, in the south, has a predict-ably higher mean annual temperature than Perugia, for instance, while Orvieto, in the south-west, registers a distinctly lower annual rainfall than Gubbio, in the mountainous north-east. Spring and early summer, as we have noted, see Umbria at its freshest and most verdant. Then the hillsides are briefly and miraculously covered in wild flowers. In high summer, droughts are common and serious. Water becomes an even more precious resource as wells dry up, just as crops require constant irrigation if they are to survive. The region may turn tinder-dry, when a spark is enough to set it ablaze. When autumn comes, the valleys of Umbria lie shrouded in mist, with only the hills rising spectrally above the sea of vapour below, reminding us of those distant days when most of the region lay beneath the waters of vast lakes. Winters can be harsh. In exceptional years, such as 1767, 1864, and 1960, Lake Trasimeno has frozen over com-pletely for up to two months at a time. In 1956 frosts destroyed as many as 90 per cent of the olive trees in some areas, driving part of the rural population permanently from the land. Snow visits much of the region annually, and is heavy enough in the mountains above Norcia for Umbria's highest settlement, Castel-luccio di Norcia (1,452 m.), to find itself regularly cut off in winter from the rest of the region. Fortunately, snow-ploughs are generally out quickly in the area, for nearby Forca Canapine is a much-frequented ski resort.

Umbria's climate, in fact, still poses problems for those inhabit-ants of the region who continue to work the land. These, it is true, are many fewer in relation even to comparatively recent times, let alone preceding centuries. The 1991 census showed that no more than 9 per cent of the active population is pri-marily engaged in agriculture today, as opposed to 56 per cent as recently as 1951. Nevertheless, even the harshest environment can be made to yield valuable crops. The great upland plain –

the Piano Grande – on which Castelluccio stands, for instance, grows Italy's best lentils. It also continues to provide pasture in summer for cattle, horses and sheep, although the days are now gone when shepherds accompanied their flocks here along the old transhumance routes from the malarial swamps around Rome – a movement of men and animals which endured from prehistory to the early twentieth century.

The patterns of rural settlement have always changed through time, of course. Even the scattered farmhouses, known as *case sparse*, which seem today one of the most characteristic features of a timeless landscape, are mainly sixteenth- or seventeenth-century in origin. These are the houses which formed part of the share-cropping system known in Italy as the *mezzadria*. Once they became established, however, they followed a remarkably stable pattern for hundreds of years. Typically, the Umbrian *mezzadria* included a house, the farmyard, a well, an oven, animal sheds and dovecots. Thousands of farmhouses of this kind survive throughout the region to this day. The house had two storeys: the lower was for animals and storing winter feed, while the farmer and his family lived upstairs. The centre of the house was the kitchen, with its huge open hearth for cooking as well as for heating water and warming the house. A large table in the centre of the kitchen served as a focus for family life. The bedrooms, which opened off the kitchen, were generally five in number. One was for the farmer and his wife, a second for the eldest son and his bride, a third for all the remaining male family members and a fourth for the women. The fifth room was used by the family to store foodstuffs, including cereals, preserved fruit and vegetables, together with cured hams, hung from hooks in the ceiling. It is still easy to find Umbrians throughout the region who were brought up in such farmhouses but it will not be so for very many more years. An unmistakable indication of changing times is provided by the Museo delle Tradizioni Popolari (Folk Museum), founded in 1975, just south of Città di Castello on the road to Perugia. Here, a well-presented display documents a rural existence fast becoming unfamiliar to the large majority of native Umbrians.

For inhabitants of the region, it is a new experience.

Traditionally, the relationship between those who resided in the towns and those who lived in the surrounding countryside was a close one. The cities of the Etruscans, for instance, often included much cultivated land within their city walls. Roman Umbria was a favoured resort of wealthy patricians, who purchased estates where they might pursue the idyllic life they read of in Virgil or Horace. In the Middle Ages, many well-off towns-people were also landowners and the Umbrian cities had a close relationship with the surrounding countryside – the *contado*, or county – which provided them with food. That Umbrians did, for many centuries, remain rooted in strategically placed settlements which served the needs of successive generations means that it is impossible to turn anywhere in the region without finding traces of a long and complex history. The walls the ancient Umbrians built in the sixth century BC still survive in Amelia. So, too, do the walls and the city gates the Etruscans erected in Perugia and the necropolises they built around the rock of Orvieto. The Romans left their mark throughout the region: in the temple at Assisi, the gates and walls of Spello, the baths at Bevagna, the theatre at Gubbio, which is still in use, the much-admired bridge at Narni, or the extensive ruins of the city of Carsulae.

Of course, much was lost, not least to the waves of invaders who came to Umbria from the north. Yet some of these built, too, and around Spoleto – once capital of the great Longobard duchy which bore its name – there are churches which are among the most important of their period anywhere. Today Umbria appears, above all, a medieval landscape, one of the greatest in Europe. In every corner of the region there are towns and villages which retain their medieval walls intact. Within those walls the towns of Umbria reveal varied evidence of the period of their greatest prosperity in the civic palaces of, say, Perugia, Orvieto, Gubbio, or Città di Castello; in the great cathedrals of Spoleto or Orvieto, or in the basilica of St Francis in Assisi; in the huge preaching churches of Assisi, Perugia, or Todi, where Francis's followers brought their founder's message to ordinary men and women. In these and many other buildings we can trace the development of medieval architecture from early Romanesque to the final flowerings of Gothic. As we shall see, the Renaissance marked the beginning of Umbria's long decline, yet the region's towns preserve buildings from that period which may be counted among the finest to be found in central Italy: the sixteenth-century church of the Consolazione at Todi, or the secular masterpiece of the Collegio del Cambio in Perugia. The latter is remarkable principally for the decoration it received at the hands of the artist who took his name from his native region – Il Perugino – but Umbria's towns are full of work which ranks among the finest of the late medieval and early Renaissance periods. The basilica of Assisi – where Cimabue and Giotto, Martini and Lorenzetti worked – is unsurpassed anywhere, and one of the pleasures of Umbria is that so much of the region's art remains in those buildings for which it was designed. Other paintings and statues survive in the many museums which are to be found in virtually every town of any size in the region. Perhaps more than anything, though, Umbria offers the rewarding experience of wandering through the towns and villages of the region – the bustle of Perugia's busy centre or the silent alleys and courtyards of a hundred tiny hamlets. It is virtually impossible to go anywhere without, unbidden, making some discovery, noticing something, that deepens our sense of the link between past and present.

To visit Umbria is, inevitably, to become aware of what is absent as well as of the great wealth of what remains. The architecture and painting of the high Renaissance and Baroque are much less well represented in this region than in Rome, not so far away. (As regards the art and architecture of the Middle Ages, the situation was reversed.) By the mid sixteenth century, the Umbrian cities had lost the independence they had enjoyed for hundreds of years and were ruled by the popes in Rome. Some characteristic features of the Umbrian landscape do date from the sixteenth to eighteenth centuries – the *case sparse*, as we have noted – but for the most part the region was becoming increasingly provincial, in comparison to its former greatness. Certainly, this is how the travellers of the seventeenth, eighteenth, and nineteenth centuries described the region in letters and books. Umbria was not even on the route for most of those from Britain and Ireland who made the Grand Tour – though the opinions of those who did visit the region, such as Fynes Morison, Addison, Boswell, Smollett or Lady Morgan, are lively as well as revealing.

It was not just outsiders who were aware of Umbria's decline, however. Native Umbrians found increasingly few outlets for their talents at home. In the eighteenth century, the Foligno-born architect Giuseppe Piermarini (1734–1808) spent virtually all of his working life outside Umbria, most of it in Lombardy, where he was responsible, for instance, for the La Scala opera house in Milan. Similarly, Francesco Morlacchi (1784–1841), a Perugia-born composer of some twenty-five operas, enjoyed a distinguished career outside the region, principally in Germany, where, having been named Kapellmeister for life at the Saxon court at Dresden, in 1811, he remained for thirty years. The Umbria that men like Piermarini and Morlacchi left behind was sadly reduced, as contemporaries made clear, and would not even begin to revive until some decades after the unification of Italy. Then, it was improved communications by road and rail, together with the rapid development of heavy industry around Terni, that brought about the transformation. Although that industry is now largely gone once more, Terni led the way – and other cities soon followed its lead, developing important industries of their own. An engaging view of how industrial Terni appeared to the first generation to experience it is to be found in the naïf art of the shoemaker Orneore Metelli (1872–1938), whose paintings hang in the city's art gallery. Like other industrial areas of Umbria, including Foligno and Perugia, Terni was heavily bombed in the Second World War. The whole region was fought over – as had happened so many times in earlier centuries – in June and July of 1944, as the Allies pushed the retreating German army back up the Italian peninsula. The loss of medieval Terni, in particular, was a heavy blow but post-war reconstruction was – in the longer view – just one more stage in the process of building and rebuilding which has marked Umbria for thousands of years. What most impresses today's visitor, perhaps, is how well Umbrians have conserved their past, while facilitating the different needs of the present. This was true, to an extent, even at the end of the nineteenth century. In 1888, Orvieto built a water-powered funicular railway to give access to the city on its remarkable site on a vast outcrop of rock; the same railway, now powered by electricity, survives today. Outstanding among more modern examples of imaginative urban planning are the escalators which give Perugians access to the ancient centre of their city from the more recent developments below; these rise steeply up to reach an eerie underground cityscape 500 years old – the houses, towers, streets and alleyways of fifteenth-century Perugia, used as foundations for the great papal fortress built in the 1540s.

If this is a particularly dramatic example of the Italian flair for design, then other, more modest, examples are on the increase. In place of the often quaintly old-fashioned art galleries (only rarely to be seen in the region now) are some excellent examples of modern museum displays. The deconsecrated church of San Francesco in Montefalco was reopened as a museum in 1990, and Spello's new museum was inaugurated in 1994; most striking of all is the superb, and splendidly annotated, display of art treasures in the National Gallery of Umbria, opened in Perugia's Gothic Palazzo dei Priori in 1994, after years of renovation work. In art, as in other things, Umbria does not devote itself entirely to its past, no matter how rich. Today there are three museums in the region which offer glimpses of the best of twentieth-century art. Spoleto has a small collection, featuring pieces by its own internationally renowned artist Leoncillo, while Città di Castello has two quite magnificent collections by Alberto Burri, who was born there. An even more recent creation is the Flash Art museum in the small hill-town of Trevi, which seems set to give Umbrians a sense of the international avant-garde.

Increasingly, Umbria is also aware of the needs of national and international tourism – it can now attract 2 million visitors a year. In addition to its artistic heritage, the region has increasingly important facilities for everything from bathing to windsurfing and horse-riding to hang-gliding – often in surroundings of outstanding natural beauty. The summer months, in particular, are packed with festivals and local feast-days which range from the genuinely old and traditional to remarkably successful innovations. Oldest of all is the feast of St Ubaldo in Gubbio. This extraordinary race involves three teams, each carrying one of the massive, wooden *ceri* or candles around the city's winding streets and up the steep mountainside to the saint's sanctuary. The origins of the festival have been much discussed but never entirely satisfactorily explained, though they may well be pagan. Not all of the 'medieval' festivals, or costume pageants, in which Umbria now abounds are genuinely old (a cynic might think that '*tradizionale*' means anything that happened last year too). Even some of the better-known pageants (which at least have some real connection with the past) have been refounded very recently. Foligno's Giostra della Quintana was revived only in 1946, and Assisi's May Day celebrations, the Calendimaggio, which hark back even to pagan times, took on their present form only in 1974.

It would be a mistake, though, to conclude that virtually all traditions in Umbria are of recent origin, or that they are laid on primarily for tourists. The visitor fortunate enough to be able to travel through Umbria at times other than the peak summer months will find genuinely ancient, and deeply felt, celebrations. Christmas and Easter are particularly rich in such events, however much these may be constantly adapted with the passing of time. The tradition of the crib, for instance – instituted by St Francis himself at Christmas in 1223 – is genuinely popular. Today there are cribs in churches, public buildings, and private homes everywhere throughout the region. They may be centuries-old works of art (like the tiny crib in Perugia's Oratory of San Bernardino) or newly made by local children; they may be private acts of devotion or part of the big show held in Spoleto each year. They may even be moving cribs, celebrated enough – like those of Petrignano or Armenzano – to draw thousands of visitors each year. Today, Christmas does not only mean cribs, however, and Gubbio now boasts what it claims to be the largest Christmas tree in the world. This is the tree outlined on Monte Ingino, above the town, which consists of fifteen kilometres of cable, 700 lights, and a fifty-metre-long star; it is visible for miles around.

Easter, understandably, has more muted commemorations during Holy Week. Some involve elaborate stagings of passion plays, others the singing of chants that have been handed down by oral tradition for centuries. The processions held in Cascia and Gubbio go back to the fourteenth century. In Assisi, a procession of hooded, barefoot penitents wends its way through a city lit only by the flames of torches. The most moving events, though, are perhaps the much less well-known Good Friday processions held in virtually all the region's villages. Then, the entire local population, often preceded by the local band playing a funeral march, walks behind a statue of the dead Christ to the local cemetery, where flowers are deposited on family tombs, before the statue is taken back in procession to the local church. On Easter Sunday, by contrast, appropriately joyful processions take place before morning mass.

Such festivals are not entirely religious. On Easter Monday in Città della Pieve, the town fountains run with wine. Food, in fact, is always associated with feast-days in Umbria. For the summer visitor, the many *sagre* now held throughout the region offer splendid opportunities to sample dishes from the regional cuisine which are not always easy to find in restaurants. Even tiny villages now hold such celebrations – usually in midsummer under the night sky – and while they may not be especially 'traditional', they are good-natured celebrations in which local people and visitors mingle easily. The dishes on offer draw on local resources, and the speciality of one place may be unknown elsewhere in the region. Montepetriolo, for instance, offers *bruschetta* with truffles, Carbonesca has polenta and sausage, Colfiorito a *ciambella* of red potatoes, and Sant'Arcangelo lake fish.

At the other extreme from these homely celebrations are Umbria's big international festivals. Perugia led the way with its Sagra Musicale Umbra, which celebrated its fiftieth anniversary in 1995. The festival, held in September, features classical orchestral and chamber concerts, as well as opera, all with international artists. Even better known is Umbria Jazz, a festival which began in Perugia in 1973 and which has featured most of the leading players in jazz from Lionel Hampton to Miles Davis, Count

Basie to Carla Bley and Us3. Many of these concerts are free and are held in Perugia's historic heart, most notably in the Piazza IV Novembre, where artists perform between the cathedral, the Palazzo dei Priori and the city's great medieval fountain. For sheer cultural diversity, it is hard to beat the sight of a New Orleans marching band making its way up Perugia's medieval Corso Vannucci. So successful has this particular venture been that many other cities in the region now host one or more of the concerts each summer, while Orvieto has initiated Umbria Winter Jazz, where some of the world's best musicians play to packed-out houses over the New Year period. Of all Umbria's music festivals, the best known internationally is the Festival dei Due Mondi (or Two Worlds Festival), which the Italo-American composer Giancarlo Menotti started in 1958; at something close to international prices, the festival offers a range of opera and concerts of classical music. Other festivals are remarkably good value. Città di Castello's Festival delle Nazioni, which makes a feature of music and artists from a different country each year, began by specializing in chamber music but now offers important choral concerts – often of unusual repertoire – and, since 1994, opera. Some of the larger concerts here are held in the open air, in the splendid gardens of one of the city's Renaissance palaces. Neither are the festivals confined to classical music or jazz, nor to the larger cities. Rock gets a look in too, with Rockin' Umbria – a more modest venture, based on the small town of Umbèrtide – but not without its top-line names.

In fact, it would be hard nowadays to stay anywhere in Umbria in midsummer without finding some festival being celebrated near by. The region knows the value of tourism to its economy. Such festivals, however, represent only a very small part of what Umbria offers the visitor today, and no one could visit the region without a sense of how much – of past and present, landscape, architecture, or art – there is to see in a remarkably compressed space. What visitors see, though, is always determined by what they expect to find. In the mid nineteenth century the first modern tourists came, like Henry James, Baedecker or Murray in hand, to discover the Gothic world classically-minded travellers of the eighteenth century had glanced at, and turned from in disgust. If religiously inclined, they came to discover the worlds of St Francis and of sacred art – the 'Umbria, the true Italia Mystica' Edward Hutton described in his *The Cities of Umbria* (1905). When of a more aesthetic bent, travellers sought out a landscape which they already knew from Renaissance art – and which Walter Pater brilliantly evoked in his essay 'Raphael' (1892), where he speaks of the 'dreamiest Apennine scenery' of Perugia, 'the richly-planted lowlands, the sensitive mountain lines in flight one beyond the other into clear distance, the cool yet glowing atmosphere, the romantic morsels of architecture, which lend to the entire scene I know not what expression of reposeful antiquity'. Pater, however, added parenthetically, but crucially, '(one hardly knows whether one is thinking of Italian nature or Raphael's art in recounting [it]).' More recent travellers have continued to evoke the past, such as the English novelist Lisa St Aubin de Terán, in *A Valley in Italy* (1994), or confronted Umbria's changing present, as when the Irish poet Macdara Woods ponders on the significance of Perugia's 'The Paradise Sexy Shop', in *Blood-Red Flowers* (1994). If Umbria provokes such diverse responses, it is because it includes both the old and the new.

The Umbria which begins by astounding visitors with the diversity of its cultural heritage, however, can easily end up bemusing them. Umbria's richness derives from a history which is at once fascinating and complex. The landscape itself is a product not only of nature – of geological and climatic properties – but also of thousands of years of human action. Anyone who remains long in Umbria, however, will certainly wish to know more of how the region came to be the way it is. This book is intended for those standing at the crossroads, not quite certain which way to turn. The directions it attempts to offer should enable readers better to plan the later stages of their exploration unaided, restricted only by the limits of their energy and curiosity.

CHAPTER TWO

Umbrians and Etruscans

✳

Umbria once looked very different from the rugged blend of mountains, hills and valleys we see today. In prehistoric times, vast expanses of the land lay beneath the waters of lakes, rivers and marshes. The huge Lago Tiberino or Tiber Lake – 120 kilometres long by thirty kilometres wide – covered much of the present region, stretching from Umbria's modern border with Tuscany in the north, via Todi, as far as Terni and Monte Ferentillo in the south. A second arm of the lake filled the valley between Perugia and Spoleto, while a third reached from Perugia, along the valley of the river Nestore, as far as Città della Pieve. Eventually, the Tiber Lake filled with alluvial sediment and slowly fragmented, giving rise to the present plains. Once, the shores of this vast lake were covered with forests of huge sequoias. In the course of quarrying in the 1980s, some of these remarkably re-emerged from the mud which had preserved them for millions of years and now constitute the so-called fossil forest at Dunarobba, near Todi. The Lago Tiberino was not the only lake in the region. A second covered a substantial area in the north-east, between Gubbio and Gualdo Tadino, while a third occupied the large plain south of Norcia, now known as the Piano di Santa Scolastica. Around a million years ago, the area in the north of Umbria which includes the modern Lake Trasimeno was part of a large basin occupying the entire Chiana valley. (Confusingly, the present Lake Trasimeno is not strictly related to the earlier Trasimene lake, which dried up – today's lake being formed subsequently by rainfall unable to escape due to an absence of natural outlets.)

The earliest traces of human existence in Umbria date from the remotest times, and it was still a watery landscape, abundant in both vegetation and animal life, that was known to *Homo erectus*, among the earliest ancestors of modern man and the first inhabitant of the region. In 1955, in a cave-dwelling on Monte Peglia, in the mountains north-east of Orvieto, archaeologists uncovered evidence of early Stone Age culture – more precisely, the Pebble culture of the Lower Palaeolithic age. The find, which included both a primitive limestone tool and the remains of deer, porcupine and sabre-toothed tiger, suggests how skilful these early hunters were, notwithstanding their still-embryonic technology. Where these first inhabitants of the region came from is not certain, but the discovery of chopping tools on Monte Peglia suggests a southern Italian, or even African, origin – perhaps from the period when the Italian peninsula was still joined both to Sicily and to the African land-mass. Other archaeological finds made in Umbria indicate, however, that from a very early date the region was subject to a mix of different cultural influences. Tools from a slightly later period – found close to Perugia, in the Tiber and Chiascio valleys, around Lake Trasimeno, and in the mountains around Norcia – were carried by nomadic peoples from the north. They may have been brought into the Italian peninsula over the Alps or along the western or eastern coastal routes, from south-eastern France or the Balkans.

Among the most important discoveries – now on display in the Archaeological Museum of Perugia – are those from Abeto, to the north-west of Norcia. These include more advanced tools, from the Mousterian culture of the Middle Palaeolithic (between 70,000 and 30,000 years BC). This was the period which saw the appearance in Europe of Neanderthal people, the first to practise magic and ritual cannibalism, and the first to bury their dead. With the passage to the Upper Palaeolithic, *Homo sapiens sapiens* appeared and humans acquired their modern physical appearance. Remains of the still more developed tools from this period have been uncovered in various parts of the region, including the Chiascio and Tiber valleys, the Norcia plateau, and in the vicinity of Perugia. The Tane del Diavolo, or

Devil's Lair – a series of caves close to Parrano, north of Orvieto – yielded up an especially important cache, including bifacial tools, incisors, and scrapers. A particularly notable discovery was made at Castiglione del Lago: a tiny soapstone statue, just over three and a half centimetres high, known as the Venus of Lake Trasimeno. Now in the Archaeological Museum in Florence, this figure of a naked female, with pronounced sexual characteristics, dates from around 30,000 BC and is of a kind which has been discovered over a remarkably wide area, including France, Germany, and Siberia.

Little evidence has so far emerged of the culture of the Mesolithic period, which began after the last ice age – around 8300 BC. However, discoveries from the Lower Neolithic have included tools of stone and bone, as well as fragments of pottery, found in the tunnels of the Pozzi della Piana, near Titignano, between Orvieto and Todi. A find from a slightly later period, made at Norcia, was especially significant, since it indicated cultural penetration from outside the region. Here, pottery fragments showed distinct similarities to the characteristically shaped and decorated ceramic ware identified with Lagozza culture, suggesting that by 2500 BC, the first contacts had been made between Umbria and Piceno to the east, across the barrier of the Apennine mountains.

If the people living in the region had contacts with others elsewhere, however, they were also beginning slowly to develop a degree of more local identity. A major discovery was made at Poggio Aquilone near Marsciano, at the end of the last century: a ditch tomb (*tomba a fossa*) from a period between 2400 and 1800 BC. The tomb is related to Rinaldone culture, characteristic of that part of central Italy which lies between the rivers Arno and Tiber. The inhabitants of the region at this time were pastoral nomads, constantly on the move as they took their flocks from one pasture to another. They came mainly from the east, and brought with them elements of Indo-European culture. Already skilled workers in stone, they soon began looking to the emergent metal cultures growing up in the coastal regions of the Italian peninsula. From the numbers of weapons found in their burial places, it seems as though they organized themselves not only in self-defence but also aggressively. Certainly there is evidence that farmers from the plains were forced to leave their settlements close by rivers and lakes, in order to take refuge on more easily defended hilltops. It was a move which set a precedent for a great deal of Umbria's subsequent development.

Despite the move towards a shared identity, the inhabitants of the region in the late Stone Age still exhibited the cultural diversity of those peoples, from the areas of the Danube and the Balkans, who would go to form the basis of Indo-European linguistic stock throughout Mediterranean Europe. This population spread over a large area of central Italy, travelling along river valleys and even making use of the easier passes across the Apennines in order to trade. During the Bronze Age (1600–1000 BC), settlements flourished in mountainous areas as well as in the valleys and foothills of the Apennines. One of the most significant discoveries from the end of the Bronze Age, made near Gualdo Tadino, is now in the Archaeological Museum in Perugia. The find contains tools (knives and chisels) and jewellery (clasps, pins and bracelets) as well as two very fine discs, covered in gold leaf and decorated with geometric designs, which have been dated to the thirteenth to eleventh centuries BC. Along with finds made at Titignano, Parrano and Terni, the Gualdo Tadino discoveries give evidence of a shared Apennine and late Bronze Age culture moving slowly through the region from north to south.

A thousand years before the birth of Christ, Umbria was being shaped by a range of diverse cultural influences from different points of the compass. An extensive necropolis unearthed near Monteleone di Spoleto in 1907 revealed cylindrical pits (*tombe a pozzetto*) containing terracotta cinerary urns. These urns were decorated in a style used in the same period in the Marches, to the east – while serpentine clasps, also uncovered on the site, resembled those found in tombs in Lazio, to the south. There is also evidence that the region's inhabitants were exchanging a nomadic life for a more settled existence. The important hoard of knives, chisels, axes, spearheads and fibulae discovered in the mid nineteenth century at Piediluco, east of Terni, dates from the early Bronze Age but was deposited only in the eighth century. The Piediluco hoard also includes elements which, while related to those of neighbouring regions, are sufficiently distinct to attest to the gradual emergence of an embryonic cultural, and even ethnic, identity.

It was in the early Iron Age, between the ninth and eighth centuries BC, that a new and truly distinctive culture began to emerge in central and northern Italy. Villanovan culture – named for a necropolis unearthed at Villanova, near Bologna, in 1853 – was diffused throughout parts of Romagna to the north, in Campania to the south, and in the Marches to the east. More importantly, it was also characteristic of an area, bounded by the Arno and Tiber rivers and extending to the Mediterranean, which includes part of modern Umbria. The Villanovans were farmers who lived in small villages, in huts made of reeds or wood. As no evidence has been found of defensive structures around their settlements, it seems likely that the Villanovans were a pacific people who, in turn, did not feel themselves threatened by their neighbours. Among the principal distinguishing characteristics of the Villanovans was their practice of cremating their dead. They placed the ashes in hut-urns – whose characteristic shape enables us to visualize what Villanovan settlements actually looked like. The Villanovans also characteristically used grey impasto biconical urns, decorated with geometrical motifs and covered by a shallow bowl or helmet. These urns were placed in *tombe a pozzetto*, dug in the earth or rock. Gradually, the *tombe a pozzetto* – each containing the relics of just one individual – were superseded by trench tombs (*tombe a fossa*), sometimes lined with stone (*tombe a cassone*). Trench tombs were almost always used for burial – that is, inhumation – but it was cremation which became a distinguishing mark of Villanovan civilization. The Villanovans also placed personal items in the graves, to assist the dead in their future lives. From the mid eighth century BC onwards, the objects deposited were often many in number and high in quality: weapons, jewellery, ceramic and metal ware, all decorated with either geometric or figurative designs. Some examples of Villanovan earthenware, found in the vicinity of Perugia and datable to the eighth century BC, are displayed in the city's Archaeological Museum.

Towards the close of the eighth century, Villanovan culture received a fresh impetus for further development. Greek colonizers arrived by sea from further south, from Sicily, Magna Graecia and Campania, in search of metals. These – especially copper, iron and tin – they found in abundance, both on the island of Elba and in the hills close to the sea. Though the colonists came initially to take from the Villanovans, they also gave much in return. It was from the Greeks that the Villanovans acquired new skills in metal-working and pottery, a taste for previously unknown luxury items, and the art of writing – a combination which led to the development of one of the most important of all early European civilizations – the Etruscan.

From its starting points in those areas in the south and along the coast most open to outside influence, Etruscan culture gradually developed throughout all of that part of western central Italy formerly inhabited by the Villanovans. The northern border was marked by the river Arno, while the southern border was formed by the river Tiber. To the west, the boundary was that part of the Mediterranean known as the Tyrrhenian Sea. Between Volterrae (modern Volterra) in the north and Caere and Veii in the south, the principal cities of western Etruria were Tarquinia, Vulci, Rusellae, Vetulonia and Populonia.

The eastern boundary of Etruria is less easily fixed, since the development of Etruscan territory was gradual and uneven. Around the sixth century, however, the Etruscans moved eastwards from their original territories in modern Lazio and Tuscany to occupy the area of modern Umbria west of the Tiber. In the process, they founded two new major centres of Etruscan culture: Perugia and Volsinii Veteres (now usually identified with Orvieto).

Since the development of Etruscan civilization was gradual and uneven, it is not possible to say, precisely, when it supplanted Villanovan culture – although the late eighth century was probably the decisive period. Besides the influence of the Greeks, Etruria also reveals the influence of other Mediterranean and Near Eastern cultures, such as those of the Phoenicians and the Carthaginians, who traded throughout the Mediterranean. Over the course of 200 years or so these influences were gradually assimilated, within historically flexible boundaries, into a distinctive culture. For all its points of contact with other contemporary cultures, Etruscan civilization would retain its distinctiveness for 500 years – in social organization and art, as well as in its use of a non-Indo-European language.

It was around the beginning of the seventh century that the acquisition of new skills, especially in metal-working, from the Greeks led to the most important social development in Etruria – the formation of an aristocracy founded on the control of trade. During the course of this and the following century, an important middle class of local craftsmen trained by master craftsmen from Greece and the Near East came into being. Etruscan society was completed by servants and an underclass of slaves, without political or civil rights. From the seventh century onwards, the Etruscan aristocracy modelled itself in important respects – including new methods of banqueting, the use of wine, and the symposium – on Greek culture. The wealth of this aristocracy is most obviously indicated today by the great number of large and richly decorated tombs that have been excavated and may now be visited. These are built underground and entered through a sloping corridor, or *dromos*. The tombs of the rich were also filled with funeral objects, often of great value and variety: jewellery and vessels in precious metals (gold, silver and bronze), together with pottery, mostly of local manufacture but sometimes imported from Greece or Asia.

At the end of the seventh century, Etruscan culture still revealed much local variation. Broadly speaking, Etruria was united by the Etruscan language spoken by its inhabitants, though in border areas other tongues were spoken and frontier towns were apparently bilingual. Unlike the languages spoken by the surrounding peoples, Etruscan is not an Indo-European tongue – posing particular problems for its decipherment – although it has been speculated that it is the relic of a language once spoken throughout the entire Mediterranean area. The Etruscan alphabet at least is well understood, being the same as that of the Greek alphabet from Cumae, brought to Etruria by Greek colonizers. It was subsequently diffused by the Etruscans throughout the surrounding regions and even, via the Alpine passes, to northern Europe, where it influenced the runic alphabet – the *futhark* – which survived in parts of northern Europe as late as the eighteenth century. Though neither the grammar nor the syntax of Etruscan is fully understood, modern scholars share some measure of agreement about how the language sounded and there is general agreement about the content of the Etruscan inscriptions that have survived. Unlike the Greeks, the Etruscans had no imaginative literature and the majority of surviving texts are funerary inscriptions, imposing considerable restrictions on vocabulary. In addition, the 10,000 or so known inscriptions are generally very short. The longest – a religious text found, bizarrely, on strips of linen wrapped around an Egyptian mummy which ended up in Zagreb – contains about 1,200 words, but this is exceptional. Exceptional too is the *cippus* from the second century BC found near Perugia and now in the Archaeological Museum there; the *cippus* is an inscribed boundary stone, recording an agreement between the Velthina and Afuna families after a territorial dispute.

Writing soon came to be associated with the powerful priestly caste of Etruscan society. Skilled in divination – the examination of animal entrails, and the interpretation of the flight of birds as indications of the will of the gods – the priests established writing schools for scribes close to religious sanctuaries. Accordingly, while surviving Etruscan votive offerings include those depicting the liver of animals, so other tablets are engraved with the alphabet. One complete example of the Etruscan alphabet followed by '*abat*' – believed to be the Etruscan abbreviation for 'alphabet' – engraved on the base of an impasto vase was discovered in Perugia, and is now displayed in the city's Archaeological Museum. The control of writing by the priesthood meant that much of the surviving Etruscan literature concerns religious matters but, as can be seen from such surviving inscriptions as that on the Perugia *cippus*, the magistrature also made use of writing for legal and civic affairs.

As the population of Etruria began to increase, the original village settlements of the area expanded and grouped together to form the rudiments of cities or city-states on the Greek model, each centre controlling an area of surrounding land. The earliest of these cities – Tarquinia, Veii, Vulci and Caere in modern Lazio, and Vetulonia and Populonia in Tuscany – were the first real urban developments in Italy. Their sites were determined by two principal factors: proximity to the metal and mineral wealth which had originally attracted outside interest in the region, and easy access to the sea, to facilitate maritime trade. As the Etruscans pushed eastwards into Umbrian territory, however, these requirements changed. The most famous city in northern Etruria, Chamars – the modern Chiusi – lay right on the modern border between Tuscany and Umbria, close to the metal-bearing hills of mounts Cetona and Amiata, but differed from earlier Etruscan cities in basing its wealth not primarily in minerals but in agriculture.

Dominating the valley of the river Chiana, a tributary of the Tiber, Chamars developed from small villages originally inhabited by the Italic-speaking people known as Umbri. Umbrians continued to form part of Chamars's population even once the Etruscans were firmly established and, as with other frontier areas, the city was bilingual. As it began to develop around the end of the seventh century BC, Chamars destroyed a number of hilltop villages in its vicinity. Having once consolidated its position, however, the city-state began to colonize the surrounding area, founding satellite settlements to the north, south and east – among them Arezzo and Cortona, in modern Tuscany, as well as the Umbrian city of Perugia. In his *Natural History*, the Roman historian Pliny claimed that, in taking over from the Umbrians the area between Lake Trasimeno and the upper Tiber valley, the Etruscans seized no fewer than 300 towns – although, even if the number may be trusted, these 'towns' must be understood as small hilltop developments of a kind to be found in the area to this day.

According to later Roman sources, such as Cato the Elder and Servius, Perugia had previously been an Umbrian settlement, but although recent archaeological discoveries have confirmed the existence of Villanovan settlements on the site of Perugia at the earliest phase of Etruscan development, these small villages only came together to form a city under the influence of Chamars in the mid sixth century BC. The fact that the inhabitants of the surrounding area were Umbrians meant that even when the villages merged, Perugia showed a distinct ethnic mix. If the hilltop site of Perugia overlooking the Tiber valley thus moved decisively from Umbrian to Etruscan control, contact between the developing city and the neighbouring Umbrians was extensive, and Perugia maintained important contacts both with nearby Bettona and with the more distant Todi, Umbrian frontier towns on the east bank of the Tiber.

To make up for its late development, Perugia devised for itself an impressive account of its (allegedly) early foundation by the Trojan Aulestes. Ocnus, a brother or son of Aulestes, was then given credit for crossing the Apennines and founding Felsina (the modern Bologna). Despite this apparent attempt to deny the role of Chamars in encouraging its development, Perugia remained dependent for some time on Chamars – as is seen by the fact that it continued to import goods, such as the black ceramics known as *bucchero* and the impressive sarcophagus discovered in the Sperandìo necropolis outside Perugia and now in the Archaeological Museum there. Elaborately embellished with a relief depicting warriors returning from a raid with prisoners and spoils, and with banqueting scenes, the sarcophagus is far in advance of any local production of the same period and bears witness to a cultural dependency on Chamars which continued into the fifth century BC.

When it eventually broke free from the political control of Chamars, some time in the fourth century BC, Perugia began to develop into one of the richest and most powerful of all Etruscan cities. As the cities of southern Etruria began to decline, Perugia became a member (and even, by some accounts, leader) of the Dodecapolis – the Etruscan League of twelve cities dedicated to mutual support and defence. Since modern scholars tend to doubt the very existence of this league – given the uneven development of urban centres throughout Etruria, it is difficult to find twelve contemporaneously important cities in the region – we need not pay too much attention to the details of this claim to Perugian pre-eminence, but there is no doubt that the city flourished for a period of several centuries.

Today, the most obvious evidence of Etruscan Perugia's

power and prosperity is provided by the long stretches of the city walls which still survive and help give shape to the modern city. Using enormous blocks of travertine, the walls were erected without defensive towers – a partial exception being made for the main city gate, the Porta Augusta, which is flanked by two huge, tapered bastions. For 1,800 years these walls survived intact – before the changing needs of the medieval city led to their being enlarged around the beginning of the fourteenth century. A number of Etruscan city gates also survive. Of these, the magnificent Porta Augusta is certainly the most impressive. Once a symbol of Perugia's military might, and now virtually a symbol of the city itself, the gate attracted the attentions of successive generations. In the first century BC, the Roman Emperor Augustus had the legend '*Augusta Perusia*' inscribed on the original Etruscan arch. A second arch, above the first, was also erected by the Romans, and a further inscription, '*Colonia Vibia*', was added by the Emperor Gaius Vibius Trebonianus Gallus (AD 251–3), a native of the city. The second gate of Etruscan Perugia was the Porta Marzia, on the road to Volsinii and Rome. Only part of the original structure remains today, for the building of a massive fortress, the Rocca Paolina, in the sixteenth century came close to obliterating the gateway altogether. Fortunately the architect, Antonio da Sangallo the Younger, moved the gate, stone by stone, a distance of four metres, incorporating it in the outer wall of the new citadel, where it is still to be seen. Over the arch itself runs a balustrade, with a figure believed to represent Jove, flanked by Castor and Pollux and their horses. The two inscriptions repeat those on the Porta Augusta. Between these two principal gates the main artery of the Etruscan city ran along a north–south axis virtually identical with that of the principal thoroughfare of the modern city, the Corso Vannucci. Two further gates – the Porta San Luca and the Arco dei Gigli – mark the western and eastern extremities of another major road crossing the city. These two principal arteries of the city crossed in the vicinity of the present cathedral, and it was this area that formed the heart of the Etruscan city, with the forum and its associated public buildings. The acropolis – with its temple, raised on a podium and richly ornamented with terracotta figures – probably lay slightly above the forum, close to the area now occupied by Piazza Piccinino. Close by, another important monument from the Etruscan period may still be visited. This is an enormous well which dates from the fourth or third century BC and gives evidence of the Etruscans' well-known skills as hydraulic engineers. Built of regular travertine blocks, the well is over thirty-five metres deep, tapering from over five and a half metres in diameter at the highest point to just over three metres at the base. Supplied by underground sources, it doubled as a cistern for the city. Although the well now lies some four and a half metres below ground, its rim was originally at street level.

Etruscan Perugia was an impressive city, with a population of perhaps 40-50,000 inhabitants. Its late development, compared to other leading Etruscan centres, seems, however, to have militated against major artistic development in the area. The discoveries made in the Perugian necropolises reveal that the finest goods continued to be imported rather than manufactured locally: *bucchero* ware from Chamars and red-figure vases from Volterra, together with ceramics imported from Campania and even Greece.

The ability to import top-quality goods from elsewhere is, of course, a clear indication of Perugia's wealth, even at a relatively early date. This wealth – like that of Chamars – was based largely on agriculture, for the city proper was surrounded by numerous small farming communities and controlled the fertile valley of the upper Tiber. Agriculture itself was becoming increasingly diversified, and while the valleys continued to produce cereals, the surrounding hills began to be covered by vines and olive trees imported from Greece – giving the Umbrian countryside, even at this early date, something of its modern appearance.

The period of Etruscan Perugia's greatest prestige and prosperity stretched from the fourth to second centuries BC, as the necropolises from this period discovered in the area testify. Burial sites, in fact, provide much information about the Etruscans – both because their literature is so restricted in scope, and because elaborate funeral rites were an important part of Etruscan culture. For the aristocracy, at least, those rites involved not only lamentation but also feasting, games, and music – as we can see from wall-paintings in tombs around Chiusi and Orvieto. Perugia itself is ringed by burial sites which lie, in the characteristic Etruscan manner, outside the city walls, along the main roads leading from the city, their location marked by an engraved stone or *cippus*. The prominence of aristocratic tombs indicates how leading Etruscan families reaffirmed their power, and the importance of their ancestors, even in death. While Etruscan society was patriarchal, with emphasis placed on the central importance of the founder of the extended family, the tombs also reveal that Etruscan women had greater rights than those accorded Greek women. Banqueting scenes show husbands and wives feasting together in an apparently equal manner. This egalitarianism extended to burials and also to sculpted urn covers, which depict both men and women, in some cases showing husbands and wives lying together atop a single urn. Wall-paintings also show Etruscan women's elaborately braided hairstyles and rich jewellery, and tombs throughout Etruria – including those around Perugia – have revealed many items belonging to women alongside objects used by men or symbolic of male power.

Even if they can boast neither the extraordinary wall-paintings of the kind found in the necropolis outside Tarquinia, nor the profusion of highly embellished urns characteristic of Volterra – both among the finest achievements of Etruscan art – the necropolises of Perugia and the surrounding countryside contain tombs of great architectural importance, some of which have yielded up rich collections of cinerary urns and funerary objects. These include weapons, decorated shields, helmets, bronze panels from a princely chariot, and black- and red-figure vases, as well as strigils, engraved bone-handled bronze mirrors, and elaborately embellished jewellery. Many of the finest can be seen today in the Archaeological Museum in Perugia.

Although Perugians continued to import the finest Etruscan manufacture from more developed artistic centres, there was extensive local manufacture. This was certainly distinctive and could, on occasion, reach a high standard. Typically, urns from

Perugian tombs are small, almost square, and adorned only with very simple decorative motifs. (The comparative crudity of the decorative work on these urns has been attributed to the irregular surface of the travertine stone of which they were made, as well as to the fact that sculptors applied colour and gilding directly, without preliminary stuccoing.) Others, however, could be much finer. Though still usually made of travertine (less frequently of limestone or terracotta), these have gabled covers, pedimented above the front panel, and are usually engraved with the names of the deceased whose ashes they contained. At their most elaborate, such urns were decorated locally – either in the high relief style typical of the workshops at Volterra or in the very low relief characteristic of Chamars. The reliefs often continued from the front of the urn around both sides, and characteristically depicted mythological scenes, or the deceased's journey to the underworld – variously made on horseback or on foot, by chariot or by wagon.

The earliest of the Etruscan tombs discovered around Perugia are those of the necropolis known as the Villa dello Sperandìo. It was in one of these tombs that the richly decorated Sperandìo sarcophagus made in Chamars was found, together with an impressive hoard of bronze objects, now on display in the Archaeological Museum in Florence. A more architecturally interesting tomb lies further outside the city, in the suburb of Ferro di Cavallo. Known as the Hypogeum of San Manno, it consists of a large barrel-vaulted rectangular room, with two square niches facing each other half-way along the longer walls. Many of the architectural details of the tomb remain conjectural today, because of alterations made during the Middle Ages when the tomb was used as a store. The tomb's barrel-vaulting, however, is characteristic of northern Etruria in general and of the Perugia area in particular – as can be seen from other examples in nearby Torgiano and Bettona. The tomb also contains an inscription in Etruscan, on the left-hand wall, carved in three rows of unequal length, the longest of which is some five metres in length. It indicates that the tomb belonged to the Precu family and was intended primarily to hold two brothers, Avle and Larth.

The most important burial site yet to have come to light in the vicinity of Perugia is the Palazzone necropolis, to the south-west of the city, on the road to Rome. Uncovered in 1842, the necropolis includes one of the most famous of all Etruscan tombs, the hypogeum of the Velimna family – better known as the Ipogeo dei Volumni. Although this striking tomb probably dates from the end of the third century BC, the site was a long-favoured one. There are indications of a Villanovan settlement in the ninth and eighth centuries, traces of sixth- and fifth-century burials, and a rich collection of tombs from the third to first centuries BC. The tombs vary in type from very simple rooms, roughly carved out of the rock, to finely designed hypogeums with several rooms, decorated in the manner of Etruscan houses, with carved doors and beamed roofs.

The tomb of the Velimna family is the finest of this kind. Dating from the third or second century BC and carved entirely out of the rock, the tomb is reached by a long, steep, staired *dromos*, at the end of which the original door is still in place. Much of the importance of the hypogeum lies in the fact that the interior of the tomb has survived complete, allowing us to envisage non-funerary Etruscan architectural and decorative work of the same period. Once past the entrance, the hypogeum consists of a large atrium, with four smaller rooms leading off; these are symmetrically arranged, two to the right and two to the left. Opposite the entrance is a corridor with three further rooms leading off, of which the central and largest room corresponds to the tablinum, the most important room in Etruscan houses, used for receiving guests and for holding the most important family possessions. Two smaller rooms, the alae, lie to the side of the tablinum. The sloping roof of the tablinum is decorated with a central beam, together with lateral beams leading down from it to the walls, carved out of the rock. The furthermost chamber has a carved ceiling. The decoration and architectural detail of the hypogeum testify to the wealth and social prestige of the Velimna family. On the far wall of the atrium, for instance, a shield embellished with a Gorgon's head is flanked by two ceremonial swords and two male heads, one representing a bard. There are also women's heads, and the decoration extends to Gorgons and serpents also. The Velimna hypogeum also speaks eloquently of Etruscan confidence in the future of their society, for the Velimna family evidently conceived of the tomb as an architectonic whole designed to hold not only present members of the family but also succeeding generations. As was Etruscan custom, the founder of the family was buried in the most prominent position in the tomb, on the far wall directly opposite the entrance, in a manner symbolic of his role as protector and model for future generations. In this case, Arnth Velimna was buried in a richly embellished sarcophagus with a carved polychrome representation of him reclining on a couch, as though banqueting. It is the most precious sarcophagus in the tomb – and one of the finest of all Etruscan funerary monuments of this period. Many urns, finely decorated with reclining figures, containing the ashes of other members of the family, line the walls of the chamber. As a group, these urns give a telling indication of a great change taking place in the Etruscan world: while the inscriptions on the older urns are in the Etruscan language, later inscriptions are in Latin. In the process, even the family name changes – from Velimna to Volumnus – a clear sign of the increasing assimilation of the Etruscans into Roman society in the first century B C.

Another undisturbed tomb from the late Etruscan period was discovered close to Perugia's main hospital, the Policlinico, just north of the city centre, in 1983. In general, it conforms to the pattern of the Velimna hypogeum. A *dromos* leads to an entrance chamber which in turn gives way to three further rooms, roughly carved out of the rock, placed in the shape of a cross. On the far wall of the chamber directly opposite the entrance to the tomb lay a sarcophagus holding the body of the patriarch of the Cutu family, again the only family member to have been buried. Around him lay urns – some stuccoed, decorated and painted – containing the ashes of his cremated relatives and descendants, ordered in chronological sequence, from the middle of the third century throughout the entire second and first centuries B C. When the room facing the entrance was filled, the family began to fill the room to the left of the entrance hall and subsequently the right chamber and, eventually, the entrance chamber itself. The objects buried with the dead were, in contrast, piled in disorderly fashion to the immediate left of the door. From the evidence of the tomb, the Cutu family was originally of the servant class but rose at the end of the third century to assume a position of greater social importance. At the very end of the period in which the tomb was used, this family too became increasingly integrated into the Roman world, adopting the Latin form Cutius in place of the Etruscan family name, Cutu.

Among other noteworthy tombs around Perugia are that of Arnth Cairnina, known as the Tomba del Faggeto, to the north, and those at Pila to the south-west, which contained rich hoards of funerary objects. It may have been at Pila that one of the most celebrated of all Etruscan bronzes was discovered, during the Renaissance. Usually known as '*l'Arringatore*' or 'the Orator', the statue – almost 1.8 metres tall – depicts one Avle Meteli. It is a late and extremely fine work which shows strong Roman influence but has an inscription in Etruscan engraved on the orator's robe. Made in a workshop at Cortona or Arezzo, the statue is now in the Archaeological Museum in Florence. One tomb well worth visiting for its lovely location as well as its design is that in the aptly named location of Paradiso, close to Umbria's border with Tuscany. Occupying an isolated position overlooking the tiny Lago di Chiusi, and with the Tuscan hills as a backdrop, the small barrel-vaulted tomb retains its stone door and stone hinges intact.

Perugia and the surrounding area reveal something of the development of Etruscan society over seven centuries, from the Villanovan culture which preceded it, until its assimilation into an expanding Roman culture increasingly dominant in central Italy. Elsewhere in Umbria, and especially around Orvieto, in the south of the region, the picture is somewhat different. For a start, while the general pattern of Perugia's development in the Etruscan period is increasingly well understood, Orvieto presents major problems. That it was an important Etruscan site, particularly between the end of the seventh and the beginning of the third centuries BC, is certain, as finds in the city and surrounding necropolises confirm. Undoubtedly the importance of the city derived initially from its dramatic and easily defended site, an isolated, sheer-sided tufa outcrop overlooking the Paglia valley, slightly north of the point at which the river Paglia flows into the Tiber. If – as seems likely – Orvieto is the Etruscan city known as Volsinii Veteres, then it was one of the most flourishing of all Etruscan cities. At least, classical authorities from Pliny the Elder, in the first century, to Orosius, in the fourth, thought so: '*Volsinii oppidum Tuscorum opulentissimum*,' Pliny called it. It may even have been the capital of Etruria, as Valerius Maximus and Livy believed. It was this city which was eventually destroyed in 264 BC by the Romans, who resettled its surviving inhabitants about twelve kilometres away to the south-west in a new city they called Volsinii Noves, or Bolsena – in which form the name recalls the original Etruscan for Volsinii: Velzna.

Archaeological investigation of the site of modern Orvieto has uncovered materials dating back to the late Bronze Age, with stable settlements in evidence during the Villanovan period of the ninth to eighth centuries BC. Numerous finds from the necropolises surrounding the city rock confirm the flourishing in the sixth century of a city – perhaps refounded by Etruscan colonists from the maritime regions, or even Chamars – whose prosperity derived from the control of land together with intensive commercial activity with its neighbours.

Like Etruscan Perugia, Volsinii was surrounded by numerous smaller centres of population politically and culturally dependent on it. In the earliest period, these settlements tended to be located close to the city itself, but in the sixth century Volsinii's territory expanded considerably. The wealth of Volsinii derived predominantly from agriculture, as is evidenced by the fact that, before the destruction of the city, its inhabitants were known as 'those who live in the countryside', and the remains of scattered villages and farms are widely distributed throughout the surrounding area.

If Orvieto was Volsinii, then it was also the site of the Fanum Voltumnae, the most celebrated sanctuary in Etruria, where representatives of all the Etruscan city-states gathered to discuss issues of shared 'national' concern, such as mutual defence in the case of aggression from surrounding peoples. On the occasion of the federal gatherings in the sanctuary, ceremonies dedicated to the god Voltumna took place, along with a variety of games and contests, while the assembly elected a supreme magistrate.

Unlike Perugia, Volsinii was also a flourishing artistic centre. As early as the sixth century BC the city had several workshops producing a variety of ceramic goods, often on Greek models, as well as decorative work in terracotta, designed for religious sites. Even more important was the local bronze work, including decorative panels for chariots and a wide range of vessels. A great deal of this was exported, and pieces from Orvieto have been found not only throughout Umbria but also in the Marches in the east, and along the Po valley, in northern Italy. It was in these workshops that another of the most famous of all Etruscan bronzes was cast: the elegant figure of a warrior in armour from the early fourth century, the so-called Mars, found in Todi. If bronze statues were an important export of Volsinii, however, the city itself was impressively endowed with bronzes of its own; Pliny records that when Volsinii finally fell to the Romans, the booty included some 2,000 bronze statues, perhaps looted from the sanctuary Fanum Voltumnae itself.

Unlike the coastal cities of Etruria, which had entered a period of decline by the fifth century, Volsinii continued to flourish, maintaining its power throughout the fourth. That power was being increasingly challenged, however, by the force that would ultimately see the end of the Etruscan world – Rome. Already in 396 BC the Romans had conquered the southern Etruscan city of Veii, and they were soon in conflict with Volsinii. Despite a twenty-year truce, the conflict was renewed at the end of the fourth century and in 294 BC a Roman army invaded the territory of Volsinii. The city-state fought back, forming an alliance first with the Gauls of northern Italy and subsequently with the Etruscan city of Velch or Vulci. The struggle continued for another fourteen years until 280 BC, when Tiberius Coruncanius was able to celebrate victory over both Etruscan centres. The extent of the Roman triumph, and of Volsinii's defeat, however, only became evident sixteen years later. In 264 BC Volsinii was torn apart by internecine strife between aristocratic and plebeian factions in the city. While an aristocracy had ruled Volsinii until the city submitted to Rome, the plebeians had subsequently taken over the civil and military government of the city. Soon they aspired to rights previously denied them: the right of marriage with aristocratic women (*ius conubii*) and admittance to the city senate (*ius honorum*). The city's aristocracy appealed for assistance to the senate in Rome, but in taking the side of the aristocratic faction, Rome destroyed Volsinii Veteres and resettled its population at Volsinii Noves. There was no notable Roman settlement at Volsinii Veteres, and although archaeological evidence has revealed that the site was not entirely abandoned, Orvieto did not rise again as a city for more than eight centuries.

During the height of Etruscan power, Volsinii was a walled city, massively fortified around the gate at its most accessible – and so defensively weakest – point at the extreme western edge of the plateau, as is evidenced by a surviving section of the Etruscan wall subsequently incorporated into a medieval dwelling. The city had other gates to the north and south which led to the two major necropolises, known as the Crocifisso del Tufo and Cannicella. Like Perugia's Corso Vannucci, Orvieto's main street – the Corso Cavour – follows the line of the principal Etruscan thoroughfare, leading eastwards from the Porta Maggiore. Along the roads running off the present Corso Cavour, the remains of numerous religious sites have been discovered, together with numerous conduits and wells belonging to the elaborate Etruscan water supply system.

The Roman destruction of the city, however, has meant that the principal Etruscan remains today are those of necropolises, dating from the seventh century BC until Volsinii's abrupt end. These necropolises once surrounded almost the entire site of Orvieto, though primitive attempts at excavation in the nineteenth century led not only to the loss of the tombs' contents but also to the virtual loss of tombs themselves – the sites being given back to cultivation as soon as the first excavation had taken place. Today, the earliest surviving tombs are those of the Cannicella necropolis to the south of the city rock, where chamber tombs from as early as the late seventh or early sixth century BC have come to light. This necropolis once contained a sanctuary incorporating a temple decorated in terracotta in the fifth century BC, and restructured in the fourth.

The larger Crocifisso del Tufo necropolis – first investigated in the nineteenth century – is still under excavation today. So far, more than 100 chamber tombs have been unearthed, and some of the most recently excavated have been found with their contents undisturbed. This fascinating site contains blocks of tombs, placed back to back, with a common wall and with their entrances on opposite sides. Each tomb belonged to a single family, and the size suggests that each would have held the remains of no more than two or three individuals who were either buried or cremated. The accompanying funeral caches consisted mostly of bronzes and many pottery vessels – including some superb examples of Greek, especially Attic, and *bucchero* vases (many of the finest objects uncovered in the nineteenth century are now distributed among museums throughout the world, including the Louvre and the British Museum).

What most immediately strikes the visitor today about the Crocifisso del Tufo necropolis is the extent to which this city of the dead reveals the Etruscans' flair for town planning. The tombs are laid out in regular fashion along roads placed at right angles to each other, apparently marked by means of small stone blocks indicating the space allotted to each family for their tombs, very much in the manner in which the ancient world planned its living cities. Closer inspection shows that the entrances, placed on the short side of each rectangular tomb, and originally closed by a massive stone door, lead down two or three steps to a single chamber lined with ledges intended to hold the remains of the dead. The tombs were topped with travertine blocks covered in turn with earth rich in clay, to prevent rainwater from entering. Each tomb was marked by a *cippus* placed on top of this layer of earth. One particularly fine example, from the second half of the sixth century, takes the form of the helmeted head of a warrior and is inscribed with the name Larth Cupures; it is now on show in Orvieto's Museo Civico. The given and family names of the dead were also carved on the stone lintel above the entrance to the tombs, where many can still be deciphered.

The fact that the Crocifisso del Tufo necropolis contains more funerary inscriptions than any other single Etruscan site makes it a particularly rich source of information about the social and cultural make-up of Volsinii during its heyday. The broad social base of Volsinii is suggested, for instance, by the existence of more than ninety different family names for the second half of the sixth century alone, with roughly the same space allotted to each family and with only a few individual tombs consisting of more than one chamber, in the manner, suggestive of higher social standing, known from the Cutu or Velimna tombs in Perugia. Early tombs in the necropolis show that the dead were of Greek origin, while those of a later date show that those buried within were, variously, of Latin, Umbrian, Oscan, or Gaulish descent – suggesting that Volsinii was very much a cultural crossroads, characterized by an ethnic and cultural mix quite different from that of the cities of maritime Etruria.

Just to the south of Orvieto, another necropolis was uncovered in 1863 at Settecamini. This disclosed two important tombs from the second half of the fourth century BC, of a kind rare in the territory of modern Umbria. Named after their discoverer, Domenico Golini, and now reconstructed in the National Archaeological Museum in Orvieto, the Golini tombs are painted with scenes representing banquets in the underworld. A tomb belonging to the Leinie family and now conventionally known as Golini I shows the preliminaries of a feast. The tomb is divided into two parts: to the left, we see game and meat hanging from hooks, while a number of servants, each of whose names is inscribed alongside the painting, make preparations around an oven and at table. To the right, the banquet itself is depicted, with the participants semi-reclining on tricliniums, surrounded by candelabras. In a feature which is characteristic of Etruscan funerary art from the fifth century onwards, both Pluto and Persephone are depicted, enthroned. The former wears a wolf-skin headdress and carries a lance with the familiar funerary symbol of an entwined serpent, while the latter holds a sceptre surmounted by a bird. The deceased is shown arriving on a *biga* or two-horse chariot, accompanied by a female demon, to join his ancestors, whose roles in life are indicated by inscriptions. The second Golini tomb is similar in representing both the journey to the underworld and a banquet. On the left wall, the funeral cortège approaches the banqueting couches, beneath which are depicted the characteristic stools on which the sandals of those feasting were deposited. The well-displayed collection in the Archaeological Museum contains other items discovered in these tombs and elsewhere in the Settecamini necropolis. They include fine red-figure ceramics – one of them, an amphora dating from between 350 and 325 BC, depicts a scene of centauromachy – and a magnificent set of bronze armour, found in the so-called Warrior's Tomb.

Today, the principal evidence of the religious importance of Volsinii is provided by the remains of the Belvedere Temple on the eastern edge of the city. This temple, unfortunately damaged during the Renaissance by building work carried on close by, was rediscovered by chance in 1828 during road construction. Facing south-east, and fronted by a large piazza, the temple measured approximately twenty-two metres in length and sixteen and a half metres in width (being slightly wider at the back than at the front), and stood on a podium reached by a series of steps leading to the façade. It was divided into two parts: the front, or *pronaos*, has two rows of four columns each, while the rear is subdivided into three separate rooms, that in the centre being somewhat wider than those flanking it. In broad outline, in fact, this temple, whose origins probably date back to the beginning of the fifth century BC, is entirely characteristic of the Etruscan style as described, in the first century BC, by the great Roman architect Vitruvius in his treatise *De Architectura*.

Also found on the site were many terracotta figures from different stages of the decoration of the temple, now to be seen in Orvieto's Museo Civico. These range from a partial figure of a horse, dating from the time the temple was built, to the later and extremely fine high-relief figures which originally decorated the façade and rear face of the temple, and which date from around the end of the fifth century. Originally mounted on stone slabs and nailed to the roof-beams, they include a powerful yet elegantly moulded male figure with breastplate from the front frieze, and other male figures, including youthful warriors. There is also a female figure, tentatively identified with the goddess Artemis, from a mythological scene which once adorned the rear of the temple. This terracotta sculpture is interesting both for its own sake and also in indicating very clearly the extent to which Volsinii differed artistically from Perugia. Volsinii *did* import work from Greece, especially in the sixth century BC – among the finds made are important red- and black-figure ceramics, including five amphoras by the admired black-figure Athenian painter Execias, and also a marble statue of a nude female figure, known as the Venus of Cannicella, which combines the attributes of a fertility goddess and of a figure from the underworld. The city, however, also produced artists of its own, who were receptive to Greek models, and the locally made temple sculptures reveal considerable affinities with the work of the celebrated artist Phidias (b. *c.* 490 BC).

Although it is not known which divinity was worshipped here, the temple was probably linked with the cult of the underworld, as is suggested by an inscription linking the name of the highest Etruscan deity – the equivalent of the Greek Zeus or the Roman Jove – with that of a divinity associated with Hades. If so, this is very much in line with the Etruscans' characteristic concern with the underworld – a concern which sometimes took a more sinister turn. A fourth-century sarcophagus discovered at Torre San Severo, to the south-west of Orvieto on the road to Bolsena, and now on display in the Museo Civico, is decorated with two superbly carved but blood-chilling scenes. One represents Achilles's sacrifice of Trojan prisoners to the shade of Patroclus, the other the killing of Priam's daughter, Polyxena, by Neoptolemus, before the tomb of Achilles; both scenes are framed by demonic figures.

Between them, Perugia and Orvieto reveal a great deal about the history of Umbria in the first millennium before Christ. It must not be forgotten, however, that the history of the region in this long period is not only the story of the Etruscans. While the land to the west of the river Tiber was Etruscan territory, the larger portion of modern Umbria lying to the east was occupied by the people who gave the region its modern name:

the Umbri or Umbrians. Culturally and ethnically, the Umbri were a distinct Italic people, speaking an Indo-European language resembling Latin. They were not confined to the present region but occupied a considerable portion of central Italy, stretching from the Tiber across the Apennines to the Adriatic coast. As we have seen, it appears that they had once settled west of the Tiber also, only to be driven from this territory during the course of the Etruscans' expansion westward. The Elder Pliny considered them the most ancient inhabitants of the Italian peninsula. Among the towns and cities of modern Umbria that were originally founded by the Umbri are Città di Castello, Gubbio, Gualdo Tadino, Nocera Umbra, Assisi, Bettona, Foligno, Spoleto, Todi, Terni, Narni, and Amelia. This is a notable list, and if the early Umbrians figure much less prominently in modern accounts of the region it is only because many fewer traces of their culture survive than is the case with the Etruscans. What does survive, however, is impressive. The walls of the southern city of Amelia, for example, go back to the fifth century BC, when the Umbrians constructed them using huge, irregular blocks of travertine, fitted perfectly together, without the use of mortar. These walls, which are still substantially in place, survived the coming of the Romans and the later waves of northern invaders, and helped shape not only the medieval city but the modern one as well.

The most extraordinary document relating to the Umbrians came to light in the fifteenth century, when seven bronze tablets were unearthed in an underground chamber, decorated with mosaics, in the vicinity of the Roman theatre at Gubbio in 1444. The tablets, now displayed in Gubbio's Palazzo dei Consoli, were written between the third and first centuries BC in the Umbrian language, using first the Etruscan and later the Latin alphabet. They contain a long inscription concerning Umbrian ceremonies and religious rites, relative to the priestly caste, the Confraternity of the Atiedii. These include detailed descriptions of ritual sacrifices of cattle and wild boar and propitiatory offerings of grain and wine to tutelary deities, along with directions for silent prayer. Known as the Eugubine tablets – taking their name from Iguvium, the Latin name for Gubbio – the texts also give us a good deal of information about the Umbrians' relations with neighbouring peoples. The Ikuvini prayed that the gods might protect them from the *Naharkum nomen*, the *Japuzkem nomen*, and the *Turskem nomen*, peoples who have been identified respectively with the inhabitants of the valley of the river Nera in the Terni basin, the population of the coast of the former Yugoslavia, and the Etruscans. The tablets add instructions on how any individuals from these ethnic groups, or from neighbouring Gualdo Tadino, unlucky enough to be seized by the Ikuvini should be sacrificed.

Despite the mutual hostility suggested by the Etruscan invasion of Umbrian territory and the stated desire to be protected from or revenged upon their enemies, the Umbrians seem to have lived in close contact with, and learned from, their neighbours across the Tiber, while remaining ethnically and culturally distinct. Border areas, for instance, were bilingual, with both Etruscan and Umbrian spoken in cities like Chamars, Perugia, Vettona (Bettona) or Tuder (Todi). The higher degree of development in Etruscan material culture also led to the importation on an extensive scale of Etruscan ceramic and bronze work into Umbrian territories. The degree of Etruscan economic and cultural influence on the Umbrian world can be seen in many of the border areas, especially those lying just to the left of the Tiber, in important centres of population such as Vettona or Arna (Civitella d'Arno). Some of the most important discoveries of Etruscan art have been made not in Etruria itself but in adjoining territories: these include the bronze statue of Mars, made at Volsinii but found at Todi, and the richly decorated parade chariot discovered in a necropolis near Monteleone di Spoleto and now in the Metropolitan Museum in New York. Border areas themselves seem not always to have been clearly marked. The upper Tiber valley, around the modern Città di Castello (the former Tifernum Tiberinum), is normally considered as Umbrian territory, yet Pliny the Younger, who owned a large estate close by, at San Giustino, on the east bank of the Tiber, placed his land in Tuscia – i.e. in Etruscan territory – and there is strong archaeological evidence of Umbrian influence on the west bank of the Tiber in the same area, as late as the second century BC.

Given that, from the fifth century BC onwards, Etruscan influence had spread not only throughout the Italian peninsula but far beyond – into central Europe, southern France and the Iberian peninsula – it is hardly surprising that areas so close to the major centres of Etruscan power should have been heavily influenced by the culture of their powerful neighbours. Nevertheless, the extent and strength of the links between the Etruscan and Umbrian worlds – and the survival of these as distinct cultures – are astonishing. As late as the fourth century AD, long after the time when one might have expected the spread of Roman power to have all but obliterated traces of former patterns of political alliance or religious practice, links between the former Umbrian and Etruscan worlds continued strong, at least locally. The best surviving indication of this is the so-called Constantine Rescript, the text of which was inscribed on a marble slab uncovered in Spello (the Roman Hispellum) in 1733. Promulgated by the emperor Constantine between AD 333 and 337, the document acceded to the petition of Spello's inhabitants to stop having to send a priest to the Fanum Voltumnae, the federal Etruscan sanctuary at Orvieto, where Umbrians had joined the Etruscans in their rites; instead, they were permitted to hold their own ceremonies and gladiatorial games. That such a practice should have survived for several centuries, eventually to be abandoned only because of the increasing difficulty of journeying between Hispellum and Volsinii, as the western empire began to decline, indicates just how close were the ties between the Umbrians and their Etruscan neighbours.

As part of their more general spread throughout Italy and beyond, the Etruscans travelled widely throughout Umbrian territories. Etruscan luxury items have been unearthed throughout the extent of these territories, not only in well-established border towns like Todi but in apparently remote mountain areas such as Monteleone di Spoleto, or the plateau of Colfiorito, north-east of Foligno, close to one of the more easily accessible Apennine passes. Nor was the influence of the Etruscans in Umbrian territory confined solely to the Umbrian taste for imported goods. Bettona, for instance, reveals extensive Etruscan influence, even today. The town's massive walls, built with huge sandstone blocks, were erected in the third or second century BC, using techniques derived from the Etruscan Perugia and similar to those employed at Todi, further south. The barrel-vaulted tomb to be seen at the side of the steep road leading up to the town is likewise very similar to the Etruscan tombs of neighbouring Perugia.

Todi is a particularly good example of the way in which an Umbrian centre internalized contacts with the Etruscan world. Like Bettona, Todi – in Umbrian Tuder, from the Etruscan *tular* or boundary – owes its importance to its hilltop position, on the left bank of the Tiber. In its Umbrian phase, the site was already occupied by a wealthy aristocracy, whose prosperity probably derived from the fertility of the surrounding countryside. A princely tomb discovered there in 1916 contained a hoard rich in bronzes and high-quality Greek ceramics (imported through the Etruscan maritime centres), including a fine bronze helmet, with relief decorations, a large red-figure bowl, and more than sixty Attic vessels. Todi's relatively early urbanization, in the fourth or third century BC, owes much to Etruscan example, and the city walls still retain important sections indicating direct contact with the Etruscans. It was in a sanctuary outside these walls that the celebrated Etruscan bronze statue of Mars was found, a votive offering from the Celt settler Ahal Trutitis. Within the city, traces of other sanctuaries from the period have been uncovered in an area corresponding to the very centre of modern Todi. One of the last great public buildings to be erected in ancient Tuder, probably in the first century BC, still survives in part and shows how, by this time, Umbrian culture was adapting itself not only in response to the Etruscans but also to the encroaching influence of Rome. The so-called Nicchioni or large Niches, in the Piazza del Mercato Vecchio, have a Doric frieze, with triglyphs and metopes; the decoration of arms and flowers is based on an artistic language, originally derived from the Hellenistic world, and characteristic of much late Etruscan work, yet which also reveals an awareness of newer Roman models.

Even as they absorbed Etruscan influences, however, Umbrian areas continued to assert their own ethnic and linguistic identity.

The separate religious identity of Spello has already been noted, and a distinctive Umbrian culture clung on at nearby Assisi. The site of the town had been occupied at least from the Iron Age and had developed as an Umbrian centre in the sixth century BC. Urbanization began late, however, reaching its height with the most active phase of building in the second and first centuries BC, under Etruscan influence. Nevertheless, the monumental inscriptions from that period are in the Umbrian language, and local planning shows a number of characteristically Umbrian features, such as the importance given in Assisi to water – springs and fountains – in the siting of religious buildings. The names of the *marones* – Umbrian magistrates responsible for building projects (like the *aediles* of the Roman world) – are also recorded, a practice unfamiliar in neighbouring Etruria. One such record is to be found beneath the bell-tower of the cathedral of San Rufino in Assisi, where an inscription marks the construction of the city's large barrel-vaulted cistern, built on a site believed to have once been dedicated to the cult of an Italic god. Another inscription relating to the *marones* from the same area – this time a stone found between Assisi and Bastia – is in the Archaeological Museum in Perugia.

If the Umbri were able to retain their ethnic and cultural identity despite the pressure exerted by the Etruscan world, then both Umbrians and Etruscans would eventually yield to an even more powerful force growing up in central Italy. As it expanded throughout the Italian peninsula and beyond, the Roman state would begin to erase those differences between the right and left banks of the Tiber which had survived for so long.

CHAPTER THREE

Roman Umbria

✳

The idea of the Etruscan and Umbrian worlds succumbing to the military might of Rome encapsulates an element of truth but it is also too simple. For a start, Rome was itself an Etruscan city. At least, some ancient historians, such as Dionysius of Halicarnassus, thought so. In the eighth century BC, Rome was still no more than a collection of tiny hilltop villages, lying between the advanced culture of Magna Graecia to the south and the developing Etruscan civilization to the north. Unlike their neighbours in Etruria, the inhabitants of these village settlements spoke an Indo-European tongue that would develop into Latin, and practised both cremation and inhumation. Though the Roman date for the founding of the city – 753 BC – is purely conventional, it was probably not long after the middle of the eighth century that the villages on the Palatine, Caelian and Esquiline hills joined up to found the nucleus of the city. By the end of the seventh century, the marshy area that would become the Forum was drained, the Quirinal and Viminal hill settlements joined up, and the first bridge was built over the Tiber, linking Etruria with Latium. By this time, Rome was already a centre subject both to the same Greek influences as had led to the growth of Etruria and to the influence of the emergent Etruscan culture itself. Rather as would happen with the Umbrians at a later date, the Romans showed a liking for Etruscan metal and ceramic work and also absorbed Etruscan ideas: the draining of the Forum, for instance, was an engineering scheme characteristic of Etruria.

Rome soon took more than material culture or technology from the Etruscans; it acquired its rulers from them also. At the end of the seventh century – though dates are very conjectural – an Etruscan dynasty ruled in Rome. Whether the first Etruscan king, Tarquinius Priscus (616–579 BC), came to power by consent, as Roman historians later alleged, or whether the strategic importance of Rome made its seizure irresistible to the Etruscans, is not certain. Tradition has it, however, that in place of its former Latin or Sabine kings, Rome was ruled by Etruscans for more than a century, during which time the city underwent a notable expansion. The temples of Fortune and Mater Matuta in the Forum Boarium, and that of Jupiter, Juno and Minerva (Tinia, Uni, and Menrva, as the Etruscans knew them) on the Capitoline hill, where the kings now lived, were both built on the Etruscan plan. The latter was also magnificently decorated with sculptures by the artist Vulca, responsible for the decoration of the temple in the Etruscan city of Veii. Though Rome preserved an identity independent of the wholly Etruscan centres to the north – Latin rather than Etruscan continued as the principal language spoken by the people – the city absorbed a great deal of Etruscan culture that shaped Roman civilization long after the fall of Tarquinius Superbus, the seventh and final Etruscan king. Many aspects of Roman religious practice were originally Etruscan. The use of the haruspex – easily recognizable by his large, pointed headdress, knotted beneath the chin, and his short-sleeved tunic, covered by a fringed cloak, fastened by a brooch – who practised divination by examining the entrails of sacrificial animals, was taken from Etruria, as was the custom of divination from observing bolts of lightning. Romans continued for centuries to send their children to the Etruscan centre of Caere to perfect their knowledge of reading and writing. It was from Etruria that the Romans took the practice of the triumph, and from Tarquinia or Vetulonia that they acquired their symbols of power.

The development of Rome at the same time as the decline of the Etruscan centres of southern Etruria closest to the city eventually led to hostilities between the Romans and the Etruscans which would herald the end of an independent Etruria. Yet the increasing military, political and administrative influence of Rome on Etruscan and Umbrian cultures may also be seen as a final stage of development of those civilizations. It was the degree to which Rome was itself Etruscanized, however, that enables us to understand certain aspects of the relationship between the city and such centres of Etruscan power as Perugia, so important in the development of Umbria.

Having consolidated its own position as one among many Italic cities by the middle of the fourth century BC, Rome began to expand its political, cultural and economic influence over a much wider area. Rome's victory over the Etruscan centre of Veii, after a decade-long war between 405 and 396 BC, allowed the establishment of the first Roman colonies on the right bank of the Tiber. Hostilities with Etruscan Tarquinia began in 358 BC and, despite lengthy truces, continued for the remainder of the century, while Caere became a Roman *municipium sine suffragio* (that is, a *municipium* without the right to vote) in 353 BC, firmly establishing the Roman presence in southern Etruria. Rome also intervened in Etruscan affairs further north, as when it supported the pro-Roman aristocratic faction in Arretium (the modern Arezzo) during a popular uprising in 302 BC. When the Etruscans, allied with the Umbrians, Samnites and Gauls, were defeated at the Battle of Sentinum (close to Sassoferrato in the Marches) in 295 BC, the ultimate victory of Rome was virtually assured.

The Roman presence in the modern region of Umbria was most dramatically marked by its destruction of Volsinii Veteres in 264 BC, and Perugia, the other leading Etruscan city in the region, seems to have accepted the inevitable, declining to challenge Roman military power. In order to facilitate their expansion throughout Etruria and Umbria, the Romans built new roads – notably the Via Amerina and Via Flaminia – which, though primarily intended to speed up military communications, also facilitated the spread of Roman cultural influence generally. The Via Flaminia, in particular – linking Rome with the Adriatic – would become the key to the Roman control of Italy and a crucial element in the development of Umbria long beyond the Roman period.

That Etruscan Perugia was content to live with, rather than resist, Roman power was notably demonstrated during the Second Punic War. Under their commander-in-chief, Hannibal, the Carthaginian army marched from Spain, through France and across the Alps, winning important victories in the north of Italy in 218 BC. In the following year Hannibal reached the shores of Lake Trasimeno, where he achieved one of his most decisive victories, inflicting a massive defeat on the Roman army commanded by Gaius Flaminius, builder of the Via Flaminia, or Flaminian Way. The famous battle took place after Hannibal's Carthaginian, Iberian and Celtic troops, closely pursued by the Roman army as they marched south, pitched camp on the northern shores of Lake Trasimeno, below the site of the present Tuoro. On the morning of 24 June 217 BC Gaius Flaminius ordered his troops to continue their pursuit of the enemy. In the early morning mist, the Romans marched through the narrow gap between the hills and the lake only to find, as the mist lifted, Hannibal's army waiting for them in battle positions. His forces divided on either side of the gap, Flaminius saw the Celtic foot-soldiers and Numidian cavalry charge down on his troops from the hills above. The charge further split the Roman army, and when Hannibal sent in his second wave of Iberians and Libyans from the east, the Romans could do nothing except attempt escape along the shores of the lake. The manoeuvre was fatal, for the terrain was not the solid ground the Romans had looked for but swampy marsh. Trapped, they died in their thousands, Gaius Flaminius among them. Testimony to the slaughter survives both in two local place names – Ossaia (from *ossa*, bones) and Sanguineto (from *sangue*, blood) – and in the cinerary pits in which the bodies of the dead were burnt, in an attempt to avoid plague. It was one of the greatest military defeats the Romans ever suffered.

Yet, even with such overwhelming evidence of Roman military fallibility at hand, Etruscan Perugia did not betray the alliance Rome had forced on it. Many of the 6,000 Roman troops who survived the battle found shelter in the city, and Perugia's gates were shut against the Carthaginians. The story in Umbrian territory was similar. The ancient Umbrian stronghold of Spoleto, where the Romans had founded a colony less than a quarter of a century previously, also stayed loyal, repelling Hannibal as he marched south. When Rome was later preparing to fight the Carthaginians in Africa, the region was equally dependable; the historian Livy mentions Perugia as one of the cities which offered the greatest support in supplying the Roman forces, offering large stores of grain and dispatching logs down-river from the upper Tiber valley to provide wood for shipbuilding.

Both banks of the Tiber soon reaped the reward of loyalty to Rome in increased prosperity in conditions of peace, though the area to the east of the river was to prove the more flourishing under the empire. Small settlements and farmhouses sprang up throughout the countryside, as the natural fertility of the region was increasingly exploited. Perugia entered a new period of affluence, and Asisium, Hispellum and Vettona all thrived. It seems likely too that many – though not all – sections of these Etruscan or Etruscanized societies benefited, for a peasant class was created, with some slaves being granted freedom and land, in an attempt to prevent the kind of social conflict between aristocrats and plebeians that had led the Romans to intervene in the affairs of Arretium and Volsinii, and to destroy the latter city.

For another century or more the Etruscan world would live on, yet signs of Romanization were increasingly evident. We have already noted, as an indication of an enduring Etruscan culture, the great bronze statue known as '*l'Arringatore*', or the Orator, found close to Perugia, with its inscription in the Etruscan language declaring that it is a votive offering by Avle Meteli intended for a sanctuary of Tece Sans – yet the inscription is to be found on the border of the orator's toga which, like his tunic and shoes, his ring, and the very manner of his representation, bears witness to the growing influence of Rome. Eventually, even the Etruscan language would give way to Latin, as in the Velimna hypogeum at Perugia, where the last urn deposited bears not only the Etruscan inscription 'Pup. Velimna', but also the Latin 'Publius Volumnius' – and it is by this Latin form that the hypogeum continues to be known.

When the hypogeum of the Volumni was discovered, some

of the outer rooms still stood empty, awaiting urns that never arrived. The date at which the final urn was deposited – around 50 or 40 BC – is significant, for in the end Perugia shared in the fate of Volsinii. Having benefited from an accommodation with Rome for more than two centuries, the city eventually fell foul of Roman civil strife in the so-called *Bellum Perusinum*, the Perugian War. In 41 BC local farmers, resentful at the prospect of losing their lands, which new laws threatened to assign to veterans of the Roman army, took Mark Antony's side in the struggle with Octavius Caesar (the future Emperor Augustus). Mark Antony's brother, Lucius, established himself within the walls of Perugia, along with Antony's wife, Fulvia. Besieged by Octavius's troops, the city was starved into submission (*Perusia fames*), and the Perugian senators who had supported Mark Antony were executed on the fourth anniversary of Julius Caesar's death – the Ides of March, 40 BC. Perugia itself was destroyed. Later, Octavius himself had the city rebuilt and granted it the title of '*Perusia Augusta*'.

Perugia was no longer, in any sense, an independent Etruscan centre and yet, in contrast to most other parts of Etruria which entered a period of sharp decline, the city flourished once more. Indeed, virtually the whole region maintained or increased its prosperity: while the countryside was rendered increasingly fertile by the reclamation of lands for agriculture by draining marshlands and swamps, urban centres boasted new forums, temples and baths. The region's inhabitants, meanwhile, continued to enjoy the benefits of Roman citizenship, to which they had been entitled since the passing of the *lex Julia* in 90 BC.

It was under the rule of the Emperor Augustus that the region of Umbria came into being for the first time as a distinct administrative entity. Anxious to acknowledge ethnic and historical distinctions within his territory, Augustus divided most of what is now Umbria into two separate regions: Umbria, the Sixth Region, which included most of modern Umbria on the left bank of the Tiber, and Etruria, the Seventh Region, comprising the territories, including Perugia, on the right. This administrative restructuring of the territory was to endure for almost three centuries, until the Emperor Diocletian added

Umbria to Tuscia to create the single region of Tuscia et Umbria.

With the Augustan reforms, the Etruscan world slowly disappeared. Yet even as they imposed a new order on their territories, the Romans did not forget the Etruscans or their culture. The Emperor Claudius himself is supposed to have written no fewer than twenty volumes on the Etruscans – though these are lost – and the historian Tacitus recorded that, in speaking to the Senate in the first century AD, Claudius also insisted on the importance of preserving the ancient discipline of the haruspex. Remarkably enough, these Etruscan diviners continued to accompany the Roman army at least into the fourth century. In 363 they were credited with interpreting the presence of a lion amid the Persian army as an omen unfavourable to the Emperor, Julian the Apostate, who was indeed killed in the battle that followed. Even in the fifth century, when the empire was near its end, the commander of the troops defending Rome against the invading Visigoths made a point of bringing Etruscan haruspices to the capital, impressed by their supposed success in saving the Umbrian city of Narni from danger, by recourse to the traditional prayers of their ancestors.

What was true of Etruria in relation to the coming of the Romans was true also of the Umbrian territories. The Romans imposed themselves on Umbria partly by military might and partly by political skill. In 299 BC they destroyed the strategically important southern Umbrian city of Nequinum, dominating the Nera valley, and founded on the same hill site the colony of Narnia (the present Narni). Just over half a century later, in 241 BC, the Romans founded a second colony on Umbrian territory: Spoletium, which would soon demonstrate its loyalty to Rome by repelling Hannibal as he moved south after his victory at the Battle of Trasimeno. By 100 BC, Cicero could list Spoletium as among the most illustrious of all Roman colonies.

The Roman progress through Umbria was slow yet certain. As a result, almost every corner of modern Umbria, especially on the left bank of the Tiber, reveals some evidence of its Roman past. In the north, for example, Gubbio flourished. The city had become a *municipium* in 90 BC, and its first-century theatre – the substantial remains of which lie today just beyond the city walls – was one of the largest in the Roman world, holding some 16,000 spectators (more than double the capacity of the theatres at Pompeii or Herculaneum, for instance).

In central Umbria, both Assisi and Spello flourished under the empire. Asisium, made a Roman *municipium* in 89 BC, was also the probable birthplace of the Roman elegiac poet Sextus Propertius (*c.* 50 BC – after 16 BC), who recalled the region in his verse. Speaking of himself, Propertius asks:

> Umbria te notis antiqua Penatibus edit
> (mentior? an patriae tangitur ora tuae?)
> quam nebulosa cavo rorat Mevania campo,
> et lacus aestiuis intepet Umber acquis,
> scandentisque Asis consurgit vertice murus,
> murus ab ingenio notior ille tuo.

> [Ancient Umbria gave you birth from illustrious Penates/(do I lie? or remember aright your fatherland?)/where misty Bevagna oozes moisture in the sloping fields/and the waters of the Umbrian lake warm up in summer/and on the heights rise the high walls of Assisi/walls made more famous by your own gifts.
> (*Elegies*, IV, i, ll. 121-126)]

Assisi today retains many more vestiges of its Roman past than the mere boast of being the birthplace of Propertius (a claim which, in any case, it shares with about a dozen rivals!). These include stretches of its walls with part of the gate leading to Perugia, the fountains now between the buttresses of the church of Santa Chiara, and the remains of its theatre and amphitheatre. Most famous among the city's Roman monuments is the temple in the Piazza del Comune, which is not only the finest Roman building in Umbria but also possesses one of the best preserved of all temple façades anywhere (the interior was converted into a church in 1539 and remodelled in Baroque style in the following century). Built at the end of the republican period or the beginning of the imperial age, the temple boasts a façade of six

Corinthian columns on plinths, surmounted by a tympanum; a lack of space on the hillside site led to the very unusual placing of the columns not at the top of the flight of steps giving access to the temple but in the middle, so that the steps thread their way delicately through the columns to the *pronaos*. Excavations beneath the modern piazza have revealed extensive remains of a large colonnaded terrace in front of the temple – once part of a larger sanctuary – giving a magnificent outlook on to the valley below.

Along that valley to the south-east lay the Roman Hispellum, today's Spello. It too benefited from a long tradition of loyalty to Rome – having, like Spoleto, repulsed Hannibal from its gates, and offering Octavius Caesar military support against Perugia. As a result, it was awarded the title of 'Hispellum Splendidissima Colonia Iulia' and granted considerable territory in the surrounding area. The town's consequent prosperity is indicated by the many monuments which still survive, in whole or in part. These include a virtually complete ring of Roman walls and no fewer than four gates: the triple-arched Porta Consolare, leading to Rome and now decorated with statues from the later empire, discovered in the sixteenth century; the massive though much altered Porta Venere, once composed of two triple-arched gates with a courtyard between; the single-arched Porta Urbica; and a gate to the north of the town, now known as the Arco dei Cappuccini. There is also an amphitheatre. It was in the vicinity of this last that the previously mentioned Constantine Rescript – giving the people of Hispellum the right to build a temple in honour of the *Gens Flavia*, where the Umbrians could gather on the occasion of their most solemn festivities – was unearthed in 1733, a discovery which revealed Spello to have been an important regional centre of paganism, just at the time when Constantine had announced the toleration of Christianity throughout the empire.

To the extreme east of the modern region, Norcia was also a Roman city. Known as Nursia, it differed from all other large centres in being neither Etruscan nor Umbrian but the most northerly of the Sabine settlements. After Rome eventually conquered its highland neighbours, at the beginning of the third century BC, the Sabines were granted Roman citizenship and in

205 BC Nursia was noted as having offered volunteers to Scipio during the Second Punic War. The city was not always associated with loyalty to Rome, however. It was the birthplace of Quintus Sertorius, leader of the democratic faction in Roman politics of the first century, who became praetor in 87 BC and was given the province of Spain. Sertorius later led the Lusitanians in revolt against Rome, and for a time controlled most of the Iberian peninsula, until being killed by treachery in 73 or 72 BC. The following year, Norcia was the scene of a battle between the Roman troops and an army of slave-gladiators; though the Romans were victorious on this occasion, they were shortly defeated by the forces of Spartacus, who moved his troops to reinforce the rebel army and inflicted on the Romans the loss of some 14,000 men. As the civil wars continued to affect central Italy, Norcia supported Mark Antony during his struggle with Octavius Caesar, the future Emperor Augustus, and, as a result, the city suffered the same fate as Perugia, being sacked in 40 BC. In Augustus's subsequent administrative division of Italy, Nursia was separated from the remainder of the modern region and placed in the Fourth Region, Samnium, which included all the territories between the river Nera and the Apennines as far as Reate, the modern Rieti. Though Rieti today belongs to the modern region of Lazio, the city's links with Umbrian territories continued for many centuries; at the nineteenth-century unification of Italy, Rieti became part of Umbria and was only separated from it in 1922.

If the Roman settlement of Umbria includes virtually all of the present region – with the notable exception of Orvieto, whose site lost its importance after the destruction of Volsinii Veteres – the Romans displayed a marked preference for the former Umbrian territories on the left bank of the Tiber. The area was not far from Rome, and notably fertile – a quality Propertius singled out for praise in another of his elegies (I, xxii). The possibilities for land reclamation promoted by widespread drainage schemes, and the suitability of the terrain for the cultivation of vines and olive trees, combined to make the territory a favourite location for wealthy Romans to own country villas. Among these was Pliny the Younger, who gave an extended and evocative account of his estate near Tifernum Tiberinum (Città di Castello):

> The countryside is very beautiful. Picture to yourself a vast amphitheatre such as could only be a work of nature; the great spreading plain is ringed round by mountains, their summits crowned by ancient woods of tall trees, where there is a good deal of mixed hunting to be had. Down the mountain slopes are timber woods interspersed with small hills of soil so rich that there is scarcely a rocky outcrop to be found; these hills are fully as fertile as the level plain and yield quite as rich a harvest, though it ripens rather later in the season. Below them the vineyards spreading down every slope weave their uniform pattern far and wide, their lower limit bordered by a belt of shrubs. Then come the meadows and cornfields . . . The meadows are bright with flowers, covered with trefoil and other delicate plants which always seem soft and fresh, for everything is fed by streams which never run dry; though the ground is not marshy where the water collects, because of its downward slope, so that any surplus water it cannot absorb is drained off into the river Tiber flowing through the fields. The river is navigable, so that all produce is conveyed to Rome by boat, but only in winter and spring – in summer its level falls and its dry bed has to give up its claim to the title of a great river until the following autumn. It is a great pleasure to look down on the countryside from the mountain, for the view seems to be a painted scene of unusual beauty rather than a real landscape, and the harmony to be found in this variety refreshes the eye wherever it turns. (*Letters*, V, 6)

This idyllic description does much to suggest why patrician Romans liked Umbria so much (Pliny's mother-in-law owned no fewer than four villas in the region). The single most decisive reason why Rome was so interested in the area, however, was quite different, and determined by the crucial position Umbria occupied in central Italy.

Foremost among the means by which the Romans came to conquer and dominate Umbrian territories was the building of the Via Flaminia after 220 BC. The importance of the Flaminian Way lay in the fact that it linked Rome, across the barrier of the Apennines, to the Adriatic coast and, beyond the Rubicon, to the Po valley and the rest of northern Italy. Just as the natural boundary of the Tiber had its importance – marking the division between the Etruscans and the Umbrians, or the Sixth and Seventh Regions – so the Flaminian Way acquired a particular significance for Rome, linking Italy north and south, east and west, and becoming one of the most travelled of all routes in Italy, not only during the Roman period but for many centuries thereafter (the modern Via Flaminia follows the line of the ancient road through Umbria almost exactly). The fact that the route continued to be used for centuries after the fall of Rome means that the settlements along the road were repeatedly built over in the succeeding centuries. Nevertheless, it is the route of the Via Flaminia which offers the visitor the greatest insight into the history of Umbria in the seven centuries of Roman rule.

The Via Flaminia began in the Forum at Rome, led along the present Via del Corso through what is now the Piazza del Popolo, and left the city by the Flaminian Gate. The road entered the modern region of Umbria in the vicinity of Otrícoli, an Umbrian city allied to Rome since the beginning of the third century BC, which the Romans called Ocriculum (from the Umbrian *okri*, a sacred hill). There, in a site below the present town, survive the remains of a large theatre, an amphitheatre, and other public buildings, including baths once decorated with a celebrated octagonal mosaic of mythological sea scenes, now displayed in the Vatican Museum in Rome. From Ocriculum, the road went north-east to Narni (known to the Romans as Narnia), at which point it divided into two, the eastern branch going via Terni (Interamna), Spoleto (Spoletium), and Trevi (Trebiae) to Foligno (Fulginium), the western branch proceeding to the now-abandoned city of Carsulae and Bevagna (Mevania), to rejoin the former stretch at Foligno. From there the road proceeded via Nocera Umbra (Nuceria Camellaria) and Gualdo Tadino (Tadinum) into the present-day region of the Marches. All of these centres still bear witness, to a greater or lesser degree, to their Roman past.

Narni, for example, retains stretches of its Roman walls, and a series of cisterns, beneath the church of Santa Maria in Pensole. However, the greatest relic of Narni's Roman past lies just outside the town: a massive bridge believed to have been built during the reign of Augustus, and long regarded as one of the great feats of Roman engineering. Originally over 160 metres in length and standing some thirty metres above the river, the bridge is partly ruined today but the remaining section bears eloquent testimony to Roman skill and to the significance accorded to the site.

It was at Narni that the Via Flaminia split into two, the older section being the more westerly. Not far away lies the best preserved of all Roman settlements in Umbria, the abandoned town of Carsulae. Lying on a plateau beneath thickly wooded hills, amid notably beautiful countryside, Carsulae was an important Roman *municipium*, probably built on the site of an earlier Umbrian settlement. Although its origins have been dated to as early as the third century BC, it was first mentioned (by the historian Strabo) only at the very end of the first century BC but soon acquired a reputation for affluence, achieving its greatest prosperity between the middle of the second and the middle of the third century. Here, a long stretch of the Flaminian Way itself remains virtually intact, though its stones are deeply rutted by centuries of heavy Roman traffic. On one side of the road, in the centre of the old town, lies the forum, surrounded by the remains of its public buildings, including the basilica, the curia, and a small temple dedicated to Castor and Pollux (the head of a giant statue of the Emperor Claudius which once stood here is now in the Archaeological Museum in Perugia). Across the way are the remains of a large amphitheatre, a theatre, and a cistern. From the ancient heart of Carsulae, it is possible to walk along the Flaminian Way as far as the still-standing Roman arch which was the city's north gate, and two large mausoleums beyond. What fate befell Carsulae is uncertain. Unlike Pompeii or Herculaneum, its destruction was not the work of a single day yet, unlike so many other Roman towns in Umbria, it did not remain continuously inhabited by successive generations after the decline of the empire. It may have suffered damage from earthquake, and the unwalled city must have been easy prey to northern invaders who passed through Umbria on their way to Rome. In any case, despite the building of a single medieval church, San Damiano, little effort seems to have been made to reinhabit the city, and many neighbouring towns – such as Acquasparta, San Gémini and Cesi – reveal that Carsulae was long used as a quarry for fresh building elsewhere.

Beyond Carsulae, the most important Roman settlement on the western route through the Martani hills was Mevania, the modern Bevagna. This small town was once an important *municipium* and retains some traces of its Roman past, most notably in some extensive mosaics from the former baths, as well as in parts of a temple, theatre, and amphitheatre. The town's complete circuit of walls, though dating from the Middle Ages, follows exactly the line of the Roman walls. From Bevagna, the Via Flaminia led to Foligno, where the western and eastern stretches reunited.

After Narni on the eastern route lay the ancient Umbrian centre of Interamna – the modern Terni – which became an important Roman city, though not always a fortunate one. While two Roman emperors of the third century AD – M. Claudius Tacitus and his brother M. Annius Florianus – were born in the city, another, Trebonianus Gallus, was murdered there in AD 253. Subject to repeated attack from the time of the northern invasions of the sixth century to the Allied bombing of the Second World War, Terni reveals comparatively few traces of its Roman past, but these include a house from the late republican or early imperial age beneath the church of San Salvatore, a cistern, and the remains of an amphitheatre built in AD 32.

The traveller who continued on the eastern route from Terni would find Spoleto the next important stop to the north, and the city still contains much evidence of Roman occupation. Already an important Umbrian centre, surrounded by walls extending for over two kilometres, when the Romans founded their colony there, Spoletium retained its importance throughout the entire Roman period, despite damage during the civil wars of the first century BC and an earthquake in 63 BC. As late as the fifth and sixth centuries it was still being improved by Theodoric and Belisarius. The birthplace of the dramatist Caius Melissus, librarian to the Emperor Augustus, the town played host to a number of emperors, including Constantine and his son, Constans, who signed decrees there. Among surviving Roman monuments is the Arch of Drusus, erected in memory of his son by the Emperor Tiberius in AD 23, which led into the Forum. To the side of the arch, beneath the present church of Sant'Ansano, are the remains of a temple which faced on to the forum, and traces of a second temple are to be found close by. Across the modern Piazza del Mercato – which corresponds to the Roman forum – a first-century Roman house, which may have belonged to Vespasia Polla, mother of the emperor Vespasian, is open to view; notable among the substantial remains are some intricate mosaic floors. The Roman theatre, also from the first century, was lost for several hundreds of years but having been restored in the 1950s is now in use for concerts; part of Spoletium's massive second-century amphitheatre – which once measured 115 by eighty-five metres – also survives. Travellers going north left the city by an impressive bridge built in AD 27, on the orders of the Emperor Augustus, to improve the Via Flaminia; though it fell into disuse when the torrent over which it passed was diverted, three tiers of arches built of huge tufa blocks can still be seen beneath the Piazza della Vittoria.

Not far from Spoleto, the north-bound Roman traveller would have passed a site famous throughout the entire ancient world for its beauty and tranquillity: the Fonti del Clitunno. Once visited by the emperors Caligula and Flavius Honorius, these limpid springs were sacred to the river god, Clitumnus, to whom temples were erected near by, their waters serving to purify white oxen destined for sacrifice. Lying amid groves of poplars and weeping willows, the Springs of Clitumnus were celebrated in verse by Virgil, in the *Georgics*, and by Propertius:

> qua formosa suo Clitumnus flumina luco
>   integit et niveos abluit unda boves
>
> [where the Clitumnus shades the lovely
> waters with its wood/cleansing the snow-
> white oxen with its wave.
>   (*Elegies*, II, xix)]

The springs were also described at length by Pliny the Younger and later famously evoked by Byron and Carducci (see pp. 285–6).

Just five kilometres from the Fonti del Clitunno, perched on a hilltop some 200 metres above the plain, stands Trevi, one of the most beautifully situated towns in all of Umbria. It was once thought that the Roman Trebiae – recorded by Pliny the Elder as being close to the Fonti del Clitunno – lay on the plain beneath the present town. Recently, however, a stretch of Trevi's walls some 350 metres long, long believed to have been built by the Goths, has been confidently identified as Roman.

Ten kilometres further north, the two stretches of the Flaminian Way rejoin at Foligno – which the Romans variously called Fulginae, Fulginia, and Fulginium – a considerable *municipium*, situated on the river Topino, though one which retains comparatively few traces of its importance under the Romans. Unlike neighbouring Spello, or the towns further south, Foligno lies on the plain. Here, the principal archaeological discoveries – including a mosaic pavement and traces of a necropolis used between the first and fourth centuries – have been made to the south-east of the modern town, in the vicinity of the church of Santa Maria in Campis. However, the regular design of the urban centre itself, so dissimilar to medieval practice, with the axes of the principal streets aligned with four bridges over the Topino, bears the imprint of Roman town planning. The importance of the entire area during the Roman period is also suggested by the proximity to Fulginium and Hispellum of yet a third Roman *municipium*, Forum Flaminii, now vanished but once located on the opposite bank of the Topino, a mere three kilometres from Foligno; the site is now occupied by San Giovanni Profiamma, whose eleventh-century church was built with Roman spoils.

Following the valley of the Topino, the Via Flaminia stretched north to Nocera Umbra, once an Umbrian centre known as Noukria and familiar to the Romans as Nuceria Camellaria. The exact location of the Roman city is not known for certain but, as with Roman settlements elsewhere in the region, it probably stood a little below the elevated site of the present town, in the vicinity of today's Nocera Scalo. Thirteen kilometres further north, Gualdo Tadino is the last sizeable town in Umbria before the Via Flaminia crosses the present regional boundary into the Marches. Mentioned in the Eugubine Tables as an enemy town, Gualdo Tadino was known to the Romans as Tadinum. As with Nocera, the Roman settlement almost certainly lay lower down than the present town, probably on the valley floor. Three more Roman stations existed along the final stretch of the Via Flaminia inside Umbria's borders; though their exact locations are uncertain, Fossato di Vico may have been the Roman Helvillum, and Sigillo was perhaps Suillum. The most substantial reminders of the Flaminian Way here are two bridges: one, from the reign of Augustus, stands just beyond Sigillo and another is to be found close by, at Scirca. Scheggia – known to the Romans as Schisa, and measured as 130 miles from Rome itself – is the last town in Umbria. Seven kilometres further on the Via Flaminia entered the Marches, and it reaches the Adriatic at the port of Fanum Fortunae (now Fano) before continuing north to Ariminum (Rimini), where an arch marks the end of the road – the point at which the Via Flaminia met up with the Via Aemilia.

The prosperity Umbria enjoyed throughout the first century of the Christian era extended into the second, as the Roman empire expanded under the Antonines to its greatest extent, stretching from Britain to North Africa and from Spain to the Arabian peninsula. Given that the Roman towns or stations have, virtually without exception, been lived in, fought over, plundered, and rebuilt throughout more than 2,000 years since the Flaminian Way was built, it is remarkable that so much of the Roman past remains visible today. Despite the region's proximity to Rome, which helped maintain stability in the region, however, Umbria could not be wholly immune to the more general decline of the empire which began with the accession, in 180 AD, of the deranged Commodus – who believed himself the reincarnation of Hercules and Mithras. Despite occasional respites, the empire was increasingly weakened by a succession of ruthless and short-lived military commanders unequal to the immense task imperial rule posed. At its far-flung edges, the empire suffered invasions from Franks, Goths and Persians, and though each wave of invaders was temporarily repulsed, the cumulative effect was to weaken Roman power still further. At the end of the third century, Diocletian endeavoured to save the empire by decentralization, providing for an administrative division into four provinces – two in the west and two in the east – to be ruled over by joint emperors. When Diocletian and his co-emperor, Maximian, abdicated in 305, however, renewed internal conflict broke out, and after victories in the west – at the Milvian bridge outside Rome in 312 – and later in the east, Constantine established himself in 324 as sole ruler of the empire. By choosing Byzantium (which he renamed Constantinople) as his capital, however, Constantine dealt a severe blow to the prestige not merely of Rome but of Italy and the entire western empire. By the end of the third century the split between the empires was complete, and they would, thereafter, have separate rulers.

Civil strife and poor government affected Umbria very quickly. One of the reasons put forward to Constantine by the inhabitants of Spello in 333 to support their request to hold theatrical and gladiatorial spectacles in their own city rather than at the Fanum Voltumnae was the difficulty caused in travelling – no more than fifty kilometres – by 'high mountains, arduous roads, and wooded areas'. The prosperous and well-tended countryside of the immediate past was already giving way to the more desolate landscape, marked by an increase in swampland and spontaneous reforestation, which would characterize Umbria in the following centuries. After the transfer of the imperial capital to Constantinople, Umbria's geographical position close to Rome was of much less account. When the capital of the western empire was transferred from Rome to Ravenna in 404, the proximity to increasingly vulnerable Rome threatened Umbria's own tranquillity and the prosperity of those who lived there. In the first years of the fifth century, the Visigoths, who had been pushing westwards into Europe for two centuries and sporadically fighting the Romans for decades in the Balkans and Greece, invaded the Italian peninsula under their king, Alaric. In 408, on their way to Rome, their armies used the route which had previously been instrumental in ensuring Umbria's prosperity – the Flaminian Way – only to lay waste to the region. Once at Rome, the Visigoths besieged the city and left only after obtaining an enormous ransom for sparing it. Two years later, Alaric returned and this time captured and plundered Rome.

CHAPTER FOUR

From the Fall of Rome to the Longobard Supremacy

✳

For Umbria, the sack of Rome marked the beginning of a long period of neglect and destruction. Alien armies passed repeatedly through the territory, along the Flaminian Way, until by the end of the fifth century the surrounding areas had been abandoned and had grown wild as their former inhabitants fled to the forbidding mountains to the east in search of safety. After the Visigoths came the Huns of Attila and the Vandals under Genseric, who sacked Rome in 455. In 476 the last western Emperor, Romulus Augustulus, was deposed and Odoacer became the first barbarian king of Italy. With the support of Zeno, the eastern Emperor, the Goths, under their king Theodoric, invaded Italy, overthrowing Odoacer. Granted the title of King of Italy by the new Emperor, Anastasius, Theodoric continued to reign until 526, without ever fully attaining power over a unified Italy. Nevertheless, Theodoric's attempt to integrate his own people with the natives of the peninsula, and an administration founded on Roman law and institutions, ensured that his reign of over thirty years was marked by comparative peace. In Umbria, there was even some move to reverse the destruction and neglect of the previous century. In 499, Theodoric travelled into Umbrian territory in order to establish an important garrison at Spoleto, where he set up camp in the amphitheatre, rebuilding the town walls and civic buildings, and setting in motion plans to reclaim the land around the city for cultivation.

This respite, however, was temporary, and the relative stability of Theodoric's reign did not long outlive the ruler, who was succeeded by his eight-year-old grandson under the regency of the boy's mother. The death of the young king seven years later, and the subsequent murder of his mother, resulted in a confused political situation in Italy which provided Justinian, emperor of the east, with a justification to attempt the reconquest of Italy from the barbarians. To this end he sent an army to the peninsula in 535, under the command of the general Belisarius. Arriving in Sicily from North Africa – accompanied by his secretary, the historian Procopius, who wrote a long history of the wars – Belisarius made his way north as far as Rome. The Goths were now commanded by an old soldier, Witiges, who recognized the superiority of Belisarius's forces, abandoned Rome without a struggle, and took the royal treasure north to Ravenna. Supported by only 5,000 men, Belisarius occupied Rome unopposed. Having taken the former imperial capital, however, he now found himself threatened by Witiges. A year-long siege followed, between 537 and 538, the defenders suffering from both famine and plague.

If the plight of the Romans was dire, that of the inhabitants of the Umbrian territories was no less so. On the direct route between the old and the new imperial capitals, they suffered as the rival armies variously marched north-east or south-west between Rome and Ravenna. Narni, Norcia, Spoleto, Todi, Assisi and Perugia – where Belisarius established his command in 536 – all suffered, first at the hands of the Goths and then at those of the counter-attacking Byzantine forces. After the lifting of the siege of Rome, Belisarius moved north again, taking the resettled site of Orvieto in 538 and marching through Umbria once more to attack Ravenna, where, after a siege, Witiges was made prisoner in 540 and taken to Constantinople.

Although Italy now seemed securely back under Byzantine control, it did not remain so for long. Two years after the capture of Witiges, and in the absence of Belisarius, the Ostrogoths again swept down through the peninsula from the north Italian plain, this time under the command of Totila. In his progress through Umbria, Totila endeavoured to ensure that the region would never again prove a military obstacle to him. His armies tore down the defences of all those Umbrian cities (including Tifernum, Perugia, Assisi, Forum Flaminium, Gualdo Tadino, Gubbio and Spoleto) that had held out against him, and sometimes destroyed the cities themselves. When Perugia resisted, it was – for the second time in its history – starved into surrender and many survivors were put to death. Belisarius returned to Italy and briefly occupied Rome before abandoning it once more. The war dragged on for a decade. In the end, it was left not to Belisarius but to his general, Narses, to defeat Totila and his army. The decisive battle was fought on Umbrian soil.

In 552 Narses marched his troops from Dalmatia and along the Adriatic coast, before crossing the Apennines to arrive at Tagina, just to the north of the present-day Gualdo Tadino. There he encountered Totila, who had left Rome at the head of an army to meet him. Exhausted by years of warfare and aware of the importance of the battle, the commanders treated with each other. Narses's attempt to persuade Totila to surrender met with a predictably negative response, but the Ostrogoth leader, anxious to gain reinforcements for his outnumbered troops, agreed to an eight-day truce. Narses immediately readied his soldiers for action and took advantage of the truce to occupy a strategically significant height to the left of his position. Totila too put his troops into battle position. The disposition of the two forces indicates well the difference between the strengths of the two armies. While Narses put his infantry into the centre, flanked on each side by archers and a small force of cavalry, Totila placed all his cavalry in the centre with his infantry behind. When fighting began, the Ostrogoth cavalry charged directly at the Byzantine forces in a desperate attempt to break up the foot-soldiers, regardless of the assault they suffered from the arrows reaching them from each side. Despite their skill, the cavalry suffered too heavy casualties to achieve their aim and the survivors turned and fled. In their flight, the first wave ran into the second, which was advancing close behind them, and into the infantry following in support. The result was first panic and then chaos. Battle not having been joined until midday, night intervened, but when the next day dawned, half the Ostrogoth force lay dead or dying on the field, while the rest were put to flight. Among the wounded was Totila himself, who died just fifteen or so kilometres from the scene of his defeat. The battle of Tagina was nearly decisive. When Narses defeated Totila's successor, Teia, a year later, in the south of the peninsula, the Ostrogoth rule over Italy was ended for ever.

For Umbria, there was little respite. The region had been marched through and fought over for decades by two opposing armies, neither of which had hesitated to destroy what was left of the region's past greatness. Whole cities vanished from the map. Arna, Urbinum Hortense, and Carsulae would be heard of no more, and the towns that remained were stripped of their protective walls and their wealth. According to Procopius, Italy was in the grip of famine – the people reduced to eating dogs, rats, nettles, grass or excrement, and dying in their tens of thousands – and the inhabitants of the region who survived fled to more remote and inaccessible areas of the region, in an attempt to escape the conflict or plague. Yet no sooner was the region back under Byzantine control than it faced a new threat: the third and most important wave of northern invaders, the Longobards (or Lombards), descended the peninsula, and yet again Umbria, with its crucial route linking Rome to Ravenna, felt the full brunt of Italy's instability.

Roman power and prosperity had, by now, long disappeared, but one legacy remained which proved strong enough to conserve some order at the time of the first barbarian invasions and would shape the future of Umbria over the following centuries of Longobard domination. Even as the Roman empire began its long decline, a new cultural force had begun to make inroads into Umbrian territory. Christianity had firmly established itself in Umbria as early as the fourth century and may have been present in the second or even the first century. Again, the region's proximity to the former imperial capital was decisive. Rome was the site of one of the earliest Christian communities, established probably during the reign of Claudius, between AD 41 and 54. Legend has both St Peter and St Paul passing through Umbria on their journeys to and from the capital, where both

were to suffer martyrdom around the year 67, and local traditions have them preaching or celebrating the eucharist in both
Bevagna and Foligno. Even if we discount these historically
improbable (and certainly unproven) tales, there is good reason
to suppose the early appearance of Christianity in the region,
encouraged not only by proximity to Rome but also by the
presence of Christian travellers journeying along the Via
Flaminia. The new religion may first have been embraced by
the communities of Hellenized Jews which seem to have existed
in Norcia, Nocera and the Umbrian mountains, where they fled
after Claudius expelled them from Rome in AD 49.

Medieval legend is notoriously unreliable, but since modern
historians estimate that Christians already accounted for half the
population of Italy, south of the Rubicon, in the third century –
well before the Emperor Constantine announced the toleration
of Christianity by means of the Edict of Milan in 313 – the
many legends of early Umbrian Christians may have some
foundation in fact. Certainly, early accounts suggest that it was
the Via Flaminia which facilitated the spread of Christianity in
Umbria. The first Umbrian martyrs – and the tale of the early
church in the region is also very much the tale of those who
died for the new faith – were supposedly from Ocriculum, now
Otrícoli, the southernmost town in the region and closest to
Rome. These were St Victor (San Vittore), executed in 168, and
subsequently St Medicus (San Medico) – properly, Benedetto, a
physician (*medico*) – whose conversion to Christianity was inspired by the miracles alleged to have occurred at the tomb of
Victor, and who followed his fellow citizen in martyrdom four
years later; relics of both saints are still venerated in Otrícoli. At
San Faustino, near Massa Martana, an underground necropolis,
where the Christian symbols of the fish and the lamb appear, has
been dated to the second century.

Aside from accounts mentioning the apostles themselves, prior-
ity in the evangelization of Umbria is given to two saints of the
late second and early third centuries: Felicianus (Feliciano) and
Heraclius (Eraclio). St Felicianus was supposedly born into a
noble and wealthy family at Forum Flaminii – the Roman
settlement on the right bank of the Topino, just to the north-

east of Foligno – in the year 159. Sent to Rome to be educated, he came into contact with the Christian community there and was noticed by Pope Eleutherius – the last of the Greek-speaking bishops of Rome who had dominated the Church since the time of Peter. The Pope put him in the care of the man who was to be his successor, Victor I. Ordained a priest, Felicianus was consecrated bishop of Forum Flaminii and Fulginae (Foligno) by Victor in 193, and given power to ordain other bishops throughout central Italy, as the needs of the growing Church dictated. Though he proselytized for almost half a century, without suffering more than a brief period of imprisonment in Assisi, Felicianus eventually fell victim to the persecution of the Christians by the Emperor Decius, who passed through Fulginae on his return to Rome after defeating the Persians. In acknowledgement of his age and fame, Felicianus was initially imprisoned rather than suffering immediate execution, but he defied all attempts to cajole or torture him into renouncing his faith – even the execution of the young noblewoman, Messalina, condemned for bringing him food. Eventually ordered to be brought to Rome, the ninety-two-year-old Felicianus expired just three miles outside Fulginae, around the year 251.

Or so, at least, goes one version of the story. In fact, the dating of the saint's life is hazy enough that another account gives 304 as the date of his death. (This is not exceptional: Brizio, an early Bishop of Spoleto, is variously recorded to have been a disciple of St Peter, ordained bishop in 93, and one of 300 Syriacs who settled in Umbria in the early sixth century.) What is certain, though, is that as the centuries passed St Felicianus's memory became increasingly venerated – he is the patron of Foligno and gave his name to a small fishing town on the shores of Lake Trasimeno, where he is supposed to have preached in 220. Nor was his fame confined to Umbria. In 970 the Bishop of Metz, a follower of the Holy Roman Emperor, Otto I, piously stole Felicianus's body, along with the relics of many other Umbrian saints, for good measure; the martyr's bones were only returned to Umbria, and then in piecemeal fashion, during the course of the seventeenth century.

Accounts of other martyrs follow similar patterns. St

Felicianus's companion, a former Roman soldier and the other great evangelizer of Umbria, was St Heraclius. Imprisoned along with Felicianus by order of Decius, Eraclio refused to sacrifice to the gods and was executed just outside the town. In Perugia, the supposed first bishop, St Constant (San Costanzo), was eventually beheaded at Foligno having survived vicious flogging and imprisonment in a burning oven, from which he emerged unscathed. Among his successors, both St Ercolanus (Ercolano) I and St Ercolanus II met a martyr's end: the former in 304 during the persecutions of Christians by Diocletian, and the second being beheaded two centuries later after unsuccessfully leading the defence of Perugia against the besieging Goths. While decapitation was the fate of many – especially under the Romans – the ghastly end of other early martyrs bears grisly witness to the savage times in which they lived. St Tutela – along with twelve other women of Bettona – was put to the sword for attempting to bury her brother St Crispoltus. St Messalina, who had brought food to St Felicianus, was flogged to death, St Rufinus (San Rufino) of Assisi was cast into the river Chiascio with a stone tied round his neck, and St Vincent (San Vincenzo), Bishop of Bevagna, died after seven nails were hammered into his head.

Of all Umbria's earliest saints, the best known – at least in Britain – is undoubtedly Valentine. Nobly born, and educated in Rome, Valentine was only twenty when ordained Bishop of Terni, in 197. He remained bishop for the next seventy-six years until eventually finding martyrdom in Rome in 273, at the age of ninety-six. If Valentine's end was unremarkable in his own day, then the old martyr's fate – to be remembered as the patron saint of lovers – is curious enough. As bishop, Valentine is said to have permitted the marriage of the pagan Roman knight, Sabinus, to a young Christian named Serapia; Sabinus subsequently converted to his wife's faith. The story continues, however, in a vein which – while it recalls classical myth – is rather less in tune with the sentimentality of modern greeting-card manufacturers. Shortly after their marriage, Serapia died and Sabinus implored St Valentine's aid in praying for his own death; the saint obliged and Sabinus's petition was quickly granted. If historical fact seems left far behind in this tale, then the early penetration of Christianity into the region around Terni is well attested. Just two kilometres out of the city, in the locality named San Valentino, after the saint, excavation of an early Christian cemetery uncovered both a fourth- or fifth-century sarcophagus, embellished with scenes from both the Old and New Testament, and a funeral stone carved with praying figures.

If legend and historical evidence are hard to separate, then we should not assume that all the stories that come down to us are untrue. By 500, there were no fewer than twenty-two bishoprics in Umbria, and the holders of many had gained a significant reputation for sanctity. Narni, for instance, boasted at least six saints out of its first ten or so bishops, and Spoleto perhaps as many as seven by the middle of the fourth century. Among the saints from Narni, the most famous was St Juvenal (San Giovenale), a Carthaginian physician and intimate of Pope Damasus I, who consecrated him bishop and sent him to Narni in 368 to organize the church there. At his death, St Juvenal's tomb became the site of one of the most important of palaeo-Christian complexes in Umbria, where Roman walls, a ninth-century mosaic, and tenth-century frescoes (among the oldest in the region) survive today. Such was the prestige of this Umbrian saint that in 850, Adalbert, Landgrave of Tuscany, stole his relics and took them to Lucca, only returning them under threat of excommunication by the Pope. A desire to obtain holy relics in order to ensure the protection of the saints at the Day of Judgement was so strong in the Middle Ages that the theft of relics was commonplace. Less frequently, remains might be gifted: those of St Crescentius (San Crescenzio) of Tifernum (Città di Castello) – who suffered during the Diocletian persecution of 303 – were ceded by an eleventh-century bishop of the town to Urbino in the Marches and solemnly relocated under the high altar of the cathedral there in 1360.

Though many Umbrian saints died for their faith, martyrdom was not the only sign of sanctity. The fourth-century St Fortunatus (San Fortunato) of Montefalco – who interestingly prefigures Umbria's most famous saint, Francis – was ploughing his fields one day when he unearthed some money which he gave away to the poor. Such spiritual consolation did he derive from his act that he became a priest and dedicated his life to charitable works. When he died, his grave became as popular a place of pilgrimage as if he had suffered martyrdom. Other saints, such as St Crispoltus (San Crispolto) or St Illuminata of Bettona, performed miracles in the biblical manner during their lifetimes. Others were associated with still more extravagant wonders. In exchange for a promise from the inhabitants of Tifernum to convert to Christianity, St Crescentius killed a dragon which had been threatening their city. It was Pope Gregory the Great himself who recorded the story of San Fiorenzo – the hermit Florian – whose prayer for a companion to relieve his solitude was granted when God sent him a bear – which subsequently looked after the hermit's sheep like a shepherd, until being killed by the saint's jealous neighbours.

That many early Umbrian saints were bishops and the deeds attributed to them unusually various is not in itself surprising, for in the early Church – and especially as the Roman empire began to disintegrate – the role of bishops was a wide-ranging one. After the fall of Romulus Augustulus in 476, leading to a fierce struggle between the inheritors of the empire and the northern invaders, it was the papacy which increasingly emerged as the third force in Italian politics. The Pope in Rome gradually took the place of the former Emperor, a process consolidated under Pope Gregory the Great in the sixth century. As this assumption of political power was added to the spiritual claims of the Church at a national level, so the process was echoed in local communities. The bishops did not confine themselves to pastoral care but took on some of the secular duties of the state officials. They administered justice, controlled education, looked after the sick and aged, encouraged agriculture and the arts and organized the defence of their cities in times of war. In this way, the early bishops set a pattern which was to last for centuries. Umbria boasts many examples of bishops whose reputations for sanctity and leadership in war and peace led them subsequently to be adopted as the patron saints of their cities. St Florus (San Florido) was born into a Christian family in Tifernum, in 520, at the time of the Gothic invasions, later becoming a priest. When his home town was devastated by the northern invaders, its walls torn down and its buildings razed, Florus set about rebuilding and fortifying the city. The work was completed in 570 and, a decade later, Florus was consecrated bishop. His exemplary life came to the attention of Pope Gregory, and when he died in 600 the bishops of Perugia, Arezzo and Urbino all came to Città di Castello to bury Florus in the cathedral whose construction he had initiated and which was subsequently dedicated to him.

While bishops like Florus and Ercolanus were deeply engaged in the contemporary civic life of Umbria, a very different but equally important manifestation of Christianity was developing in the region – one which would exercise an enormous influence for the next 1,000 years, not merely locally but on the whole of western European culture. Monasticism did not begin with St Benedict, but no single individual was as dominant in the shaping of monastic life in the west as this son of a Roman official born in Nursia (now Norcia), around 480. (The remains of a Roman building beneath Norcia's cathedral are traditionally identified as Benedict's birthplace.) In the east, monasticism owed much to the Rule of Basil the Great (c. 330–79), Bishop of Caesarea, who emphasized the importance of community, labour, and the study of the Bible but did not entirely shift the emphasis away from the ascetic ideal of a life of contemplation and renunciation. At its extreme, eastern asceticism was epitomized, around 420, by the Syrian St Simon Stylites, who endeavoured to remove himself from worldly temptation by retiring to live at the top of a series of columns – the last some eighteen metres high – where he spent the last thirty-seven years of his life. Though the most celebrated ascetic, Simon Stylites was not alone and examples abound of anchorites living in trees or at the bottom of dry wells, dependent on charity for their very survival. In 514 this eastern tradition manifested itself in Umbria very directly, when some 300 Syrians, fleeing the persecutions of the Arian Emperor Anastasius (491–518), arrived in the region and formed tiny anchorite communities in caves in the remote areas of Monteluco and in the Nera valley. At the same time, the young Benedict, who had abandoned his studies in Rome – in despair at the dissolute life he found there –

retired to a life of contemplation and mortification in a cave on Mount Subiaco, in the Sabine hills. In the course of a three-year stay, Benedict gradually gathered around himself a small group of followers and began to formulate the principles of the ideal Christian existence that would become the basis of his Rule. A simple hermitic repudiation of the world was wrong, and self-denial inadequate, Benedict came to believe. Instead, he argued for the value of a life of prayer and work – the latter understood to include both intellectual and manual endeavour – summed up in the motto 'ora et labora'. In 529 he founded twelve small monastic communities each with a dozen members, a kind of monastic organization based on that of St Basil, and of which several examples could be found in Umbria. A victim of local jealousy and even of a plot against his life, Benedict later left central Italy, moving south towards Naples. There he established the monastery of Montecassino, where he completed his Rule, the basis of one of the most important religious movements of the Middle Ages. This movement of renewal was not restricted to men, for Benedict's sister, St Scholastica (tradition would have them twins), also removed herself to Montecassino, where she supposedly met her brother just once a year until her death in 543, close to the nunnery she had founded near by.

In a time of extreme political upheaval, with social life continually disrupted by the waves of invaders moving up and down the peninsula, the Benedictine monasteries offered not only a spiritual example, characterized by the monks' vows of poverty, chastity, and obedience, but a much-needed model of social organization and stability as well. Pope Gregory the Great, whose account of Benedict – though unburdened by any effort to distinguish fact from fanciful fiction – is the source of our knowledge of the saint, suggests Benedict's political significance for his age in the story of his supposed meeting with the Ostrogoth leader, Totila himself. According to Pope Gregory's account of the saint's life, Benedict quickly gained credit with Totila when he immediately saw through the King's subterfuge of sending one of his soldiers into the monk's presence masquerading as his royal master. As a result, Totila listened to Benedict's condemnation of the destruction his army had caused to the regions through which it passed and heard the predictions that he would capture Rome, reign nine years, but die in the tenth – prophecies which were in fact to be fulfilled – after which the King supposedly promised the monk to restrain his troops from further massacres.

Benedict's Rule sought to establish a source of authority at a time of a near-total collapse of social order, but though Benedictine rule was indisputably authoritarian – for Benedictine abbots had great power in their communities – it was also, in other respects, notably egalitarian. All monks were considered of equal status regardless of their social standing at birth, personal possessions were abandoned in favour of common ownership, and each community was independent and elected its own abbot. Benedictine monasteries gradually became centres of prosperity and security in times of want or danger. Inspired by a belief in the dignity of manual labour unknown in the Roman world, the monks began the reclamation of lands lost to cultivation with the decline of the Roman empire: marshes were drained, canals were constructed, mills and oil-presses were built, and livestock farming encouraged. Monasteries became important economic and commercial centres, employing lay helpers in the fields and selling surplus produce. Benedict's Rule did not confine the business of the monks to physical labour, however, nor even to such arts as medicine, but to a spiritual and intellectual life. Called frequently and regularly to prayer, the monks were also obliged to study, and not only the sacred writings but also the classical authors. In time, the celebrated Benedictine scriptoriums gave rise to great libraries whose role in the preservation of classical culture and its transmission to later times was incalculable, while the abbeys themselves became models of social organization imitated throughout Europe. In Umbria, monasticism took so great a hold that by the tenth century there were perhaps as many as 300 monasteries in the territory, some of them both wealthy and powerful, holding as many as 2,000 monks.

The contemporary importance of monasticism is easy enough to understand. Just twenty-five years after the death of St Benedict, Italy saw the arrival of yet more invaders from the north, and this time ones whose influence would be the most far-reaching and long-lasting of all. The Longobards – or Lombards – were a Germanic people, originally from the shores of the North Sea, who arrived in northern Italy in 568 under the leadership of Alboin. Rapidly conquering the north Italian plain, they established a kingdom, with its capital at Pavia, which was to last for more than two centuries. Although their base remained in the north, the Longobards soon moved south through the Italian peninsula to found two duchies, which enjoyed near autonomy from Pavia, and, as a result, were able in the course of time to survive the fall of the northern kingdom. One of these duchies was Benevento in the south of Italy and the other was centred on Spoleto, in Umbria.

The Duchy of Spoleto, which extended out from its Umbrian capital to include parts of the Abruzzo, the Sabine region and the Marches as far as the Adriatic, was created under the rule of Faraold I in 571, and existed – at least in name – for almost 700 years, until 1250. With the founding of the duchy, the territory of the present Umbrian region was split into three. Within the duchy lay the cities of Spoleto, Terni, Norcia, Trevi, Bevagna, Foligno, Forum Flaminii, Spello, Assisi and Tadino. Orvieto, which had still not regained anything approaching the status it had enjoyed under the Etruscans as Volsinii, remained in Tuscia, which also included Tifernum. Between these, the remainder of the Umbrian centres – including Otrícoli, Narni, Amelia, Todi, Bettona, Perugia and Gubbio – remained in Byzantine hands, in a slim ribbon of land linking Rome with the Exarchate of Ravenna.

The imposition of Longobard rule in Italy was not without its problems. According to Paulus Diaconus, author of the eighth-century *Historia Langobardorum*, it began badly enough when King Alboin was killed at the instigation of his wife, Rosmund – understandably vengeful after her husband forced her to drink out of a cup fashioned from the skull of her father. For a decade following Alboin's death in 574 there was near anarchy, with Longobard dukes ruling small parts of their conquered territory according to their own lights. Only when menaced by the external threat posed by a Byzantine–Frankish alliance did the

Longobard nobles gather to elect a single ruler, Authari. From this moment onwards, however, the impact of the Longobards on Italy increased considerably.

In Umbria, they were not content to pass through, like previous invaders from the north, pillaging and destroying on their way to some other destination. Instead, they settled on the land and, in time, became assimilated to the indigenous population. Although few signs remain of the earliest period of Longobard settlement, the important necropolis (whose contents are now on display in Rome) discovered at Nocera Umbra in 1898 indicates the strategic importance accorded to this centre along the Via Flaminia. Even Spoleto, the centre of Longobard power, reveals scant trace of its prestige, with no public building of any description remaining. The reason lies in the nature of Longobard society. While not destroying the former Roman centres they occupied, the Longobards built very little of their own, at least in stone. Though civil and ecclesiastical power remained centred in the cities – and the Longobards defended these cities against the Byzantines and the Franks – the highest authorities did no more than occupy existing Roman buildings. The Longobards were a predominantly military people who dedicated themselves to hunting and the rearing of livestock, especially horses. Even within the cities, land was returned to pasture, and most new buildings were constructed of wood instead of more durable materials, at least until the mid seventh century.

Nevertheless, the Longobards did not merely impose their own culture on the lands they occupied. The process of acculturation began early, albeit in minor ways. Traditional dress was abandoned in favour of clothing made after Byzantine models, and new forms of pottery replaced traditional Longobard work. Longobard tombs reveal the widespread use of gold-leaf crosses and of shrouds embroidered with crosses. Such small borrowings, however, were merely symptomatic indications of much profounder change taking place in Longobard culture. Originally Arian – a form of Christianity they had adopted as a result of their contacts with Byzantium to the east – the Longobards gradually converted to Roman Catholicism after 600 (notably through the influence of Theudolinde, wife of Alboin's successor,

Authari). Though King Rothari – whose reign between 636 and 652 saw the publication of an Edict (643) which represents the most notable attempt to codify Longobard law – remained an Arian, his successors were all Catholics.

As a result, it is in the sphere of religious building that we can most easily discern the Longobard presence in Umbria today – and here too that we can perceive the interaction of the new with indigenous cultures. Despite the comparative lack of monuments of indisputably Longobard origin throughout all the territories they occupied in Italy, there are, nevertheless, some particularly celebrated examples of Longobard religious architecture in Umbria – products of the building programmes of the mid seventh century, marked by the flourishing of sculpture, painting, and associated crafts. The dating of the church of San Salvatore just outside Spoleto has long been disputed, largely as a result of the notable use made of materials from earlier Roman buildings. Together with the extensive remodelling it has undergone, this has led to suggestions that the church may have originated anywhere between the fourth century and the late eighth or even early ninth century. It seems likely, however, that San Salvatore was either originally built, or significantly restructured, during the period of Longobard rule in Spoleto. Today, the diverse nature of the inspiration for the building is especially evident. Originally the façade was divided into two levels, the upper having a pediment above fluted pillars, while the lower was preceded by a porch, supported by columns with Corinthian capitals, taken from earlier buildings. The doors were decorated in a manner giving clear indication of Roman influence but given a Christian turn by the addition of the monogram of Christ; by contrast, the decorative motif above the rounded arch of the central window on the upper level of the façade shows eastern sources of influence. The interior of the church – built on a basilical plan – reveals three aisles divided by pairs of fluted Doric columns supporting a massive entablature. At the end of the nave are three apses – the two outer ones square, the central one semicircular. The square presbytery has four pairs of fluted Corinthian columns, again supporting a heavy entablature, all taken from earlier buildings. Though elements of the architecture are heavy and even awkward in places, the overall effect is impressive – and remains so whether San Salvatore is a palaeo-Christian construction (in which case it would be one of the earliest surviving Christian churches in the world) reworked by the Longobards, or whether it originated in this later period.

The importance of Spoleto and the surrounding area, as well as the flourishing of architectural skills at an early period, may also be gauged from another building, not far away. The church of San Salvatore a Campello presents similar problems of dating to its namesake in Spoleto. Still better known as the Tempietto del Clitunno – or Little Temple of Clitumnus – this small church, close to the Springs of Clitumnus, has been much discussed. Variously held to be a small Roman temple from the late empire, a palaeo-Christian edifice, and a Longobard foundation, this San Salvatore was also built with material taken from earlier buildings – perhaps from the 'holy temple', dedicated to the god Clitumnus, which Pliny the Younger mentions. It now seems as though the building dates from two different periods, the first phase being the construction of a single chamber with a barrel-vaulted roof, the second its extension and decoration, including the construction of the temple-like façade with its four columns and two semi-pilasters supporting the entablature and pediment. Again, this apparently classical building is given a Christian turn, by means both of an inscription on the architrave dedicating the church to the 'SCS DEVS ANGELORVM QVI FECIT RESVRRECTIONEM' – or 'The Holy God of the Angels who made the Resurrection' – and by the decoration of the pediment with a cross flanked by bunches of grapes, vines and flowers. Frescoes in the interior of the church, depicting Christ the Redeemer with Sts Peter and Paul and with angels, have been dated to the eighth century.

The San Salvatore churches both have considerable artistic importance. So, too, does the abbey church of San Pietro in Valle, situated in the Nera valley, across the mountains to the south-east of Spoleto. The abbey itself, moreover, once possessed great political power. Built on the site occupied by the hermitages of John (Giovanni) and Lazarus (Lazzaro), two of the

Syrian monks who arrived in Umbria after fleeing the persecutions of the Emperor Anastasius, the building of the abbey represented an important stage of Longobard expansion into the Valnerina. It was begun by the Duke of Spoleto, Faroaldo II, who, when he was deposed by his son, Trasamond II, about 720, retired to the abbey as a Benedictine monk, dying there in 728. In the centuries that followed, San Pietro in Valle flourished. Like other Benedictine foundations, the abbey benefited from donations of lands given by their proprietors, either for spiritual reasons or as a means of ensuring the protection the increasingly powerful monasteries offered. Though not immune from attack – it was nearly destroyed by the Saracens who invaded the Italian peninsula in the late ninth century – San Pietro survived, and the rebuilding included the construction of defensive fortresses, designed to ward off further attacks. By 1190 the abbey was so powerful as to be in conflict with the city of Spoleto itself. Most of the present building dates from later periods – after the early-tenth-century restoration which followed the Saracen depredations, the abbey was enlarged and embellished at different times, including the late twelfth century when the cloister was added, and when the interior of the church was decorated with a particularly important cycle of pre-Giottoesque frescoes, which mark a significant break with Byzantine models and the beginnings of an independent Umbrian tradition of painting (see p. 213). Some traces of the abbey's origins do remain, however, notably the Longobard reliefs set in the outer walls and the present high altar, which was constructed using other important carved stones from the earliest period. The stone altar frontal – commissioned by Hildericus, Duke of Spoleto between 739 and 742, who was buried in the church, along with his predecessors, Faramond II and Trasamond II – is especially remarkable for the signed portrait of the artist, who described himself as Ursus Magester, or Master Ursus.

Other Umbrian monasteries also flourished under the Longobards – such as San Benedetto, close to Assisi on the wooded slopes of Monte Subasio, and the monastery at Monteluco, above Spoleto. Typical of the generally remote locations of these early foundations is the abbey of Sant'Eutizio which lies high in the hills in an isolated position near Preci, in the Val-castoriana, north-west of Norcia. Protected by its isolation, the abbey prospered, especially between the ninth and thirteenth centuries, when it benefited from numerous gifts of land. One such donation was made in 907 by Ageltrude of Benevento, wife of Duke Guido III of Spoleto, who gave a church, lands and houses near Iesi in the Marches. Similar grants and fiscal privileges by successive rulers, including the Dukes of Spoleto, Holy Roman Emperors, and popes, meant that at its height the monastery controlled no fewer than 100 fortified villages and churches. Indeed, by the end of the twelfth century, Benedictine foundations in Umbria controlled as much as a third of the region's territory. Sant'Eutizio's social and economic power throughout an extensive area stretching beyond Umbria across the Apennines to the east was matched by its cultural influence: the school of surgery in neighbouring Preci, famous for centuries, had its origins in the abbey's infirmary, and among the manuscripts copied in the scriptorium are documents from the eleventh century in local dialect – the first examples of the written use of the vulgar tongue in the entire region.

As Benedictine monasticism extended its influence throughout Italy and much of western Europe – England was evangelized by a Benedictine monk, St Augustine of Canterbury, and the Venerable Bede, Alcuin, and St Anselm were all Benedictines – Longobard power also slowly grew and then, rather more suddenly, declined. The height of that power had been reached in the mid seventh century under Grimwald I, who achieved a union of the northern kingdom with the Duchy of Benevento and succeeded in defending the joint territories against the predations of Byzantines, Franks and Slavs alike. Even when conflicts arose over the question of succession after Grimwald's death, the Longobards remained dominant. Under Liutprand (712–44), the northern kingdom attempted to unify Italy by subjugating the duchies of Benevento and Spoleto and by endeavouring to conquer Rome and the Exarchate of Ravenna. Periodic attempts by Liutprand and his successors, Rachis and Aistulf, to occupy the narrow corridor of land linking Rome with Ravenna threatened the so-called *ducatus perusinus*, or

Duchy of Perugia, which administered the Byzantine cities of Umbria. In 748, Perugia itself was only saved from assault at the hands of the army of Rachis camped beneath its walls by the intervention of Pope Zacharias. The *ducatus perusinus* survived, and Rome too resisted the Longobard threat, but the days of the Exarchate of Ravenna were numbered. When it eventually fell to Aistulf in 751, the defeat signalled the end of Byzantine rule in central Italy.

The very power of the Longobards, however, eventually led to their own downfall. Increasingly alarmed at the continuing threat they posed to Rome, Pope Stephen II invited the Frankish king, Pepin the Short, to cross the Alps and enter Italy. Pepin did so and, having taken back the Exarchate's lands from the Longobards, he gave them to the Pope. Twenty years later, Pope Adrian I similarly called for assistance on Pepin's son, Charlemagne. In 774, at the age of thirty-two, Charlemagne seized the Longobard capital of Pavia and, having forced King Desiderius to abdicate, had himself crowned 'King of the Franks and Longobards' with the iron Longobard crown. Although the Duchy of Spoleto remained nominally independent, its rulers came increasingly to be of Frankish origin.

Charlemagne's intervention provided a temporary respite for the papacy. It also initiated what would be, in the longer term, one of the most persistent sources of conflict in Italian politics, and one of the most important factors shaping the future destiny of Umbria – the struggle for power between the papacy and the Holy Roman Empire. The Church of Rome had long been in possession of extensive lands – known as the Patrimonium Petri or Peter's Patrimony – but, since these had been freely given by donors, it had possessed them simply as a private landowner. However, in 728 the Longobard king, Liutprand, gifted to the papacy the lands in northern Lazio he had conquered from the Byzantines – the so-called Donation of Sutri. From that moment on, the Church – as the possessor of territory acquired by conquest – could be considered not only a spiritual but a temporal power. With the acquisition of the lands seized by force from the former Exarchate of Ravenna, the Papal States took on a more significant dimension and became a signal fact in the life of central Italy. That the papacy harboured political ambitions was becoming increasingly apparent in the mid eighth century, as the production of the so-called Donation of Constantine reveals. This was a document purporting to show that, back in the fourth century, the Roman Emperor and Christian convert Constantine had, on leaving for the east, given the papacy authority in perpetuity over Rome and all the provinces and cities of Italy. (Though in fact a contemporary forgery, the Donation of Constantine was considered credible for 700 years until the humanist Lorenzo Valla demonstrated otherwise in the mid fifteenth century.)

As the Church asserted its political power, another political force was emerging – the Holy Roman Empire. Like the Papal States, it too would last for 1,000 years. On Christmas Day, in 800, Charlemagne knelt before the high altar in St Peter's in Rome to receive the imperial crown from Pope Leo III. Though the Holy Roman Emperors looked to the papacy for guidance on spiritual matters, they soon came into conflict with the Church on matters of temporal power. When, after Charlemagne's death in 814, his extensive empire began to break up, Italy fell to the share of his grandson, Lothair, who also inherited the imperial crown. The question of who really ruled in Umbria was, for centuries, complicated by a split between the pretensions of the various contenders for political authority and the ability of these to assert it. While the nominally independent Duchy of Spoleto came increasingly under the control of the Franks, the papal lands fragmented into a multitude of largely autonomous local powers, free of any effective central authority. The very name of Umbria disappeared entirely, as it ceased to correspond to any political reality.

The centres of power were now monasteries, castles, small cities and the lands surrounding each of these. The fragility of this power is evident, however, for while certain centres, especially the increasingly important and well-ordered monasteries, grew in wealth and influence, others declined, or were destroyed, as the Carolingian empire broke up in the wake of Charlemagne's death. Tadino, for example, suffered repeatedly as a result of its vulnerable position on the Via Flaminia, exposed to warring armies moving north or south, who reduced it to little more than a village. While under Frankish rule during the ninth century, it was destroyed by invading Saracens and shortly afterwards was given to Monaldo, count of Nocera. In the late tenth century, an attempt by the rebuilt town to free itself from the control of Nocera met with a fierce response from the troops of the Holy Roman Emperor, Otto III, who razed it to the ground. Abandoned by its inhabitants, Tadino began to revive only in the twelfth century – and then in a slightly higher location, close to the Benedictine abbey founded there in 1006. The story was similar throughout the region. Norcia was sacked by the Longobards in 576 and by Saracens in 829 and 890; rebuilt, it continued to form part of the Duchy of Spoleto until 962, when the Emperor, Otto I, gave it to the Church. Città di Castello was sacked by Saracens in 857, and Magyars in 917, before being similarly gifted to the papacy in 962. The ancient city of Gubbio, which formed part of the Donation confirmed by Charlemagne (who stayed there briefly *en route* to his coronation in 800), had been partly destroyed by the Longobard king, Desiderius, in 772, and was totally demolished by invading Magyars in 924. In the south, Terni – under somewhat tenuous papal control – was also raided by Magyars, and twice sacked by Saracens. Only very rarely did cities in any part of the modern region escape the destruction wreaked by invaders, especially the Saracens, who launched repeated attacks on the peninsula from their base in Sicily. Narni, which had been part of a donation to the Church made in 817, was unique in having twice successfully repelled these Saracens, in 876 and 882. The magnitude of its feat was belatedly recognized in the twelfth century by the Arab geographer Al-Idrisi, who, when commissioned by Ruggero II of Sicily to illustrate the whole world on a silver sheet weighing 150 kilos, indicated Narni as Nârawm, the only city in Umbria, besides Todi, to be so distinguished.

For two centuries after the death of Charlemagne, the Umbrian territories were fought over and fragmented, while their inhabitants found themselves subject to repeated changes of ruler, as shifts in the balance of military power, or political necessity, dictated. For parts of Umbria, these were genuinely dark ages. A once great city like Perugia, for instance, is virtually lost sight of in historical record for 250 years, after the intervention of Pope Zacharias saved it from destruction at the hands of the Longobard king, Rachis. When it re-emerges into faint light in the eleventh century, it is a largely autonomous power constantly engaged in boundary skirmishes with the neighbouring powers of Chiusi (1012), Cortona (1049), Assisi (1054), and Todi (1056).

The hostilities which marked the relations between the Umbrian city-states at this period took place, at least nominally, within the context of the much wider conflict between the Empire and the Church. As so often before, Umbria found itself at the crossroads of this long struggle, caught between the imperial German armies to the north and the Roman papacy to the south. While the Empire fought to assert its supremacy in Umbrian territory, so too did the Church. In theory, of course, much of the region had formed part of the Papal State for centuries, ever since Pepin the Short had presented the Byzantine territories to Pope Stephen II in 754. The actual boundaries of this grant, however, were conveniently vague, and had come to be identified with a great swathe of land running across Italy, from the Tyrrhenian Sea to the Adriatic. At the beginning of the twelfth century the area was becoming a patchwork of small city-states – nominally allied to Church or Empire – but each given to conducting its affairs, as far as possible, without reference to either.

Since the Holy Roman Emperor, Conrad II, resided in Perugia in 1038, the city's allegiance seems then to have been to the Empire, yet it fought on the side of the Church only the following year, against the imperial city of Todi. Soon it was habitually engaged in conflict with other imperial cities, including Assisi, Foligno, Città di Castello and Gubbio. By 1068 its links with Rome had evidently been consolidated, for Pope Alexander II made his residence here. From this time onwards, as the German emperors staked their claims to rule Italy, and the popes grew from being little more than Roman despots to a major political force, the cities of Umbria came increasingly to declare themselves either Guelph or Ghibelline – that is, to

define themselves by their allegiance to the papacy or to the
Holy Roman Empire, respectively. Even two centuries later, at
a time when local interests were put much higher than loyalty
to either side, harsh penalties could be enacted against those who
did not respect nominal allegiances: one hapless Perugian was
sentenced in 1269 to have his tongue cut out for uttering an
insult to King Charles of Anjou, a French ally of the papacy.
Not that Guelph Perugia was altogether auspicious for popes,
either, for no fewer than four of them died in the city in less
than a century, three apparently by poisoning (the Perugians
blamed it on the water). One of these unfortunates was Innocent
III, whose body was stripped of both clothes and jewels on the
night following his death in 1216. In 1264, Urban IV also died
in mysterious circumstances and, in 1304, Benedict XI – visiting
Perugia in an endeavour to mediate between warring factions in
Florence – was given a plate of poisoned figs by a nun with
Ghibelline sympathies. (The Perugians, perhaps running out of
space, then stored the bodies of all three popes in the same
tomb.) The fourth pope to meet an untimely end in Perugia was
Martin IV, who reputedly died of a surfeit of eels, for which
Dante consigned him to Purgatory as a glutton (*Purgatorio*, xxiv,
22–3). Largely as a result of these misfortunes, Perugia was also
the site of several conclaves which saw the election of Honorius
III (1216), Clement IV (1265), Honorius IV (1285), Celestine V
(1294), and Clement V (1305).

The struggle between Church and Empire forms an important
part of the history of Umbria in the three centuries following
the year 1000. In the twelfth century, Frederick I, Barbarossa,
having failed to limit the power of the new communes on the
Lombardy plains in the north of Italy, turned his attentions
elsewhere, and Umbria was now subject to renewed military
incursions. Eventually it was Barbarossa's grandson, the cultured,
intellectual warrior Frederick II – called *Stupor mundi* or the
Wonder of the World – who asserted imperial power in central
Italy, launching attacks on the region from his southern Italian
base in Apulia. Frederick had a personal interest in Umbria, for
he had been baptized in the cathedral at Assisi and had lived,
when a young child, both in Foligno and Spoleto. Once

emperor, he promised to confirm the Church in all the territories – including the Duchy of Spoleto – it then possessed or
claimed. Having quarrelled with the Pope, however, Frederick
reneged on his promises and sent his troops to capture a number
of Umbrian cities, including Gubbio, Nocera, and Foligno.
When he was excommunicated by the Pope he declared the papal
territories annexed to the Empire and, processing through
Umbria, took up residence in Foligno. There he held a parliament in the cathedral and began to impose his rule throughout
the divided region. Advancing south to Rome, Frederick took
the papal cities of Spoleto and Terni unopposed – though his
troops later devastated other Umbrian centres, including Montefalco in 1249. Only after Frederick's death in 1250 did the
struggle between Guelph and Ghibelline begin to ease.

CHAPTER FIVE

The Rise of the Communes

✳

For all its importance, the conflict between the papacy and the Holy Roman Empire does not provide a total explanation of the complex and confused story of Umbria between 1100 and 1250. Profound economic and social changes were taking place in the region, as throughout much of central and northern Italy. To begin with, there was fresh population growth after a long period of stagnation. For the first time for centuries, towns began to expand once more. In some cases, old settlements were abandoned and new towns rebuilt near by: so much of the land that had been drained by the Etruscans and Romans had returned to unhealthy malarial swamp during the previous 500 years that Gubbio, Gualdo Tadino and Trevi all moved to a neighbouring location at a higher altitude. New settlements also began to appear where none had been before. The names of many of these – Arboreto, Bosco, Canneto, Farneto, Fratta, or Pantano, for example, each deriving from a local topographical or other natural feature – give clear indication of a renewed desire by Umbrian men and women to dominate their environment. Communications improved, and new roads linked monasteries, castles, and villages as well as the major towns and cities. Although an agricultural economy remained significant through-out the region, the older feudal order was increasingly challenged by a barter economy centred on the towns. Surplus produce from the surrounding countryside was exchanged at town mar-kets for the growing number of locally produced goods on sale there. While the dominant social groups in the towns remained the clergy and nobility, newly important social groups were emerging, including craftsmen, merchants, physicians and lawyers. It was among these groups that new political and administrative structures arose, as citizens came together to discuss matters of common interest – the strengthening of city walls to provide defence from hostile neighbours or the building of roads and bridges to permit trade with friendly ones. Such groups of citizens had no real legal status, and power usually still resided with the ecclesiastical authorities, but the local bishop frequently encouraged the coming together of leading citizens for the common good of the city. In many cases, the Empire and the papacy vied with each other to create such communes and invest them with specific powers, in an attempt to bring the cities more securely into their own sphere of influence. Terni, for instance, owed allegiance to the Empire for most of the second half of the twelfth century, after Barbarossa camped outside the city in 1155; after the deposition of the imperial legate, however, Pope Innocent III paid a visit in 1198, to reclaim Terni by establishing a commune there. Gubbio, by contrast, became a commune under imperial rule and always remained Ghibelline.

In fact, whether nominally under imperial or papal sway, the new communes enjoyed a great deal of autonomy, in many cases amounting to the political independence they were generally careful not to claim. (There were exceptions: Cascia, for instance, became an independent republic in the twelfth century, forming a small buffer state between the Papal States and the Kingdom of Naples.) The communes passed legislation, minted their own currency, dispensed justice and contracted (and broke) alliances, with little or no consultation with emperor or pope. Once constituted, they also quickly endeavoured to enlarge their own spheres of influence, extending their power into the surrounding countryside, bringing feudal lords under their control and freeing serfs who would then form smaller rural communes, possessing a certain degree of autonomy of their own, but primarily designed to foster the interests of the dominant city. The power of the larger communes could be very widespread: Perugia received the submission of the Isola Polvese (thereby acquiring the important resource of Lake Trasimeno) in 1139,

Città di Castello in 1180, Castrum Plebis (Città della Pieve) in 1188, Nocera in 1202, and Gualdo in 1208.

As the city-states grew, however, so too did mutual antagonism between near-neighbours. Increasingly, the inhabitants of the region saw themselves, first and foremost, as *perugini*, or *assisani*, or *orvietani*, as the case might be, thereby setting a pattern for the *campanilismo* – or intense local patriotism – that remains a very real feature of Umbrian life even today. In contrast both to the demographic fluidity of earlier times, and to the contemporary situation in northern Europe, Umbrians were becoming rooted in their birthplace. Whereas its necropolises reveal that Orvieto had been a notably cosmopolitan city under the Etruscans, a census carried out in 1292 showed that of the city's 2,816 citizens only fifty-eight had lived elsewhere, and of these no more than nine came from outside Umbria. Such immobility led to local antipathies and antipathy soon resulted in open hostility. Perugia and Assisi, for example, lie less than twenty kilometres apart, on opposite banks of the Tiber, facing each other across the plain, the one clearly visible from the other. Yet the two cities fought each other for hundreds of years. It is true that Perugia's sympathies were generally Guelph, while Assisi remained staunchly Ghibelline throughout the eleventh and twelfth centuries. Yet even when Assisi rebelled against the Empire, the hostilities against Perugia – now nominally an ally – continued unabated. Only following a treaty concluded between the two cities in 1228 did a more lasting peace occur – and then their combined armies were soon to be found besieging another nearby city, Foligno.

At the beginning of the twelfth century, power resided in the hands of a small group of leading citizens, the *boni homines* (or 'good men'), who chose one or more of their number to act on behalf of all whenever occasion demanded. As the century wore on, a more permanent arrangement became desirable and the *boni homines* chose a number of consuls – their name echoing Italy's Roman, and specifically republican, past. These consuls were the supreme magistrates of the city and the commanders of the army in times of war. In comparison to more northerly cities, the Umbrian communes were of late foundation. While the communes of Pisa, Genoa and Milan came into existence at the end of the eleventh century, consular rule in Umbria began in the twelfth: Perugia, for example, had consuls from 1130, Gubbio from 1163, Spoleto from 1173, Assisi from 1184, and Bevagna from 1187. Chosen from among the local nobility, and numbering – depending on time and place – anything between two and twenty, they remained in office for one year. In 1139, for instance, Perugia's consuls were ten in number – two for each of the city gates – though the number was subsequently increased to sixteen and later reduced to thirteen. Gubbio had at first two, then four, then eight – divided equally between nobles and plebeians. This particular division, however, also draws attention to another complicating factor and one of the principal difficulties besetting the emergent communes. While caught between Empire and papacy on the one hand, and mutually antagonistic on the other, communes were also riven by internal disputes – both between rival Guelph and Ghibelline factions and between different social groups.

In their consular phase, the communes were usually dominated by the nobility, who provided the majority of consuls. The changing economy of the cities, however, saw the growth of an ever more powerful middle class of merchants and craftsmen, whose interests were often at odds with those of the nobility and who increasingly demanded a greater share in government. Before long, the consuls were replaced by a *podestà* (from the Latin, *potestas*: authority or power). Unlike the consuls – who had been chosen exclusively from the local population – the *podestà* was always brought in from elsewhere, in order better to ensure impartial government. His appointment was hedged around with many conditions: not only must he be an outsider, and not related to anyone in the city in which he was to serve, but he was advised – and sometimes obliged – to abstain from all private contact with citizens, neither walking nor talking with them, during his term of office. The *podestà* did not, strictly speaking, rule the city but was, rather, the guarantor of law within it. As such he had an enormously important role, for the commune controlled every secular aspect of the lives of the men and women who lived there. Internally, it regulated the supply of water and food, employment, law, education, civic and domestic building, road construction and sanitation. The commune was also responsible for the relations of the city-state with the Church authorities and the nobility who owned land in the surrounding countryside – called the *contado* – as well as the state's relations with other communes. Perugia, which had its first *podestà* – a Roman named Cazullo – in 1191, stipulated that he must be not only an outsider, but also of noble birth, and a Guelph. The situation was similar elsewhere, though particular circumstances varied. Spoleto specified that its *podestà* should be a foreigner, who had been neither banished nor excommunicated, and who needed the support of 200 counsellors to be elected for a term of six months. These were not, of course, democratic elections in any modern sense. Not only was the electorate tiny and drawn from restricted social groups, but outside interests – notably the Church and the Empire – had frequently to be consulted. So it was Pope Gregory IX who gave Assisi the freedom to elect Breve da Viterbo *podestà* in 1237, while Foligno's *podestà* was elected only with the permission of the Emperor. Spello, meanwhile, could elect its *podestà* only with the approval of Perugia.

Rule by *podestà* did not end disputes within the medieval cities of Umbria. As the communes expanded to control increasing areas of the surrounding countryside, large landowners often moved into the town, where they built large fortified houses for themselves. Rivalries between families became commonplace and even – as with the Baglioni and Oddi families in Perugia, the Trinci and Vitelleschi in Foligno, or the Monaldeschi and Filippeschi in Orvieto – legendary. Today, the best reminders of these rivalries lie in the tower-houses still to be found within the walls of many Umbrian cities. These severe, vertical examples of domestic-cum-military architecture once dominated the cities of central and northern Italy. The most celebrated of all surviving examples of city towers are found today outside Umbria: in Bologna – where the Torre degli Asinelli is over ninety-seven metres high – and in the small walled town of San Gimignano in Tuscany, whose fourteen surviving towers, out of a reputed total of over seventy, still present an impressive sight, even to twentieth-century eyes long accustomed to high-rise buildings. In Umbria, the best single example is the Torre degli Sciri – a massive structure, forty-six metres high – in Via dei Priori in Perugia, once famed for its reputed 500 towers. Virtually all Umbrian towns, however, retain examples of these towers, and a few smaller centres, such as Pissignano, in the Vale of Umbria, are still dominated by them. Primarily defensive in purpose – families could escape their enemies within the city walls – the towers were sometimes erected in such proximity to each other as to serve equally as a means of attack. In Narni, tower-houses were built so close together that three thirteenth-century towers were joined together in the fourteenth century to form the basis of the Palazzo del Podestà (now the Palazzo Comunale). The desire to turn the towers from defensive to offensive structures must also have had something to do with the extraordinary height of some of them, though height was evidently also an unmissable indication of a family's prestige – or ambitions.

The struggle for supremacy between rival families led to bitter and frequently bloody disputes being fought throughout the streets of Umbrian cities. Nominally, at least, such feuds were conducted under the colours of Guelph or Ghibelline – in the late twelfth century the Florentine notary, Brunetto Latini, himself exiled for his Guelph politics, wrote in his encyclopaedic work *Li Livres dou Tresor*: 'War and hatred have become so multiplied among the Italians, that in every town there is division and enmity between the two parties of citizens.' Frequently, however, internal conflict was based on economic rather than narrowly political or tribal differences, as the nobility and other magnates who had previously dominated the communes found their dominance increasingly under threat from the emerging middle class.

The power of this new class was founded, above all, on trade. Between the end of the twelfth century and the beginning of the fifteenth, Umbria – lying between Tuscany and the Lombardy plains to the north, Rome and the Kingdom of Naples to the south, and with the Adriatic to the east and the Tyrrhenian to the west – was an area of commercial exchange of international importance. Men, money and goods all passed through the region, with great regularity. While Umbria was itself a notable producer of prized goods – paper from Foligno, fine textiles from Perugia, saffron from the area around Norcia – it was as a centre of exchange that the region particularly flourished. Roads through Umbria linked Rome and southern Italy with the great trading route which passed through Liguria into Provence and up the Rhône valley to northern Europe; the trans-Apennine roads connected the Adriatic port of Ancona with Pisa and Livorno, and hence the Levant with the western Mediterranean. The great trading city of Venice sent goods through Umbria – starting with a sea journey to Rimini and then continuing by land across the Apennines via Urbino, Città di Castello, Perugia, Marsciano and Orvieto, and on to Pitigliano in Lazio and so to the port of Talamone, from where ships sailed for Barcelona.

As a result of its central position in this trade, Perugia became an important market in both raw materials and finished goods: grain from Provence and Spain, wool from Provence, Catalonia, Navarre, and England, silk from southern Italy and the East, together with woven cloth from France and England, and twills from Ireland. Fairs became an important part of Umbrian economic and social life. The All Saints' Fair in Perugia – still celebrated today as the Fiera dei Morti – is the oldest fair in central Italy. Foligno and Assisi also had large fairs and there were others in Città di Castello, Fratta (now Umbèrtide), Gubbio, Gualdo Tadino, Rieti, Pietrafitta, San Mariano, Panicale, Castiglione del Lago and Valiano.

The life of the merchant could, it is true, be financially hazardous, for warfare disrupted trade and market fluctuations were commonplace. It could also be physically dangerous: trade was subject to the risks posed by piracy and shipwreck at sea and violent brigandage by land; in 1199, a group of monks inadvertently overlooked the corpse of the murdered *podestà* of Orvieto, later explaining that they mistook it for no more than the body of 'some merchant who had been killed by robbers'.

Even so, the period between the twelfth and fourteenth centuries was essentially one of prosperity, both for merchants and tradespeople. Understandably, both these groups were much concerned with the politics of their commune (or, later, *signoria*), since the power or weakness of their city had rapid financial repercussions. As a result, they formed themselves into corporations or guilds. These guilds – the *arti* – were professional and trade organizations whose members were part of the popular faction within the cities, and they soon set up a political grouping of their own – the *popolo* – to represent their interests. Though the *popolo*, which had its own military organization, did not – as the word might suggest – actually represent *all* the people, it did considerably extend the political base. A rival figure of authority took his place alongside the *podestà*. This was the *capitano del popolo*, who, like the *podestà*, was obliged to be an outsider and one who kept himself apart from the citizens. The office of *capitano del popolo* dates from around the mid thirteenth century in Umbria; Perugia had a captain from 1250, Città di Castello from 1255. Although different cities show local variations, the *podestà* and the *capitano del popolo* carried out the main administrative functions of the city between them.

Throughout Umbria, the merchant, exchange and wool guilds were especially powerful but the guilds – divided into major and minor – showed some variation from city to city. Orvieto, for instance, had no fewer than twenty-five guilds in 1300, the complete list giving a vivid insight into the make-up of the medieval town. They were judges and notaries, merchants, woollen-drapers, shoemakers, coopers, butchers, blacksmiths, tanners, tailors, bricklayers, fish and game merchants, taverners, spicers, carpenters, millers, salt and oil-sellers, rope-makers, innkeepers, barbers, greengrocers, limers, vessel-makers, tilers, carters and muleteers, and makers of grindstones. The development of the system of guilds led to a gradual democratization of the communes, as the new middle class came to take over many of the civic functions previously open only to the nobility. Since the guilds often made careful stipulations concerning the observance of particular religious feasts, marking these feast-days with popular processions, they also did much to contribute to the pattern of urban life. Moreover, the wealth of the more important guilds frequently enabled them to contribute notably to the fabric of their cities, through the construction of their own seats and the endowment of new churches.

Despite the extent, and variety, of internal divisions, the thirteenth century was, for many cities in Umbria, the period of their greatest splendour. The increased power of the communes resulted in a comparable growth of administrative structures, which led in turn to the most ambitious urban building programme in the region since the height of the Roman Empire. This was the age which saw the laying out of public spaces, flanked by important civic and religious buildings, as well as a marked growth in the number of private dwellings and other churches. Although the urban renewal of the thirteenth century has parallels in other parts of Italy, Umbria is particularly rich in surviving examples of such building projects. In many towns throughout the region – including Perugia, Orvieto, Gubbio, Todi, Città di Castello and Bevagna – the main squares still reveal the essential structure of the medieval civic space – the physical embodiment of the different social and economic groupings of the day, and the place where the great public debates and celebrations took place. Often, such spaces occupied sites favoured by much earlier inhabitants of the region. The principal piazza in Perugia corresponds to the centre of the Etruscan city and the Roman forum, while that of Città di Castello also occupies the position of the forum, at the very centre of the walled city; as a variation, Assisi's Piazza Comunale lies on the site of the colonnaded balcony fronting the Temple of Minerva, leaving the nearby site of the Roman forum for the Cathedral of San Rufino.

Of all these great squares, one of the finest is the Piazza IV Novembre in Perugia. Certainly the sloping piazza was considered as an architectonic whole; newly paved, it was designed to be flanked by the Palazzo dei Priori (the priors were city magistrates), the Palazzo del Podestà, and an already existing Romanesque church (later enlarged and transformed into the present Gothic cathedral), as well as to hold the city's principal fountain. The Palazzo dei Priori – or Palazzo Comunale – remains today, as it must always have seemed, a building of striking beauty as well as civic dignity. Designed by two otherwise unknown Perugians, Giacomo di Servadio and Giovanello di Benvenuto, it was originally built between 1293 and 1297, added to in 1346, and later extended between 1429 and 1443. The severe symmetrical mass of the original building – the later addition gives the now distinctive flowing curve to the longer side – is offset by the warmth of the pink and white stone used for its construction, the delicacy of the Gothic tracery of the two rows of three-light windows, and the fan-shaped stairway, leading up to the huge doorway of the principal chamber. The two large symbolic bronzes – the Guelph lion and the Perugian gryphon – placed above this stairway confirm the desire at once to assert Perugia's independence and to embellish the city, for the sculptures, which date from 1274, are believed to be the earliest surviving medieval examples of bronze casting by the *cire perdue* method, a technique used by both the Etruscans and Romans but subsequently lost. The later history of the building confirms its continuing importance. In 1328 the adjoining church of San Severo was demolished, along with other neighbouring buildings, to allow for the extension of the civic palace. The enormously impressive and magnificently decorated doorway – the *portale delle arti* – on the longer side of the palace was added in 1346; on this occasion the city was evidently determined to have the best central Italy could provide, for while the design of the arch recalls the architecture of Florence, the decoration suggests Siennese influence. Beauty, however, was never an end in itself, and a more bellicose addition is still to be seen above the fan-shaped stairway – the keys and chains of the city gates of Siena, which were hung in sign of triumph between the figures of the gryphon and lion after the Perugian victory over the Siennese at the Battle of Torrita in 1358.

Of the Palazzo del Podestà, almost completely destroyed by fire in 1534, only traces remain, incorporated into the Archbishop's Palace, adjoining the present cathedral. Fortunately, the Fontana Maggiore, or Great Fountain, also situated on the piazza, survives. When built, it represented not only an essential addition to the growing city, as its principal source of water, but also an eloquent indication of civic pride; today it remains both a symbol of Perugia and one of the most significant achievements of medieval sculpture anywhere. Planned two decades previously, the fountain was built between 1275 and 1278, possibly to a design by Fra Bevignate, the overseer of public works in Perugia, with the aid of the Venetian hydraulic engineer Boninsegna, who was summoned from Orvieto to construct an acqueduct for the city. The decoration was the work of the sculptor Nicola Pisano and his son, Giovanni; the former had already won fame for his work on the pulpits in the cathedral at Siena and in the cathedral baptistery at Pisa, while the latter was still at the beginning of a career which would culminate in the magnificent relief carvings of the pulpits of the Duomo in Pisa and the church of Sant'Andrea in Pistoia. The Fontana Maggiore consists of a twenty-five-sided lower basin and a dodecagonal upper basin in marble, completed by a heavy bronze column and basin decorated with three bronze nymphs, designed by Giovanni Pisano and cast by a local craftsman, known only as 'Rubeus' (or 'Red'). Around the lower basin, no fewer than fifty panels testify to the city's independence and political allegiance (the gryphon and Guelph lion again), to its classical past and Christian present (two Roman eagles and scenes from both Roman and biblical history) and to its present secular culture (representations of the Liberal Arts, Philosophy, and the Labours of the months of the year). Around the upper basin are represented kings, saints, prophets, and other figures from myth and history, including Aulestes, the Trojan hero and supposed founder of Perugia, along with Matteo da Correggio and Ermanno da Sassoferrato, respectively *podestà* and *capitano del popolo* of Perugia in 1278; there are also reliefs of the sources of Perugia's contemporary prosperity, represented by Lake Trasimeno, source of fish, and Chiusi, source of grain. The fact that the two basins of this remarkable fountain are slightly out of alignment – driving the viewer continually around the fountain in search of a nonexistent point of rest – cannot help but suggest Perugia to have been a dynamic city, in no sense ready to rest on its already substantial political and artistic achievements as it entered the fourteenth century.

Perugia's medieval town planning was especially impressive, but it was far from unique. Both Todi and Bevagna, for instance, retain virtually intact medieval squares. Todi's Piazza del Popolo contains no fewer than three thirteenth-century civic buildings, along with a cathedral built in the same period. The earliest – today seen in a much restored condition – is the Palazzo del Popolo (or Palazzo del Podestà), which was begun in 1213, heightened by one storey between 1228 and 1233 and eventually completed in 1267. The Palazzo del Capitano, which adjoins the Palazzo del Popolo, on one of the rectangular piazza's longer sides, shares with it the characteristic feature of having been built over an open loggia, though its arches are considerably wider and more massive. The proximity of these two buildings makes it easy to see how the architects thought of the square as an architectonic whole, while remaining open to contemporary developments in architectural style. Here, both buildings are predominantly Romanesque in inspiration, yet the Palazzo del Capitano has an arched doorway, triple-lancet windows, and a pointed gable running above the three first-floor windows, unmistakably marking a transition towards Gothic. After completion, the two differently-sized buildings were brought together by means of a broad external stairway leading up from the piazza. Close by, on the shorter, southern, side of the piazza, directly opposite the cathedral, is the contemporary Palazzo dei Priori, begun in 1293 and substantially enlarged between 1334 and 1337. Particularly severe in its original conception – a feature emphasized both by the battlements and by the tower added to the palace between 1369 and 1385 – the palazzo today appears somewhat softened by the remodelling of the windows in a gentler Renaissance style in 1513, by the orders of Pope Leo X. The eagle, cast in bronze in 1339, to be seen on the palace wall high above the piazza, is the symbol of Todi.

Though less obviously monumental, the Piazza Silvestri in the tiny town of Bevagna presents a similar grouping of civic and religious buildings. The Gothic Palazzo dei Consoli, dating from 1270, is built on a simple rectangular plan, two storeys high, with a double row of double-lancet windows above a massively arched open loggia at street level, and with a wide, open stair ramp to the side. Across the virtually intact medieval square are two of the finest Romanesque churches in Umbria – San Silvestro and San Michele Arcangelo, both of which date from around the very end of the twelfth century. The former is the work of Master Binellus, who signed his name along with the date (1195), and the same master-builder, aided here by Master Rodolfus, was likewise responsible for San Michele.

Not all cities in Umbria have preserved their principal squares in quite such unchanged conditions as Perugia, Todi, or Bevagna. Even so, the signs of the vitality and confidence, as well as the power and prosperity, of the region's medieval communes are apparent throughout the whole of Umbria. Orvieto, for instance, retains both the Palazzo Comunale, built in the first half of the thirteenth century but heavily remodelled in the sixteenth century, and also the Palazzo del Capitano del Popolo. The latter, built in the warm local tufa, is one of the earliest civic buildings in central Italy, dating from the mid thirteenth century. Its architect is anonymous, but the sources of inspiration from the building emphasize once more the importance of Umbria's position in the centre of the Italian peninsula, for while the civic model for the palace is to be found among the public buildings of northern Italy – Bergamo (late twelfth century), Como (1215) or Milan (1228–33) – the evenly spaced diaphragm arches which support the roof of the palace's single great chamber find a direct source in the refectories and infirmaries of the leading Cistercian monasteries to the south – Fossanova, in Latina (1208) and Casamari, in Frosinone (1217). Externally, the palace reveals several features typical of many thirteenth-century civic buildings. Like the later palaces of Todi or Bevagna, it is constructed over the transverse barrel vaults of what was originally an open loggia at ground level (though the filling in probably took place as early as the end of the thirteenth century). Even more characteristic is the flight of stairs leading up from street level to the council chamber and first-floor balcony. Here, as in Perugia, Todi or Bevagna, the exterior stairway and massive doorway symbolize the people's ease of access to the single large hall that served as the meeting place of their leaders.

Like the public buildings of Perugia, Orvieto, Todi and Bevagna, the Palazzo dei Consoli in Gubbio also has a broad external staircase (fan-shaped, like Perugia's), giving access to the council chamber. Dramatically situated high above the town, on the steep slopes of Monte Ingino, the Palazzo dei Consoli faces the Palazzo del Pretorio across a wide balcony called the Piazza della Signoria. Completed in 1338, the Palazzo dei Consoli is yet another of the finest civic palaces in Italy. Attributed to an architect by the name of Angelo da Orvieto, the Palace of the Consuls bears some resemblance to the earlier Palazzo del Capitano in Orvieto, notably in the massively impressive barrel-vaulted hall which served as the council chamber and which occupies the entire first floor of the palace – the ground floor again consisting of a loggia composed of a series of transverse barrel vaults. Across the exposed open space of the piazza, with its commanding view of the town and surrounding countryside, lies the Palazzo Pretorio, started in 1349 but unfinished. The appearance and placing of the three-storeyed palace suggest that the space was planned as a whole, expressive of the commune's power over the town and the surrounding countryside below. Whether or not Angelo da Orvieto was also responsible for the design of the Palazzo Pretorio, as has been suggested, it is certain that he also built the unfinished Palazzo Comunale at Città di Castello – only the ground and part of the first floors were completed – at an uncertain date during the first half of the fourteenth century. Although this palace reveals, in the pointed forms of its doors and windows, a quite different source of influence from the rounded forms of Orvieto or Gubbio, the importance of creating a civic space remains paramount, for the Palazzo Comunale lies next to the cathedral, across a square from the civic tower, and close to the thirteenth-century Palazzo del Podestà.

The rise of the communes in Umbria was founded on the increasing secularization of civic administration, often encouraged by the ecclesiastical authorities. The church, however, retained a crucial place at the centre of medieval life, as the vast number of surviving churches and convents reminds us. Indeed, civic and religious life were so closely connected that not only are the principal churches and the main civic buildings of most towns grouped closely together, but the principal city square often grew up around an existing ecclesiastical building. Perugia's Piazza IV Novembre, for example, was bounded on one side by a large Romanesque church, originally built between 936 and

1030, which later formed the nucleus of a new cathedral (two earlier cathedrals stood on sites now occupied by the monastery church of San Pietro and the church of San Domenico), while the Piazza Silvestri in Bevagna likewise contained the town's two largest churches for many years before the building of the Palazzo dei Consoli in 1270. The main squares of Città di Castello, Foligno and Todi were all created in direct relationship to the cities' already existing cathedrals. As the population of the region's urban centres grew, however, so too did the towns' wealth and sense of civic dignity, giving rise to a sustained church-building programme – characterized both by the building of the great Umbrian cathedrals, and the large number of preaching churches of the Franciscan, Dominican, and Austin friars.

In Perugia, plans were laid for a new cathedral shortly after the building of the Palazzo dei Priori, the Palazzo del Capitano del Popolo and the Fontana Maggiore. The intention of Fra Bevignate, the monk who was overseer of the town works, was not to begin from scratch but to adapt an existing Romanesque church, transforming its nave into the transept of the new building. As it transpired, the first stone was not laid until 1345 and even then work soon stopped, being taken up again after more than a century in 1437 and continuing until 1587. Whereas Perugia was given a new cathedral close to the principal civic buildings, the Palazzo del Popolo (1213–33), the Palazzo del Capitano del Popolo (1290), and the late thirteenth-century Palazzo dei Priori in Todi were built around the square occupied by a cathedral since about the year 1000, when the local bishop still ruled the city. In Foligno, the Palazzo Comunale was erected between 1262 and 1265, opposite the cathedral built in the previous century – and when the Trinci family came to rule the town in the fourteenth century, they built their own great house, the Palazzo Trinci (1389–1407), on another side of the same elongated piazza. Città di Castello's Palazzo Comunale and the civic tower were similarly erected in direct relationship to the existing Romanesque cathedral.

Sometimes local constraints – especially, in this hilly region, the difficulty of the terrain – forced cities to modify the basic pattern of grouping all the principal civic and religious buildings around a single open space. Even so, the placing of such buildings was never haphazard. Since the site of Assisi's Roman forum, where the Cathedral of San Rufino had been built in the mid twelfth century, was rather restricted, the town's Palazzo Comunale and Palazzo del Capitano del Popolo were erected on a piazza close to the Roman temple instead. In Gubbio, the Palazzo dei Consoli and the Palazzo del Capitano del Popolo were built on their separate balcony site because the city's cathedral, higher up the town, hugs the hillside so tightly as to need substantial internal buttressing, its bell-tower being located, most unusually, above the choir. The cathedral itself, however, occupies an important site which had been marked out for public buildings since the time of the Longobards – and one whose symbolic associations Federico da Montefeltro, Duke of Urbino, who ruled the city in the fifteenth century, also exploited when he built his ducal palace opposite the cathedral. Spoleto's vast cathedral, meanwhile, dominates the far end of a unique, fan-shaped piazza, specially opened up, at the extreme edge of the upper city, at a time, during the late twelfth century, when episcopal power in the city was at its height. Approached from the old Roman centre of the city, the cathedral towers over the surrounding buildings, as its designers clearly intended it should – and it continued to dominate the city until the mid fourteenth century, when Pope Innocent VI asserted *his* authority over Spoleto by building the even more massive fortress – the Rocca Albornoz – which sits menacingly above the town and surrounding countryside.

As with their public buildings, Umbria's cities vied with each other in the size, and the richness of the decoration, of their principal places of worship. The building of many cathedrals, in particular, was protracted over several centuries. Parts of the ninth-century cathedral church of Spoleto survive, even today, incorporated into the present Romanesque building, erected in the second half of the twelfth century. The superb large mosaic of the Redeemer enthroned between the Madonna and St John the Evangelist, by the artist Solsternus, dates from 1207, and the lower part of the façade is preceded by a Renaissance portico, built between 1491 and 1504. The incorporation of Spoleto's coat of arms here also serves to remind us of the civic uses to which the cathedral square was always put. One of the streets leading to the piazza today is called the Via dell'Arringo. Called the *arengo* in Perugia, and the *arrengha* in Norcia, the *arringo* was one of the earliest forms of communal decision-making, in which citizens took decisions by acclamation (the word is the origin of the English 'harangue').

Among the region's cathedrals, the most magnificent is the Duomo of Orvieto, one of the greatest of all European cathedrals. After having been abandoned for centuries after the destruction of Volsinii Veteres by the Romans in 264 BC, Orvieto had returned to prominence only in the twelfth century. By the thirteenth century it was again flourishing, to the extent that popes took up residence or even, as in the case of Martin IV in 1281, were crowned there. At this time, Sant'Andrea, close to the Palazzo Comunale and civic tower, was the town's principal church. In 1290, work began on the cathedral which was concluded only in the seventeenth century (the present bronze doors being put in place as late as 1970). While the thirteenth-century growth of Orvieto, in terms of population, wealth, and prestige, makes the building of a great cathedral unsurprising, the particular circumstances in which it came to be built are remarkable.

In the mid thirteenth century, the Church's doctrine of transubstantiation – the teaching that the bread and wine at communion are turned by the priest's consecration into the real body and blood of Christ – had not found universal acceptance, despite having been formulated as long ago as 787 at the Council of Nicaea, and having subsequently been declared an essential dogma by the Lateran Council in 1215. The story is told that one of those who had doubts about the doctrine was a Bohemian priest, Peter of Prague, who spent the night in the town of Bolsena while *en route* to Rome. As he celebrated Mass the following day, his doubts were answered when the host in his hands miraculously spilled blood on the linen corporal cloth. Pope Urban IV, who was residing in Orvieto at the time, heard of the miracle and had the blood-stained cloth brought to the city. On 11 August 1264 he instituted the feast of Corpus Christi (the Body of Christ), to be celebrated on the Thursday after Trinity Sunday. To help ensure the wider acceptance of the doctrine, the Pope had the Office and Mass of the Feast prepared by no less a figure than the leading theologian of the late Middle Ages, St Thomas Aquinas, who was also in Orvieto at the time. The cloth that Urban IV had brought to Orvieto is still in the city and is preserved today in the elaborate, enamelled silver-gilt reliquary, made in 1337–8 by Ugolino di Vieri, which for centuries was carried through the streets of Orvieto in the great Corpus Christi procession which remains one of the major dates in the city's calendar.

If the Holy Corporal is the most precious relic of the miracle at Bolsena, then Orvieto cathedral is the most prominent testimony to it. From virtually the time of the miracle itself, Orvieto town council determined to build a church appropriate to commemorate so auspicious an event and so worthy a city. They could not, however, decide on what form that church should take, and a quarter-century of wrangling preceded the laying of the first stone on 13 November 1290. Progress thereafter was relatively swift, at least initially, for the nave was completed by 1308. This first stage – sometimes attributed to the great Florentine builder and sculptor Arnolfo di Cambio – is itself quite splendid. Built in alternating horizontal bands of grey and white in basalt and travertine, the plain rectangular basilical plan of the church is relieved externally by a series of semicircular chapels running along each flank, and harmonized internally by the elegant correspondence between the series of columns separating the nave from the aisles and the flanking chapels. When work stopped in 1308, however, the cathedral still lacked both a façade and a roof. Faced with apparent structural problems caused by the building's size and the vast height of the nave, Orvieto called in the Siennese master-builder Lorenzo Maitani, and it was he whose design for the façade transformed the original Romanesque church into one of the great masterpieces of Italian Gothic.

Seen from any angle, the Duomo reveals itself as a remarkable building. Glimpsed in silhouette from afar, it towers over the skyline of Orvieto as dramatically as the rocky outcrop on which the city stands dominates the surrounding countryside. Like the cathedrals of Pisa, Siena or Florence, in neighbouring Tuscany, the Duomo declares Orvieto as a city to be reckoned with. Yet it is not the size alone that impresses, for Maitani created a church in which an essentially simple approach to architectural form is radiantly transformed by some of the most imaginative and accomplished sculpture and polychrome mosaic work of the age. Remarkably, two large and very beautiful preparatory drawings of the façade, made in pen on parchment, survive (they are today in the Museo dell'Opera del Duomo). Dating from about 1310, when Maitani took over the construction of the cathedral, at least one of them is almost certainly by Maitani himself. In an age when the term 'architect' was still quite unknown, the drawings are notable for revealing the extent to which the façade – which famously resembles a Gothic picture frame – was conceived of as an architectural whole from the very beginning. From the time he was summoned to Orvieto in 1310 until his death in 1330, Lorenzo Maitani devoted himself to the Duomo – and this despite known excursions to Perugia in 1317 (to work on a fountain), Siena in 1322 (to give advice on building a new cathedral there), and on military service in 1325. Orvieto thought so highly of him that he was appointed *capomaestro* for life, granted Orvietan citizenship and the privilege of carrying arms, and allowed to nominate his own assistants. In the years and centuries after his death, Orvieto summoned as distinguished a line of architects as it is easily possible to imagine to carry on his work. Among those who contributed to the cathedral's completion and present state were Lorenzo's son, Vitale, followed by Nicolò Nuti (1331–5 and 1345–7), Meo Nuti (1337–9), Andrea Pisano (1347–8) and his son Nino Pisano (1349), Andrea di Cecco da Siena (1356–9) and Andrea Orcagna (1359–62); in later centuries, Sano di Matteo superintended the works between 1406 and 1410, to be followed by, among many others, Antonio Federighi (1451–6), Michele Sammicheli (1509–36), Antonio da Sangallo the Younger (1540–41), Ippolito Scalza (1567–1617), and Carlo Maderno (1619), while when the façade was struck by lightning in 1795, the restoration was entrusted to Giuseppe Valadier (1797–1806). The artists called to embellish the interior were equally distinguished, including, in the fifteenth century alone, Gentile da Fabriano, the Beato Angelico, Benozzo Gozzoli and Luca Signorelli, who began his magnificent fresco cycle of the *Last Judgement* there in 1499.

The Duomo in Orvieto is the supreme achievement among late medieval cathedrals in Umbria, the greatest expression in the region of civic pride combining with religious piety. What makes the building still more remarkable, however, is that for much of the period of its construction Orvieto was almost ceaselessly embroiled in internal conflict and in waging war on its neighbours. For a long while the city had been riven by disputes between rival factions, notably the Guelph Monaldeschi family, supporters of the papacy, and the Ghibelline Filippeschi, who favoured the imperial cause. Shortly after Lorenzo Maitani began work on the cathedral, these disputes broke out again in a particularly bloody way. In 1313, Henry VII, Count of Luxembourg and King of Germany, arrived in Italy in order to be crowned emperor. Having met with a less than enthusiastic reception from both Florence and Siena, he turned towards Orvieto, raising the hopes of the town's Ghibelline faction. So apprehensive were the Guelphs of what might lie in store that they offered control of Orvieto to the Ghibellines, on condition that the city was not given over to the German army. The Ghibellines declining to accept these terms, fighting broke out on 16 August and, after two days, a Ghibelline victory appeared all but complete. On the following day, however, Guelph reinforcements arrived, encouraging that faction, only for the Ghibellines to receive the aid of the lord of nearby Baschi, with 800 knights and 3,000 imperial infantry, along with troops from Todi, Spoleto, Amelia and Terni. So overwhelming did this force appear that the Bishop of Orvieto offered the city to the Ghibellines, who immediately demanded the expulsion from the city of their rivals. When the departing Guelphs were at the city gates on their way to exile on the morning of 20 August, no fewer than 1,200 Perugian cavalry appeared in their support, and in renewed fighting the leading Ghibelline commanders were killed. A massacre followed in which 4,000 Ghibellines died – including women and children hurled from the city-rock

– while 300 Ghibelline houses were put to the flames. On 24 August 1313, just eight days after the beginning of the fighting in which so many lives were lost, the Emperor, Henry VII, whose presence had sparked off the bloodshed, died at Buonconvento, near Siena. For the next two years a directory of five Guelph nobles ruled the city, destroying what remained of Ghibelline houses and towers in the city and the surrounding *contado*, and removing the Ghibellines from the list of citizens. However, having entered into the Guelph League – along with Perugia, Assisi, Spello, Bevagna, Montefalco, Trevi, and Spoleto – the Orvietans were defeated in two major battles, at Montecatini in August, and again at Montefiascone in November 1315. Disillusioned, the city dismissed its leadership of Guelph nobles and reinstated the popular faction. Guelph and Ghibelline, nobles and the *popolo*, Monaldeschi and Filippeschi: to these internal rivalries, Orvieto added warfare with neighbouring cities among which Siena – the most prominent source of architects, artists and builders, including Maitani himself – was chief. Yet it was in just such unlikely circumstances, amid the physical destruction of large parts of the city, and the immense human and economic toll caused by continual warfare, that the Duomo of Orvieto was built.

Orvieto, Spoleto, Todi, Gubbio, Città di Castello, Perugia: even so incomplete a list of Umbrian cathedrals indicates the richness of ecclesiastical architecture and artistic activity in the region during the late Middle Ages. Nevertheless, the cathedrals, notwithstanding their individual distinction, give only a partial sense of the extraordinary extent of church-building which took place in Umbria during the thirteenth and fourteenth centuries. As towns grew, the old parish system became increasingly inadequate to the needs of the urban population, while leaving sometimes large impressive churches where few people now lived – the isolated churches of Santa Maria in Pantano, close to Massa Martana, or Santa Pudenziana at Visciano near Narni, both seventh- or eighth-century in origin, are two outstanding examples which survive to this day. While the erection of cathedrals might indicate true piety as well as civic pride, they did little to satisfy the real spiritual needs of ordinary people, as

the two great mendicant friars of the early thirteenth century –
St Francis of Assisi (1182–1226) and the Spanish-born St Dominic
(c. 1170–1221) – quickly discovered.

When St Francis embarked on his mission, he found inspiration and consolation in the tiny, rough country churches then
dotted throughout the Umbrian countryside – hut-churches
such as the still-surviving San Damiano, just beyond Assisi's
walls, or the Portiuncula, now contained within the huge basilica
of Santa Maria degli Angeli, on the plain below Francis's home
town. Since such churches were wholly unsuited to the throngs
Francis and his followers attracted, the Franciscans began to
build large preaching churches in cities and towns throughout
Umbria. Before long the even larger churches of the Dominicans
started to appear, together with the churches of the Augustinians,
or Austin Friars. If the mendicant churches did not perform the
same civic function as the cathedrals, they nevertheless helped
shape Umbria's medieval cities and towns, in ways that can still
be appreciated today. While cathedrals were sited on the principal, and usually central, piazza of the cities, whether pre-
existing or especially opened up, the churches of the Franciscans,
Dominicans and Augustinians were generally disposed in a very
regular fashion around the perimeter of the city walls. In order
to accommodate the crowds drawn to hear the preaching friars,
the churches gave on to large open spaces, many of which –
those in front of the basilica in Assisi, Gubbio's San Francesco or
Perugia's San Francesco al Prato (St Francis-in-the-Field), for
example – have been respected in subsequent town planning and
still exist.

What was principally required of these churches was the space
to accommodate large congregations, clear sight lines such as
would allow those present to see the preacher, and acoustical
clarity permitting his words to be heard distinctly by all present.
A large unbroken wall surface, appropriate for the narrative
fresco cycles which reinforced the preacher's message, was a
desirable bonus. The architecture which resulted was not
uniquely regional – like the Dominicans, the Franciscans were
soon to be found throughout the whole of Italy and far beyond
– and both orders were consistent and influential advocates of

the new Gothic forms gaining ground throughout Europe. Yet, with their particular and consistent religious programmes and the urgency with which they were built, the mendicant churches gave Umbrian religious architecture a unifying theme that the great cathedrals – competing one with another to glorify their various cities – could never supply.

The great prototype for the Franciscans was San Francesco at Assisi. Along with the Duomo at Orvieto, the basilica is one of the two finest Gothic churches in Umbria. Unlike the Duomo, however, it also provided a model for many, and much humbler, churches throughout the entire region. San Francesco was begun, amid much controversy, just two years after the saint's death, at the behest of Brother Elias, the then General of the Order. A huge double church, composed of two buildings, erected one on top of the other, visible for miles around, the basilica is far grander than any other example of Franciscan building – and was felt by many to be a quite inappropriate memorial to a man whose whole message had been a call to simplicity and humility. Nevertheless, the Upper Church at Assisi was to prove an influential model since, despite the eye-catching decorative splendour of its frescoes, it is architecturally quite plain: an unembellished Latin cross with an aisleless nave. It is a space designed for preaching, where nothing intrudes to obstruct the congregation's view of pulpit and altar. The undoubted sense of grandeur of the church is imparted almost exclusively by the harmonious relationship between the length, breadth and height of the building. In essence, the Franciscan church, with its clear plan, comforting simplicity, and evident sense of purpose, is a solid, three-dimensional representation of the directness of St Francis's spiritual message.

Begun in 1228, the basilica in Assisi was substantially complete by 1239, although it was not to be consecrated for another fourteen years. Though it had no obvious architectural dependence on local sources – the cathedral at Angers in France has been suggested as a prototype – the Upper Church, with its flat-screen façade and airy interior, is echoed by a number of later churches in Umbria. In Assisi itself, there is the church of Santa Chiara, the Franciscan sister-church, built at the opposite end of town between 1257 and 1265, in honour of St Clare, St Francis's first female follower. Other examples include the churches of San Francesco al Prato in Perugia (1230), which also echoes the pink and white facing typical of Assisi's churches, San Francesco in Terni (built in 1265 but enlarged to three aisles in 1437 and subsequently much altered), and the late-thirteenth-century church of San Francesco in Gualdo Tadino. Less impressive than these, other early Franciscan churches conform even more obviously to a common pattern, being built of roughly hewn stone to a simple rectangular plan, covered by simple wooden roofs, and lit by narrow lancet windows. Such buildings were never intended to add lustre to the cities or satisfy local pride: the product of limited funds and sometimes limited skill, these hall-churches fulfilled the Franciscan order's most basic needs, that of providing an appropriate space in which their founder's message could be preached. Just as the Franciscan order changed with the years, however, so too did their churches, and from the simple rectangular plan of the early buildings came more elaborate designs, such as the cruciform plan in which a transept with choir and flanking chapels were added to the rectangle. Most striking of all the variants on Franciscan churches in Umbria is San Fortunato in Todi. This church dwarfs all other buildings in the town, including the cathedral – and makes a remarkable impression on anyone approaching Todi, especially from the direction of Orvieto or Terni. Building began in the late thirteenth century and the eastern half of the church was largely complete by 1328, though the western half and the lower part of the (still unfinished) façade were terminated only in the following century. Although similar in many respects to the other Umbrian hall-churches, San Fortunato's extreme breadth in relation to its height gives it a very distinctive appearance; one leading architectural historian has described it as being built on a Brobdingnagian scale, squatting 'like a huge hangar on the hill'. Unlike its simpler predecessors, San Fortunato is a vaulted Gothic hall whose aisles give on to rows of chapels, and whose four wide bays terminate in a huge, seven-sided apse. It is a church built, in fact, to accommodate the changing nature of the Franciscan movement. Originally lay in inspiration, the order became increasingly clerical in the century after the death of its founder, resulting in a need for more altars at which Franciscan priests might fulfil their daily obligation to celebrate Mass. Yet the builders of San Fortunato were not unmindful of the origins and continued purpose of Franciscan churches. So, despite its size, the comparative complexity of design, and the introduction of rows of columns to support the vaulted roof, the church was conceived in such unified terms, and the conception executed with such skill, that the pulpit could be placed high up on the wall facing the right-hand aisle and yet remain easily visible to the entire congregation throughout the church.

San Fortunato is exceptional, yet it exemplifies the way that the region's Franciscan churches embody considerable variety within the constraints placed on them by their unifying purpose. In fact, few towns in Umbria are without a Franciscan church. Some – like Stroncone (1213) or the church of the Speco di San Francesco (1213) – claim to have been founded by the saint himself, though the existing buildings are of later date. Others, like Corciano (1223), can trace their origins back to the saint's lifetime. The large church of San Francesco in Gubbio was built in the mid thirteenth century by the desire of the Spadalonga family, with whom St Francis stayed when he visited the town in 1206–7, and other thirteenth-century Franciscan churches include, besides those already mentioned, Bevagna (1275), Amelia (1287), Acquasparta (1290) and Umbèrtide (1299), to-gether with the less precisely datable churches of San Gémini, Gualdo Tadino and Foligno. Not all the early churches survived, of course; indeed, the Franciscans of Nocera Umbra had built a second church in the town by as early as 1336, after invading troops had sacked and destroyed their first. Apart from Todi's San Fortunato, other notable fourteenth-century Franciscan churches include San Francesco at Montefalco (1336–8), now the town museum, where Benozzo Gozzoli was later to paint a famous fresco cycle on the life of St Francis.

If the Franciscan churches of Assisi or Todi might make a visual impact by sheer size alone, then the churches of the Dominicans – less hampered by Franciscan ideals of humility – often made more deliberate efforts to impress. It may be idle to speculate on how such huge buildings appeared to medieval eyes, but it is striking that a church such as Perugia's San Domenico (begun in 1305) still dominates part of the city skyline at the end of the twentieth century, while Foligno's mid-thirteenth-century San Domenico is large enough to have been converted into a new auditorium for Umbria's third largest city as recently as 1994. Like their Franciscan counterparts, the huge wooden-roofed Dominican hall churches are still to be found today throughout the entire region. Among the best surviving examples, besides those mentioned, are the churches of San Domenico in Città di Castello, Gubbio, Narni, Orvieto and Spoleto.

By the end of the fourteenth century, most of Umbria's cities and larger towns centred on their great public buildings, fountains, and cathedral or other principal church, while the mendicant foundations were regularly disposed around the city perimeter, close to the defensive walls. This urban plan imprinted itself strongly enough throughout the region to survive, to a remarkable extent, the next six centuries of social and economic change, giving Umbrian towns the medieval appearance many retain to this day.

It would be a mistake, of course, to think that the townspeople of the Middle Ages saw their cities as we see them through late-twentieth-century eyes. Certainly they must have been aware of the splendour of their cities, when compared to the smaller settlements of the surrounding *contado*. They had the benefit not only of carnivals, fairs, and the great religious holidays and guild processions, but also, in the case of cities like Perugia or Orvieto, the splendour of occasional visits by popes and other dignitaries. Unlike their rural neighbours, who suffered frequent hardship from destruction of their homes, and the theft or destruction of their crops by pillaging troops, city-dwellers felt themselves protected behind sturdy city walls, and enjoyed access to their town's grain stores as well as belonging to a community with both the financial resources to buy supplies from elsewhere in times of shortage, and the military capacity to defend its food convoys. Yet perhaps the most that might truly be said of life in the towns was that it was preferable to that in the surrounding countryside.

Certainly there could be no complete assurance that the city would not come under siege, or even be assaulted, taken, and sacked. In the case of siege, there would certainly be shortages of food and perhaps also of water. In the case of internal violence between opposing factions, or if a city resisted an outside enemy and was subsequently taken, the results could be terrible indeed. The violence wreaked on Orvieto in 1313 has already been mentioned, but the case was not exceptional, and the list of Umbrian cities devastated between the thirteenth and sixteenth centuries is a long one. It was the Saracen troops of Frederick II who, in 1249, destroyed the town of Coccorone, which was later rebuilt as Montefalco. The same troops also burned neighbouring Bevagna in the same year, and that town was destroyed once more, with great loss of life, in 1375, by the army of Foligno. Foligno's own territory was devastated in 1414 by King Ladislas of Naples, and the city seized and its leaders killed by papal forces in 1439. Often the violence must have seemed quite random, the unforeseeable result of decisions taken far away, by persons unknown to them, and for reasons largely obscure. Following the Congiura dei Pazzi, or Pazzi conspiracy, of 1478 – when the Pazzi family attempted to murder their Medici rivals during Mass in the cathedral in Florence, killing Giuliano and wounding Lorenzo dei Medici – the Medici blamed the Pope, Sixtus IV, and sent troops against the papal territories to the south. Having failed to take their target, Perugia, they sacked instead all the towns and villages on the road between that city and the Tuscan border – and having been forced to retreat by an approaching papal army, they returned as soon as it had withdrawn, to devastate the entire region again. As late as 1527, the region suffered grievously at the hands of the troops of the German Emperor, Charles V, who passed through Umbria on their way to lay siege to Rome, and again on their return. Few towns on their route escaped. In the north, Borghetto di Tuoro and Passignano were pillaged and put to the torch; in Città della Pieve, to the west, 700 people were killed. Amelia, Lugnano, Acquasparta, Trevi, Bevagna, Foligno, and Assisi were all captured and sacked. The scale of the devastation was reminiscent of the sufferings inflicted on the region by Totila 1,000 years before. Indeed, a description of the effects of warfare on the city of Todi and its *contado*, in the *Chronicle* written by Gian Fabrizio degli Atti (d. 1536), who lived through the attack, vividly recalls Procopius's account of Italy in the Gothic wars:

... there was a great famine in Todi and the surrounding countryside, and by day and night many people could be heard screaming 'Help us, have mercy.' And each day more people were seen to fall dead in the streets or be discovered lifeless in their homes. Many horses, donkeys, dogs, cats and unclean animals were eaten. In Montecastrilli, two cooking pots full of mice were found in the house of a peasant. Elsewhere it was said the flesh was cut off two hanged men and eaten. In the city itself more people were forced to live on grass and roots than on bread.

Warfare was terrible but medieval cities could also be dangerous in times of peace. Almost invariably they were violent places, marked by murder, riot and pitched battles between city magnates and the popular faction or rival families. It is no exaggeration to say that the most admired Umbrian city squares – the Piazza IV Novembre in Perugia, for example, where on separate occasions the cathedral was turned into a fortress, and its steps used to mount cannon, in the course of fighting between rival families – literally ran with blood. Religion, too, could be violent. In 1259 a hermit called Ranieri Fasani began flagellating himself in public in the streets of Perugia, to atone for his sins. He was soon imitated by others, who formed themselves into companies, known as the *Disciplinati*. Moving in procession, they whipped themselves, for the love of God, until blood streamed down their backs, passing barefoot from city to city, until they numbered thousands and were familiar not only in the cities of Umbria, but also in Tuscany and Romagna. Even popular entertainments depended on such violence. For centuries, until it was finally abolished in 1425, opposing teams of Perugians, representing different parts of the city, met in the same great square to contest the Battle of the Stones. The game began with the mere hurling of rocks in an attempt to disable opponents. It so frequently ended, however, with the employment of any available weapon – despite legal penalties, including the cutting off of the hand of anyone caught breaking the rules – that the city's rulers, who found it useful for toughening men for real fighting, were eventually forced to ban it.

Worst of all the perils of urban life in the Middle Ages, perhaps, was plague. For most of the city's inhabitants, life consisted of being crammed, several to a room, in garrets or airless quarters in back courtyards off the twisting maze of the same narrow streets and alleys that appear so picturesque today. Amid the filth of towns in which sanitation was virtually unknown, the urban poor were always vulnerable to disease, not least the pest. Of all outbreaks of pestilence, the worst was the Black Death which devastated most of Europe between 1347 and 1350 and which, with subsequent epidemics, reduced the population of Europe by a half or more by 1400. The Black Death arrived in Umbria in 1348, resulting in 100,000 deaths. Cities saw their populations cut dramatically in the space of a few months: Città di Castello lost a third of its inhabitants, while in Spoleto seven in every ten townspeople died. Among the victims of the pestilence in Perugia was the celebrated physician Gentile da Foligno, whose *Consilium de peste*, written just months previously, was a notable early account of the plague. The physical symptoms of the disease were fearful: violent fever, sweating, delirium, unbearable thirst, discoloration of the skin, and buboes the size of eggs or apples swelling in the groin or armpit. Perhaps worse were the psychological effects, for the plague came close to breaking down the entire fabric of medieval society, as still healthy people abandoned parents, spouses, and children in terrified attempts to save themselves, leaving the bodies of families and neighbours piled up in the city streets. Ignorant of the causes of the plague and virtually power-less as a result to prevent its spread, those who lived through the pestilence could only attribute it to the actions of a malign fate or accept it as the just actions of a wrathful God intent on punishing a wicked and ungrateful people. Umbria was far from unique, of course, in its experience of plague. Boccaccio de-scribed the terrifying effect of the Black Death on Florence at the beginning of the *Decameron*, and artists such as Orcagna and Francesco Traini luridly portrayed it in their *Triumph of Death* frescoes (these are to be found, both in sadly reduced states today, in Santa Croce in Florence and the Camposanto in Pisa, respectively). In Umbria, though, the Black Death must have appeared even more apocalyptic than elsewhere, for the outbreak in 1348 was preceded by a famine and followed by an earthquake, which devastated the area around Spoleto. Further outbreaks of plague hit the cities of Umbria in 1362–3, 1371, 1390 and 1399, while in the next century the plague returned in 1418, 1429, and 1443–4. In 1522–4 the pestilence affected a third of the total population of the region, claiming as one of its victims the painter Pietro Vannucci, Perugino, who died in Fontignano, where he was working, in February 1523. A massive outbreak of the plague occurred in 1663–4 (making its way to London by the following year), and another in 1716 claimed 4,000 victims in Perugia alone. The frequency with which the plague struck is indicated by the widespread appearance in the region's churches of paintings and statues of St Roch and St Sebastian, the two most popular plague saints, whose aid was invoked in times of peril (the former is usually represented with the plague-like symptom of a discoloured wound in the inside of his upper thigh, while the many arrows piercing the latter recall classical belief that disease resulted from Apollo's arrows). Today, the most potent evocation in Umbria of what townspeople felt when plague struck is to be found in the Perugian church of Santa Maria Nuova. There, a standard painted by Benedetto Bonfigli in 1472 shows Christ unleashing thunderbolts on Perugia – the general shape of the city is still recognizable today – while the Virgin, joined by St Benedict, St Scholastica and the Blessed Paolo Bigazzini, endeavours to placate her son's wrath.

CHAPTER SIX

From Commune to Signoria

※

The growth of the towns and cities of Umbria which took place from the twelfth century onwards forms part of the wider political, economic and social history of northern and central Italy in the Middle Ages. When these cities had declined under the onslaught of successive waves of invaders passing back and forth through the region, at the fall of the Roman Empire, their inhabitants had endeavoured to escape marauding armies by seeking the safety of remoter areas, so that power centred increasingly on the large monasteries and castles in the country-side. Having expanded once more, however, as their populations increased, the cities again began to take control of the surround-ing countryside. This they did both by armed force – including the destruction of the castles of the feudal nobility – and by the extensive purchase of land by townsfolk made affluent by profits from trade. Unlike the majority of towns in northern Italy, which possessed no more than small strips of land beneath the city walls, the towns of Umbria came to possess large tracts of the surrounding territories, recalling the Etruscan cities of earlier centuries, and giving rise to what were essentially city-states. The countryside was made increasingly to serve the towns. Massive deforestation took place, as a growing urban population found in Umbria's extensive woodland a ready source of material for building, heating, cooking, and manufacture. The hills around the towns were more intensively planted than before, especially with the prized crops of grapes, olives and fruit. In order to maximize efficiency, and thereby profits, agricultural land needed to be properly tended and communications to be improved. In 1279, at the time of the building of Perugia's great public fountain, the city's administrators were also concerning themselves with canalization in the surrounding *contado*; in the following year, they determined to build a road from Perugia to Marsciano, to ease the passage of men, beasts, and merchandise across the marshy valley. Twelve years later, in 1292, there was an attempt to control the waters in the area between Trevi and Montefalco, and in 1342 work was carried out on strengthening the banks of the Tiber and straightening the course of the Genna from Pila to the Nestore.

Such work was not effected without difficulty and – despite determined efforts, and the considerable sums of money expended – there were repeated setbacks. Swampland proved particularly resistant to efforts at improvement, and the combination of rapid deforestation and a rudimentary technology added to the difficulties of draining the vast tracts of marsh that still characterized the areas around Lake Trasimeno, and the Tiber valley. The problem would in fact endure for several hundred years, and even at the beginning of the fifteenth century much of the Vale of Umbria, from Foligno to Spoleto, was still marshy – a problem exacerbated by the near-total deforestation of Monte Subasio, which led to Assisi being forced to make strenuous efforts to encourage reforestation with oaks and chestnuts.

Even more importantly, the rise of the Umbrian communes was accompanied by continual conflict between neighbouring cities, with the result that valuable reclamation work might be undertaken only for the results to be undone by enemy soldiers. Only when more immediately pressing matters intervened did the cities maintain friendly (or at least neutral) relations with their neighbours. Then, diplomatic activity was often intense – in the year 1260 alone, Perugia's ambassador, Maffeo 'Cinturalie', travelled to Assisi in January, the Tuscan cities of Siena and Lucca in March, Fabriano, across the Apennines, in July, and Orvieto in September, before returning to Assisi in October. Yet peace was invariably short-lived, so that Perugia was constantly engaged in warfare for a period of several hundred years.

For the men and women who laboured in the countryside, the situation was frequently grim. To add to the dangers posed by pillaging troops, there was the ever-present risk of crop failure. As a result of long summer droughts or intense winter colds, crops failed with depressing regularity – and would continue to do so for centuries. In the fourteenth century alone, there were notable dearths in 1328 and 1329, 1345, and 1384, when the upper Tiber valley was constantly at the mercy of passing troops. One recourse for Umbrians of the time was once more to seek shelter from the wars of the city-states in the remoter mountain areas of the region. There, new settlements arose, especially at altitudes between 900 and 1,150 metres, in sites where water, cultivable land, and the resources of still untouched forests made the prospect of habitation attractive. (That most such villages – Castel San Giovanni di Cascia, or Castelluccio di Norcia, for instance – were heavily fortified does suggest, however, that their inhabitants did not believe that mere isolation would secure their safety.) In the later Middle Ages, the mountains of Umbria were not, in fact, the marginal areas they were later to become, and the mountain passes of the Apennines were regularly crossed by merchants, pilgrims and farmers, as well as soldiers. Then, the mountainous east of Umbria was extensively inhabited. Between the thirteenth and fifteenth centuries, the density of population in the mountains around Norcia was fifty inhabitants per square kilometre, only slightly less than the fifty-eight inhabitants per square kilometre in Perugia; today, by contrast, the density of population in the commune of Perugia has risen to 323 inhabitants per square kilometre, while the commune of Norcia has no more than seventeen. So different was the demographic pattern of mid-fourteenth-century Umbria that rates of taxation were often higher in mountain areas than on the hills or in the valleys of the region.

The warfare that plagued Umbria in the twelfth and early thirteenth centuries was still conducted, at least nominally, in terms of the wider conflict between the Holy Roman Empire and the Church. After the death of Frederick II in 1250, the Empire's position became progressively weaker, while the fortunes of the Church correspondingly revived. In 1305, however, a Gascon, Bertrand de Got, was elected pope. As Clement V, the new Pope moved the seat of the papacy from Rome to Avignon, where it was to remain for the next seventy years. Except in the minds of a few idealists (such as Dante), Rome now became just one more Italian city, greatly declined in size, increasingly dilapidated, and even semi-rural, with land inside the walls returned to agriculture and the site of the Roman forum itself given over to pasture. Politically, the city became a prey to internal conflict between opposing aristocratic factions. The support accorded Cola di Rienzo (1313–54) – a plebeian who briefly ruled Rome, inspired by a vision of the city rising above factionalism to reclaim its former pre-eminence – was enough to persuade the Pope in Avignon to reassert the power of the Church in Italy. To this end he sent a legate to the Church States to try to bring them once more under direct papal authority. The man chosen – and the dominant figure in Umbrian history of the mid fourteenth century – was not an Italian at all but a Spaniard: Gil Alvarez Calvillo de Albornoz, known in Italy as Egidio Albornoz.

Gil Albornoz had been born around 1310 in Cuenca and had distinguished himself in several ways before arriving in Italy: of noble birth, he had studied law, had fought with distinction against the Moors at the Battle of Tarifa in 1340, had served as Chancellor at the Court of Alfonso XI of Castile, and had been made Archbishop of Toledo at an early age. Summoned to the papal court at Avignon, Albornoz was sent to Italy in 1353. For the most part, reaction in Umbria was guarded. On 22 October Perugia welcomed the cardinal, with gifts, feasts and tournaments, while endeavouring to perceive his intentions. In the north of the region, Gubbio provided no opposition, nor did Foligno, while the southern cities of Terni and Narni – long at odds with each other – allowed themselves to be reconciled. Spoleto, however, was a different case, for the city was proud of its imperial history and Albornoz had need of recourse to military action to take the city and impose on it the rule of his nephew, Blas Fernández, as governor; the Spoletines responded by setting an ambush at Piediluco, in which Blas and his son were killed.

1. Etruscan Arch, or Arch of Augustus, Perugia (3rd century BC)

2. Etruscan necropolis called the 'Crocefisso del Tufo', Orvieto (6th–3rd century BC)

3. Ipogeo dei Volumni, in the Palazzone necropolis, Perugia (2nd–1st century BC)

4. (*Above*) Roman theatre,
Gubbio (1st century AD)

5. (*Left*) Roman bridge, known
as the Bridge of Augustus, on
the Via Flaminia, Narni (1st
century BC)

6. The Springs of Clitumnus, at Campello: a spot sacred in antiquity, described in the 1st century AD by Pliny and Propertius, where the poet Giosuè Carducci first hailed 'Umbria Verde!' or 'Green Umbria!'

7. Church of San Salvatore a Campello, or the Tempietto del Clitunno; perhaps built using materials from Roman temples at the nearby Springs of Clitumnus (4th century)

8. Church of Sant'Angelo, Perugia (5th–6th century)

9. Church of San Salvatore, Spoleto (4th–9th century)

10. Abbey of San Pietro in Valle, in the Nera valley (10th–11th century)

11. Abbey of Santi Fidenzio e Terenzio, near Massa Martana (11th century)

12. Piazza IV Novembre, Perugia, with the city fountain (1275–8), the Palazzo dei Priori (1293–1443) and the cathedral (1345–1490)

13. Palazzo dei Priori and the Corso Vannucci, principal thoroughfare of Etruscan, Roman, medieval and modern Perugia

Albornoz now made his intentions abundantly clear, and the systematic control he was soon to impose on the papal territories owed little to the region's love of the Church but much to the force the cardinal threatened or employed. In 1367 Albornoz moved to establish his authority in Perugia, now striving to maintain its independence. The city, already weakened by plague, found itself under attack by a mercenary force called the White Company, led by the Englishman Sir John Hawkwood. Known to the Italians as Giovanni Acuto, Hawkwood so distinguished himself as a ruthless but efficient soldier of fortune that he eventually acquired a fine castle at Montecchio, near Castiglion Fiorentino, just over the Umbrian border in Tuscany, and is remembered in Florence, which he long served, by a memorial in the cathedral, painted by Paolo Uccello. In Umbria, he is remembered with less affection, for his company devastated large tracts of the region's territory, twice defeating the Perugians who, in the second battle, lost both their *podestà* and their military commander. With Perugia weakened, though not entirely defeated, Albornoz felt free to move against the cities in the territory under Perugian influence, and he soon occupied Assisi, Nocera and Gualdo. When Pope Urban V entered Italy from Avignon, Albornoz was able to present him with the keys of all the cities of Umbria, with the sole exception of Perugia (which eventually came to an accord with the Church in 1370).

Egidio Albornoz left two notable legacies to Umbria. The first were the so-called Egidian Constitutions, named after him. Given at Fano in the Marches on 13 April 1357, the Constitutions endeavoured to lay down norms for the organization and administration of the papal territories – now divided into seven provinces – which would override the multitude of local ordinances. So successful were the Constitutions that they remained in force for almost five centuries, until 1816. Albornoz's second legacy substantially survives to this very day. These are the great fortresses erected at the warrior-cardinal's command: among them, the massive fortress of Spoleto, which still dominates the city and surrounding countryside, Assisi's imposing Rocca Maggiore, the sombre grey castle at San Giacomo, and the great citadel at Narni. Less militaristically, Albornoz also contributed

to the development of Assisi, to which he devoted much attention, ordering the construction of the Porta San Pietro, the finest
of the city's gates, enlarging the monastery of San Francesco,
and causing his military architect, Matteo Gattapone, to build
the Cappella di Santa Caterina in the Lower Church at Assisi, to
hold his own tomb, close to the spot where his murdered
nephew and his son are interred (Albornoz's body was later
returned to Spain and reburied in Toledo cathedral).

Despite the enormous transformation he brought about in
Umbria, Albornoz's achievements seemed, for more than a half-
century after his death, to be destined to come to nothing. Both
during the exile of the papacy in Avignon and again during the
Great Schism – which saw two contenders, one at Rome and
one at Avignon, vying for the papal throne between 1378 and
1417 – the Umbrian cities continued in their old ways, claiming
freedom from papal authority and vaunting their independence.
The result was a situation of near anarchy, leading to repeated
military and economic crises, to which the increasingly divided
ruling oligarchies of the communes proved unequal. Diplomatic
indecisiveness in external affairs and an inability to reach clear or
implementable decisions internally led to a widespread feeling
that only strong government by a single individual could give
the cities the authoritative direction they desired. And so, one by
one, they turned from being communes to *signorie* – from
republican government to rule by a single lord.

There was no clear pattern in the region as to how the
transformation from commune to *signoria* actually occurred. In
some cases, the city nobles supported a single individual out of
dislike of the *popolo*; in others it was the *popolo* who preferred to
back a single lord in order to curb the power of the city
nobility. Many of the *signorie*, however, came into being as the
result of political decisions – the lords, or *signori*, often being
podestà or *capitani del popolo* whose terms of office were extended,
by agreement, beyond the stipulated term. Other *signorie* were
created as the results of ruthless acts by powerful nobles anxious
for personal power. In 1334 the Guelph noble Ermanno Monaldeschi became lord of Orvieto by arranging for the murder of a
relative and potential rival, and staging a coup in which he

challenged the power of the newly appointed *podestà* and the *capitano del popolo* before they had had time to settle into their posts. Monaldeschi's supporters voted in council for the suspension of the Orvietan constitution and, abandoning the simplicity of previous civic titles, elected him *Vexillifer populi et vexillifer iustitie Urbisveteris toto tempore vite sue* – Standard-bearer of the People and Standard-bearer of Justice for Life. In Ermanno Monaldeschi's case, 'life' was to be no more than three years but the days of the commune were over (and the later history of Orvieto was repeatedly marked by bloody quarrels between different branches of the Monaldeschi family). In Foligno, the Trinci family established their supremacy in the city after 1353, by offering allegiance to the Church in return for Albornoz's support against their hereditary enemies, the Vitelleschi.

Perugia was a case apart. By the middle of the fourteenth century the city was unrivalled in wealth and might among cities in the region, and was beginning to attract the unwelcome attentions of even quite distant powers. The ambitious Visconti family of Milan, for instance, made incursions into Umbria as early as 1350, at first in support of their Ghibelline ally, Giovanni Gabrielli, who was endeavouring to wrest Gubbio from the control of Guelph Perugia; soon, however, they were acting independently in the region, in their own interest. On 19 January 1400, the council of Perugia – beset by internal strife, debt and plague, and with marauding enemy forces in the surrounding countryside – presented their city to Giangaleazzo Visconti, son of Galeazzo II, and heir of Milan. It was the era of the Viscontis' greatest triumph in central Italy, for Siena had accepted their rule just eight days previously and, on 20 January, Assisi and Gualdo Tadino followed Perugia's lead. As it turned out, the Visconti *signoria* was to be short-lived, for Giangaleazzo died in 1402 and his wife presented Perugia to Pope Boniface IX in the following year. The Church, however, was unable to hold on to the city for long: in 1408, having recently taken Rome, King Ladislas of Naples turned his attentions to Umbria, occupying Terni and Orvieto. Perugia's leaders then freely offered the city to Ladislas, in order to save it from a more feared enemy at its gates. Though Ladislas left Umbria shortly afterwards, he returned in 1414, devastating Montefalco, Bevagna and Todi, only to fall seriously ill in Perugia. Leaving the city in July, he returned home to Naples where he died less than a month later, in August 1414.

The enemy Perugia had feared in 1408 was one of a new breed of men who did much to shape the fortunes of Italian cities during the fifteenth century. These were the *condottieri*, the great mercenary leaders who thrived in the political confusion rife in much of Italy. Three of the very greatest of these were themselves Umbrian: Braccio Fortebraccio da Montone (1368–1424), the Perugian Niccolò Piccinino (1386–1444), and Erasmo da Narni, called Gattamelata (1370–1443), this last a *condottiero* in the service of the Venetian Republic and commemorated at Padua, where he died, by a monumental equestrian statue, one of the greatest masterpieces of Donatello. Of these three great military leaders, it was Braccio Fortebraccio who made the greatest impact on Umbria itself and whom Perugia so feared.

Braccio was born into a noble Guelph family, lords of Montone, a small hill-town dominating a stretch of the upper Tiber valley between Città di Castello and Umbèrtide. He spent most of his youth in Perugia, until he was exiled, along with other members of the nobility, in 1393. His exile was to last for no fewer than twenty-three years, during which time Braccio never lost his aspiration to return; when, eventually, he achieved his ambition, it was to become lord of the city. In 1394 Braccio led a company which laid siege to Fratta (now Umbèrtide), but was taken prisoner by the Perugians and released only after agreeing to renounce the *signoria* of Montone. Braccio then passed, by turn, into the service of the Cardinal-Archbishop of Bologna, and King Ladislas. When the King turned his attention to Florence in 1408, Braccio remained in Umbria, where he captured Todi and the territories between that city and Perugia, on Ladislas's behalf. In 1410, Braccio attacked Perugia itself, managing to reach the third circle of the city's walls before being compelled to retire after a fierce action which lasted all night, and during which women joined in the city's defence, pouring boiling water, oil, and wax on the heads of the besieging troops. Braccio retreated only long enough to regroup, however, and soon defeated his pursuers in a battle at nearby Torgiano. Having quarrelled with Ladislas – who had been led to believe that the *condottiero* intended to betray him – Braccio passed into the service of the Roman pretender to the papacy, John XXIII, and helped him recapture Rome itself. In his absence, the Umbrian cities he had so recently taken shifted their allegiances to Ladislas, but after a forced march through hostile territory, Braccio recaptured his home-town of Montone on 29 July 1413. A year later, John XXIII appointed Braccio to safeguard Bologna, during his absence at the Council of Constance, naming him Count of Montone, and declaring Montone henceforth outwith Perugian control. Once established in Bologna, Braccio quickly occupied the whole of Romagna, only to lose his gains when the Bolognese rebelled on learning of the deposition of John XXIII.

Braccio left Bologna with 4,000 cavalry, besides his infantry, and rode towards Perugia. At Sant'Egidio, on 12 July 1416, he defeated the Perugian forces after a battle lasting seven hours; two days later, he defeated another army at Colfiorito, in the hills above Foligno. On 16 July 1416, after twenty-three years' exile, Braccio entered Perugia and was proclaimed *signore*. His *signoria* was to last for eight years, during which period Braccio strengthened the fortifications and did much to improve and embellish the city. In order to pay for these works, Braccio made military incursions both inside and outside Umbria: taking the area around Norcia and raiding the *contado* of Lucca. By the time Pope Martin V, who had been elected at the Council of Constance, passed through the region on his way to Rome, Braccio was *signore* of all of Umbria and southern Tuscany, and hence the real power in the lands which, in theory, belonged to the Church.

Predictably enough, Martin V was not prepared to accept this situation for long and he soon made attempts to wrest control of Spoleto and Assisi from Braccio. When Braccio refused to treat, the Pope promptly excommunicated him. The situation in central Italy had become so grave that Florence now endeavoured to make peace between the Pope and Braccio, who travelled to Florence accompanied by representatives of all of the Umbrian cities under his control. The result of the negotiations was an agreement that, if Braccio would regain Bologna for the Church, the Pope would accept Braccio as his lieutenant in Umbria. Braccio returned victorious to Perugia only to depart once more in 1421, this time to assist Queen Joanna of Naples who, in return, made him Prince of Capua and Constable of the Kingdom of Sicily. Leading his forces through the Marches and the Abruzzo, and taking all the towns and castles that lay in his road, Braccio entered Naples on 7 June 1421. Now Braccio put conditions on the Pope: in return for relinquishing those cities he had captured in the Abruzzo, he insisted that the Pope grant him the *signoria* of Città di Castello, which he did, leaving Braccio free to take the city on 3 September 1422. Back in Naples, Braccio was named Viceroy of the Abruzzo by a grateful Queen Joanna. He found, though, that his successes did not endear him to others. The Pope excommunicated him for a second time and Braccio found himself with no ally but Florence, itself threatened by the Milanese. On his departure from Naples to lay siege to L'Aquila, in the Abruzzo, Braccio is said to have left his wife a crown and a suit of mourning, to serve as circumstances dictated. During the first stage of his assault, Braccio knew his accustomed success, taking all the towns and fortresses in the surrounding area, cutting off the city's supply routes and seeing off attempts to relieve the city. On 2 June 1424, however, Braccio – though aided by his fellow Perugian Niccolò Piccinino – found himself facing fresh Milanese forces under their great commander, Francesco Sforza. In the course of the battle that followed, Braccio was struck from his horse (allegedly by another Perugian whose family had been killed by Braccio's supporters). Wounded, Braccio refused aid and food and died later the same day. Possessed of great personal courage, and admired for his tactical skill and for the discipline he imposed on his troops, Braccio was one of the most notable of all *condottieri* – a warrior whom Machiavelli singled out, in *The Prince*, as one of those men who were, in their time, the arbiters of the destiny of Italy. And yet, almost immediately after Braccio's death, the Umbrian territories he had conquered returned within the Pope's sphere of influence – and after more than sixty years the reforms and administrative structures Cardinal Albornoz had put in place began to work. By guaranteeing the *signori* who followed Braccio the peaceful possession of their cities and lands, in return for acknowledging – not least by taxation – the supremacy of the Church, the papacy endeavoured to take a firm grip on Umbria.

So far as Perugia was concerned, it was not an easy task. For another hundred years the city endeavoured to maintain its independence and extend its influence throughout Umbrian territory. In the process, it gained the reputation as the most brutal and savage *signoria* in the whole of Italy. Two Perugian families in particular – the Baglioni and the Oddi – were engaged in a bloody rivalry which endured for centuries. In the early fourteenth century the Baglioni were already notable members of the city government, but it was in the following century that they came to dominate the life of Perugia, and no account of Umbria would be complete that did not take account of their fearsome doings.

When Malatesta I (1390–1437) married the niece of Braccio Fortebraccio, he received from him the *signoria* of the small town of Cannara. Despite having previously fought against the Pope, Malatesta now saw the papacy as the best guarantor of his own interests and engaged in the enterprise of securing Perugia's submission to the Church. As a reward for Malatesta's success, the Pope appointed him to rule Perugia on his behalf and gave him the lordships of Spello, Bastia, Collemancio, Bettona and Torgiano, to add to that of Cannara. When Malatesta died, the Pope divided these *signorie* among his sons: Guido (1425–1500) taking Spello, Ridolfo I (1430–1501) inheriting Cannara and Bettona. The greatest prize, Perugia, went to the eldest son, Braccio I (1419–79), who consolidated his position, and that of the Church, by taking military control of the entire region as far as the mountains of Spoleto and Norcia. In 1459, Pope Pius II visited Perugia and Braccio celebrated the occasion with tournaments and feasting. Even with papal backing, however, Braccio could not feel his position secure and in the following year, fearful of a conspiracy against him by his cousin Pandolfo and his son Niccolò, Braccio had them killed in Perugia's main square.

Braccio died in 1479, to be succeeded by his brother, Guido, whose *signoria* was marked by threats both from outside and within the city. The appearance in Perugia of Pope Sixtus IV gave rise to fears that the Church was unwilling to allow Guido the same degree of independence that Braccio had enjoyed. Within the city, the ancient quarrel with the Oddi was renewed. Three years after Guido came to power, the Baglioni and the Oddi fought a pitched battle in the square between the cathedral (on whose steps artillery was placed) and the Palazzo dei Priori, which left 130 dead. A new magistrate was created in the city to try to avoid any such clashes in future but to little avail. In 1488, an apparently minor dispute concerning land boundaries near the lakeside town of Passignano saw a renewal of hostilities, with the Baglioni now occupying the cathedral and turning it into a fortress. After three days' fighting, the Oddi were expelled from the city and their property divided up among the Baglioni. The Oddi retired no further than the town of Castiglione on the western shore of Lake Trasimeno, from where they commenced hostilities which soon involved all the surrounding territory and drew in the families of the Vitelli of Città di Castello, and the Medici of Florence, as well as the Pope in Rome. In 1491 the Oddi endeavoured to take Perugia by surprise but when their expected reinforcements failed to appear, Fabrizio and Bertoldo degli Oddi were seized and killed, and fifty of their supporters hanged from the windows of the Palazzo dei Priori. Three years later, a further attempt to seize Perugia ended in bloody farce when 200 Oddi supporters were trampled underfoot as they made a precipitate retreat after mishearing an order; three captured Oddi brothers were first flung from the windows of the Palazzo dei Priori and afterwards hanged there.

The threat to the ruling Baglioni did not come only from the Oddi, however. In 1500, the most prominent members of the Baglioni were the five sons of Guido – Gentile, Astorre I, Adriano I, Marcantonio, and Gismondo – and the three sons of Ridolfo – Troilo, Giampaolo and Simonetto. A plot to murder all of these was hatched by Carlo and Giulio Cesare Varano, the lords of Camerino in the Marches, Girolamo della Penna, a Perugian who hoped to gain the *signoria* for himself, and two other of Malatesta's grandchildren: Federico (called Grifonetto) and Carlo (called Bargiglia). The occasion chosen for the attempt was the wedding of Astorre I to Lavinia (herself offspring of two feuding Roman families, the Colonna and the Orsini), which was to be followed by no fewer than twenty days of feasting and jousting costing 60,000 florins. One evening after the wedding, all of the Baglioni family, who had heard Mass and dined together, retired to their separate homes. The plotters, by contrast, gathered at the house of Bargiglia, from where at the appointed hour each went to the home of his designated victim. All the leading Baglioni in the city died that night, with the single exception of Giampaolo, who evaded his would-be assassin, Grifonetto, by escaping across the rooftops and managing to reach the house of his brother, Troilo, who lived outside the city. On the following day Giampaolo returned to Perugia, accompanied by Vitellozzo Vitelli of Città di Castello. All the conspirators had fled except Grifonetto, who appeared before Giampaolo to seek his cousin's pardon. It was an unwise decision, for he was brutally killed on the steps of the church of Sant'Ercolano. Giampaolo's revenge was fierce. The Rione di Sant'Angelo – a district of Perugia traditionally hostile to the Baglioni, whose inhabitants had refused to celebrate Astorre's wedding – was sacked and its houses burned, the inhabitants themselves having sensibly fled. Appointing his cousin, Adriano, to govern the city in his stead, Giampaolo turned his attentions to Foligno, where the conspirators had taken refuge. Giampaolo fought and defeated these enemies before turning on the Oddi in Cortona, who had taken advantage of Giampaolo's absence at Foligno to march on Perugia. At Borghetto di Tuoro, on the shores of Lake Trasimeno, Giampaolo was victorious once more, Carlo Oddi dying in battle and Pandolfo – the last of the family – being taken prisoner and strangled.

On assuming power in Perugia, Giampaolo was careful to consolidate his position. He sent envoys to the newly elected Pope, Julius II, who then visited Perugia from 12 to 21 September 1506. In February of the following year, on his victorious return from Bologna where he had fought in support of the Pope, Giampaolo celebrated with three days of feasting and jousting which afforded an opportunity for reconciliation between the Perugian nobles and between the nobility and the people. In 1510 he was appointed captain-general of the Venetian forces and, three years later, on the death of Julius II, visited Rome to pay his respects to the newly elected Leo X. For a further seven years, Giampaolo ruled Perugia without serious threat to his position. When Leo X invited him to Rome in 1520, however, Giampaolo hesitated and took up the invitation only after receiving many guarantees as to his safety. The initial hesitation was well-justified: on his arrival in Rome, Giampaolo was imprisoned, tortured, and eventually beheaded in the Castel Sant'Angelo on 11 June 1520.

A fresh struggle for power broke out among the Baglioni family. At first, Giampaolo was succeeded by Guido's son, Gentile (1466–1527) – a priest, though married to Giampaolo's cousin, Giulia Vitelli – who governed with the approval of Leo X. Gentile fled Perugia, however, when Giampaolo's sons, Orazio and Malatesta, approached at the head of a hostile force. When both of these were themselves imprisoned in Rome, Gentile returned to Perugia, leaving the troops of Orazio and Malatesta to support themselves by pillage in the area of Bettona and Cannara. A papal force sent to Umbria to deal with this problem succeeded in capturing a great number of these soldiers, and among those hanged were two cadet members of the Baglioni family: Sforzino and Costantino. Orazio now managed to escape from Rome and return to Perugia while Gentile – charged with treasonable contact with the Emperor Charles V, who besieged and captured Rome in 1527 – was taken prisoner and stabbed to death. Not content with this death, Orazio took his revenge, in the course of July and August 1527, on any of Gentile's relations unlucky enough to fall into his hands. Malatesta, who arrived when the slaughter was complete, at first took power in a Perugia stricken by famine and plague alongside his brother, only to quarrel with him over Orazio's desire to kill two more of Gentile's relations, who had been captured near Foligno. The quarrel was resolved when Orazio departed Perugia, to be killed fighting the following year.

The story of Perugia under the Baglioni is one of despotism

and terror, jealousy and treachery – an epoch so steeped in bloodshed that the city's cathedral itself was washed with wine and consecrated anew. Yet the supremacy of the Baglioni was also the age of the Early Renaissance, when learning was respected, when artists and sculptors from elsewhere – the Beato Angelico, Piero della Francesca, Agostino di Duccio – worked in Perugia, when Benedetto Bonfigli, Perugino, and Pinturicchio helped create a native Umbrian art, and when the young Raphael began his own illustrious career in the city. If it is worth considering this disturbing juxtaposition of political savagery and artistic refinement, however, it is also worth asking why, in the end, the full potential of Renaissance culture was never realized in Umbria. For all the indisputable achievements of mid-fifteenth- to mid-sixteenth-century painters and the presence of occasionally very fine buildings of the same period, the region today still presents the appearance of a medieval world largely untouched by the achievements of the Renaissance. Today it may seem unrealistic to expect any Umbrian city to rival Florence or Rome, Venice or Naples, yet it is striking that none offers a real parallel to smaller centres of Renaissance culture, such as Mantua or Padua, Ferrara or Urbino, either. There is no simple answer to why this is so, but the very abundance of cities with aspirations to local independence did not help the emergence of a single dominant centre anywhere in the region – and it was not only Perugia that was weakened by years of internecine strife. In the south of the region, Orvieto and Spoleto – which had both formerly profited from their usefulness as refuges for the popes during incursions by foreign armies with designs on Rome – suffered from neglect once the city began to seem more secure in the late fifteenth century. In the north, Gubbio was always going to be a satellite of Urbino across the Apennines once it fell into the hands of the Montefeltro family.

As the largest and most prosperous city in the region, however, Perugia might have become a much more important cultural centre than was, in fact, the case – and humanism certainly made inroads there. Indeed, from the early fourteenth century, Perugia had a university, and the scholars who taught there were among the most eminent of their day: among them, the jurist and poet Cino da Pistoia (*c.* 1270–1337), the jurist Bartolo da Sassoferrato (1313–57), and the Perugian-born Baldo degli Ubaldi (1327–1400), author of *Summula respiciens facta mercatorum*, considered the founding text of commercial law. The prestige of the university continued into the fifteenth century, through its law and medical schools and classical studies, while the teachers included the great mathematician Luca da Pacioli (1445–1517). In 1483 Pope Sixtus IV gave the university a new home in a fine palazzo built between 1453 and 1483, in Renaissance style, by Gasperino di Antonio and Bartolomeo Mattioli da Torgiano (the building survives in what is now the Piazza Matteotti). Yet, unlike comparable centres elsewhere, Perugia never developed a distinctive humanist culture of its own.

With one notable exception, the humanists of Umbria were, at best, men of the second rank. In the fourteenth century, the first stirrings of a new sensibility can be seen in the work of the Foligno-born Dominican theologian and Bishop of Foligno, Federico Frezzi (1347–1416), whose long allegorical poem, *Quadriregio*, reveals the influence of Petrarch and Boccaccio, as well as of Dante. In the fifteenth century, Pacifico Massimi, from Ascoli in the Marches, was present at the Baglioni court in Perugia, fulsomely dedicating his heroic *Poema Triumphorum* to Braccio I. Meanwhile, the Perugia-born Lorenzo Gualtieri (1425–96), poet and soldier of fortune, wrote his *Altro Marte* in praise of the celebrated *condottiere* Niccolò Piccinino, from nearby Magione. Gualtieri, however, did not only write but also held office in Perugia, and it was this dual role as writer and political adviser that distinguished the great humanists of the fifteenth century. Consequently, it was the lack of a real political role in the declining *signorie* which most obviously militated against the emergence of a strong humanist culture in Umbria. Antonio Pacini (1420–89), from Massa Martana, for example, was at one time tutor to another renowned Umbrian *condottiere*, Bartolomeo d'Alviano (1455–1515). This famous captain of fortune imbibed sufficient humanism to write poetry, a commentary on his own military exploits, to give his birthplace a fine library, and to found the academy of Pordenone in the north of Italy, whose lordship had been bestowed on him by the Republic of Venice as a reward for his services. Just as Bartolomeo d'Alviano left Umbria in order to find success, however, so too did Pacini, who departed to serve the Medici family at their court in Florence.

Massimi, Gualtieri and Pacini were all comparatively minor figures. Umbrian humanism did, however, boast one exceptional name: that of Giovanni Pontano (1426–1503), better known by his Latinized name as Pontanus. Pontanus was born at Cerreto, into a family already noted for a succession of distinguished lawyers, theologians and scholars. Aged fourteen, he went to Perugia to study and began to compose verses. While he was still at university, his family home was sacked and burned, and on leaving Perugia Giovanni travelled to the Aragonese court at Naples, where he had relations. It was there that he acted as adviser to the Aragonese princes and took over the Academy which he made famous and which took his name – the Accademia Pontiana. Pontano might, however, have returned to lend glory to Umbria in 1465, for in that year he was offered the Chair of Rhetoric of the university in Perugia. Instead, he declined, and in 1471 became a citizen of Naples. There he not only consolidated his literary fame as a writer of sensuous Latin verse and as pioneer of the long didactic poem, but also became Secretary-General of State. Pontanus's career is thrown into stark relief by the career of his younger contemporary, the humanist Angelo Poliziano (1454–94), Politian, from the Tuscan hill-town of Montepulciano, just across the Umbrian border, above Lake Trasimeno. As Pontanus had studied in Perugia, so Politian studied in his home university of Florence. He then proceeded to the court of the Gonzagas at Mantua, as Pontanus had gone to Naples. When Politian was offered a Chair at the university of Florence, however, he returned home and spent the remainder of his life within the orbit of the Medici, becoming a prime contributor to Florentine cultural life.

The problem in Umbria, in other words, was the lack of a political culture strong enough to attract talented and ambitious outsiders into the region, or to persuade Umbrian-born men of learning to remain. Similarly, it was political, rather than simply economic, weakness that prevented the art of printing – which did so much to disseminate humanist culture throughout Europe – from striking strong roots in Umbria, despite its remarkably early presence there. After Gutenberg's invention of the press and movable type in Mainz in the 1450s, printing arrived in Italy in 1465. Predictably enough, the printing press soon made its way to Rome (1467) and Venice (1469). Less predictably, perhaps – until one remembers that the Flaminian Way was still the principal route for those travelling between Venice and Rome – presses were to be found both in the small town of Trevi and in Foligno by 1470. In Foligno, a local goldsmith, Emiliano Orfini, joined forces with the German printer Johann Numeister to produce works which included the first edition of Dante's *Divine Comedy*, which appeared on 11 April 1472 and was one of the earliest books in the Italian language to be printed in Italy. Despite this precocious start, however, printing took many years to establish itself firmly in Umbria. For Johann Rothmann, who worked at Trevi, the lure of Rome was too great and in this, as in so many other areas, Umbria found itself marginalized in relation to the political, commercial, and artistic centre of Rome.

The single best surviving example of Renaissance humanist culture in Umbria is, happily, a magnificent one: the Collegio del Cambio in the Palazzo dei Priori in Perugia (which deserves far more than the fleeting glance sometimes bestowed on it by tourists in a hurry). For this fifteenth-century exchange, the Deruta-born humanist Francesco Maturanzio provided an intellectual plan – confidently fusing Christian and classical cultures – which the painter Perugino used to create what is not only one of the best examples of his harmonious art but one of the finest examples of Renaissance art in the whole of Italy. Beneath a ceiling depicting Apollo in his chariot, surrounded by representations of the planets, God the Father gives his blessing to Old Testament prophets and classical sibyls alike. Figures from ancient Greece and Rome embody the classical virtues of Prudence and Justice, Fortitude and Temperance, while Christian revelation is made manifest in two complementary scenes: the Nativity and the Transfiguration. A small *trompe l'œil* self-portrait of the artist – phlegmatic, unlovely, but intensely human – completes the scene. In one small luminous space, past and present, ancient and modern, seem to co-exist happily a near-perfect synthesis of classical and Christian, human and divine.

Perugino worked on the frescoes in the Collegio del Cambio between around 1498 and 1500 – one of the very bloodiest periods in the history of Baglioni rule. By the time the artist died in 1523, however, the family's domination of the city was all but over.

In 1527, with Italy in general disarray under the onslaught of the imperial forces of Charles V, Umbria became the scene of fierce fighting, with town after town falling to the invading forces. Malatesta Baglioni headed northwards to Tuscany in a vain attempt to defend Florence, which eventually fell in August 1530 after a long siege in which 22,000 died. Malatesta returned to Umbria, taking up residence in Bettona, where, far from opposing the passage of imperial troops through his territory *en route* from Florence to Rome, he prudently gave a subvention for their support. When he died in 1531, the supporters of Gentile made their presence felt once more, in support of Grifonetto's son, Braccio II, who was also backed by Pope Clement VII. An opposing faction in the family advanced the claims of Ridolfo II and Giampaolo II, sons of Malatesta and Orazio respectively. At Clement VII's death, Ridolfo and Giampaolo triumphed briefly, expelling Braccio II from Perugia, only to be expelled themselves by the new Pope, Paul III.

The end now came quickly. As long ago as 1424, Pope Martin V had established that Perugia and other Umbrian cities would not be liable to pay the papal salt tax, and this privilege – acceded to by subsequent popes – was held dear by the Perugians. When, on his second visit to the city in September 1539, Pope Paul III rescinded his predecessors' concession by fixing a salt tax of three *quattrini* per pound of salt, the Perugians were incensed, not just by the tax but by the additional fact that they were already obliged to acquire their salt from the papacy's own saltworks. They began by sending ambassadors to treat with the Pope but he refused to revoke the tax. On 2 March 1540, the people gathered in five of the city's churches to choose twenty-five delegates to meet with the papal vice-legate to discuss the price of salt. Again, the Pope refused to treat with them, and prepared for a showdown – the so-called Salt War. On 5 June 1540, papal troops under the command of Pierluigi Farnese, son of Paul III, entered Perugia and the ascendancy of the Baglioni was effectively over. Having devastated much of the surrounding *contado*, the Pope chose the Baglioni stronghold on the Landone hill as the site of a massive display of strength. There he caused the architect Antonio da Sangallo the Younger to build the Rocca Paolina, or Pauline Fortress, and had inscribed on it the legend *'Ad repellandam Perusinorum audaciam'* (For curbing the audacity of the Perugians). Some 138 houses belonging to the Baglioni were destroyed, along with ten churches. Fortunately, Sangallo used other houses as the foundations of the new fortress, the result being those subterranean and eerily empty medieval streets still visible today as a reminder of a dynasty whose *signoria* in Perugia had endured for more than a century.

CHAPTER SEVEN

St Francis and His Followers

✳

From the earliest days of Christianity, Umbria had never been short of saints. In the third century there were the early proselytizers who preached the new religion to a pagan world. There were the many martyrs – one partial source lists over 100 names – who died for the faith at Roman hands. Some men and women won reputations for the holiness of their lives, whether they chose to live within the secular world or retire from it, while others performed miracles. Warrior-bishops gained a martyr's crown for defending their cities against the invaders who plundered the region in the centuries after the fall of Rome. In the sixth century it was an Umbrian, St Benedict, who transformed contemporary Christianity to such an extent, by giving early medieval men and women a new pattern of social organization, that he helped shape the future of the whole of Europe, whose patron saint he now is.

St Benedict, though born in Norcia, nevertheless spent most of his life outside Umbria. St Francis of Assisi, by contrast, remained very closely connected with the region throughout the whole of his life, and in particular with the area in which he was born. In this attachment to his birthplace, to its people and its language, Francis offered a new pattern of Christian living for the thirteenth century. The very success of Benedictine monasticism over seven centuries had tended to suggest that religion was primarily a matter for professionals. What Francis offered to an increasingly secularized world was a model of Christian living open to all. By example, he suggested that sanctity need not be something remote in time or place, to be admired from a distance but impossible to emulate. Francis showed that it was possible, as he endeavoured to live out the life of the gospel in the here and now, to achieve holiness not as a bishop but as a layman, not as a nobleman but as one of the people. In doing so, he brought religion close to ordinary, everyday human experience and transformed the nature of sainthood from a sanctity of function to the *imitatio Christi*, the imitation of Christ. The result was not only to make Francis the most revered saint of his day but, paradoxically, to turn him today into the most universal and modern of saints. Today, Francis is remembered throughout the length and breadth of Umbria: by tiny churches he knew – San Damiano or the Portiuncula – and by the vast basilicas at Assisi and Santa Maria degli Angeli, on the plain beneath the town, in the remote mountain hermitages he frequented – the Carceri, Lo Speco, or Monteluco – and by the great Franciscan churches to be found in every town in the region. He is remembered too by the many images to be seen in churches, monasteries, and museums everywhere, by some of the greatest artists of the Middle Ages and Renaissance – Cimabue, Giotto, the Beato Angelico, Gozzoli, Piero della Francesca, or Perugino. Yet the saint from Assisi is also the patron of all Italy and the patron of the worldwide Green movement. He has given his name to one of the great cities on the west coast of the United States. He is the subject of innumerable biographies, from that of his contemporary, Thomas of Celano, to that by the French Academician of American descent, Julien Green. And St Francis has been celebrated too, in the twentieth century, in other media; in music by composers as different as Olivier Messiaen and Karl-Heinz Stockhausen, in film by directors as varied as Roberto Rossellini, Franco Zeffirelli, and Liliana Cavani.

Francis was born in Assisi, then a town of around 10,000 inhabitants, in 1181 or 1182. The great variety of biographical or hagiographical accounts which appeared in the years after his death make many of the details of his life uncertain. By tradition, he was the son of a cloth-merchant, Pietro di Bernardone, and of Pietro's French-born wife, Pica. This tradition would have the future saint christened not as Francis, or Francesco, but as

Giovanni, his name having supposedly been changed in honour of his mother's country of birth. Francis grew up in comfortable surroundings and spent his youth in a fashion which different biographers chose to call carefree or dissipated. Though not noble by birth, Francis's social position meant that he received an education which taught him some Latin – his surviving prose works are in that language – and French, the language of chivalry and courtly love, whose values shaped not only his early years as a soldier but also his later, spiritual life. In 1195, Assisi was the scene of a singular event of which the young Francis must have been aware, and at which he may well have been present: the baptism in the cathedral of San Rufino of the infant son of the Emperor Henry VI and the Queen of Sicily, who would grow up to be the immensely powerful emperor Frederick II. As a fourteen- or fifteen-year-old, Francis saw something of a world beyond the confines of Assisi when he accompanied his father on one of the mercantile expeditions that took place annually to northern Europe, following the road that led north, via Florence and Lucca, to Genoa and then west along the coast of southern France and up the Rhône valley towards the cloth centres of Bruges and Ghent.

Francis grew into manhood in the politically charged world of Assisi, where in 1198 the popular faction (the *minores* or minors) rose up against the town's nobles (the *maiores*), leading to the expulsion and subsequent exile of the latter in the neighbouring city of Perugia. Four years later, the traditional hostility between the two cities turned into open warfare. Inspired by the chivalric ideals of his day, Francis joined the Assisian cavalry and in 1202 took part in a ferocious action on the plain at Collestrada, close to the Tiber crossing, where he was captured by the Perugians and imprisoned. He was held captive for a year, being freed only when a general peace was concluded between Perugia and Assisi. Under the terms of this peace, Assisi saw an enforced reconciliation between its *maiores* and *minores*, which marked the effectual triumph of the former, leading to the return of those nobles who had been expelled from the city in 1198.

· Francis too returned home. He was, we read, a sick man, and, by some accounts, a changed one also. Thomas of Celano – a contemporary of Francis and his first biographer – tells the story that, meeting a knight reduced to abject poverty, Francis gave him clothes of his own to cover his nakedness. The story recalls the action of St Martin, who divided his cloak in half to share it with a naked beggar, but we need not, for this reason, disbelieve it. Martin's path from serving in the Roman army to a life of Christian service is one that Francis was shortly to follow. In the year following his return from imprisonment, Francis seems to have been torn between the ideals of chivalry and courtly love which had inspired his youth, and a desire to find another way of life. As he slept one night, he was visited by a vision of a splendid palace, of knightly accoutrements, and a beautiful lady which, a voice proclaimed, were reserved for Francis himself.

Francis's experience of war had so far been very local and fighting against a town clearly visible across the plain from the walls of Assisi was perhaps not sufficiently in line with chivalric ideals to gain the rich rewards promised him. While Francis had been fighting at Collestrada, crusaders had left Venice to conquer Jerusalem; by 1204 they had captured Constantinople and were spreading out, taking prizes throughout the eastern Mediterranean. So – inspired by thoughts of what the twelfth-century troubadour Jaufré Rudel called *terra lonhdana* (the distant land) – Francis joined a band of knights being raised by Walter of Brienne to ride south to Puglia, one of the principal gateways to the east. He got no further than Spoleto. Taken ill once more, he heard voices asking of him what he was doing, and telling him to return home.

Back in Assisi, Francis transformed the chivalric values that had guided him thus far into spiritual ideals. He sought the service not of an earthly lord but of a heavenly one. He exchanged his knightly dress for a rough tunic, and instead of marrying in the flesh, he espoused *Madonna Povertà*, Lady Poverty. He also exchanged the pursuit of chivalric glory for what his contemporaries saw only as a source of shame and pain: the service of those who lived on the margins of society – beggars, for example, or even lepers, the most despised and feared outcasts of medieval society. In the thirteenth century, lepers were entirely separated from the rest of that society, bearing as they did the obvious marks of divine displeasure on their ulcerous and gangrenous bodies. They were obliged by law to live outside areas inhabited by the healthy, to carry rattles warning of their approach, and were forbidden to touch anything used by others. Herein lies the significance of the story of Francis, at the very outset of his ministry, dismounting from his horse to kiss a passing leper. And in his identification with all the outcasts of his age lies the significance of the title Francis chose for himself: *ioculator dei*, God's fool, a title taken from one of those disreputable itinerant entertainers of medieval society.

The decision Francis made to turn his back on worldly success in order to follow Christ was taken before the crucifix in the small church of San Damiano (St Damian) in 1206. (By tradition, the crucifix is that displayed today in the church of Santa Chiara in Assisi.) In one version of this story, Francis felt himself called to restore the Church, riven by clerical corruption and lay indifference, by the crucified Christ who commanded him with the words: 'Repair my house, which you see is in ruins' – a prefiguring of the celebrated dream of Innocent III, depicted by Giotto, among many other artists, in which the Pope sees Francis (or, it must be said, St Dominic, as ecclesiastical expediency dictated) holding up the Roman basilica of St John Lateran, on the point of collapse. Pietro di Bernardone was understandably perplexed and distressed at his son's decision to abandon both his chivalric ambitions and the comfortable mercantile background into which he had been born, and they quarrelled. In order to help restore the church of San Damiano, Francis had sold his horse and some of his clothes. Taken before the spiritual court of Assisi by his reproachful father, who had provided the money, Francis removed the clothes he was wearing before the Bishop of Assisi – who became one of his earliest protectors – and declared that henceforth he would own no earthly father but only 'Our Father who art in Heaven'.

Such stories often seem too obviously exemplary to be taken literally, yet it is clear that, however much his early biographers made the life of Francis conform to their own needs, something exceptional did happen in Assisi in those early years of the thirteenth century. The kind of spiritual renewal and ecclesiastical reform that Francis's visions and conduct promised were not, in fact, something unique to him. A return to a primitive, evangelical Christianity – the New Testament *metanóia* – lay at the heart of the message of other reformers. In the mid twelfth century, Arnold of Brescia – a pupil of the philosopher Abelard – had spoken out in Rome against the degeneracy of the Church, and even after the Pope had Arnold executed, the voice of reform would not be silenced. Northern Italy saw the rise of Waldensians and Catharists, while the millenarian movement of Joachim of Flora, convinced that the Second Coming was at hand, was influential in the south. The Church's response was twofold: a brutal repression of what it declared to be heresy (the Albigensian crusade which led to the destruction of the Catharist strongholds of south-western France and the indiscriminate slaughter of their inhabitants was launched by Innocent III in 1209) and a parallel attempt to absorb reformist movements less radically antagonistic to the Church's authority into its own orthodoxy.

Francis and his followers stayed within the orthodox fold by restraining themselves to an implicit criticism of the contemporary Church and clergy. Francis took literally the words of Christ to the apostles in Matthew X, 7–10: 'Preach, saying, The kingdom of heaven is at hand./Heal the sick, cleanse the lepers, raise the dead, cast out devils: freely ye have received, freely give./Provide neither gold, nor silver, nor brass in your purse,/ Nor scrip for your journey, neither two coats, neither shoes, nor yet staves: for the workman is worthy of his meat.' To a Church already devoted to luxury and the pursuit of political power, this undoubtedly presented a challenge. It was not, however, quite the same challenge as that offered by the followers of Peter Waldo of Lyons – a contemporary of Francis – who preached the common ownership of all goods and taught that the Church of Rome was the scarlet woman of the Apocalyse. As a result, Francis was not only able to avoid the charge of heresy levelled at so many spiritual reformers of his day but had his primitive Rule accepted by Innocent III, to whom he presented it at Rome in 1210.

By this time Francis had already gathered about him a small

group of brothers – Bernardo da Quintavalle, Pietro Cattani, Egidio d'Assisi, Angelo Tancredi, among others – who came from all sections of society, and included the learned and the illiterate, contemplative mystics and men of an active missionary bent. However diverse the movement Francis had started, however, two things were clear. First, his was a lay movement – and Francis was never a priest. Secondly, the movement was also a popular one – the very name later given his order, Friars Minor, recalls the *minori*, the popular faction in the Assisi of his day. Francis and his companions now lived and preached close to Assisi: at first, at Rivotorto and later at the Portiuncola, the tiny chapel now dwarfed by the huge basilica of Santa Maria degli Angeli which, built literally over and around the Portiuncula, dominates the plain below Francis's home-town.

Yet though Francis continued to be attached to the places close to where he had grown up, some remnants of his former ambitions remained. Leaving Pietro Cattani as leader of the brothers in his absence, Francis set off once more for the East, crossing the Apennines to set sail from the Adriatic port of Ancona; again Francis was thwarted, for his ship was caught in a storm and he was cast up on the shore of Dalmatia, from where he was forced to return to Italy. A subsequent attempt to travel to Morocco also came to nothing as Francis, increasingly prone to illnesses brought on in part by self-mortification, fell sick in Spain. When Francis's companions did eventually reach Morocco, the movement had gained its first martyrs: six friars, including Bernardo da Calvi, were killed there in 1220. These missionary expeditions were the first of many undertaken by the Franciscans, who, in a short space of time, had sent groups of brothers not only throughout Europe but still further afield. Fra Giovanni (*c.* 1200–1252), from Pian di Carpine (now Magione), travelled at the behest of Innocent IV across eastern Europe and Russia, as far as China – anticipating Marco Polo by some thirty years. There he presented letters from the Pope to the son and successor of the Tartar ruler Ghengis Khan and, on his return, wrote the *Historia Mongolorum*, a crucial text in the West's developing attempt to achieve an understanding of the East. Eventually, Francis himself, with the determination which marked his life, finally succeeded in his own ambition of visiting the East. In 1219 he again departed from Ancona, to make his way to the court of the Sultan Al-Malik al Kamil, before whom he preached the gospel. Although failing to convert him, Francis gained the Sultan's respect, not least by refusing all the gifts offered him, and was given a safe conduct to visit the Holy Land.

On his return to Italy, however, Francis discovered problems awaiting him which he had not foreseen. To lead the life which Christ had commended to the apostles had once seemed a challenging but straightforward task. The Church, however, despite its willingness to entertain the movement Francis had started, continued to look uneasily at the growing band of itinerant friars who wandered the countryside, homeless, and subject to no internal discipline. While the Bishop of Assisi, Pope Innocent III, and Francis's protector, Cardinal Ugolino de' Conti (the future Pope Gregory IX), all saw value in the spiritual renewal the Franciscan movement embodied, they also recognized that the movement could serve the interests of the Roman Church only if it could be brought firmly within existing ecclesiastical structures. So, in 1220, the Pope persuaded Francis to relinquish the post of Superior – which Francis himself persisted in regarding as that of first among equals – to Pietro Cattani and, after Cattani's death the following year, to Brother Elias. Francis himself, unwilling to see his followers adopt an existing monastical rule – whether Benedictine or Augustinian – made two attempts to establish a new Rule to supersede the simple one of 1210. When the second of these attempts was accepted, by Pope Honorius III, on 29 November 1223, the Franciscan order came formally into being.

The last three years of Francis's life were a compound of disappointment at the course the movement was taking (anticipating the bitter divisions which would afflict it shortly after his death), a strenuous commitment to preaching undertaken with astonishing energy for one who suffered increasingly from crippling sickness and near-blindness, and moments of mystical ecstasy. Francis continued to wander the roads of Umbria. He would stay in such modest hermitages as the Carceri, Lo Speco, or Monteluco – each to be found among thick woods on remote mountain sites in the areas of Assisi, Narni, or Spoleto. While travelling, Francis might spend the night on one of the so-called '*letti di San Francesco*' or 'beds of St Francis' – the simple stones he chose in remembrance of the Christ who had nowhere to lay his head – examples of which are still recorded today in popular tradition, at Collicello or Castel Rigone, for instance. It was this sense of the saint's attachment to his native Umbria that Dante evokes in writing of Francis's birthplace, Assisi, in Book XI of *Paradiso* in the *Divine Comedy*:

> Intra Tupino e l'acqua che discende
>   del colle eletto del beato Ubaldo,
>   fertile costa d'alto monte pende,
>
> onde Perugia sente freddo e caldo
>   da Porta Sole, e di retro le piange
>   per grave giogo Nocera con Gualdo.

> [Between Tupino and the water that
> tumbles from the hill chosen by the
> Blessed Ubaldo (i.e. Monte Ingino, on
> which Gubbio stands), a fertile slope
> beneath the high mountain, whereby
> Perugia feels cold and heat, through
> Porta Sole, and behind Nocera laments
> its heavy yoke with Gualdo.]

As he wandered throughout Umbria, legends grew up around Francis: of his preaching to the birds near the small town of Bevagna, of commanding the swallows to be silent as he preached at Alviano, near the region's south-western border with Lazio, of reproaching the huge wolf that had been terrorizing the townspeople of Gubbio, until the wolf repented and the townspeople promised to leave it sufficient food each day for its needs. Such stories remind us not only of much earlier Christian legend concerning the close relationship between saints and the animal world but also of pagan myth, and there is no doubt that much of the attraction of St Francis to the people of the Umbrian countryside lay in bringing an increasingly remote

Christianity back in touch with the instinctive, natural religion of their ancestors. Early biographers – and artists – zealously recorded these miracles, but Francis's first companions were not misled: when, in 1245, they heard that a collection of such miracles was to be made, they reminded their brothers that 'miracles did not make sanctity but manifested it'. If the miracles attributed to Francis recall an earlier, pagan Umbria, then other stories remind us of what Francis himself endeavoured to achieve: the Imitation of Christ or 'to follow naked the naked Christ' in the disturbing words of another itinerant preacher. Back in the early years of his ministry, Francis had spent the Lent of 1211 fasting alone on the Isola Maggiore in Lake Trasimeno; the boatman who transported him found on his return most of the two small loaves Francis had taken as his only sustenance still uneaten after forty days. At Christmas time in 1223, at Greccio, in the mountains near Rieti, Francis remembered the birth of Christ by recreating, in a cave, the stable, complete with ox and ass, where the infant Jesus came into the world. So powerful an effect did this assertion of Christ's humanity – so different from the image of Christ in Judgement that characterized much earlier Christianity – have on the villagers present that it was claimed that many observed Francis holding the infant Christ himself in his arms (and later hagiographers went one stage further in asserting that Francis himself had been born in a stable between an ox and an ass). It was in this way at Greccio that Francis not only initiated the tradition of the Christmas midnight mass but that of the *presepe* or crib – one of the most popular and enduring of Umbrian traditions, in which model and some-times moving cribs are still lovingly recreated at Christmas time throughout the region, in churches and private homes alike.

It was in the following year of 1224, however, that Francis most directly manifested that human identification with the suffering Christ that was his most striking contribution to thirteenth-century spirituality. Having ascended Mount La Verna, in the Tuscan province of Arezzo, to meditate, Francis was visited at night by a six-winged seraph, bearing an image of Christ crucified, who imprinted on Francis the stigmata, the marks of the wounds Christ himself had suffered on the cross:

the lance-wound in the side and the marks of the nails on his hands and feet. This was the Francis whom later piety would soon transform into an *alter Christus*, a second Christ. After receiving the stigmata, Francis lived for only another year. A sick man, he was cared for in the Bishop's palace at Assisi until, shortly before his death, he asked to be taken to the Portiuncula, where he died, in October 1226, aged about forty-five.

At his death, Francis's fame was such that canonization proceedings were immediately begun and, less than two years later, on 16 July 1228, he was proclaimed a saint. In that same year, work was begun on the vast basilica at Assisi, where he is buried and which stands as the greatest monument to him in Umbria. It is impossible, even today, not to be simultaneously impressed with the basilica, dominating as it does the town of Assisi and the plain beneath, and to recognize immediately how at odds it is with the values of the saint's own life. Yet it was the very fame of Francis that caused contemporaries to wish to celebrate his life and which led, paradoxically, to the near-betrayal of all he had endeavoured to preach.

During the year before he died, Francis had written a Testament, which he intended as a supplement to his Rule, and which he enjoined his followers not to gloss or interpret. Yet glossing or interpreting the saint's teaching was just what had to be done. Francis had preached poverty, but so impressed were contemporaries by his sanctity that they had begun to help ensure their own salvation by bequeathing possessions and moneys to the Franciscan brothers. What was to be done with these worldly goods? Within a year of the saint's death, Giovanni Pareti – who had succeeded Elias of Cortona as superior of the order – appealed for a ruling to Pope Gregory IX, Francis's former protector, and the man who had canonized him. In the bull *Quo elongati* (1230), the Pope declared that the saint's Testament was not binding and that the friars were permitted to own necessaries; he also appointed *nunzi* to administer the order's finances. By the 1230s, the Franciscan movement had grown to such an extent that it was thought appropriate to reorganize it, and the order was divided administratively into thirty provinces, thereby undermining its itinerant character. At the same time, a priest, Alberto da Pisa, was appointed at its head, thus weakening the order's lay character. All of this, of course, had the effect of bringing Franciscans increasingly under the control of the Roman curia, and by 1245 Pope Innocent IV declared all the order's goods to be the property of the Church.

For some, this was too much. The order split into 'spirituals', who continued to insist on the need for evangelical poverty, and 'conventuals', who accepted the institutionalization of the order. The more the Franciscan movement grew, the more painful a thorn in the side of successive popes did the question of poverty become. Neither Nicholas III, in 1279, nor Clement V, in 1312, was able to resolve the matter, despite their bulls on the issue. To complicate matters, the notion of 'theoretical' poverty was added to the fact of 'practical' poverty. Eventually, Pope John XXII, who had himself promulgated several bulls on the subject, was confronted, in 1322, by the declaration of the chapter of Perugia that Christ and the apostles had possessed no property at all, either individually or in common. This view struck so deep at the heart of the medieval Church that the Pope hastened to reject it with a bull in the same year and, in the following year, he declared the opinion heretical. The spirituals now refused to give way and the Franciscans' general − Michael of Cesena − went so far as to offer his support to the Holy Roman Emperor, Ludwig of Bavaria, who supported the election of Nicholas V as anti-pope. So, not only was the charge of heresy − which Francis had managed to avoid in his lifetime − levelled at his followers but, within a century of the saint's death, the movement he had founded to celebrate the unity of creation was deeply embroiled in the politics of the Catholic Church.

Of course, the later troubled history of the movement does not represent the whole of the story. Despite internal divisions, the order continued to grow in prestige. It was fast establishing a foothold in the leading universities of Paris, Bologna and Oxford, and would count among many other distinguished brothers William of Ockham, Alexander of Hales, Roger Bacon and Duns Scotus. St Bonaventure was a Franciscan who became general of the order and wrote a biography of its founder. St Anthony of Padua was likewise a Franciscan, whom later hagiography, like the fourteenth-century collection of Franciscan legend, the *Fioretti*, presented in ways – as in the story of him preaching to the fish – which made him a second St Francis, as Francis had been a second Christ. Among its tertiaries – the order's lay members – the Franciscans could count men as distinguished as Dante, who eulogized Francis in the *Paradiso*, and made St Thomas Aquinas tell his story.

The Franciscan movement changed the manner of thinking and acting for the thirteenth century in other ways also. Not only did Francis give the common people the sense that a Christian life was something which they too might aspire to imitate, he also gave them images which would become among the most potent in later Christian iconography: the Madonna and Child on a human scale, the crib, and the image of the suffering Christ-made-man on the cross. Francis's appeal to the marginalized and outcasts of his age was also extended to another section of the population whose opportunities to express a spirituality had been long suppressed – women.

Among the earliest followers of Francis in Assisi was a young girl, born into the noble family of the Offreduccio, called Chiara, or Clare. Born in 1194, she left Assisi four years later when her parents were expelled in the wake of the popular uprising in the town. On her return she soon came under the influence of Francis, who was just setting out on his ministry, and, by tradition, was personally instructed by him. In 1212 she left her parents' house to go to visit Francis at the Portiuncula, and by 1215 she was abbess of the church of San Damiano, where she instructed members of her family and friends in the spiritual values of Francis. Like her mentor, Clare too started an order – the Clarisse or Poor Clares – founded originally on the primitive Rule of Saint Francis and later based on a more elaborate Rule, confirmed by Pope Innocent IV, just before Clare's death in 1253. Renowned in her lifetime as a contemplative – and credited with twice saving the town of Assisi from being sacked by the Saracen forces of the Emperor, Frederick II – Clare held firm to the ideal of absolute poverty – owning nothing and living by alms alone. Yet like the Franciscans, the Poor Clares soon found themselves caught up in the wider ecclesiastical controversy about poverty.

While Clare was canonized just two years after her death, a new Rule was approved in 1264 by Urban IV, in which he refused to confirm the privilege of poverty granted to Clare in 1228. Despite this crucial change, the Poor Clares retained their importance for women of the thirteenth century and beyond by offering them the opportunity to elect a life of contemplation or of service to the community. The order thus stood out against the abuses of earlier female monasticism, which included the enforced seclusion of supernumerary daughters in enclosed orders with the result – as ecclesiastical attempts to stamp out the abuses make clear – that reluctant nuns became the sexual prey of male religious, and some nunneries notorious centres of immorality.

The example of St Francis was also important to women in another way, for just as Francis was convinced – though a layman – of having been singled out by God, so his example allowed women to break free of the cultural constraints which defined woman, first and foremost, by her gender – her body and her relationships to men. Divine revelation, vouchsafed by visions, allowed exceptional women, at least, to counter both the anonymity and passivity imposed on them and their 'natural' subordination to men. It is particularly striking that three famous women religious (two of them saints) of the thirteenth century were all born in Umbria. St Margaret (c.1247–97) – usually called St Margaret of Cortona, but born in Laviano, near Castiglione del Lago – was particularly celebrated for her life of piety. The other two women were visionaries: St Clare (c. 1268–1308) of Montefalco, the hill-town across the valley from Assisi, and the Blessed Angela (1248–1309) of Foligno, the town lying on the plain at the opposite end of Monte Subasio from Assisi. While nominally under the direction of priestly confessors, these women derived such contemporary prestige from their mystical visions – their direct communication with God, epitomized by Angela's assertion that 'You are me and I am You' – that they turned their spiritual directors into mere spokesmen for themselves. So inspired were their contemporaries by these holy women that canonization proceedings were quickly started after their death and proceeded rapidly. Only the Church was reluctant to endorse a phenomenon which so obviously called into

question male authority – with its immediate repercussions both
for the role the early fourteenth century had allotted women
and the ecclesiastical structures of the Church itself. So, while
the canonization proceedings for St Clare of Montefalco – noted
for her charitable works, her learning (though she was unedu-
cated) and her prophetic gifts – were virtually complete two
years after her death, she was not in the end declared a saint until
1881, and then only thanks in part to the strength of local
feeling, for the pope who canonized her was Leo XIII, who was
elevated to the papal throne after having been Bishop of Perugia.
The canonization of Margaret of Cortona – whose life was
devoted to nursing the sick poor, preaching the need for repent-
ance, and personal penance – took almost as long, not being
completed until 1728 (though the diocese of Cortona had celebrated her feast since 1515). The Blessed Angela – whose
visionary writings, recorded by her amanuensis Brother Arnaldo,
speak of the joy of personal sacrifice amid universal human
suffering – still awaits her canonization.

St Francis left one other great legacy to his age and to
Italian culture – his writings. Some of the finest Italian poetry
of the thirteenth century came from the Franciscans. Thomas
of Celano not only wrote the first biography of St Francis but
is also the reputed author of the *Dies Irae*, one of the most
powerful eschatological texts of the Middle Ages – reminding
a sinful humanity of the Four Last Things: Death and Judgement, Heaven and Hell. A more significant and prolific poet,
Jacopone da Todi (1236–1306) was a lawyer from the town of
Todi who turned to religion after the death of his young wife,
whom he discovered, after she was killed when a floor collapsed
at a wedding, to have been wearing a hair-shirt. Abandoning his
profession, he spent ten years in self-mortification before entering
the Friars Minor in 1278, where he became known both as one
of the most prominent of the Franciscan 'spirituals' in their
conflict with the 'conventuals', and an outspoken critic of Pope
Boniface VIII, whom he openly defied in a manifesto written in
1297 (Boniface was the pope Dante described as seeing in Hell,
during the pontiff's own lifetime). Jacopone ferociously attacked
Boniface in one of his poems (*Laude*, LVIII):

O papa Bonifazio,   molt'hai iocato al monno:
pensome che ioconno   non te porrai partire.

[O Pope Boniface, you have made very merry with the world:
I think you will not be able to leave it so happily.]

Jacopone's attack was not merely a personal one, however, for what he lamented was the direction the Franciscan movement was taking:

Tale qual è, tal è: non c'è religione.
Mal vedemmo Parisi,   c'hane destrutto Ascisi:
co la lor lettoria   messo l'ò en mala via.

[Things are as they are: religion is no more.
To our misfortune Paris has destroyed Assisi:
With its teaching it has set it on the wrong path.
(*Laude*, XXXI)]

Nor was Jacopone's achievement confined to the *Laude*, though no fewer than ninety-three of them survive, and neither was his writing confined to irony or invective. Among the Latin works attributed to him stands another of the finest and most enduring religious works of the Middle Ages, the *Stabat Mater*, a poem which continues Francis's own humanization of the story of Christ and the passion with its central image of the weeping mother at the foot of the Cross — and one set to music by composers as different as Palestrina, Pergolesi, Rossini, Verdi, Dvořák, and Szymanowski.

Just as the Franciscan movement continued to be dominated by the figure of its founder, however, so too is the poetic achievement of the Franciscans overshadowed by a single work of Francis himself. The *Cantico del Sole*, or *Canticle of the Sun*, remains today not just the single greatest expression of the vision of harmony Francis offered to the world but one of the earliest and most significant texts of Italian literature — what might, not unreasonably, be called the first Italian poem. It is written, in rhythmic prose, in Francis's local Umbrian dialect, and composed in two parts: the first and greater section in 1224, and the final praise of Sister Death in the very last days of the saint's life.

Cantico del Sole

Altissimu, onnipotente, bon Signore,
tu so' le laude, la gloria e l'honore et onne benedictione.
Ad te solo, Altissimo, se konfano,
et nulle homo ène dignu te mentovare.

Laudato sie, mi' Signore, cum tucte le tue creature,
spetialmente messor lo frate sole,
lo qual'è iorno, et allumini noi per lui.
Et ellu è bellu e radiante cum grande splendore:
da te, Altissimo, porta significatione.

Laudato si', mi' Signore, per sora luna e le stelle:
in celu l'ài formate clarite et pretiose et belle.

Laudato si', mi' Signore, per frate vento
et per aere e nubilo et sereno et onne tempo
per lo quale a le tue creature dài sustentamento.

Laudato sì, mi' Signore per sor'acqua,
la quale è multo utile et humile et pretiosa et casta.

Laudato si', mi' Signore, per frate focu,
per lo quale ennallumini la nocte:
ed ello è bello et iocundo et robustoso et forte.

Laudato si', mi' Signore, per sora nostra matre terra,
la quale ne sustenta et governa,
et produce diversi fructi con coloriti flori et herba.

Laudato sì, mi' Signore, per quelli ke perdonano per lo tuo
    amore,
et sostengo infirmitate et tribulatione.

Beati quelli ke 'l sosteranno in pace,
ka da te, Altissimo, sirano incoronati.

Laudato si', mi' Signore, per sora nostra morte corporale,
da la quale nullu homo vivente pò skappare:
guai a'cquelli ke morrano ne le peccata mortali;
beati quelli ke trovarà ne le tue sanctissime voluntati,
ka la morte secunda no 'l farrà male.

Laudate e benedicete mi' Signore et rengratiate
e serviateli cum grande humilitate.

[*Canticle of the Sun*

Most high, omnipotent, good Lord,
Yours be the praise, the glory and honour and every
    blessing.
To you alone, Most High, these things belong,
And no man is worthy to speak your name.

Be praised, my Lord, with all your creatures,
Especially, good Brother Sun,
Who gives us the day, and enlightens us.
And is beautiful and radiant with his great splendour.
And tells of you, Most High One.

Be praised, my Lord, for Sister Moon and the stars:
In heaven have you made them: shining, precious and
    beautiful.

Be praised, my Lord, for Brother Wind
And for cloudy skies and clear ones and for all weather
By means of which you give sustenance to your creatures.

Be praised, my Lord, for Sister Water,
Which is most useful and humble and precious and chaste.

Be praised, my Lord, for Brother Fire,
By which you light up the night:
And he is beautiful and cheerful and robust and strong.

Be praised, my Lord, for our sister Mother Earth
Who rears and feeds us
And brings forth various fruits and coloured flowers and
    herbs.

Be praised, my Lord, for those who forgive others for love of
    you
And bear sickness and tribulation.

Blessed are those whom you keep in your peace
For by you, Most High One, will they be crowned.

Be praised, my Lord, for our Sister Death
Whom no one living can escape.
Woe to those who die in mortal sin,
And blessed be those who do your most holy will
For the second death will do them no harm.

Praise and bless My Lord, and thank
And serve him with great humility.]

Even after the death of Francis, Umbria continued to be prodigal
in men and women whose lives or faith made them exemplars.
Among Franciscans alone, we may point to St Agnes (1197–
1253) and the Blessed Beatrice (d. *c.* 1260), sisters of St Clare;
martyrs such as the Blessed Giacomo and the Blessed Filippo,
who were murdered by foreign mercenaries sacking Bevagna in
1377, or the Blessed Andrea from Cascia (d. 1532), who was
killed while preaching the gospel in North Africa; ascetics such
as the Blessed Pietro Crisei (1243–1323) from Foligno, or the
Blessed Angelina from Spoleto (d. 1450); the Beata Angelina
(1357–1435) from Marsciano, meanwhile, devoted her life to
founding convents dedicated to the education of young women.

Of all later Franciscans to make their mark on Umbria,
however, the most celebrated was born outside the region. This
was St Bernardino of Siena, born in 1380 in Massa Marittima in
the province of Siena, where his father was governor, and who
would become the greatest popular preacher of his day. Or-
phaned at a young age, the young nobleman joined the Observant Franciscans in his early twenties, dedicating himself to a life
of mendicant poverty. Only in 1417, however, did Bernardino
begin the preaching that was to take him on foot throughout all
of northern and central Italy for the remainder of his life.
Possessed of an emotional language and style, which he had
carefully cultivated, Bernardino inveighed against the vices he
perceived as characterizing the Italian cities of his day: fraud,
usury, witchcraft, superstition, sexual deviancy, and luxury. In
an age of power-seeking he preached humility, in cities riven by
hatred and division he preached love and reconciliation, and in a
mercantile society much given to the pursuit of wealth he spoke
of the spiritual value of poverty. Bernardino also remembered

the poor themselves – those who had not elected to live a life of poverty – and inspired the foundation of lending institutions – the *monti di pietà* – to assist them. All this was to be done, Bernardino insisted, in devotion to the Holy Name of Jesus, and the engraved monogram, IHS, shown in the multitude of portraits of the saint to be found in the region and elsewhere, was Bernardino's invention; one given to the town of Montefalco by the saint himself in 1444 is still to be seen in the museum there.

Bernardino's message was not, however, an easy one and his impassioned sermons, preached to huge crowds, could inspire hatred as well as love. His denunciation of usury, for example, was nourished by anti-semitism, so that in pursuit of his endeavour to reconcile the inhabitants of Spoleto, when he preached in the town in December 1425, he succeeded in abolishing all the privileges accorded to Jews in the town. Similarly, his preaching against superstition in Todi in 1428 resulted in the burning of an alleged witch named Matteuccia di Francesco. Misogyny, like anti-semitism, was never far from the surface of Bernardino's message and found a receptive audience. Female luxury and the wearing of false hair were singled out for attack, and Bernardino created bonfires of the vanities wherever he preached, on which false hair and personal ornaments were joined by cards, dice, song-books and musical instruments. Bernardino's asceticism, like that of other mendicant preachers of the fifteenth century, was well received by an audience as anxious for the return to the spiritual values he preached as for the peace he championed. Even the great Franciscan preaching churches were not large enough to hold the crowds who flocked to hear him. When Bernardino spoke at the Portiuncula at Santa Maria degli Angeli on 31 July 1440, he is supposed to have attracted an audience of 200,000. Perugia – then living through one of its bloodiest periods under the Baglioni – had a sculpted and polychromed pulpit built specially for Bernardino; it survives today and is to be seen on the right of the side doorway of the cathedral, giving on to the city's main square.

Virtually every city in Umbria was the scene of a spectacular preaching mission, during which Bernardino might preach several times a day, speaking for three or four hours at a time. In the space of just a few months in 1425–6, for instance, the preacher visited much of Umbria. He spent September to November in Perugia – where the bonfire of the vanities he lit included seven bales of women's hair; at the end of November he was in Montefalco, endeavouring to reconcile rival political factions; in the following month he helped reform the statutes of Spoleto; in January 1426, Bernardino was at Todi and then Orvieto, where he also amended the city statutes as a way of ending the rivalry between different factions of the Monaldeschi family, before travelling to Gubbio, where he preached the Lenten sermons. These series of sermons that Bernardino gave – those given at Siena in the last year of his life amounted to fifty – gave him time to get to know the cities he visited and an opportunity to propose solutions to their particular problems. In 1437 he became Vicar-General of the Observant Franciscans, causing their number to rise more than tenfold, but six years later he resigned the post to return to preaching.

By then, Bernardino – who had founded a school of theology at the convent of Monteripido in Perugia, and is also said to have declined the sees of Siena, Urbino and Ferrara – was a sick man; in 1440, Perugia had gifted him a donkey to ease him on his travels. His last journey of all took Bernardino once more along the Umbrian roads he knew so well. Setting out from Siena on 29 April 1444, he spent three days on the island in Lake Trasimeno where St Francis had spent the Lent of 1211, and then proceeded by way of Perugia, Santa Maria degli Angeli, Foligno, Spoleto, Terni and Piediluco, to his destination of L'Aquila in the Abruzzo, where he died on 20 May. Just under six years later, in 1450, Bernardino was canonized by Pope Nicholas V.

Despite the misogyny, anti-semitism, and rigid puritanism which were the obverse of Bernardino's message of peace and love, it is hard not to be impressed by the reactions his preaching provoked. It is not so much the early canonization – the Church which had twice charged him with heresy was always alert to the need to reclaim the potentially subversive by containing it within the elastic bounds of its own orthodoxy. Nor is it just our knowledge of the vast crowds he attracted and their receptiveness to his message. It is, rather, the extraordinary way in which Bernardino's rules for living a more Christian life were taken up, first by Perugia and then by other Umbrian cities – Spoleto, Orvieto, Assisi, Foligno and Todi – which incorporated the saint's precepts into their statutes. There is also the vast number of paintings of the saint: images which multiplied rapidly, making the slight, aged, emaciated preacher, with sunken but ardent eyes, one of the most immediately recognizable saints in Renaissance iconography. Above all, perhaps, Bernardino's message of Christian charity is evoked most tellingly in the monument that Perugia – always the saint's favourite city – erected at communal expense, next to the Franciscan church of San Francesco al Prato, shortly after Bernardino's canonization. The Oratory, or Oratorio di San Bernardino, designed by the Florentine artist Agostino di Duccio, lies just beyond the old city walls. In contrast to the severe medieval cityscape within, the sheer beauty of the oratory's façade – with the soft pinks and blues of its polychromed marbles, the delicate tracery of sculpted fruits and flowers, and the depiction of the saint himself kneeling in prayer surrounded by flights of angelic musicians – serves to remind us today that, even in the violent city that was Perugia under Baglioni rule, the gentler message of Bernardino did not go entirely unheeded.

CHAPTER EIGHT

The Church State

✳

The defeat of Perugia in the Salt War decisively signalled the end of Umbria's long period of independent power which had begun with the rise of the communes in the late twelfth century. After 1540, it was no longer possible even to conceive of any Umbrian city withstanding the encroachment of papal authority and imposing its own rule on the region. By the end, in fact, even Perugia's aspirations were little more than a throwback to earlier times and bore little relation to existing political realities. Throughout much of the region, the Church had begun to exert real, rather than merely nominal, control as early as the mid fifteenth century. Terni, for instance, had passed into effective papal jurisdiction by 1420, to be followed by Foligno in 1439, Orvieto by 1450 and Assisi by 1460. At times, exhausted by debilitating bouts of internal strife, these cities virtually delivered themselves up to papal government. In Orvieto, the *signoria* fell when the local tyrants, Gentile and Arrigo Monaldeschi della Vipera, were overthrown in 1449 by a rival branch of the family, the Monaldeschi della Cervara, who killed Gentile and banished Arrigo – with the result that the government of the city was placed in the hands of Pope Nicholas V in the following year. On other occasions, local hatreds and papal ambitions coincided. Foligno – where the *signoria* of the Trinci family had endured for more than a century, extending its control to the neighbouring towns of Assisi, Spello, Montefalco, Trevi and Bevagna – was occupied during an internal crisis by the army of Pope Eugenius IV under the leadership of Cardinal Giovanni

Vitelleschi; the cardinal being himself a member of the family which had been the most bitter rivals of the Trinci, he had Corrado Trinci, the last lord of the city, executed along with many of his supporters.

The final stage in the imposition of papal rule took place during the late fifteenth and early sixteenth centuries during the reigns of Popes Alexander VI (1492–1503) and Julius II (1503–13). Rodrigo Borgia, Alexander VI, endeavoured to place the stamp of papal authority on the region by sending his children to conquer or rule the territory. The Pope's infamous son, Cesare Borgia, having abandoned his ecclesiastical career in 1499, headed a military expedition which proceeded through Umbria on its way northwards to occupy Romagna, which henceforth became an established part of the Church State. Lucrezia Borgia, the Pope's nineteen-year-old daughter, took up her appointment as governor of Spoleto (in place of the more usual cardinal), on 15 August 1499, after a six-day progress from Rome. She stayed in the city only a short time, however, before appointing a deputy to rule in her place – and moving north to take as her third husband Alfonso I of Este, establishing herself at the centre of the brilliant Renaissance court at Ferrara – though she continued to receive the substantial revenues yielded by Spoleto and the surrounding countryside.

In fact, not quite all of the present region of Umbria fell immediately into the orbit of the Church State. Gubbio, which had belonged to the Montefeltro family of Urbino in the Marches, continued outside papal control, even when the Della Rovere family replaced the Montefeltro in 1508; only in 1624 did the last of that family, Francesco Maria II, solemnly cede his lands to the Church – and even then Gubbio continued to be associated administratively with the Marches until the unification of Italy in 1860. Despite the seizing of Città di Castello for the Church by Cesare Borgia in 1503, the ruling Vitelli family, long-time allies of the papacy, continued to exercise effective jurisdiction throughout the sixteenth century. Their near neighbours in the upper Tiber valley, the Marchesi Bourbon del Monte, who ruled a tiny territory centred on Monte Santa Maria Tiberina, a small town perched high on a hill dominating the border area between Perugia and the Grand Duchy of Tuscany, did even better, defending the independence of their miniature state until the French invasion of 1798. Driven by the nepotism which marked so much Church government, the papacy was even capable of carving newly independent states out of its own territories. Julius III made his nephew, Ascanio della Corgna, ruler of a small marquisate (later a duchy) centred on the town of Castiglione del Lago on Lake Trasimeno and encompassing the lands as far as Castel della Pieve (which the Pope Clement VIII elevated to an episcopal see in 1600, giving it city status as Città della Pieve). This small state remained independent until 1643, when it was incorporated into the Grand Duchy of Tuscany, eventually returning to the Church in the eighteenth century. Of all such independent states, the tiniest and most unusual was Cospaia, an unprepossessing village on the Umbrian border with Tuscany, which preserved its independence for almost four centuries between 1441 and 1826. Its existence arose from a loan of 25,000 gold florins raised by Pope Eugenius IV from Cosimo dei Medici, of Florence, to help defray the costs of the Council of Basle; in return, the Pope ceded Borgo San Sepolcro to Florence. When the boundaries were redrawn, however, the Florentine surveyors took the Rio della Goraccia as the relevant border, while the papal surveyors used the Rio Ascone. Between these two small tributaries of the Tiber, which enter the river a mere 500 metres apart, lay the village of Cospaia. Despite repeated attempts by its neighbours to incorporate it into their territories in the centuries that followed, Cospaia survived – as a tax-free haven and bandit hideout – for the next 385 years.

In so far as the existence of these pockets of land independent of papal power indicate Umbria's lack, at this period, of distinct regional identity, they are worthy of note. In terms of the overall picture regarding the region in the sixteenth century and beyond, however, they are of little real account. For the most part, the Papal State was increasingly sure of its hold on its territories throughout central Italy. As the threat to the internal stability of the Church State receded, so too did the Umbrian territories cease to be a matter of immediate concern to a papacy more preoccupied with external threats posed by the Turks in the east and Protestantism across the Alps. Closer to home, the popes concerned themselves with the rebuilding of Rome, in an attempt to restore the city to its former glory as the worthy capital of a powerful political state. In such circumstances, what remained of the old nobility was permitted to enjoy status, privilege, and even a measure of power – so long as their territories continued to supply the Church with the wherewithal to finance its policies, at home and abroad.

In place of their lost political and economic independence, the cities of Umbria now found themselves subject to a clerical administration and a fiscal policy which saw taxes double between 1492 and 1525 and then double again, in real terms, by 1600. Successive popes may have loathed each other – as Julius II detested his predecessor, Alexander VI – but they were at one in their determination to consolidate the Papal State, bringing to completion a business started almost two centuries previously by Innocent VI and his legate, Cardinal Albornoz. The results for Umbria were fateful, for the region began to suffer from the economic and cultural stagnation which would, in the course of the next three centuries, turn once vibrant political and artistic centres into sleepy provincial towns. Power, talent, and the wealth generated from the land all began to drain away from Umbria towards Rome. While the capital's population began to grow – it was over 100,000 by the early sixteenth century, in comparison to fewer than 20,000 in the first half of the fourteenth century – the towns of Umbria had embarked on a slow decline that would not be halted before the present century. The population of Perugia, which was around 30,000 at the beginning of the fourteenth century, dwindled to a mere 13,000 in the nineteenth; the once-flourishing city of Orvieto, with an early-fourteenth-century population of approximately 30,000, was reduced by 1762 to just 5,625 inhabitants.

These changes did not happen overnight, but while work might continue on such massive building projects as Orvieto cathedral, even as the city population slowly contracted, new building projects of such vision and scope would not be undertaken again in Umbria. Nor would new public buildings, like the Palazzo dei Consoli in Gubbio or the Palazzo dei Priori in Perugia – at once architectural masterpieces and potent symbols of local independence – again be needed by a state in which power and administration were increasingly centralized. In place of the civic projects of the past, Umbrian taxes went to build the Rome of the popes. The construction of St Peter's began in 1506; two years later, Raphael commenced work on the Vatican apartments, and in 1512 Michelangelo began his great fresco of the *Last Judgement* in the Sistine Chapel. The greatest building project of the first half of the sixteenth century in Umbria, by contrast, was the building of the Rocca Paolina, the huge fortress Pope Paul III had erected in Perugia to ensure the permanent submission of the town's inhabitants to papal authority – a symbol of Church rule so hated by the Perugians that they tore it down at the first opportunity three centuries later.

The situation was perhaps worst for that part of the Umbrian population which still lived in the countryside. As the region's slow economic decline resulted in under-investment in agriculture, the sixteenth century saw famines as severe as those which marked earlier centuries – such as those in 1504, 1526, or 1529, following plague. A remarkable hailstorm in 1538 resulted in poor crop yields, and towards the end of the century there were notable shortages in 1584, 1590 and 1591. By the sixteenth century, most of the region was marked by a pattern of settlement which had begun to emerge in the late Middle Ages. To escape from pillaging troops, Umbrians tended to live as far as possible in a walled village or *castello* (from the Latin *castrum*, or fort), rather than in an unfortified village (or *villa*). These walled villages are the 'castles' remembered today by so many place-names throughout the entire region: Castel Giorgio, Castelleone, Castelluccio, Castelmonte, Castel Rigone, Castel Ritaldi or Castelsantangelo sul Nera, for example. Behind the walls of these settlements, usually situated on hilltops or other easily defended sites, villagers might at least enjoy security from the casual violence of soldiers passing through the region.

The difficulties of rural existence did not end with the securing of protection from the worst vagaries of uncontrolled warfare. As the region's cities and towns grew in prosperity, the wealthy merchant class bought increasingly into land. Soon they joined the older feudal and urban nobility as substantial landowners, either forcing peasant farmers to become tenants or leaving them almost impossibly small properties of their own. These last were forced to eke a generally scanty living from their minute holdings, for the most part to be found in remote and mountainous areas of the region. Occasionally they prospered, with the farmer or his wife taking their produce to local markets to barter, or even sell, until they had accumulated enough money to expand their holdings. Most, however, were eventually forced to abandon their land as winter snows and summer droughts, insufficient capital and the constant threat of pillage took their toll. If they were lucky, such farmers might find places as tenants on holdings elsewhere, but most were constrained to fall still further socially and economically, becoming a source of cheap labour to those luckier or more skilful neighbours who bought up their land after they had failed.

In contrast to these small peasant farmers, urban proprietors owned increasingly large tracts of land. Since they rarely managed to consolidate their properties, however, Umbria soon became a patchwork of plots of land, owned by a single individual but often divided geographically by considerable distances – a pattern which significantly worked against any real improvement in agricultural practice. These urban landowners were generally absentees, preferring to remain in town, while living off their rents and the profits from such prized cash crops as grapes, olives, and fruit, which found an easy sale in city markets. Those who worked the land found themselves in turn faced with shorter and shorter leases.

This very particular relationship between Umbria's medieval cities and their *contadi* developed into a share-cropping system – the *mezzadria* – which was to dominate the region's agriculture for 500 years. Once much praised for preventing the extreme social upheaval evident in other peasant societies of the fourteenth century – Umbria saw no equivalent of the French Jacquerie of 1358 or the English Peasants' Revolt of 1381 – the *mezzadria* can now be seen rather differently: as socially coercive in principle and often harsh in practice. While appearing to offer the peasant farmer greater liberty, by freeing him from the feudal service of earlier centuries, the *mezzadria* too frequently combined some of the more onerous features of feudalism with the uncertainty engendered by short-term leases. From the beginning, the contract a notary drew up between landowner and farmer imposed leases of four or five years, later reduced to a mere one or two years. Notarial contracts also included many feudal-type clauses. The farmer was obliged to live on the land with all his family, and precise stipulations were made as to the tasks they should perform there and when these should be carried out. If the farmer wished to marry, the landowner's permission was required, and in some cases the contract obliged the farmer to employ labourers at his expense until his children were of an age to work in their turn.

The greatest benefit of the *mezzadria* system seemed to be that the farmer without capital to purchase a land-holding of his own could, nevertheless, become self-sufficient through his own labours. In fact, although the division of goods implied by the very name *mezzadria* was 50/50 between landowner and farmer, actual conditions were less favourable. While grains, vegetables, fruit, beans, acorns and hemp were divided equally, oil and wine were divided 60/40 in the owner's favour, and some contracts imposed still less equitable division of produce. The cost of seed was also borne by the farmer, the landowner's role being limited to advancing the necessary capital to purchase it. When crops were harvested, the owner's share of the produce was to be taken to the city or his storehouse at the farmer's expense. Contracts specified the number of offerings, whether of farm animals, eggs, or finished products made from wool, flax or hemp grown on the farm, due to the owner every year. The farmer had a duty to supply the owner with wood and the obligation to take his own share of olives or grain to the owner's press or mill, and pay for their use. In many cases, the notary's contract specifically enjoined the *mezzadro* to 'conduct himself with all due submission, obedience and respect'.

In a situation of physical and economic vulnerability, it is not altogether surprising that country people were tempted to move from the land to what they perceived as the comparative safety and freedom of the cities. The particular relationship between the Umbrian city-states and their *contadi* meant, however, that it was in the interests of the most powerful social groups within the towns to ensure that countryfolk stayed on the land, ensuring adequate food supplies for their urban neighbours and (not entirely incidentally) increasing the personal wealth of the large numbers of urban landowners. Far from changing this relationship between the cities and their *contadi*, the Church's new power in Umbria reinforced it, for the new nobility the papacy created also confirmed its novel status by buying land. So Perugia repeatedly obliged recent immigrants into the city to return to the countryside to build houses on the land, and directed them as to the labour they should perform there. In 1469, the statutes of Assisi concerned themselves directly with leases and the *mezzadria*, obliging labourers and their children to remain on the land, and specifying the farmer's obligation to supply the landowner with half of all he produced, to be delivered to the city at the farmer's expense. Eighty years later, in 1549, the statutes of Todi directed that all the grain produced in its territories be brought to the city. The statutes of Gubbio, meanwhile, directed in 1678 exactly what work was to be carried out by the *mezzadri*, month by month: ploughing, sowing, ditching, and harvesting, besides specifying that the landowners' share of the produce be delivered, at the farmers' expense, directly to their houses. It was because they had virtually no choice that the *mezzadri* accepted the disadvantageous conditions imposed on them by notarial contracts, and that the system of *mezzadria* endured until the present century.

There was still worse for the hapless rural population. The Church's imposition of a strong central authority in its territory did not even eradicate the centuries-long danger of finding one's house burned or goods stolen by marauding troops. While the papacy had put an end to the warfare between the city-states, it had also created a situation in which banditry thrived throughout its territories, as the poorest members of the old nobility sought to live by brigandage. By the end of the sixteenth century, it was estimated that there were no fewer than 27,000 bandits in the papal territories. In Umbria these outlaws were particularly active around Spoleto, and in border areas – especially the

mountains of Cascia and Gualdo Tadino, and in the hills surrounding Lake Trasimeno and Orvieto – where they could
more easily evade papal jurisdiction, when pursued by papal
troops, by crossing into neighbouring states. In the early part of
the sixteenth century, Umbria suffered from notorious brigands
like Petrone di Vallo di Nera and his associate Girolamo Brancaleoni, known as Picozzo, son-in-law of the notable *condottiere*
Saccoccio, who fought for the Venetian Republic. From the
stronghold of Pissignano, a small fortified village on the hillside
overlooking the Vale of Umbria, they raided the countryside
for two decades until, on 9 September 1523, they murdered the
young governor of Spoleto, Alfonso Cardona, and his escort,
after agreeing to a meeting on the bridge over the Nera close to
Vallo. The outrage was too much and a military force was sent
after the perpetrators. Picozzo was never caught but Petrone,
who managed to evade capture for many months in the wild
countryside around Sellano and Monteleone, was eventually
captured and burned alive by his pursuers. In the second half of
the sixteenth century, matters got still worse, with travel through
the region becoming increasingly hazardous. Then the bandit
Petrino Leoncilli devastated the lands around Spoleto, even
managing to penetrate the papal fortress there; he attacked
Terni, and in Cascia took the city-governor prisoner. Eventually,
and to general surprise, the papal-legate in Spoleto made a pact
with Leoncilli which spared the outlaw's life. Few brigands were
so fortunate. Late-sixteenth-century popes all acted vigorously
against bandits, putting to death no fewer than 5,000 men in
Rome in just five years between 1590 and 1595, and when
Alfonso Piccolomini, leader of a band of 500 outlaws, was
captured near Città di Castello, he was promptly beheaded.

If the increase in brigandage was the most dramatic result of
the imposition of papal power – and papal taxes – on Umbria, it
was not in the longer term the most serious. With power in the
hands of a clerical élite, opportunity for men of talent in the
region was much restricted, a weakness exacerbated by the failure of the papacy to promote any economic initiatives such as
those that were enriching Milan, Venice, or Florence. Umbrian
trade and manufacture – including such formerly prosperous

trades as wool and leather – began to decline. The decline was a slow one, and throughout much of the sixteenth century the region, with its still fine road network, remained an important area of commercial exchange. The growth of the new nobility, encouraged by papal policy, led to an increase in the purchase of land, and a consequent lack of capital investment in trade or manufacture, which put a further brake on mercantile activity. In 1569 this growing crisis was exacerbated by Pius V, who expelled from the Church State the Jews who had lived in Umbria since the first century – contributing notably to banking in the region – confining them to ghettos in Rome and Ancona. The great medieval fairs began to lose their international and even national importance, giving way to a much larger number of smaller fairs of merely local significance. This commercial fragmentation was echoed elsewhere, for while the large-scale transfer of capital into land initially resulted in the creation of very large estates, these were subsequently broken up into very many smaller ones. It was in the late sixteenth and seventeenth centuries that Umbria began to take on its now characteristic appearance, dotted with *case sparse* – farmhouses scattered throughout the countryside, virtually within hailing distance of each other, rather than being gathered together for protection behind castle walls. Over the course of the next three centuries, only the medieval fabric of once-flourishing towns and villages of Umbria would be left to bear witness to the wealth, power, and civic pride once to be found in such abundance throughout the region.

While Umbria suffered economically from papal policy, it did little better in other ways. In the sixteenth century the region began to suffer the obscurantist tendencies of the mid-sixteenth-century Counter-Reformation. In the years immediately following the subjection of Umbria to papal authority, the Church State saw the introduction of the Holy Office (1542) and the Index of prohibited books (1559). A more general fragmentation and provincialization of intellectual life followed. Occasionally, it is true, Umbria could reveal the cultural vitality of earlier centuries and even show the rest of Italy the way – as when Federico Cesi (1585–1630) of Acquasparta founded the

Accademia dei Lincei in 1603. This, the foremost of Italian academies, aimed to replace the intellectual laziness of outmoded Aristotelianism with a modern attitude to experimental science based on observation rather than dogma. It included among its members Galileo and the mathematician and physicist Evangelista Torricelli. However, the academy met, predictably enough, in Rome – although Galileo was a guest of Cesi in his palazzo in Acquasparta in 1611. Cesi himself wrote the Academy's constitution in 1623, but when he died, in 1630, the Academy died with him. Although the example of the Lincei led to a massive growth of important academies throughout Italy – and by the nineteenth century, virtually no town was without one, and many had several – few of those founded in Umbria were of any real importance. Academies at Spoleto and Perugia combined valuable scientific, with literary and antiquarian, study, but many (perhaps most) are well summed up by the name chosen for one at Gubbio, the *Accademia degli addormentati* or Academy of Slumberers.

Not all of Umbria, however, was asleep. Not surprisingly, the principal public buildings of the late fifteenth and sixteenth centuries were erected in areas where papal authority did not yet obtain and the old *signori* still held sway. Gubbio, for instance, was part of the territory of the Montefeltro family of Urbino and it was for the great Duke Federico – patron of Castiglione and Vespasian, Uccello and Piero della Francesca – that the ducal castle of Gubbio was built in the 1470s. In a compressed site high on Gubbio's hill, next to the cathedral, the palace occupies the symbolically important position formerly occupied by the Longobard administrative centre, the Corte, from which it takes its name. The architect was most probably Luciano Laurana, responsible for the great palace in Urbino itself, aided by the Siennese master Francesco di Giorgio Martini. Certainly the simple door of *pietra serena*, leading to the arcaded loggias of the elegantly proportioned courtyard, constructed with a mixture of stone and red brick, together with many interior details, such as the great chimneypieces, recall the palace in Urbino. (Unfortunately, much of the fine interior decoration has been lost or transferred elsewhere, including the Duke's study of inlaid wood, now in the

Metropolitan Museum in New York.) At the death of Guidobaldo Montefeltro in 1508, Urbino passed into the control of the
Della Rovere family, and it was the countesses Elisabetta and
Eleonora Della Rovere who were responsible for commissioning
the rebuilding of the old *pieve* of San Gervasio as a great basilica
in honour of Gubbio's patron saint, Ubaldo, between 1514 and
1525. Here, a fine Renaissance doorway leads on, via the cloister,
to the large five-naved church that holds both the uncorrupted
body of Ubaldo and the three *ceri* or complex wooden towers
raced around the city and up the steep mountainside to the
basilica every 15 May, in honour of the saint.

Gubbio demonstrates the influence of the Montefeltro and
Della Rovere families who, between them, dominated the city
for virtually the entire period between the end of the commune
in 1384 and the territory's incorporation into the Church State
in 1624. Città di Castello similarly gives evidence of the power
of its principal ruling family, the Vitelli. Lords of the city in the
fifteenth century, the Vitelli continued as effective rulers even
after Cesare Borgia brought the area definitively within the
orbit of the Papal State in 1503. Built on a flat site overlooking
the Tiber valley, close to the borders of Tuscany, Città di
Castello is more Tuscan than Umbrian in appearance, both
because of the frequent employment of Florentine architects and
because of the yellowish sandstone of which so many of the
town's buildings are made. In order better to remind the citizens
of who ruled them, the Vitelli built no fewer than five palaces in
different quarters of the small city, employing Antonio da
Sangallo and Giorgio Vasari as architects. The finest of these
palazzi is the Palazzo alla Cannoniera, built for Alessandro Vitelli,
a *condottiere* in the service of the Medici, by Antonio da Sangallo
the Younger between 1521 and 1532. Now occupied by the
town's picture gallery – the finest collection in Umbria after the
National Gallery in Perugia – the palace has a garden façade,
decorated with graffiti by Cristoforo Gherardi, to designs by
Vasari – the now neglected gardens were once famous. Just eight
years later, the even larger Palazzo Vitelli a Porta Sant'Egidio
was constructed to a plan by Vasari for Paolo Vitelli, a soldier
who served, by turns, the Emperor Charles V and Pope Paul III.

Just within the walls at one of the city gates, the palace has an extremely long and elegant façade, giving on the present Piazza Garibaldi, a vestibule frescoed by Gherardi, and a fine salone on the first floor or *piano nobile*; the extensive gardens, terminating in a large, frescoed *palazzina*, are used for outdoor concerts during the town's summer music festival. Besides these and the other Vitelli palaces, Città di Castello retains a considerable number of other late-fifteenth- and sixteenth-century *palazzi*, chief of which is the Palazzo Albizzini, built in a severe Tuscan style, which now houses part of the exceptional collection of the work of Alberto Burri (1915–95) that is to be found in the home-town of this most important of twentieth-century Umbrian artists.

Along with Gubbio and Città di Castello, the small lakeside town of Castiglione del Lago also remained independent of papal control during part of the fifteenth and sixteenth centuries. Today, it still holds the Della Corgna family's grandiose ducal palace, whose impressive sixteenth-century remodelling is variously attributed to Vignola or Alessi. The fine decorative frescoes are the work of Giovanni Antonio Pandolfi and the Florentine Salvio Savini, who also worked in the Della Corgna palace in Città della Pieve.

If the sheer size of the *palazzi* in Gubbio, Città di Castello and Castiglione make them stand out, there was, even within the Papal State, a very considerable amount of building in the later fifteenth and sixteenth centuries among both the old nobility and the new, as the *nobilizzazione* or ennoblement of the state's populace gathered pace. Not all of the palaces were built from scratch, for in many towns nobles added new façades to existing houses and towers that they remodelled and knocked together. Even so, there was a great deal of architectural activity throughout the region. The Cesi family built notably, both in Todi and in Acquasparta. In the former city, the late-sixteenth-century bishop's palace, next to the cathedral, was built by Vignola for Angelo Cesi, whose private residence, the Palazzo Cesi, designed by Sangallo the Younger, stands close by. The former lords of Todi, the Atti, whose *signoria* had ended in bloody vendettas with the Cesi, now lived peaceably in their own *palazzi* in the town. An even finer and much grander Palazzo Cesi dominates the centre of the small town of Acquasparta. Designed by the Milanese Giovanni Domenico Bianchi in the second half of the sixteenth century, it boasts an impressive interior courtyard, fine inlaid wooden ceilings, and a collection of *cippi* and inscriptions plundered from the neighbouring Roman site of Carsulae.

Orvieto, which was for long a convenient and secure refuge for popes fleeing Rome when the capital was menaced by hostile armies, retains a considerable number of substantial palaces built for both the old and the new nobility, many of which benefit from the presence in the city of distinguished architects engaged on the still-unfinished cathedral. Broadly speaking, the earlier *palazzi* took their inspiration from Florence, the later ones from Rome. So, the Palazzo Pietrangeli has a *cortile*, or inner courtyard, which seems to come direct from Florence (and is now thought to be by the Florentine architect Bernardo Rossellino). The Palazzo Gualtiero was designed by the Florentine Simone Mosca (1492–1553), and the Palazzo Crispo was built for Tiberio Crispo, nephew to Pope Paul III, to a design by Sangallo the Younger. Ippolito Scalza, director of works at the cathedral for fifty years, from 1567 to 1617, came from Orvieto itself and designed a series of *palazzi* for the city, including the vast Palazzo Clementini (1567–9), with its fine doorway, and the Palazzo Buzi (*c.* 1580), and was also responsible for the remodelling of the Palazzo Carvajal-Simoncelli, which boasts an impressive portal and is embellished with the seigneurial inscription in Spanish: '*Carvajal de Carvajal por comodidad de sus amigos padrón*' (Carvajal de Carvajal owner of this house for the comfort of his friends).

In Spoleto, which enjoyed long periods of affluence in the sixteenth and seventeenth centuries, the building of *palazzi* was also extensive, and the influence of Rome even stronger. The Palazzo Rácani, from the first quarter of the sixteenth century – whose doorway, and the arched windows of the upper floors, reveal its dependence on Roman models – has decoration attributed to Giulio Romano. Later palaces include the Palazzo Vigili (now Pompili), the late-sixteenth- and early-seventeenth-century archiepiscopal palace, built on the supposed site of the former

Longobard palace, the Palazzo Campello, the Palazzo Mauri (which today holds the City Archive and Library and is home to the Accademia Spoletina), the later-seventeenth-century Palazzo Ancaiani, close to the old Roman theatre, and, from the eighteenth century, the Palazzo Collicola, the largest of the residences of the Collicola family, erected between 1717 and 1730 by Sebastiano Cipriani. A tiny theatre, the Teatro Caio Melisso – named for a Spoletine friend of Maecenas, the great Roman patron of the arts – survives as testimony to the lively cultural life of Spoleto during the seventeenth century.

The cities of Umbria provide plentiful evidence of the increasing ennoblement of the population of the Church State; so, too, do many of the smaller towns and villages. Even in what, today, seem almost impossibly remote locations – Cerreto di Spoleto, for example – substantial houses with large rusticated doorways give evidence of the affluence and social aspirations of at least a small section of society through the sixteenth and into the seventeenth and eighteenth centuries.

Nevertheless, the single greatest building enterprise of the sixteenth century in Umbria told a very different story. Between 1540 and 1543, the suppression of Perugia's aspirations to local autonomy was marked by the building of the Pauline fortress, or Rocca Paolina. Such was the Perugians' enduring hatred of this Bastille-like symbol of papal domination that only a very little of the fortress now survives. The written and graphic testimony of many artists and travellers is sufficient, however, for us to know how remarkable a structure it was.

Barely three weeks after the entry into Perugia of the papal troops, under Pierluigi Farnese, son of Pope Paul III, work began on the construction of the fortress. The principal architect was Antonio da Sangallo the Younger, who had previously built the Palazzo Farnese (begun 1513) in Rome for the Pope, when he was still Cardinal Farnese. What was intended, from the outset, was not simply a fortress occupying the strategically important Landone hill, with its commanding view of the Tiber valley and the road to Rome, but a symbol of papal power over the city, a building which would eclipse the Palazzo dei Priori, the emblem of Perugia's days as an independent city-state. Military necessity and political design also combined in the destruction of the quarter of the town on the Landone hill which was the stronghold of the Baglioni family – resulting in the loss of 200 houses, more than thirty defensive towers, two convents, a hospital, and seven churches, including one of Perugia's finest, Santa Maria dei Servi. More happily, the need for dispatch in erecting the fortress led Sangallo to use some of the Baglioni houses and towers as foundations, vaulting over the medieval streets and courtyards and thus preserving them. Paul III interested himself personally in the construction of the Rocca to such a degree that he visited the site no fewer than seven times in the three years it took to build. He seems, however, to have shown scant interest in preserving any part of Perugia's past that did not meet with his own aims, so that one of the city's surviving Etruscan gates, the Porta del Sole (on the site of the present Piazza Matteotti), was lost; fortunately Sangallo did save the Etruscan Porta Marzia, by taking it apart stone by stone and re-erecting it just four metres from its original position, though the process also destroyed its function as a city gate and turned it merely into an ornament for the new fortress.

The near-total destruction of the fortress – initiated in the revolutionary year of 1848 and carried on after the unification of Italy in 1860 – makes it hard fully to appreciate the Rocca's overwhelming impact on the city. The principal fortress itself covered both the Colle Landone and the Colle del Sole, occupying a space centred on the present Piazza Italia and Carducci Gardens at the end of the city's main thoroughfare, the Corso Vannucci. From the angle created where the present Viale Indipendenza meets the Via Marzia – the walls of the fortress can still be seen here – a long, fortified corridor ran downhill to a large defensive outwork, situated at a traditionally weak point in the city's defences, on the plain below (terminating in what is now Piazza Partigiani). Apart from its principal military function, the upper fortress also held the Papal Palace (or Palace of the Governor), designed by Galeazzo Alessi, and richly decorated by artists who included Raffaellino del Colle, Dono Doni, Cristoforo Gherardi, and Giorgio Vasari.

The Rocca Paolina – much admired architecturally by Vasari,

in his 'Life' of Sangallo – was certainly the most important work of military and civic architecture built in Umbria during the sixteenth or seventeenth centuries. In order to secure the frontiers of the Papal State, however, other defensive structures were renewed or built, including the impressive Castellina in Norcia, which still dominates the principal square of the town. It was designed for Paul III's successor, Pope Julius III, by another leading architect, Jacopo da Vignola (1507–73), best known for his work in Rome, including the Villa Giulia, and the church of the Gesù.

Such works were deemed necessary because, however peaceful it might appear in comparison to previous centuries, the Papal State faced more than the internal threat from disaffected cities and the increasing number of outlaws. Little more than thirty years after 1494, when the armies of the French King, Charles VIII, had swept through Italy on their way to Naples, Rome was sacked by the troops of the German Emperor, Charles V, in 1527. On that occasion, Pope Clement VII took refuge in Orvieto, remaining there between December 1527 and June 1528. In order to ensure the city's water supply in case of siege, the Pope commissioned Antonio da Sangallo the Younger to design a well, which involved excavating a sixty-two-metre-deep hole to the base of the rock on which Orvieto stands, in order to reach the spring water to be found there; the resulting well is known as the Pozzo di San Patrizio, or St Patrick's Well, after the story, familiar from medieval legend, of the Irish saint who was able to reach the delights of Paradise only by passing through infernal regions. Above ground, the monumental well consists today of a large, low cylinder embellished with lilies, which were the emblem of the Farnese family to which Pope Paul III – Clement VII's successor – belonged. Into this cylinder are set two doorways, diametrically opposite each other. From these doorways, two quite separate brick stairways – one for the descent, the other to return to the surface – each of 248 steps, spiral around the well's central shaft. The broadness of the steps permits the easy passage of the mules or donkeys used to carry up the water, and the transfer from one stairway to the other is effected by means of a tiny bridge cutting diagonally across the base of the well, just above water-level. Seventy-two windows opened into the central shaft provide sufficient illumination for the stairways from above, although the last stages of the descent are made in gathering gloom as well as falling temperatures. As it happened, Sangallo's remarkable architectural and engineering skills served only to provide a curiosity, for Orvieto was never besieged and the well was never needed.

Churches were another matter. Nothing in Umbria begins to match the conception of the great medieval cathedrals, but since work was still continuing on these massive ventures, most – including both Orvieto and Spoleto – bear architectural as well as decorative testimony to the artistic revolutions of the sixteenth and seventeenth centuries. Less happily, so also do many of the mendicant churches of the thirteenth and early fourteenth centuries, which were frequently subjected to internal, and occasionally external, remodelling – not always of a high standard. Of new churches, one interesting and diverse group is associated with the renewal of Marian devotion encouraged by the widely circulated sermons of St Bernardino and confirmed by Sixtus IV's apostolic constitution, *Cum praecelsa* (1477), in which he spoke of the spiritual motherhood of Mary. Such churches were usually built on sites associated with the miraculous apparition of the Virgin.

The earliest such church is the Madonna delle Lacrime (Our Lady of the Tears), which stands on the road leading down from the hilltop town of Trevi. Designed by the Florentine Antonio Marchesi from Settignano in 1487, it has a Latin cross plan, a magnificently carved doorway by the Venetian Giovanni di Gian Pietro (1495), and much fine decoration, including a chapel frescoed by Lo Spagna and a *Visitation of the Magi* by Perugino. Built shortly afterwards is the recently restored sanctuary of the Madonna dei Miracoli in Castel Rigone in the hills above Lake Trasimeno, erected in 1494, largely at the expense of the commune of Perugia, as a votive offering to the Virgin for having been spared the plague. Standing just outside the walls of the old fortified village, the church was built by Lombard masons on the plan of a Latin cross and boasts a fine doorway (1512) by Domenico Bertini da Settignano, called Topolino, a pupil of

Michelangelo, and a splendid altar by Bernardino di Lazzaro. Among the artists who worked on the spacious and well-proportioned interior of the church were Bernardo di Girolamo Rosselli, Gian Battista Caporali, and Domenico Alfani. Not far from Castel Rigone, just outside the lakeside town of Passignano, stands another Renaissance church dedicated to Mary, the sixteenth-century Madonna dell'Olivo. Mongiovino, standing close to the road between Perugia and Città della Pieve, has a Marian sanctuary begun in 1513 by the north Italian architect Rocco di Tommaso. A centrally planned church with an octagonal cupola, the sanctuary has two fine doorways (1525–6), set on opposite sides of the building, sculpted by the architect aided by Giuliano da Verona, Bernardino da Siena and Lorenzo da Carrara; the interior has frescoes from the 1560s by the Dutch painter Heinrich van den Broek (known in Italy as Arrigo Fiammingo) and the Pisan Niccolò Pomarancio, who worked frequently in the area.

The finest of all these churches, and one of the most beautiful and intriguing churches of any period in Umbria, is Santa Maria della Consolazione at Todi. Like many other of these churches, Santa Maria della Consolazione was built on a site where an image of the Virgin was reputed to perform miracles. The intrinsic interest of the church is enhanced by the mystery surrounding the architect. The central plan and high dome atop a square balustraded balcony are completed by four apses which appear, at first glance, to be identical – in fact, three are polygonal and the fourth semicircular. These features all suggest the hand of one of the age's greatest architects, Donato Bramante (1444–1514), and link the church at Todi with Bramante's original plan (never executed) for St Peter's in Rome. This, in turn, points up the resemblance to Bramante's churches of San Biagio alla Pagnotta and Santi Celso e Giuliano, in Rome (both trial runs for the much larger St Peter's), as well as to the Marian churches of the Madonna di San Biagio outside Montepulciano in Tuscany, built by Antonio da Sangallo the Elder, also erected to commemorate the miracles worked on the site by an image of the Virgin, and Santa Maria delle Carceri at Prato by Giuliano da Sangallo, the elder Antonio's brother. The Todi church is

also related to the small Roman church of Sant'Eligio degli
Orafi in Rome, designed by Bramante and Raphael (which was
later to provide a model for another Umbrian church, Santa
Maria Nuova in Assisi (1615)). Santa Maria della Consolazione,
however, is apparently by none of the architects with whose
work it bears such affinities but rather by the virtually unknown
architect Cola da Caprarola (fl. 1494–1518), although, to complicate matters still further, the church bears a very close resemblance to some imaginative architectural sketches by Leonardo
da Vinci, dating back as far as 1489, now in the Institut de
France in Paris. In fact, an extraordinary number of celebrated
architects are known to have had some hand in the building of
the church, including Baldassare Peruzzi (Bramante's assistant
and successor in Rome) in 1518, Sangallo the Younger in 1532,
and subsequently Vignola (1565) and Alessi (1567), while Valentino Martelli of Perugia designed the drum, the cupola and the
cornices of the windows (1589).

Whatever the exact genesis of the church – and none of the
many studies has been able to sort out the confusion satisfactorily
– Santa Maria della Consolazione impresses initially by the
elegance and apparent simplicity of its exterior, as well as by its
magnificent setting at the foot of Todi's hill. The exterior
simplicity is only apparent, however, for the observer is soon
aware of the subtle use of both semicircular and triangular forms
for the pediments of the windows and of Corinthian and Ionic
orders for the finely carved capitals of the pillars, and of the four
eagles (1601–4) by Antonio Rosignoli which stand at the four
corners of the balustraded terrace. The immense yet harmonious
interior of the church impresses both by its spaciousness and
luminosity.

Santa Maria della Consolazione is, by any standards, an outstanding building, but in both its innovativeness and its scope it
remains exceptional among Umbrian churches of its time. Only
the basilica of Santa Maria degli Angeli built over the tiny
Franciscan church of the Portiuncola on the plain below Assisi
rivals the church in ambition, though it falls short of it in
achievement. The grandiose design of the three-naved church
with its semicircular apse and an immensely high dome is by

Galeazzo Alessi; begun in 1569, the church was completed over a century later in 1679. An earthquake in 1832 caused the collapse of most of the nave and the basilica was rebuilt between 1836 and 1840 with a modified façade, itself replaced in the 1920s by a pastiche seventeenth-century front almost grotesquely at odds with the humble Franciscan site the basilica supposedly honours.

For the most part, projects of such scale or architectural merit as the churches of Todi or Santa Maria degli Angeli were reserved for Rome, rather than the Umbrian territories of the Papal State. Instead, the inhabitants of the region contented themselves with remodelling existing churches, either wholly or in part. Sometimes the results were happy – though rarely entirely so. The late-thirteenth-century church of Santa Maria Maggiore in Spello, for instance, does not greatly gain from the profusion of Baroque altars added to its original simple single-aisled interior. The sixteenth-century additions, however, include inlaid wooden choir-stalls (1512–20) by Pier Nicola da Spoleto, a finely sculpted tabernacle (1515) by Rocco di Tommaso over the main altar and an imaginatively decorated stone pulpit (1545), over an appealing, if decidedly secular, sculpted grotesque mask, by Simone da Campione; there is also another fine tabernacle (1562) by Gian Domenico da Carrara in the Chapel of the Sacrament (1478), to the left of the presbytery, as well as the glory of the church, the early-sixteenth-century Baglioni chapel. To the left of the main aisle, this chapel boasts three serene and luminous frescoes (1501) by Perugino's pupil, Pinturicchio – who, in the manner of his master in the Collegio del Cambio, added a *trompe l'œil* self-portrait – and a floor of Deruta majolica (1516). It is a sobering thought that this beautiful chapel was commissioned by one member of Perugia's ruling Baglioni family in the very same year, 1500, as most other family members were murdering, or being murdered by, each other in the infamous wedding massacre.

The frescoes of the Cappella Baglioni are, of course, only one indication of what is best among later additions or alterations to medieval churches, and there are few towns in the region whose churches do not afford fine Renaissance paintings. So far as architectural changes are concerned, however, the situation is less clear. If the elegant loggia Ambrogio di Antonio Barocci added to the front of the cathedral at Spoleto is harmonious enough, it does little truly to enhance the earlier façade – and the same might be said of a similar loggia given to the cathedral at Narni. At least additions such as these do not radically alter the church for the worse, but all too often the medieval churches of Umbria were transformed in line with the different tastes of the times in ways which do little more than reveal the increasingly provincial nature of local taste. The rough-stone church of San Francesco in Città di Castello is far from the worst offender, and if what started life as a simple mendicant church is certainly embellished by the Vitelli Chapel that Giorgio Vasari added in line with the ideas of Brunelleschi and Michelangelo, then the later Baroque remodelling of the remainder of the once plain interior is merely banal.

Despite Umbria's proximity to Rome, in fact, the Baroque, though widely present in the region, is only rarely – and never outstandingly – successful. In Perugia, for instance, many of whose churches reveal Baroque remodelling, the single ambitious Baroque church – San Filippo Neri (1627–34), by the Roman architect, Paolo Marucelli – is both derivative of Santa Maria della Vittoria in Rome and somewhat incongruously placed with its right flank running along the steep and narrow Via dei Priori, so that its façade is only easily visible from the furthest extremity of the tiny piazza on to which it faces. Spoleto shows a good deal of Baroque influence – not altogether surprisingly, as it was much frequented in the seventeenth century by Roman nobles, including the Barberini family. Maffeo Barberini, elected Pope Urban VIII in 1623, had been Bishop of Spoleto between 1608 and 1617, and his nephew Cardinal Francesco Barberini, who succeeded him as bishop later in the century, called Luigi Arrigucci from Rome, where he had previously worked for the family, to transform the interior of the cathedral in Baroque style. It was Francesco Barberini too who commissioned Gian Lorenzo Bernini's bronze bust of Urban VIII, which stands above the central door inside the cathedral, one of the few notable pieces of Baroque sculpture in the region. Another is to be found likewise in Spoleto, in the church of San Filippo Neri, begun after Roman models by the local architect, Loreto Scelli, with an impressive façade, high cupola, and elegant interior; in the sacristy there, the church's patron is commemorated by a marble bust by the Bolognese sculptor, Alessandro Algardi, examples of whose work are also to be found in San Pietro and San Domenico in Perugia. Meanwhile, Orvieto has – in Francesco Mochi's *Virgin* and the *Annunciating Angel* (1605–9) – two innovative works by Bernini's teacher.

Despite such exceptions, the seventeenth and eighteenth centuries were a time of increasing political marginalization and economic and cultural malaise for Umbria. The sharp decline in the economy which affected most of Italy in the early decades of the seventeenth century was followed by a century or more of stagnation. In Umbria, the power of the surviving feudal nobility and the new papal nobility was enhanced by economic conditions which further encouraged the wealthy to eschew the risks involved in investing capital in mercantile or commercial enterprises and to purchase land. So long as the old and new landowners in Umbria continued to pay the ever heavier taxes exacted by Rome, the 'most parasitic and rent-rich city of Italy' as the historian Giuliano Procacci has described it, the popes were content to leave the region well alone, and cultivate their capital. Umbria was effectively forgotten, such identity as the region had formerly possessed being now subordinated to that of the Papal State itself and this at a time when the international prestige of the papacy was at its lowest ebb. With no capital investment, agricultural improvements were limited or non-existent, and while the region evidenced no growth in manufacturing it simultaneously declined as a centre of trade and commerce. The control of the clergy over every aspect of civil as well as ecclesiastical administration removed almost all avenues of advancement for the ambitious and talented except a career in the Church itself. Though one of the leading intellectuals of the papal court in the first half of the eighteenth century, Leone Pascoli (1674–1744) – an early proponent of monetary and agricultural reform – was a native of Perugia, his ideas made no real impact in his lifetime. Only during the reign of Pope Pius

VI (1775–98) did the papacy begin some cautious reform. Even then, such reform was bitterly opposed by a landowning class which had come to see the Church as its surest support in defence of the status quo, and was suspected by others who, not without reason, saw any move towards reform as an aberration of Church policy.

Cultural life in general was much impoverished. The decline which took place between the sixteenth and eighteenth centuries may be charted through the accounts of such foreign travellers who, in the course of the Grand Tour, had (as they usually thought) the misfortune to travel through Umbria, *en route* for more rewarding locations. When the French writer Michel de Montaigne passed through the region in 1581, he still found much to admire. The area around Otrícoli, he recorded in his *Journal de voyage*, was 'infinitely pleasing . . . all wooded but very fertile and densely populated'. Narni, Terni, and Spoleto were all praised, Montaigne lamenting only that there was no butter to be had and that everything was cooked in oil. (At Foligno, he bestowed on the hostelries the high praise that they were almost as good as those in France – although he added that there was no fresh fish, and that Umbrians did not know how to cook vegetables.) The stretch of the Via Flaminia between Spoleto and Foligno was in good condition, Montaigne found, leaving him free to admire the local scenery and wonder whether Trevi, on its olive-covered hill, really was the town surrounded by olive groves that Servius had described 1,200 years before. Only when he began the long ascent to the Apennines did the country become 'dry and barren' – though Montaigne noted that even in the mountains not an inch of cultivatable land was left untended.

It was these same 'most stony and barren' mountains which provided the English writer Fynes Morison with his first sight of Umbria, which he described in his *Itinerary* (1617). Even the Vale of Umbria Morison thought stony though 'fertle' [*sic*], and he drew attention to the promiscuous cultivation of crops there: 'yeelding together in the same field, vines, corne, Almond and Olive trees'. In general, though, he still considered the area 'most fruitfull'. Rome-bound, Morison did stop to observe the fourteenth-century fortress and aqueduct at Spoleto, but what is striking about most travellers in this period is how *little* they saw. Montaigne mentions only the Roman ruins of Ocriculum (Otrícoli), and neither he nor Fynes Morison even glanced at Assisi, though it lay close to their route.

Neither did Joseph Addison, who travelled in Italy between 1701 and 1703, though he was fascinated by the surviving monuments linking modern Italy to ancient Rome. In his *Remarks on Several Parts of Italy* (1705), he admired Raphael's famous *Madonna* in Foligno and marvelled at the height of the 'Gothick' acqueduct at Spoleto, but he reserved his greatest praise for the Augustan bridge at Narni – 'one of the stateliest ruines in Italy' – and the Cascata delle Marmore near Terni, which he called the 'famous Cascade' and considered finer than all the 'water-works at Versailles'. Addison's preference for Roman remains was shared by most eighteenth-century literary travellers, who were, for the most part, men of classical education. James Boswell, who visited the cascade on 14 February 1765, described it in his *Journal* as 'prodigious wild' and added 'Read Virgil's description thrice; was quite in Aeneid'. This was a reference to a passage in the seventh book of Virgil's poem, which many contemporaries chose to read as an allusion to the Cascata delle Marmore. Dryden translated the lines thus:

> In midst of Italy, well known to fame,
> There lies a lake (Amsanctus is the name)
> Below the lofty mounts; on either side
> Thick forests the forbidden entrance hide.
> Full in the centre of the sacred wood,
> An arm arises from the Stygian flood,
> Which, breaking from beneath with billowing sound,
> Whirls the black waves and rattling stones around.
> Here Pluto pants for breath from out his cell,
> And opens wide the grinning jaws of hell. (vii, 563–71)

Boswell is nowhere else so enthusiastic about what he sees, however, and vouchsafes little more about his stay in Terni, in June 1765, than that his travelling companion, Lord Mountstuart, cried out in his sleep, 'Boswell, what are you upsetting your chamber-pot for,' and recording that, in Foligno, 'My Lord told me many bawdy stories.'

Other eighteenth-century travellers were more forthcoming but also critical of what they saw. Tobias Smollett, a notoriously querulous but much more indefatigable and receptive tourist than most, enjoyed the ruins of Ocriculum, the 'romantic' town of Narni, with its 'stupendous' bridge and the 'astonishing' Cascata delle Marmore, all of which he described in Letter XXXIV of *Travels through France and Italy* (1766). In marked contrast to seventeenth-century travellers, however, he also found the roads, even the Via Flaminia (still the single most important route through the region), notoriously poor; between Terni and Spoleto, he recorded, 'the road winds along a precipice, which is equally dangerous and dreadful'. Though he evidently took an interest in the countryside through which he passed, noting Spoleto, 'Assisio' and several other towns along the way, Smollett stopped at none before he reached Foligno. There he was subject to an adventure which, while comic, suggests how inward-looking Umbria had become under papal rule:

In choosing our beds at the inn, I perceived one chamber locked, and desired it might be opened; upon which the cameriere declared with some reluctance, '*Bisogna dire a su' eccellenza; poco fa, che una bestia è morta in questa camera, e non è ancora lustrata.*' 'Your excellency must know that a filthy beast died lately in that chamber, and it is not yet purified and put in order.' When I enquired what beast it was, he replied, '*Un'eretico Inglese.*' 'An English heretick.'

In a spirit of fairness, Smollett added that 'I suppose he would not have made so free with our country and religion, if he had not taken us for German catholics.'

Unlike most eighteenth-century travellers through Umbria, Smollett was not bound for an Apennine pass but had elected to travel through the region as an alternative to the more westerly route through Tuscany he had taken when travelling south. He therefore took the opportunity to visit Perugia, which had 'some elegant fountains, and several handsome churches, containing some valuable pictures by Guido [Reni], Raphael, and his master Pietro Perugino'. Though admiring the city and Lake

Trasimeno, Smollett was again critical of the road which took him into Tuscany; it was, he wrote, 'so unequal and stony, that we were jolted even to the danger of our lives'.

Such criticism is neither unique to Smollett nor even to British travellers of the period. Goethe, who passed through Umbria *en route* to Rome in 1786, had many complaints of his own – and this despite the fact that he could be the most enthusiastic of tourists. Making his first visit to Italy at what he considered the late age of thirty-seven, he wrote on one occasion: 'I left Perugia on a glorious morning and felt the bliss of being once more alone. The situation of the town is beautiful and the view of the lake charming. I shall remember them both.' The German poet's uncontained joy at reaching the Temple of Minerva at Assisi – 'the first complete classical monument I have seen' – is, in these days of easy and careless travel, quite touching. Yet Goethe turned away 'in distaste' from the 'dreary' basilica of St Francis, which he dismissed as being built like a 'Babylonian tower' – and was given more personal reason to dislike Assisi when he was accosted by armed ruffians and accused of being a smuggler – a charge dropped after some coins changed hands. Most importantly, Goethe anticipated many nineteenth-century travellers in detailing evidence of the economic and cultural decline he saw everywhere about him in Umbria. Agriculture was in a poor way: he noted olive trees covered in ivy, a dearth of pasture everywhere, due to the overcultivation of maize, and a lack of manure for fertilizer. 'This Italy, so greatly favoured by Nature,' he commented, 'has lagged far behind all other countries in mechanical and technical matters.' As a result, there was much poverty, characterized by poor housing and food shortages, especially in winter, so that the poor 'suffer like dogs for a considerable part of the year'. Their social superiors, meanwhile, Goethe found to be ignorant and bigoted: a papal captain asks if it is true, as he has been assured by his priest, that Protestants are permitted to marry their sisters, and everywhere Umbrians are 'all bitter rivals: they indulge in the oddest provincialism and local patriotism, and cannot stand each other'. Contrasting the poverty of the Church territories with the prosperity of neighbouring Tuscany, Goethe concludes that the Papal States 'seem to stay alive only because the earth refuses to swallow them'.

When reform did take place it was forced upon Umbria from outside. French Revolutionary ideas spread quickly to Italy after 1789 and after Napoleon had occupied the whole of northern Italy in a campaign which lasted less than a year, between May 1796 and April 1797, he was hailed by many Italians as a liberator. The first French troops to set foot in Umbria passed through the region early in February 1798 on their way to Rome, where the Roman Republic was set up in the same month. Nominally independent, though effectively a French protectorate, the Republic adopted a constitution based on that of Year III and began an administrative reform of the former papal territories which saw Umbria divided into two departments: Trasimeno, with its administrative centre at Perugia, and Clitumnus, centred on Spoleto.

Umbrians of revolutionary persuasion now took to wearing cockades and Phrygian caps. In Perugia, all emblems of the papacy – including the statues of Popes Julius III, Sixtus IV, and Paul III – were torn down and destroyed. Liberty trees were set up, especially in the north of the region but also, though less frequently, in the south. The first appeared in Città di Castello, to be followed by others in Fratta, Perugia, Passignano, Castel Rigone, Magione, and even Todi and Orvieto. Religious processions were banned, monasteries and convents closed, and their goods confiscated. Yet while some welcomed the French presence, others quickly turned against change. Throughout the region, Catholic zealots banded themselves into guerrilla armies under a variety of names: Viva Maria, the Insorgenti (or Insurgents) and Armata Cattolica (or Catholic Army). This last group, centred on the small commune of Castel Rigone, began by tearing down the liberty tree there and attacking Jacobin supporters before proceeding to Città di Castello, where they incited a rebellion, resulting in a massacre of their opponents. Having advanced as far as Perugia, they were met by a detachment of French troops who pursued them to Magione, where the rebels were put to flight or killed. The Insorgenti, based in Valnerina and the mountains around Norcia and Cascia, at first engaged the French, and then turned, as did all these bands, to brigandage. Viva Maria – a militia which originated in southern

Tuscany and spread south into Umbria, making their headquarters in the Franciscan monastery in the hilltop village of Preggio – became a byword for violence and pillage in the region, massacring not only Jacobins but also Jews – who had been admitted as full citizens of the Roman Republic after their expulsion from the Papal States in 1569.

Such upheavals were, however, of short duration. Austrian troops soon appeared in Italy to put an end to the Roman Republic and restore the papacy to power, and in 1801 Napoleon signed a concordat with Pius VII. Only after Napoleon had declared himself the successor to the Holy Roman Emperor did the political situation in the region change once more. On 10 June 1808, Umbria was annexed to France and made a single province, Trasimeno, with its centre at Spoleto. The new administrators set quickly to work, endeavouring to give impetus to the stagnant economy, encouraging and protecting fresh initiatives, and endeavouring to restore the university at Perugia. Once more, convents were suppressed, ecclesiastical goods expropriated, and all the clergy were obliged to swear allegiance to the Emperor; most of the Umbrian hierarchy refused, though the bishops of Perugia, Spoleto and Città della Pieve did so and each was rewarded with the Légion d'Honneur.

The fall of Napoleon in 1814 led to the rapid departure of the French from Umbria, and Pius VII, now freed from his imprisonment in France, passed through the region in June, on his way to Rome. Some trace of the experience of French rule did remain. In his encyclical *Motu proprio* (1816), for example, Pius VII noted that 'our state still lacks that uniformity which is so useful to public and private interests, because having been formed by the gradual agglomeration of different territories, presents a variety of usages, laws and privileges which are naturally different so as very often to render one Province foreign to another and at times even to result in differences between different towns in the same Province'. Despite these sentiments, Umbria was once again broken up in 1816. There were now two legations, centred on Perugia and Spoleto, comprising most of the present region, with the exception of Gubbio (still linked with Urbino) and Orvieto (which was administered from Viterbo until 1853). More importantly, the administrative experience acquired by lay Umbrians during the Napoleonic years was immediately lost as the clergy once more took over responsibility for civil affairs.

Pius VII found it expedient not to inquire too closely into the conduct or political sympathies of Umbrians during the years of Napoleonic rule – despite being encouraged to do so by his more zealous advisers such as the Spoletine, Cardinal Annibale della Genga (the future Leo XII). Even so, with the restoration of the papacy, Umbria largely returned to its previous condition of stagnation and neglect. While the last decades of the eighteenth century had seen an expansion of the area of cultivated land – mostly recovered from marsh or wood – and the extension of the *mezzadria* to higher hills and the mountains, the Umbrian countryside was again struck by one of the periodic famines which had affected the region in the seventeenth and early eighteenth centuries. The famine of 1816, which followed on a typhus epidemic, was particularly severe. Trade further declined as the neglected road network deteriorated into crisis, and the once great fairs of the Middle Ages were now replaced by a plethora of tiny fairs and markets – 449 fairs and seventy-one markets by 1865 – most of scant importance even within the Papal States themselves. Such small-scale manufacture as had previously existed now tended to disappear: the woollen and silk manufactures of Perugia were lost and only linen and hemp manufactures remained. The towns contracted and even the centre of Perugia was semi-deserted, peopled only by a much-reduced and needy population, poorly clothed and worse fed.

This was the Umbria vividly described by the Irish writer Sydney Owenson, Lady Morgan, in *Italy* (1821), an account of her travels in the country in 1819–20. Mindful of the region's history and possessed of a Romantic responsiveness to landscape largely unknown to her eighteenth-century predecessors, Lady Morgan was also acutely alert to contemporary poverty and degradation. Passing from healthy, affluent Tuscany into Umbria, she was struck by the contrast between 'the Paradise of the natural scenery, [and] the wretched, ragged groups, who stretching forth their squalid forms from the black dens of

Passignano, give the first specimens of the condition of the subjects of the Papal dominions'. About Perugia, with its 'narrow, dirty, gloomy streets [and] high, dismantled, and dreary palaces', Lady Morgan had especially strong views:

Under the late French regime, the city of Perugia was governed by a military prefect, who introduced much of the order and discipline of his profession into its society. He gave gay entertainments, held assemblies, and obliged the old murky, time-worn nobles, to throw off their dusty great coats . . .

Perugia is now under the jurisdiction of a priest, the Prelato Spinola, with the title of Governor. There are, of course, no balls – no assemblies; and the nobles are at liberty to resume their great coats, in which (by the by) we saw some of them perform that weary pilgrimage, the Corso, in coaches which seemed to have existed since the time of FORTE-BRACCIO.

We left Perugia as the dawn broke upon the towers of its horrible fortress; but yet not so early but misery was awake; and the same cries which ushered us into its gloomy walks, now followed us out.

The story is similar elsewhere. Foligno has 'all the generic features of a provincial city in the Roman States – neglect, sadness, and desolation', and Narni is 'this truly feudal and papal little town, where gloom and poverty tell their tale, amidst forts and churches . . . sad and desolate as it moulders'.

Lady Morgan, it is true, was not without a political agenda of her own – and when scenes such as the 'clusters of grey and formless hovels teemed with a naked and starving peasantry' bring to mind contemporary Ireland, the Irish patriot is anxious to remind her English readers that they did not need to look to Catholic Europe to find penury and suffering. Even so, the picture she paints recalls many images from less immediately interested writers. Cyrus Redding, in his *History and Description of Modern Wines*, published in London in 1833, drew attention to the primitive state of Italian viticulture and argued that, in the Roman States, wines might be much better than they are were it not for the fact that there is no incentive for improvement offered to country-people 'trampled by . . . the feet of native tyrants'. There is little reason to disagree. Over 87 per cent of the entire population of Umbria now lived in the countryside, most on large estates, owned by the Church or by absentee proprietors who preferred to let their lands at low rates to middle-men, who enriched themselves in turn at the expense of *mezzadri*, forced to cultivate them with long out-of-date agricultural techniques. The towns, by contrast, were depopulated and idle. In the census of 1861, following the unification of Italy, Perugia's population had shrunk to just 14,885, of whom a mere 452 were engaged in any kind of manufacture.

Not surprisingly in the circumstances, Umbrian discontent readily manifested itself in the wake of political upheaval elsewhere. Following the 1830 Revolution in Paris, Italy rose and the papal forces were expelled from the region. For a while the papal territory was reduced to Lazio, though the intervention of the Austrians soon restored the status quo. The failure of the 1830 Revolution could not suppress the growing discontent which manifested itself among the small middle class and the more enlightened aristocrats whose aspirations to political reform were aired in masonic lodges and in new political societies such as the Carboneria. Dissent so swelled between 1831 and 1846, during the pontificate of the reactionary Gregory XVI, to whom social or economic change seemed a matter of supreme indifference, that even the papal administrators became alarmed and began to press for cautious reform. The election of the moderate Pius IX in 1846 seemed a good omen, as did the arrival as Bishop of Perugia of Gioacchino Pecci (later Pope Leo XIII), a friend of the liberal Catholic politician Gioberti, and a man in touch with the most advanced Catholic political circles of the day. When revolution broke out once more in 1848, however, the hopes of the moderate reformers were quickly dashed, as the hierarchy retreated behind the walls of reaction. For many Umbrians, in any case, moderation was not enough. The Perugians, for example, wasted no time in beginning the demolition of the most hated symbol of papal rule, the Rocca Paolina – the honour of beginning the demolition being conceded to Count Benedetto Baglioni, descendant of the Baglioni family, over the ruins of whose houses the fortress had been erected more than three centuries previously. Umbrians participated actively in the events of 1848–9, adhering to Mazzini's short-lived Roman Republic and endeavouring to defend it from the French troops sent in defence of the Pope.

Italian aspirations to independence were short-lived, being thoroughly crushed by the summer of 1849, but the events set in motion a wave of underground political activity which continued until the remaining moderates abandoned all hope that the papacy might itself effect real reform and joined with the liberals in support of the national leader, Cavour. For a short while in 1859, Umbria now moved to the forefront of the Risorgimento. In June of that year, Perugia rose in rebellion against the papacy and formed a provisional junta, offering the city to the Piedmontese Vittorio Emanuele II, soon to be the first king of a united Italy. The papal government responded decisively, sending a detachment of Swiss troops to take back the city. Following fighting after their entry into Perugia, the papal forces burned houses, looted shops, sacked the monastery of San Pietro and killed innocent civilians. The Perugian massacres were soon infamous not only in Italy but throughout Europe and were widely used as a propaganda tool against the Pope. The Rocca Paolina once more provided a symbolic focus for Perugian discontent and, just a month after the Piedmontese forces entered the city, General Gioacchino Napoleone Pepoli signed a famous and well-publicized decree, turning over the remains of the fortress to the city authorities, who proceeded to demolish what remained intact after 1848.

CHAPTER NINE

The Kingdom of Italy
and the First Republic

❋

When the Kingdom of Italy was proclaimed on 17 March 1861
– leaving the papal territory reduced to Rome, itself incorporated into a united Italy in 1870 – Umbria became one of the
new provinces. The revolutionary change some Umbrians had
looked for, however, continued to elude them. The lack of real
unity between the more advanced political circles and the mass
of people in the countryside prevented a popular uprising and
left Umbria to the moderates who took control of regional
administration. Economic renewal failed to follow on political
change, and for some time most Umbrians were, if anything,
worse off than under the papacy. In 1861, no fewer than 84 per
cent of them were illiterate (a figure which had only dropped to
49 per cent half a century later). The already weak Umbrian
economy was ill-prepared to thrive in conditions of financial
stringency, exacerbated by the abolition of internal customs
tariffs, which led to inflation and virtually destroyed what little
cottage industry remained to the region. Even more than elsewhere in Italy, Umbria exemplifies Gramsci's notion of the
Risorgimento as a failed national revolution, for the *mezzadria* –
for long the source of the social and economic woes of the
Umbrian peasantry – remained untouched. Those who had
found it hard to survive with dignity before 1860 discovered
themselves liable to new local and national taxes. They also
found themselves liable, for the first time for centuries, for

national military service. The result was a resurgence of banditry in the region. Bands operated in the area of Assisi, Gualdo, and Gubbio (where more than 1,000 outlaws were captured in November 1869 alone), and around Orvieto (where they were not dispersed until 1877). The last bandit was captured, at Coccorano di Valfabbrica, only in March 1901.

It was now the new communes, often controlled by the landowners themselves, which proved resistant to economic initiatives, failing to provide the capital investment necessary to endow the region with an adequate infrastructure or to modernize local agriculture. There was, it is true, some shift in the pattern of landownership but this did not extend to the acquisition of land by those who worked on it. In 1871, 6.65 per cent of landed proprietors owned 65.5 per cent of the land available. While the Church's share of land was diminishing – at the end of the eighteenth century, the Church possessed 27 per cent of all the land in Umbria and, in some areas, over 50 per cent – the nobility held on to theirs, and the rapidly expanding middle class increased their share. It was the farmers who hoped for land but hoped in vain.

If the situation of the *mezzadri* was bad – and they were continually in debt and more than ever dependent on cash advances from landowners to buy seed for planting each year – then the plight of the *braccianti* or day-labourers was worse. Kept within the orbit of the landowner by the cession of a house, the *bracciante* was forced to turn his hand to any task available to support himself and his family, whether in the countryside or by seasonal emigration. Barely surviving on a diet of maize bread and vegetables, the poorest of these labourers and many women in the countryside – weakened by a combination of poor diet, frequent pregnancies and long periods of breast-feeding – fell prey to the scourge of pellagra. In the last decades of the nineteenth century and into the twentieth, especially in the hills of the upper Tiber valley and around Lake Trasimeno, the disease – marked by a disfiguring skin condition and leading to madness – was a constant danger for those whose diet did not allow them to replace the energy their work required. In the mountains and in the northern part of the region, emigration became a necessity for many whom the Umbrian economy could no longer support. Throughout several decades thousands – some 85,000 between 1882 and 1911 and a further 18,000 in 1913 alone – left for France and Germany or on occasion for the New World, as in 1901 when 6,000 Umbrians departed for Brazil.

To this sombre picture of life in the Umbrian countryside in the half-century after national unity must, however, be added a more optimistic counterpart. Communications were beginning to improve once more. There was much–needed investment in roads, and the railway finally arrived in the mid-1860s: the first train from Foligno to Rome ran on 6 January 1865 and Perugia was connected with Florence and Foligno by December 1866. In the south of the region, an even more momentous change was taking place, one that would give Umbria a much brighter future and a quite different image. From the 1870s onwards, Terni became the principal site in central Italy of the large-scale industrial activity that had previously been lacking. The city was chosen for economic and strategic reasons. It possessed, in the river Nera and the Marmore waterfall, important sources of hydro-electric power on which its future prosperity would be founded. From a military viewpoint, Terni also had the advantage of a geographical position far from the coasts and national frontiers. (The city's central position in the peninsula even gave rise to a proposal in 1867, before Rome was incorporated into the national territory, that it become the capital of Italy – a suggestion that predictably met with no more favour than the idea, mooted in the early years of the Irish Free State, that the national capital move from Dublin to Athlone.) Massive state and private investment led, in the space of a few years, to the development of, among others, a national ordnance factory in 1875, the Terni steel works in 1886, the Centurini jute mill, and chemical industries. While large areas of the Umbrian country-side saw the population fall, Terni experienced a massive population growth, almost doubling from 15,773 to 29,361 between 1881 and 1889 alone. Having been only the eighth most populous city in Umbria in 1881, it became the second by 1911, surpassed only by Perugia – a position it continues to hold today. Known as the 'Manchester of Italy', the small medieval town was massively transformed. By the end of the century, the area within the old city walls covered just 605,310 sq. m. while the area of the steelworks alone amounted to 703,550 sq. m. In industrial terms, Terni dominated the region: in 1911, it possessed a mere 6.8 per cent of regional business but employed 33.1 per cent of the workforce and boasted a massive 78 per cent of the industrial plant. Umbria became the third most important region in Italy, after Lombardy and Piedmont, for the production of electricity. Such rapid industrialization was not effected without problems: the rivers around Terni became heavily polluted and the Cascata delle Marmore – admired for centuries by travellers through the region – was reduced to a trickle as its waters were diverted.

To most Umbrians in the early twentieth century, such disadvantages seemed a small price to pay for the revival of a region that had seemed virtually embalmed for two centuries or more. If Terni led the way, other centres soon followed suit. In the south, Terni's neighbour, Narni, produced electricity and developed a chemical industry. Spoleto opened up lignite mines and started a cotton manufacture, Campello saw the development of a chemical industry, and of fertilizer and glue production based on agricultural by-products, while even Assisi saw the emergence of chemical and fertilizer manufacture. In comparison to Terni, industrial development at Perugia was slow, being confined principally to small and medium-scale woollen and textile manufacture, so that as late as 1898 one newspaper correspondent contrasted Terni and its wealth-producing machinery with Perugia, where technical progress had brought no more than sewing-machines and coffee-grinders. It was only in 1907 that Perugia saw the creation of what would become – and still remains – its most important manufacturing industry, the chocolate and confectionery firm Perugina, which, after the First World War, would also become the first Umbrian commercial concern of truly international importance.

The belated modernization of Umbria brought with it not merely economic but the beginnings of political and social change. The quietist image of the region under the long years of the *ancien régime* had already begun to crack during the revolutionary years of the early nineteenth century, yet even after Italian unification, cultural life remained dominated by conservative voices. (The most remarkable Umbrian voice – in a very literal sense – was that of Domenico Mustafà (1829–1912), one of the last of the great *castrati* – director of the papal choir in the Sistine Chapel at Rome, shortly before the reform of church music by Pius X in the first decade of the twentieth century – whom Wagner once considered for the role of the magician Klingsor in his last opera, *Parsifal*.) For a while, it is true, Umbria became a centre in Italy of the modernist movement in the Roman Catholic Church – a European-wide movement which endeavoured to reconcile religion with modern philosophy, positivist science and prevailing liberal-democratic politics. The ensuing battle between the modernists and theological conservatives was ended, however, when Pius X intervened to condemn modernism in an encyclical in 1907. In Umbria, modernists – including a number of seminary rectors – were dismissed from their posts and placed in tiny and remote country parishes where it was reckoned that they could do least harm.

If the Church was still closed to new ideas, however, Umbria was opening up in other ways. In the new industrial centres, socialism was gaining ground, leading to the development of a working-class consciousness which would eventually transform 'Green' Umbria into 'Red' Umbria – one of the leading left-wing regions in Italy. In the general election of 1996, in fact, Umbria was the third most left-leaning region, recording a left-wing vote of 57 per cent in the Senate elections (against a national average of 44.1 per cent), and 57.2 per cent in the elections for the Chamber of Deputies (43.3 per cent). Particularly strong in Terni, in the first years of the century, the socialists built up a political organization which allowed them to return a deputy to the Italian parliament as early as 1909, when they obtained over 22 per cent of the regional vote.

If the lives of working-class men were transformed by the arrival of large-scale industry in the region in the late nineteenth century, so too were the lives of women. It was not that women had not worked before in Umbria – indeed, it had become expected that in the prevailing harsh economic crisis the wives and daughters of agricultural labourers would play their part in the family economy, by working in the fields at harvest time. (The importance of female labour in agriculture has far from disappeared even today, least of all in the tobacco-growing areas of northern Umbria, where older women can still be seen taking their place in the fields during late August and September, alongside a more recent source of cheap labour, African immigrants.) That women were a ready source of cheap labour – more docile and less prone to striking – was, of course, what induced the new industries of Umbria to employ women in such numbers. The jute mill in Terni, for instance, counted no fewer than 280 women among its first 315 employees, and 1,100 out of 1,300 in 1893. In fact, the household experience of women ill prepared them for factory life in an age of such rapid social transformation, and they were much criticized as slow and ill-educated workers. This did not cause industrialists to employ fewer of them but did permit the factory-owners to shift female workers around, as short-term exigencies seemed to demand, to pay them very low wages, and keep them in their place by sacking them at the slightest provocation. The story of the women who entered the Terni workforce and helped sustain the new industries during the late nineteenth and early twentieth centuries is, predictably, not a happy one. Yet in some places, notably the Centurini mill, female workers developed a sense of their own possibilities which led them, during the First World War, to produce trade union leaders, like Carlotta Orientale, whom management could not ignore, even in an environment where traditional patriarchal attitudes were still strong.

In 1919, in the first general election after the First World War, it seemed as though socialism had triumphed entirely in the region, as in the country as a whole, for the Partito Socialista Italiano, or PSI, gained an absolute majority of the votes cast in Umbria, with 50.9 per cent, with industrial workers joining forces with farm labourers (in the countryside around Orvieto the socialist vote exceeded 80 per cent). The agricultural workforce now demonstrated actively against the landowners in various parts of the region in protests which occasionally turned to violence, as in 1920 in the small town of Panicale, where five demonstrators were shot dead. The socialist triumph was short-lived, however. The first fascist group was formed at Perugia on 23 January 1920 – at a meeting attended by just fifty-one people, who included all of those who would later dominate local fascism. The first clash with the socialists took place the following day. By March 1920, Perugia saw violent attacks on communist, anarchist and Catholic, as well as socialist, gatherings. Perugia, indeed, was to hold a prominent position in fascist mythology, for it was in the Hotel Brufani there, in October 1922, that the fascist quadrumvirs coordinated the March on Rome, at the time of Mussolini's assumption of power. By then, the popularity of socialism was waning dramatically. In the 1921 elections, the PSI's share of the popular vote had halved to 25.39 per cent – and it would halve again in 1924 to 12.8 per cent. In these same elections, the fascists triumphed with no less than 78.8 per cent of votes cast. For Umbria, it was a period when the old conservative landowning class reasserted itself economically and socially, while the fascists took political control of the region (most members of the fascist hierarchy, as well as local administrators, were landowners or members of the prosperous urban middle class). Only a few liberal or socialist intellectuals, led by Aldo Capitini, opposed fascism in the regional capital, leaving the industrial workers of Terni as the only substantial anti-fascist group in Umbria in the course of the next two decades.

The return of men from the First World War saw women once more marginalized in the workplace, and the subsequent rise of fascism resulted in the victory of those social groups who most determinedly resisted economic and social reform at regional level. The particular problems of Umbria – and other parts of central Italy – had been recognized since the early years of the century, when it was acknowledged that Italy's problems could not be categorized by an easy division between a prosperous industrial north and a backward agricultural south. Yet all attempts at agrarian reform failed once more as conservatives played on the fear of peasant smallholders, declaring it a 'sacred duty' to preserve the *mezzadria* against both the collectivizing tendency of the socialists and the spread of lease-holding. The result was that the interwar *mezzadria* was as much a backward-looking social contract as it had been at the time of the Church State. There were some improvements in agriculture during the 1920s and 1930s – the introduction of chemical fertilizers, improvements in crop rotation and a substantial increase in mechanization – but for most of those who lived on the land the situation remained bleak. Bread and vegetables remained the staple diet throughout the region, supplemented by salt cod and a little pork. A survey in 1927 showed that of 35,327 *case coloniche*, or farmhouses, in the province of Perugia, only 10 per cent could be considered in a good state of repair, 50 per cent were barely acceptable and fully 40 per cent were considered to be unacceptable. The farmhouses lacked water, electricity, and proper sanitation, while their inhabitants were under-educated and suffered regularly from such diseases as tuberculosis, bronchitis and typhoid.

When Italy entered the war on the side of Germany in June 1940, Terni immediately assumed a central importance as the region's major industrial centre. By July 1940 the workforce stood at 30,000 as opposed to a figure of 24,000 between 1937 and 1939. As the war turned in the Allies' favour, the significance of Terni was felt in a very different way. In more than 100 bombing raids, over 2,000 people were killed and much of the old medieval city was lost for ever. By the end of the war, the removal of industrial plant to fascist-controlled northern Italy meant that the value of Umbrian industry was reduced by 45 per cent in relation to its value in 1939.

Before that time came, however, Umbria was to suffer once more the fate of being a battleground for foreign armies. As so often in its history, the region's geographical position gave it an unwanted strategic importance. The darkest days came in June and July 1944. The fascist regime having fallen the previous year, Umbria had been occupied by German troops for eight months. Partisans were now operating widely in the region – especially in the south but also in the upper Tiber valley, around Lake Trasimeno, and in the mountains above Gubbio. Rome fell to the Allied forces on 4 June 1944. Despite heavy resistance,

British and Commonwealth forces (the Americans were employed elsewhere) fought their way north, entering Umbria on 13 June, and capturing Narni. On the following day, Orvieto, Terni and Todi all fell to the Eighth Army, advancing on a broad front. On 16 June, Spoleto and Foligno were taken; on 18 June, Assisi. By 19 June, British units had reached the southern and eastern shores of Lake Trasimeno, just short of the Germans' Albert Line. Though Perugia fell to Allied troops on 20 June, it was not until 2 July that Foiano, just across the border in Tuscany, was taken, facilitating the advance on Florence. In northern Umbria, progress was slower still – and the fighting yet more savage. For some weeks, partisans had been harassing the Germans from the mountains above Gubbio. On 22 June, as a reprisal for one partisan attack, the Germans took forty innocent civilians hostage and machine-gunned them to death on the outskirts of the town; similar incidents took place elsewhere in the region, and are today remembered by plaques and stone memorials marking the sites of the massacres. From the end of June until 25 July, when Gubbio was finally liberated, the German artillery pounded the city from the mountains, in their efforts to slow down the advance of the Allies along the plain below. With democracy restored, the socialist and communist-led opposition to the regime which had been clandestinely present throughout the fascist period now helped organize the political and union structures destroyed by Mussolini. In the 1946 referendum on the question of whether Italy should retain its monarchy or become a republic, 71.9 per cent of Umbrian votes were cast in favour of the republic.

The Second World War also effectively put an end to the *mezzadria*, which had endured in Umbria for so long. In the 1930s, fascism had continually endeavoured to increase food production but it was only with the urgent need for domestic food production induced by the war itself that the agricultural work-force recognized the economic power they possessed. In the summer of 1945, farmers went on strike at harvest time in an attempt to effect a more equitable division of produce, and at Duesanti, near Todi, the red flag was raised (though the ringleaders of the rising were arrested and imprisoned). Unions took an ever more important role in organization and promoted a day of strikes throughout the region in solidarity with those in the countryside. In 1948 another small uprising took place when demonstrators took over the small village of Agello near Magione, setting up road-blocks and endeavouring to prevent the arrival of the *carabinieri*; this time nineteen arrests were made. By now the complaints of those in the countryside were familiar and are well remembered by older Umbrians today: a lack of drinking water and electricity – the former might have to be fetched from wells hundreds of metres away along dirt tracks liable to turn to thick mud after rain, while gas or oil lamps were still the norm for lighting and cooking. Heating required abundant supplies of wood – and there was no proper sanitation.

With the economic growth of the 1950s, the *mezzadria* finally began to disappear as possibilities of employment arose in northern Italy or in Germany. Together with natural catastrophes like the great freeze of 1956 – which destroyed fully 90 per cent of olive trees, one of the principal sources of income, in parts of the region – such opportunities persuaded many to abandon an ancient way of life which left them increasingly out of touch with the modern world. Fewer and fewer were content to live in poor housing (fully two-thirds of farmhouses throughout the region were considered in need of major repair in 1957), on an impoverished diet (country people continued to eat badger, porcupine and hedgehog as sources of protein), while lacking personal transport or even radios that would put them in touch with an environment beyond their fields. In 1951, Umbria was still a predominantly rural society with an agricultural economy: 56.3 per cent of Umbrians lived in the countryside as opposed to a nationwide average of 42.2 per cent. Between 1951 and 1961, while the active workforce declined by 9 per cent, the agricultural workforce fell by no less than 34.3 per cent. A survey conducted in 1964 in the middle Tiber valley between Torgiano and Todi makes it clear why: 42 per cent of farmhouses had no electricity, 83 per cent lacked mains water and 92 per cent were without proper sanitation. By the 1960s, with new possibilities of industrial employment, the *mezzadria* was gone.

Umbria now presents a very different aspect. Despite the

region's still predominantly agricultural appearance, less than 9 per cent of the active population is engaged in farming. Industry and manufacture employs 32 per cent and almost 60 per cent work in the service sector. The 1994 unemployment rate of 10.3 per cent placed Umbria midway in national unemployment statistics, contrasting with the regional extremes of just 4.9 per cent in Trentino-Alto Adige, and as much as 22.4 per cent in Sicily. Most manufacturing enterprises today are of small or medium size. They are to be found, for the most part, in industrial zones around the larger cities, from Città di Castello in the north to Orvieto in the south, and in the industrial belt that runs from Magione, past Perugia, to Foligno, allowing for relatively easy access to the national communications network, by way of the *superstrada*, or dual carriageway, linking the region to the main north–south motorway, the Autostrada del Sole. Terni, once the industrial model for Umbria, is today still struggling to extricate itself from the economic crisis into which the closing of heavy industry plunged it in the 1980s. Among varieties of manufacture, textiles and clothing are important in and around Perugia, from internationally known names such as Luisa Spagnoli, and newer enterprises like Ellesse, at Ellera. Textiles have long enjoyed economic importance in the region, and so too has paper production, for which Umbria has been famous since the late Middle Ages, especially in Foligno and Perugia. Other industries which remind us of earlier days include the industrial processing of food products: now, most notably, olive oil and wine, as well as foodstuffs for livestock. The food industry, generally, has a particular importance in the Umbrian economy. Buitoni is one of the best-known names – in its various plants throughout the country it produces some 40 per cent of Italy's pasta – but other firms, such as Ponte, enjoy national distribution. The chocolate and confectionery firm of Perugina was, back in 1930s, the first Umbrian commercial enterprise to gain an international reputation, when it began selling its products in New York, as well as in Europe. Today, Baci – chocolate kisses – are the best-known line, but the industry is sufficiently renowned for Perugia to have been named 'Città del cioccolato' in 1994. Many Umbrian wines, like those from Orvieto and from newer regions such as Torgiano, enjoy international prestige, and Montefalco hosts a nationally important wine week each year, at Easter. Mineral water production in the region – from such sources as San Faustino, San Gémini, and Nocera – is still growing in importance. One last form of manufacture which has a real economic importance in the region, as well as being of particular interest to tourists, is ceramic ware. With a largely unbroken tradition since the late Middle Ages, Deruta remains the most important area for ceramics, boasting a quite extraordinary number of factories and workshops which, between them, make everything from mass-produced items to very fine hand-decorated pieces. The area between Gubbio and Gualdo Tadino is also important, especially for the black ceramics known as *bucchero*, as is Orvieto.

Umbria is rightly proud of an industrial heritage which did so much to change the face of a moribund region in the late nineteenth century – and visitors would do well to ignore such guides as lament any sign of industrial activity around Umbria's medieval towns or sneer at the notion that Terni is worth a visit for anyone interested in industrial archaeology. Even so, much remains to be done if the region is to increase in prosperity through its manufacturing industries. The public sector alone in Umbria today employs the same number of people as all the industrial sector: around 100,000. Most significant among other activities in the services sector, predictably, is tourism. Umbria attracted around 2 million visitors in 1994. They come today for many reasons. Religious tourism brings pilgrims from all over the world to Assisi and Cascia. The beaches and watersports of Lake Trasimeno are important attractions, not only for Italians but for the German, Dutch, Belgian and English visitors to be seen in the lakeside towns in the summer months. The attractions of Etruscan, Roman, medieval and Renaissance Umbria draw many more. So too does the ease of access, by road and rail, to art centres elsewhere in central Italy – Rome, Florence, Siena, or Urbino. Music festivals bring others to Spoleto for opera, Città di Castello for chamber and choral concerts, Perugia and Orvieto for classical music, jazz and rock. Most visitors come, at least in part, for a sight of Green Umbria, for the peace of the hills, mountains, rivers and streams of one of the most beautiful landscapes anywhere. Visitors return to the region – as so many do – because, once there, they discover that Umbria is not one place but many, a crossroads where north and south, east and west intersect and where great monuments and humble settlements bear witness to a unique past in a living landscape, even today.

CHAPTER TEN

Umbrian Painting and Painting in Umbria

✳

Since art historians recognize the existence of the Umbrian school of painting, it may seem redundant to ask whether Umbrian painting really exists. The 'Umbrian School', however, properly refers to a group of painters working in the region between around 1460 to 1520, whose best-known figure is Pietro Vannucci, Perugino. Attempts to locate certain essential features in 'Umbrian' art throughout a longer chronological span tend to a simplistic reduction of art in the region to a restricted number of (frequently mystical) features, often arbitrarily attributed to artists of quite different characteristics. In the process, such attempts inevitably deny – or at least obscure – the variety and diversity of cultural influence in Umbrian painting. In fact, the region's central position on the Italian peninsula and its importance as a site of cultural exchange have rarely proved more significant than in its visual art. In the early Middle Ages, the Flaminian Way – linking Ravenna to Rome – made the region particularly susceptible to the older but still strong Byzantine traditions of the former city and to the novel artistic currents emerging in the latter. In the later medieval period, Umbria felt the influence of the different styles of Rome, Florence and Siena. The Renaissance saw not only the absorption by local painters of the new aesthetic currents of Florence, the Marches and northern Italy, but also the emergence of a vital native artistic culture. Moreover, the presence from the thirteenth century onwards both of vibrant independent city-states and of the nationally significant artistic centre of the great basilica of St Francis at Assisi brought many leading artists to the heart of the region. An account of painting in Umbria must consider the work both of artists native to Umbria and of those who, for whatever reasons, have left important records of their activities within its borders. Today, their work may be seen either in the churches, abbeys, convents and public and private buildings for which they were designed, or in one of the region's many art museums: the Galleria Nazionale dell'Umbria in Perugia, the Pinacoteca Comunale in Città di Castello, or in such smaller museums as those of Gubbio, Assisi, Orvieto, Spoleto, Terni, Montefalco or Spello.

Such an account will most usefully begin in the early eighth century. Despite the wealth of Etruscan and Roman remains, only a few examples of earlier painting (other than vase-paintings) have survived in the region. The most important of those that have come down to us are the detached paintings from the Golini tombs, now in the Archaeological Museum in Orvieto. Among extant Roman mosaics are the second-century marine scenes in the baths at Bevagna and a depiction of Orpheus and the Furies from the same period in Perugia. The first post-classical art to survive today is that to be found in the palaeo-Christian Tempietto del Clitunno. Some frescoes are still to be seen there which date from the early eighth century – that is, about a century after Pope Gregory the Great endorsed the use of art in the Christian Church. Though poorly preserved, these depictions of Christ the Saviour with Sts Peter and Paul and angels reveal close stylistic links both with the Byzantine mosaics of San Vitale at Ravenna and with the frescoes of Santa Maria Antiqua at Rome, dating from 705–7 – and it is no coincidence that the Tempietto lies on the direct route from Ravenna to Rome. A fresco from the late eighth or early ninth century survives in another palaeo-Christian church not far away: a jewelled cross in the apse of San Salvatore, at Spoleto. As the capital of the Longobard duchy, Spoleto had a particular importance in the High Middle Ages and there are extensive eleventh-century frescoes to be found in the Crypt of St Isaac the Hermit, beneath the church of Sant'Ansano. These scenes – *Christ in Glory, The Beheading of John the Baptist* and *The Last Supper* – clearly reveal surviving Byzantine influence, as do both the superb mosaic of the enthroned Christ, signed by Solsternus, on the façade of Spoleto's cathedral, and the twelfth-century frescoes in the Assumption chapel of Santa Maria Infraportas at Foligno.

Fine as these early examples at Spoleto and Foligno are, the fresco cycle in the abbey church of San Pietro in Valle, in the Valnerina, north-east of Terni, is of a quite different order of achievement. The Benedictine abbey was originally built by Faroaldo II, the Longobard Duke of Spoleto, and contains much distinguished early art, including the remarkable altar front, datable to 739–42, which bears a self-portrait of the sculptor who signed himself 'Ursus Magester', and the ninth-century statues of Sts Peter and Paul which stand on either side of the lateral door leading from the nave into the cloister. The fresco cycle consists of almost thirty biblical scenes, divided between the Old Testament on the left-hand wall of the nave and the New Testament on the right. Here, before our eyes, the solemn rigidity of Byzantine art yields to the new and freer forms of artistic representation emerging in Rome – and the similarity of the frescoes to those in the Roman church of San Giovanni a Porta Latina, dated 1191, has led to a similar date being proposed for the San Pietro in Valle cycle. Among the finest features of these frescoes are the powerful (almost Blake-like) Adam surrounded by animals in *The Naming of the Beasts*, a vigorous Noah receiving God's warning of the impending Flood, and the finely differentiated members of his family aboard the Ark. The evident concern to represent individuals in distinct fashion, which marks one of the most obvious moves away from Byzantine tradition, is carried on in the New Testament scenes, notably that in which Christ washes the feet of the apostles. The basilical form of the abbey church not only encouraged the complete frescoing of the flat wall surface of the nave – the individual scenes are separated by rich decorative painted frames – but allows the cycle to be seen with particular clarity today. Other early frescoes, such as those by Bonamico in the Perugian church of San Prospero, survive in the region, but the San

Pietro cycle is among the most important of its kind in the whole of Italy, and the most rewarding painting in Umbria in the period prior to the decoration of the Lower Church in the basilica at Assisi.

The basilica of St Francis is, nonetheless, unique. Nowhere in Italy is there so rich and complete a representation of the art of the late thirteenth and early fourteenth centuries. Even a partial list of those who worked on decorating the church is a roll-call of the greatest contemporary masters: Jacopo Torriti, Cimabue, Giotto, Cavallini, Pietro Lorenzetti and Simone Martini, for example. (It must be said that simply listing names is a good deal easier than making certain attributions as to individual responsibility for surviving works, and the long-standing dispute as to whether Giotto was responsible – either alone or in part – for the St Francis cycle in the Upper Church may never be resolved to everyone's satisfaction.)

Cimabue, however, was working in the Lower Church around 1280, and as part of his fresco of the *Virgin and Child with Angels* – closely related to the great *Santa Trinità Madonna* now in the Uffizi – the Florentine artist painted what is still the single most famous representation of St Francis. Along with his assistants, Cimabue was also responsible for much of the decoration of the choir, transepts and crossing of the Upper Church, though this work is today in very poor condition. The finest scene, the great *Crucifixion* on the south wall of the transept, is virtually a negative now due to chemical changes in the pigments but remains a restless, swirling depiction of a transcendent moment shaking heaven and earth. When they were first painted, Cimabue's frescoes were in themselves a source book for native Umbrian painters, for Cimabue's own varied influences are evident – Byzantine, Pisan, Roman, and native Tuscan. One Umbrian painter who was influenced was the so-called Master of St Francis, responsible for the St Francis cycle in the Lower Church. The same painter also absorbed the influence of the Pisan, Giunta Pisano, as may be seen from the two fine crucifixes of 1272, painted for the Franciscan church of San Francesco al Prato in Perugia (and today in the city's Galleria Nazionale dell'Umbria). The new sculpture played its role, too: Nicola

Pisano worked on the fountain in Perugia and the Siennese Arnolfo di Cambio on his great tomb for the Cardinal de Braye in Orvieto at the end of the thirteenth century, while Lorenzo Maitani executed his astonishing reliefs on the façade of Orvieto at the beginning of the fourteenth. By this time, Umbrian artists had access to an extensive and advanced artistic vocabulary and diverse stylistic influences, without needing to leave the region, by virtue of the range of artistic activity taking place in Assisi and elsewhere.

In Assisi, apart from Cimabue, a series of Roman painters – including Torriti, Filippo Rusuti and the Isaac Master – worked in the Upper Church in the 1290s. The poor condition of some of the frescoes, aggravated by their height, makes it hard to appreciate detail, but the boldness of conception of certain scenes – *Esau and Isaac*, for instance – is evident, as is the introduction into these paintings of important architectural features, visible in the Pentecost scene in the lunette of the entrance wall (to the left of the door).

This architectural element is much more striking, however, in the great St Francis cycle attributed to Giotto, and probably painted in the 1290s. However often seen and however familiar from reproduction, the cycle never fails to impress. Partly, this is a matter of sheer size and easy visibility. In part, too, it depends on the magnificent setting of the paintings in the four bays into which each wall is divided on each side of the nave, reinforced by the dazzling fusion of actual architectural features with the illusionistic pillars and cornices painted to contain the different scenes. More important, though, are the dramatic qualities of individual scenes and the cycle's overall narrative cogency, taking Francis from his first calling through the principal events of his mission to his death and posthumous miracles. The mood of the different scenes is remarkably varied, including exhortation to popular piety (*The Institution of the Crib* or *Preaching to the Birds*), or to institutional reform (*The Dream of Innocent III*, with St Francis preventing the collapse of the church), apocalypse and divine revelation (*The Fiery Chariot*, or *St Francis Receiving the Stigmata*) or sympathetic grief (*Death of Francis* and *The Mourning of the Clares*). The specifically painterly qualities of these frescoes are equally impressive: the composition of such scenes as *St Francis Giving His Cloak to the Beggar*, with its simple geometrical forms and bold blocks of colour, or the relationship between different decorative elements of the church, as in the scene on the mountain where St Francis's gaze leaves the painted frame to alight on the roundel of the Virgin and Child above the church door – taking the observer from one element to another as the saint is transported from the earthly realm to the divine.

If the cycle necessarily sought to invoke the divine or other-worldly – in line with its primary function as a visual aid for the Franciscan preachers – so too does it remain unprecedentedly rooted in the Umbria of its day. In his depiction of the Evangelists in the Upper Church, Cimabue had rendered the buildings of contemporary Rome, but Giotto localizes such reference in his depiction of Assisi's Roman temple (in *St Francis and the Madman*) and the Portiuncula (in *Death of St Francis*). Equally importantly, he suggests a concern with local landscapes – the rugged, forbidding mountains of *The Miracle of the Spring* and the gentler, wooded countryside in which St Francis preaches to the birds – a concern which will recur again, and often, in Umbrian art.

Giotto was extravagantly admired by his contemporaries – Dante foremost among them – and the Assisi cycle has been described by the art historian John White as 'one of the supremely important events in the history not only of Italian but of European art'. It is the more remarkable, then, that the basilica contains other, later, works entirely worthy to be ranked alongside these frescoes. In part, this was due to the importance the Church accorded St Francis and the consequent seriousness with which it regarded the construction and decoration of the basilica dedicated to him: from the Brief of Pope Innocent IV at the consecration of the church in 1253 to the bull promulgated in 1288 by the Franciscan Pope Nicholas IV, which expressed the need to 'preserve, repair, build, alter, enlarge, adapt and decorate' the basilica. Cimabue and Giotto had been brought from Florence, Torriti and Rusuti from Rome; in the early fourteenth century, it was the turn of the Siennese masters Simone Martini and Pietro Lorenzetti.

Martini and Lorenzetti had both learnt much from the greatest Siennese painter of the previous generation, Duccio di Boninsegna. When Martini came to Assisi – sometime between 1316 and the early 1320s – he was already celebrated for the great *Maestà* in Siena's Palazzo Pubblico. Now he decorated the whole of the recently built chapel of St Martin in the Lower Church: designing the stained glass and marble inlay floor, as well as painting the frescoes. The result is the most complete Italian Gothic decorative scheme to survive anywhere. The frescoes themselves depict the fourth-century St Martin, whose life as a soldier, monk and protector of the poor offered numerous parallels with St Francis's own. Martini, though, offered a quite different artistic vision from those of the St Francis Master in the Lower Church or Giotto in the Upper. Like Giotto, he showed a concern with spatial composition, placing his figures carefully in precisely delineated and suggestively shadowed architectural settings of great elegance, but in contrast to Giotto's simplicity of construction and direct handling of colour, Martini crowded his paintings with animated contemporaries, shown in courtly modern dress, rendered with endlessly subtle shadings of colour. In a scene such as Martin's investiture as a knight – a scene which would surely have appealed to the young Francis, brought up on tales of chivalry – Martini offers a varied group of richly garbed knights, one sporting a sparrowhawk on his wrist, and a fancifully dressed group of musicians. If they have little of the spirituality of Giotto's work, Martini's frescoes embody a courtly vision of life which makes it easy to see why he was Petrarch's favourite painter.

Given that Pietro Lorenzetti was also a Siennese painter brought up under the influence of Duccio, his work in Assisi – painted over several years, probably in the 1320s – could scarcely be more different from Martini's. Even his earliest contribution is a fine work: a *Madonna and Child with St John the Baptist and St Francis* in which the grace and decorative elements (the fresco is framed in paint as though it were a wood-framed polyptych) are strengthened by the dynamic relationship between the infant Christ who peers upward at Mary who in turn looks across the painted frame to St Francis who is lost in contemplation of the

Holy Child. Even such a work, however, scarcely hints at the dramatic and expressive power of Lorenzetti's fresco cycle on the life of Christ, in the crossing of the Lower Church. Each scene repays close attention but two stand out: the *Crucifixion* and the *Deposition*. In the former, Lorenzetti displays what he had learnt from Duccio (and shared with Martini), in his depiction of the animated crowd beneath the three crosses – a troop of mostly indifferent soldiers, finely dressed in the style of Lorenzetti's day – while in the bottom left corner of the composition a swooning Mary is sustained by her sorrowing but helpless companions. In contrast to the intricate, colourful group below, Christ presents a stark figure against a menacingly blue-grey sky, thronged by a host of anguished angels who suggest the impact Cimabue's *Crucifixion* in the Upper Church made on Lorenzetti. Comparable in stature to anything in the basilica, the *Deposition* is an even finer work, in which two small groups of mourning figures are connected diagonally across the picture by the body of Christ while the cross from which the body is being taken divides the composition vertically in two. To the right, one figure bends and tenses in an effort to pull the nails from Christ's feet, a second figure supports the dead body, and Mary Magdalene kneels to kiss Christ's bloody feet. To the left, a figure on a ladder gently delivers the body into the hands of a sorrowing Mary, accompanied by two other women, one of whom kisses Christ's hand with infinite reverence while the other – her uplifted hands frozen in a gesture of despair – wordlessly expresses the horror of the scene. Here, Lorenzetti has left behind the decorative elements still present in the crucifixion scene – the mourners' cloaks recall Giotto's blocks of sombre colour – while the sky behind has darkened to deep grey. The whole is a work in which a powerful composition is suffused with an extraordinary degree of drama and pathos.

Other talented painters would work in Assisi but, with the contributions of Martini and Lorenzetti, the finest phase of the decoration of the basilica was complete. It left Umbria with a treasure-house of the greatest art of the late thirteenth and early fourteenth centuries and an unsurpassable source of reference for local artists. Besides the Umbrian Master of St Francis – who attracted followers of his own – the Assisian Puccio Capanna worked in the basilica and also in the sister church of Santa Chiara, where he left an important fresco, the *Virgin and Child*, in the Cappella del Sacramento.

Any brief attempt to trace the influence on native Umbrian painters of the great artists who worked in Assisi must end in confusion, for the level of artistic activity there was extraordinarily high – especially given the turmoil of the times (Martini and Lorenzetti worked in Assisi during a period when the city was constantly at war and during which it was sacked on more than one occasion). Moreover, the growth and increasing affluence of other city-states meant that the work of masters from elsewhere could be seen widely throughout the region. In Perugia, the Roman Pietro Cavallini (or a follower) began the decoration of the Sala dei Notari in the Palazzo dei Priori, Duccio painted a panel of the *Virgin and Child* for the church of San Domenico, and Meo di Guido was present in the city in the 1320s. Some painters – the Maestro del Farneto, for instance – moved between Assisi and Perugia, and other parts of the region were equally open to a wide range of influence. The Master of the Cross of Gubbio worked in the north of the region, as did Gubbio's leading local painter, Guido Palmerucci, who was active between 1316 and 1345 and whose work can be seen in the city art museum and in the ducal palace. To the south, the Master of San Felice di Giano reveals the continuing influence of backward-looking Roman style in work which is, nonetheless, of high quality (now in the Galleria Nazionale in Perugia). For Orvieto, the Florentine Coppo di Marcovaldo painted a *Madonna and Child* in the 1260s and Simone Martini a polyptych in 1321 (these works are today in the Museo Civico and the Museo dell'Opera del Duomo). The Siennese-influenced Ugolino d'Ilario (known from 1350), meanwhile, worked in the cathedral –as did Cola Petruccioli (active after 1362), whose work is also to be found in Spello. Among the most characteristic Umbrian painters of the late fourteenth century was the Foligno-born Giovanni di Corraduccio, whose art shows a further source of influence, that of painters from the Marches. Like so many others, he worked in Assisi, and also at Montefalco where he –

or a close collaborator – provided the frescoed scenes from the life of St Anthony Abbot to be seen today in the church of San Francesco, now an important local museum.

Besides indicating, by their activity, the itinerant life of fourteenth-century painters, Giovanni di Corraduccio and Cola Petruccioli are important for having introduced International Gothic to Umbria. As the name suggests, this late-medieval style transcended national as well as regional boundaries and is to be seen as far apart in Europe as Valencia and Dijon to the west and Prague and Budapest to the east. In Italy, International Gothic made an important impact both in the Lombard cities of the north and in Naples to the south. It was particularly influential in central Italy, however, where the greatest exponent of the style was Gentile da Fabriano, whose home town lies just the other side of the Umbrian border in the Marches. Best known for the gentle, courtly and gloriously colourful *Adoration of the Magi* in the Uffizi in Florence, Gentile also worked in Umbria: his early *Virgin and Child*, painted in the first decade of the fifteenth century for San Domenico in Perugia, is today in the Galleria Nazionale there. It is a characteristically magical painting in which Gentile depicts the throne on which the Virgin sits as made of living wood, bursting into leaf. Gentile's fresco of the same subject, dating from 1425, is to be found just inside the door of Orvieto cathedral, on the left wall of the nave.

Among Umbrian artists, the most notable exponent of International Gothic was Ottaviano Nelli (*c.* 1375–after 1444), whose style – characterized by a harmony of composition, smoothness of execution and delicacy of colour – seems to have developed at much the same time as Gentile's. His *Virgin, Child and Saints*, in Perugia's Galleria Nazionale, is dated 1403 – making it contemporary with Gentile's earliest work. The central panel of the polyptych depicts a playful infant, intent on seizing the lily its mother holds. Among Nelli's finest work in Umbria are the ambitious fresco cycle, *The Life of the Virgin*, which the artist painted between 1408 and 1413 in the church of San Francesco, and the *Madonna del Belvedere* in Santa Maria Nuova, both in Nelli's home-town of Gubbio. Other works by him are to be found in the Chapel of the Palazzo Trinci in Foligno, in Santa

Maria delle Grazie in Città di Castello, and in the Cappella della Piaggiola in the village of Fossato di Vico Alto. Nelli's work overshadows that of most of his Umbrian contemporaries, though the Foligno-born Dominican friar Bartolomeo di Tommaso (known 1425–55) was a considerable artist whose work provides a conspectus of central Italian influences of his day – Siena, Florence and the Marches. It is seen to best advantage in the triptych of the *Virgin and Child, with Saints* in San Salvatore in Foligno and, in more dramatic vein, in some recently restored frescoes in the Cappella Paradisi in Terni's Franciscan church, where his representation of Hell, Purgatory and Paradise draws closely on Dante's *Divine Comedy*.

Even as International Gothic flourished, a very different sensibility was developing in central Italy. The change is embodied most remarkably in the frescoes painted collaboratively by Masolino and Masaccio in Santa Maria del Carmine's Brancacci Chapel in Florence. Masolino's work represents the culmination of the elegant, courtly, idealized world of late Gothic, while Masaccio forsakes idealization for a resolutely solid, naturalistic representation of the human figure set in an equally solid world whose manner of spatial representation is quite distinct from the stylized backgrounds favoured by earlier painters. Masolino's work is represented in Umbria only by a frescoed *Virgin and Child with Two Angels* (1432) in the church of San Fortunato in Todi, and none of Masaccio's scanty output is to be found in the region. The artistic revolution they helped bring about very quickly manifested itself, however, by means of the substantial presence of their contemporaries and of painters from the next generation: Piero della Francesca, the Beato Angelico, Benozzo Gozzoli, and Filippo Lippi. These artists, in turn, had a decisive influence on painters native to the region shortly after mid-century, leading to the beginnings of the Umbrian School itself.

It was for the church of San Domenico in Perugia that the Beato Angelico painted the polyptych now in the Galleria Nazionale dell'Umbria. It is a mature work, probably executed shortly after the celebrated *Annunciation* in Cortona, revealing something of the artist's innovatory treatment of the traditional altarpiece, in which the depiction of the enthroned Virgin with

Child surrounded by garland-bearing angels is utterly characteristic of Angelico's quiet lyricism, the artist adding to his habitual
painterly concern with gracefulness of line, wealth of detail and
wide range of colour, a spirituality derived from his vocation as
a Dominican friar. The Beato Angelico worked in Umbria on
one further occasion, in 1447, when he began the decoration of
the San Brizio chapel in Orvieto cathedral, only to be interrupted
by a summons to Rome from Pope Nicholas V.

Despite his limited representation in Umbria, Angelico exercised a considerable influence on the region's painters, both
through his works in Cortona and easily accessible Florence and
through the frequent presence of his best-known pupil, Benozzo
Gozzoli. This influence, it is true, has not always been considered
very positively: Gozzoli's fresco *Journey of the Magi*, in the
Palazzo Medici-Riccardi in Florence, depicting members of the
Medici as the three kings, has been (not inaptly) described as a
'clamorous episode of political propaganda', and his *Life of St
Francis* cycle in Montefalco has, in the past, been dismissed as
'decorative trifles'. It is not a judgement likely to be shared by
all today, even if it must be admitted that, whatever he learnt
from the Beato Angelico, it was not his master's spirituality.
Beginning in 1450, Gozzoli painted, for Montefalco's church of
San Francesco, a *Life of St Jerome* series, followed by the more
ambitious *Life of St Francis* in the central apse. Since the basilica
at Assisi can easily be seen across the Vale of Umbria from
Montefalco, Giotto's work is inevitably brought to mind – the
more so as Gozzoli sticks closely to the most familiar episodes of
the saint's life – and the comparison can hardly be anything
other than damaging. The mostly gentle, unassuming scenes
Gozzoli painted, however, are not only a result of the artistic
sensibility the artist absorbed from the Beato Angelico but an
acknowledgement of the great accretion of Franciscan legend
which had softened and sometimes sentimentalized the saint's
life in the two centuries since his death. By the mid fifteenth
century, Francis had indeed become the *alter Christus* implied by
Gozzoli's rendering of his birth in a stable, with ox and ass
looking on. Gozzoli also faithfully represented Montefalco and
the surrounding countryside in his account of St Francis blessing

the town. It was both a conscious acknowledgement of the continuing importance of Franciscanism there (St Francis himself knew the town well and, less than a decade before, in 1444, St Bernardino of Siena had presented his monogram to the church, where it may still be seen), and a deliberate localization of his art, which would soon become a marked feature of the Umbrian School. Gozzoli's work is also to be seen in many other Umbrian cities, including Perugia, Foligno, Narni, Terni, and Orvieto.

To ask whether Piero della Francesca was an Umbrian painter points up both the value and the futility of such a question. When Piero was born in Borgo San Sepolcro in 1416, the town was part of Umbrian territory: in the years immediately before and after his birth, it belonged, variously, to Città di Castello (with which it retains strong links), the Church and Fortebraccio. Yet while most of his work was done outside the modern region – in San Sepolcro, Arezzo, Monterchi and in the Marches – Piero is an Umbrian artist in a way which far transcends narrow provincialism or local loyalty. Twentieth-century critics from Roberto Longhi to Carlo Bertelli have emphasized the importance of the landscape of the upper Tiber valley to Piero's art. One of the painter's greatest masterpieces – the *Resurrection* at San Sepolcro – reveals why, for the work rejects the more exotic treatment of landscape in Andrea del Castagno's painting of the same subject which was Piero's most obvious model, in favour of a sombre, late-winter landscape of the sparsely vegetated, undulating hills of the area – a dead world to which the risen Christ will bring life. Of course, Piero's solemn, mystical art is only partly concerned with this landscape but it is the fusion, through geometry, line and colour, of the universal and the local, the divine and the human, that Piero expresses in his work – and which had an enormous impact on Umbrian painters who followed him.

The single work of Piero's to be found in Umbria today is a superb polyptych from the monastery of Sant'Antonio, now in the Galleria Nazionale in Perugia, and recently restored. The central panel shows the Virgin and Child, seated on a decidedly modern (i.e. Renaissance) throne, with the figures of St Anthony of Padua, St John the Baptist and St Clare to the left and St

Francis, St Elizabeth of Hungary and St Agatha to the right. Below, the predella's three scenes include St Francis receiving the stigmata, while above the Annunciation takes place within an arcaded, shadow-shot, Renaissance cloister, exquisitely painted.

Although the dating of the painting is uncertain, current opinion favours 1459 or 1460, making it exactly contemporary with Agostino di Duccio's decoration of the façade of the Oratory of St Bernardino (1457–61), and confirming these years as the period when Renaissance ideals took firm hold in Perugia. The 1450s and 1460s were also the time in which the art of native Umbrian painters began to make its greatest impact in the region. Benedetto Bonfigli (1420–c. 1496) was engaged in those decades (and beyond) in frescoing the Priors' Chapel (now part of the Galleria Nazionale) in the Palazzo dei Priori. The first phase of his work, done in the 1450s, concerns the life of one of Perugia's patrons, St Louis of Toulouse, while the second – still unfinished at Bonfigli's death – deals with the life of another of Perugia's three patrons, St Ercolanus. While the earlier frescoes remain essentially late Gothic works, the later ones show Bonfigli responding to Piero della Francesca's handling of space. Moreover, the St Ercolanus frescoes have the added interest of Bonfigli's detailed depiction of Perugia at the close of the Middle Ages, the old walled city still crowded with defensive towers. By contrast, Bonfigli's St Bernardino *gonfalone* – depicting the saint with Christ and a host of angelic musicians hovering over a vivid civic scene – is itself essentially a decorative late Gothic work which nevertheless depicts Agostino di Duccio's Renaissance Oratory, next to the thirteenth-century church of San Francesco al Prato. A further representation of Perugia – the city is recognizable in these depictions even today – appears in Bonfigli's *Christ Unleashing Thunderbolts on Perugia*, in the city church of Santa Maria Nuova; other works by the artist can be seen in San Fiorenzo and in the parish church of Civitella Benazzone.

The other leading figure of the first wave of the Umbrian School was another Perugian artist, Bartolomeo Caporali (1420–1503/5), whose mainly Florentine influences included Gozzoli.

Caporali's is an elegant, colourful art in which liveliness and minute attention to natural detail are preferred to profundity or the spatial experiments of Piero. His work is well represented in Perugia and the surrounding countryside. Among his finest productions are a *Pietà* (1486) in Perugia's cathedral museum and a beautifully restored *Adoration of the Shepherds* in the Galleria Nazionale; outside the city are a Crucifixion panel in the church of San Michele Arcangelo on the Isola Maggiore in Lake Trasimeno and frescoes in the churches of Santa Maria at Montelabate and the church of Fanciullata, near Deruta.

Most eclectic of the mid-century Umbrians was Fiorenzo di Lorenzo (*c.* 1440– *c.* 1525). Initially influenced by Gozzoli, Fiorenzo went on absorbing the lessons of his contemporaries, to the extent that attribution is a problem (Caporali's *Adoration of the Shepherds* was thought Fiorenzo's until recently). The artist's work is still represented in the Galleria Nazionale, however, and includes an early *Madonna and Child* and a late *Nativity*.

Like Bonfigli and Caporali, Fiorenzo came from Perugia, which, as the last really important *signoria* in the region, was fast establishing itself also as the principal centre of artistic production. Other cities, however, also produced important artists. Foligno, for instance, was the birthplace of Nicolò Alunno (*c.* 1420–1502), whose work is to be found not just in his home-town but very widely throughout the region and beyond (the polyptych he painted for the town of Cagli in the Marches is now in the Brera in Milan). Having, like so many contemporaries, fallen under the influence of Gozzoli's work in Montefalco, Alunno learnt also from artists whose works he encountered across the Apennines, such as Antonio Vivarini and Carlo Crivelli. The differences in his work become particularly evident in comparing the Gozzoli-influenced *Gonfalone della Fraternità dell'Annunziata* of 1466 (now in the Galleria Nazionale) and the late *Crucifixion, with Saints Francis and Bernardino of Siena* of 1497, in Terni's Pinacoteca Comunale, in which Alunno has forsaken Gozzoli's sweetness for a theatrical composition and dramatic use of line and colour. Works from the intervening years are widely distributed: some of the best are in the cathedral and museum of Foligno and the civic galleries of Nocera Umbra,

Spello, and Gualdo Tadino. Gualdo was also home-town to the painter Matteo da Gualdo (*c.* 1435–after 1503), whose stylized, elongated *Madonna and Child* is to be seen in the Galleria Nazionale. Matteo's work is also to be found on the façade and inside the Oratorio dei Pellegrini in Assisi, where other frescoes are by Pier Antonio Mezzastris (*c.* 1430–*c.* 1506) of Foligno, good examples of whose art can also be seen in his native city.

The work of these and other artists from throughout the region demonstrates considerable variety but also, at times, tension between different sources of inspiration not always ideally synthesized. Whether, by themselves, they would be thought of as an 'Umbrian' school is more than a little debatable. What, more than anything else, did pull them together was the presence of a single outstanding painter in Umbria in the second half of the fifteenth century – Pietro Vannucci, called Il Perugino.

Perugino was born in the small town of Castel (now Città) della Pieve around 1448 and died of plague in the village of Fontignano, where he was frescoing a tiny church, in 1523. During his lifetime, he was both an enormously productive and a greatly admired painter, called to work in Rome and Florence and sent commissions by such northern cities as Milan, Bologna and Venice. Equally important in extending his influence within Umbria were his two most distinguished pupils, Pinturicchio and the young Raphael. It was Raphael's father, the painter Giovanni Santi, who compared Perugino to Piero della Francesca and Leonardo da Vinci as the greatest artists of modern times:

> Due giovin par d'etade e par d'amori
> Leonardo da Vinci e 'l Perusino,
> Pier della Pieve, che son divin pictori

> [Two youths alike in age and loves
> Leonardo da Vinci and the Perugian
> Pier della Pieve, who are divine painters.]

What marks out Perugino from his Umbrian contemporaries is both the extent to which he absorbed the lessons of contemporary masters – the compositional mastery and concern with architecture of Piero della Francesca, and the naturalism of his

Florentine teacher, Verrocchio, for example – and the development of a feeling for landscape which took his depiction of the Umbrian countryside to unsurpassed poetic heights. Vannucci was also an artist of exceptionally wide range and sure technique. He was, for instance, at home equally with fresco painting or the new oil painting, introduced into Italy in the mid fifteenth century. He was also capable, in his early years, of working collaboratively, in the Urbino architectural style of Piero della Francesca and Luciano Laurana, on a series of small panels representing *Miracles of San Bernardino* for the Oratory in Perugia, and of painting on the largest scale in such monumental compositions as his highly influential *Christ Consigning the Keys to St Peter* in the Sistine Chapel. Perugino was sympathetic to the elaborate humanist scheme devised by Francesco Maturanzio which he painted in the Collegio del Cambio in Perugia, and unsurpassed in his rendering of the popular devotional themes – such as the Nativity – he painted so often. He was also an exceedingly fine portrait painter. The vastness of his output ensured that Perugino's work betrays an unevenness of quality – and like all major artists he employed many assistants in his work – but at its best his warmly coloured art has an unsurpassed lyrical intensity. It is an art which risks a sentimentality generally held in check by the painter's lack of self-delusion. In his life of the painter, Giorgio Vasari reported that this devotional artist was a man little given to religion and one unable to believe in the immortality of the soul. It is a reading of the man given considerable support by the brutally honest self-portrait Perugino painted, and illusionistically 'hung' on the wall of the Collegio del Cambio – the coarse, unsmiling, unlovely face of the artist who created some of the sweetest madonnas and most graceful youths of Renaissance art. One of the Perugino's most admired works is the *Transfiguration* in the Collegio del Cambio, but perhaps his most decisive achievement for central Italian art was the transfiguration of the Umbrian countryside, especially the hilly area around Lake Trasimeno, that features so often in his work. Bonfigli and Caporali used Umbrian scenes as backgrounds to their religious subjects but it was Perugino who, in his classical and Christian works alike, transformed his native region into an eternal landscape in which Love and Chastity might struggle for supremacy (as in the painting in the Louvre), where Mary, Mother of God, might become betrothed, or the shepherds adore the infant Christ. It would be Perugino's work, as much as anything, which would lead nineteenth-century visitors to the region to see Umbria as the 'Galilee of Italy'.

Despite the extensive presence of Perugino's work in collections around the world, his art is superbly represented in Umbria. Besides the paintings already mentioned, the Galleria Nazionale has an early *Adoration of the Magi* (c. 1475), the *Madonna della Consolazione* (1496) and a late *Transfiguration* (1517). Notable among works elsewhere in the region are the frescoed *St Sebastian* (1505) – the plague saint who provided Perugino with another of his favourite, or most requested, subjects – in the tiny church of San Sebastiano at Panicale, the *Assumption* altarpiece (1513) in Corciano, and the frescoed *Epiphany* (1504) painted in the Oratory of Santa Maria dei Bianchi in his home-town of Città della Pieve.

Of Perugino's immediate followers, two stand out. The first is one of the greatest figures of all European art – though today most notable for his absence in Umbria – Raffaello Sanzio (1483–1520), called Raphael. A pupil of Perugino (and a possible collaborator in the decoration of the Collegio del Cambio), Raphael worked both in Perugia and Città di Castello in the first years of the sixteenth century. Now, just three works remain in the region: a double-sided *stendardo* in the Pinacoteca Comunale in Città di Castello, and some early frescoes in the oratories of Sant'Agostino and San Severo in Perugia. The remainder of Raphael's Umbrian output has been long dispersed – mostly looted by the French during the Napoleonic period. Some of Perugino's finest paintings went the same way: the *Betrothal of the Virgin*, which once graced a chapel in Perugia's cathedral, is now in the museum at Caen, and Raphael's extraordinary reinterpretation of the same theme after Perugino's example is now in the Brera in Milan (Città di Castello, for whose Franciscan church the picture was painted, feels the loss deeply to this day). Among other dispersed paintings from Raphael's Umbrian period are the *Madonna of Foligno* (now in the Vatican Museum), a *Crucifixion* (formerly in San Domenico in Perugia and now in the National Gallery in London) and the *Deposition* painted for Atalanta Baglioni (now in the Galleria Borghese in Rome).

The second important pupil of Perugino was Bernardo di Betto, called Il Pinturicchio (1454–1523). Like Raphael, Pinturicchio was greatly impressed by Perugino's handling of the complex relationship between foreground figures and architectural settings, as can easily be seen in the Vatican fresco of *Christ Consigning the Keys to Saint Peter*. Whereas Raphael developed this relationship in the direction of a simplified, more monumental approach, Pinturicchio tended to a colourful narrative art which lacks profundity but is fecund in decorative detail. Pinturicchio also worked widely outside Umbria, notably in Rome (where Raphael spent most of his short life), and in Siena, where he frescoed the Piccolomini chapel in the cathedral. Fortunately, he is also represented by fine work in Perugia (the Sala del Consiglio of the Palazzo dei Priori), Spoleto (the cathedral), and – best of all – in Santa Maria Maggiore in Spello. There, Pinturicchio decorated the Cappella Baglioni (1501) with three separate fresco scenes: an *Annunciation*, *Adoration of the Shepherds and Arrival of the Magi*, and a *Dispute in the Temple*. These, and the frescoed sibyls in the chapel vaulting – not to mention the framed self-portrait 'hung' on the chapel wall – reveal clearly Pinturicchio's enormous debt to Perugino, while the painter's own decorative sensibility helps bring to mind the whole history of fifteenth-century Umbrian art to which these frescoes provide a glorious coda.

One other major painter was working in Umbria at the end of the fifteenth century but, as Pinturicchio seems to look backwards, Luca Signorelli (*c.* 1445–1523) points forward to a High Renaissance art in which Umbrian painters would play almost no role. Signorelli himself, in fact, was born not in Umbria but in the border town of Cortona, and his style was formed on the example both of Piero della Francesca and, as regards his interest in figure painting, of the Florentine, Antonio Pollaiolo. While he is understandably well represented in his birthplace, it is worth seeking out some of the least-known frescoes in Umbria: those Signorelli painted in the tiny church in Morra, which include a version of the artist's celebrated *Flagellation*, now in the Brera. Signorelli's masterpiece, however, is the San Brizio chapel in Orvieto cathedral, which the Beato Angelico had started to fresco before being called to Rome in 1447. Half a century later, Signorelli began six scenes centring on the Day of Judgement: *The Preaching of the Antichrist, The End of the World, The Resurrection of the Dead, The Last Judgement, The Elect* and *The Damned*. Signorelli's work could scarcely be more different from the Baglioni chapel frescoes on which Pinturicchio was working simultaneously. While the latter's imaginative refinement gives no hint of the turmoil affecting the region (the Baglioni family were murdering each other in Perugia as the Spello chapel was being built), Signorelli's seem to speak of the cataclysm of the present day, as well as of the end of time. The decade in which Signorelli worked, in fact, saw not only French armies marching past Orvieto's rock on their way to Rome, but the religious and political tumult brought about by the fervid preaching of the Dominican friar Savonarola in Florence, before he was burned at the stake in 1498. It is to the earthly chaos Savonarola's uncompromising ascetism brought about that Signorelli alludes in his *Preaching of the Antichrist*, and the artist's stress on human responsibility is emphasized by his presentation of the devils of later scenes in human form, rendered demonic by the grotesque grey, green, pink and purple of their flesh. Signorelli's attraction to the dynamic figure studies of Pollaiolo is evident throughout the cycle – in the laboured movements of the dead emerging from their tombs, for instance – but nowhere more so than in the contortions of the bent, twisted, fleeing, flung and tortured damned. Dante, whose portrait Signorelli painted elsewhere in the chapel, obviously lies behind the artist's depiction of these eschatological scenes, yet Signorelli's artistic vision is far different from that of Bartolomeo di Tommaso in the comparable scenes he painted in Terni just half a century before. Thirty years later, after another Sack of Rome, Michelangelo would pass Orvieto on his way from Florence to Rome, where he would paint his own *Last Judgement* in the Sistine Chapel.

By the time Michelangelo's great work was finished, the last city-state in Umbria would have fallen definitively under papal control. Painting did not stop in the region, of course, but while the papacy diverted Umbrian revenues towards the rebuilding of Rome itself, the region began its long slide into becoming a cultural and political backwater. By 1523, when he died, even Perugino's time had passed and Raphael, already long lost to Umbria, was also dead. For the most part, Perugino's contemporaries were content to learn from him. The best of these is perhaps Giovanni di Pietro, Lo Spagna (*c.* 1450–1528), who quickly absorbed the lessons of Raphael also, but there is often fine work by many local artists of the time to be seen throughout the region, including that by Tiberio d'Assisi (*c.* 1470–1524), Giannicola di Paolo (*c.* 1462–1544), Mariano di Ser Austerio (known 1493–1527), and Pier Matteo d'Amelia (known 1467–1508), who also worked with Fra Lippo Lippi on the Florentine artist's superb frescoes in the Duomo at Spoleto. Most local painters of the next generation – and there were many – tended to take their lead from Raphael. They include Berto di Giovanni (known 1488–1529), Sinibaldo Ibi (*c.* 1475–after 1548), and Eusebio da San Giorgio (1465/70–after 1540), whose fine *Adoration of the Magi* (1505) in the National Gallery in Perugia shows how quickly a talented painter could acquire the younger master's artistic vocabulary. Other sixteenth-century Umbrian artists looked elsewhere: to Michelangelo in the case of the gifted Perugian Domenico Alfani (*c.* 1480–*c.* 1553) and the Assisian, Dono Doni (d. 1575), or in the case of the eclectic Bernardino di Mariotto (known 1498–1566) to Pinturicchio, Signorelli, and Crivelli.

As native inspiration failed, more important artists from outside Umbria occasionally worked in the region or sent commissioned works to it. Among a handful of sixteenth-century works worth searching out, the best is a characteristically vibrant and dramatic *Transfiguration* by Rosso Fiorentino (1494–1540), in the cathedral of Città di Castello. The north Italian Il Pordenone (*c.* 1484–1539) left a fresco in Alviano, and Spoleto cathedral has a *Madonna and Child* by the Bolognese Annibale Carracci (1560–1609). By the end of the sixteenth century the centres of artistic excellence and connoisseurship were indisputably elsewhere, and even a cursory glance at the region's museums will confirm the dearth of talent discernible in most of the ecclesiastical and civic buildings of Umbria. The occasional surprise – an appreciable *Christ in the Garden* by Guido Reni in San Pietro in Perugia (which also has paintings by Lanfranco and Guercino), or Guercino's *Mary Magdalene*, now in the Pinacoteca Comunale in Spoleto – merely confirms such works as the exceptions they are. Such local vitality as existed in the years of Umbria's decline is best seen today in the region's popular art: particularly in painted and ceramic votive tablets, of which there are notable collections in the Diocesan museum in Spoleto and the church of Madonna dei Bagni near Deruta. Here, in contrast to the remote concerns of Counter-Reformation theology with which more ambitious art frequently concerned itself, popular piety found an often vivid artistic expression. The eighteenth and nineteenth centuries reveal scarcely a painter whose name is known outside the region – though Francesco Appiani frescoed the cupola of the Baroque church of San Filippo Neri in Perugia. A revealing indication of the backward-looking culture that marked the last decades of the Papal States is provided by the presence in Umbria of the French artist Jean-Baptiste Wicar, whose principal source of inspiration was Perugino, and whose works include copies of looted paintings by the master himself.

Fortunately, the story of Umbrian painting is not simply one of decline. The twentieth century has again seen the emergence of artists who must be considered important in national and even international terms. Among the leading painters of the second wave of Futurism was Perugia-born Gerardo Dottori (1884–1977), a signatory of the *Manifesto dell'aeropittura* of 1929, examples of whose art are to be seen in the Palazzo della Penna in Perugia, where they are displayed in an appropriately modern and European context, alongside work by the German conceptual artist, Joseph Beuys. Spoleto, too, has produced an important modern artist in the sculptor Leoncillo Leonardi, known as Leoncillo (1915–68). Leoncillo began as a figurative artist: *Roman Mother Killed by the Germans* (1944) is a wartime work and *Portrait of Elsa* (1948) dates from the immediate post-war years.

In line with many other artists caught up in the political and artistic debates of post-fascist Italy, Leoncillo endeavoured to combine an awareness of history with a formalist aesthetic but, following his association with the *Informale* group, his work – largely polychrome and enamelled ceramics – turned increasingly in the direction of abstraction. He did not disdain traditional cultural reference, however, and if such works as *Red Wind* (1958) and *White Cut* (1959) make great play with their turbulent terracotta and enamel surfaces, the lacerated surface of *St Sebastian* (1962) alludes to iconography familiar enough in Umbria, while still laying primary stress on surface and texture. Leoncillo's *St Sebastian* is to be found, along with other of his pieces, in the Museo Comunale d'Arte Moderna in Spoleto, which also holds works by important twentieth-century Italian artists such as Carla Accardi, Giuseppe Capogrossi, Mario Ceroli and Renato Guttuso. Not too far away, in Trevi, the Flash Art museum (connected to the international art magazine of that name) is another gallery devoted to modern art, specializing in exhibitions of the contemporary avant-garde in Italy and elsewhere.

Among twentieth-century Umbrian painters, one above all stands out as an artist of world stature – Alberto Burri. His status was most recently confirmed in the context of a major exhibition, *The Italian Metamorphosis 1943–68*, held in the winter of 1994–5 in the Guggenheim Museum in New York, shortly before his death in February 1995. Burri was born in 1915 in Città di Castello, where he endowed a museum of his work on two sites: in the fifteenth-century Palazzo Albizzini in the city centre and in converted tobacco-drying sheds a little further out. At the outset of his career in the immediate post-war period, Burri repudiated the figurative in favour of a concern with the materials of art – notably degraded and discarded industrial materials like sacking, tar, and iron – which he sewed, stretched, creased, slashed or glued to make collages as meticulously composed as the paintings of Piero della Francesca yet which self-consciously draw attention to, rather than away from, their materials. This continuing concern of the artist's is emphasized in the titles of several important series – *Tars*, begun in 1949, *Sacks*, started in the following year, and later *Iron*, *Woods*, and

Plastic. In 1951, Burri was one of the signatories of the Origine group manifesto, which argued against an outmoded figurative/ abstract antithesis in favour of a morally valid expressive quality. This position took the artist close to contemporary American Abstract Expressionism, while his techniques had a profound influence on the collages of Robert Rauschenberg, who first encountered Burri's work in 1952. In the course of his long career, Burri explored, with equivalent degrees of restlessness and coherence, a wide range of materials, including wood, plastic and cellotex. The master of the discarded has also worked with gold with notable success, as in the design of some wonderful brooches or in *Black and Gold* (1992–3). He has explored colour – in the masterly *Red Black* (1955) or the vivid *Sestante* (1982) – and its absence, in the *Sacchi* or *Grande Cellotex 4* (1975). Among his most distinctive works of the sixties were *Combustion* (1963) and *Red Plastic* (1964), in which he used fire both as a tool and a pigment. The conversion of the former tobacco-drying sheds to use as a studio allowed Burri to work on an even larger scale. If the surfaces of some later work became less disturbed, his late production retained its vigour, as in the Ovidian *Metamorfotex* (1991). Visitors to Umbria will come to admire the work of Giotto in Assisi, Perugino in Perugia, Pinturicchio in Spello and Signorelli in Orvieto; it would be a pity if they were to leave without visiting Città di Castello, to explore the art of Alberto Burri.

CHAPTER ELEVEN

Food and Wine

✳

In Umbria, as in the rest of Italy, food plays an important part in everyday life. Moreover, the region is not only a wine-producing area of long standing but, in terms of quality, an increasingly important one. If cooking is important throughout Italy, however, there is, as Elizabeth David rightly pointed out to British readers several decades ago, no such thing as Italian cooking. Rather, there is a series of regional cuisines – any one of which may relate closely to that of its immediate neighbours – which, in the country as a whole, reveals quite profound differences based on geographical location and history, so that, to take extreme examples, the cooking of the Val d'Aosta bears scant resemblance to the fare on offer in Sicily.

Overall, Umbrian food is not unlike that to be found either in southern Tuscany or in northern Lazio, yet it nevertheless retains dishes and variations on dishes which are to be found nowhere else in the country. Indeed, to be accurate, one might say that there is no such thing even as a single cuisine within the region, for foods and dishes that are widely eaten in, say, Perugia may be wholly unknown in Orvieto. What does unite Umbrian cooking, however, is simplicity and the conservative demands of the region's inhabitants. As a still important agricultural region, Umbria continues to reflect seasonal availability and bases its eating on a limited range of high-quality meat (including game), vegetables, pulses, grain and olive oil. In a region so prodigal in olive trees, olive oil is predictably important (and regional production is now organized, rather like wine, into six DOC areas: Lago Trasimeno, Colli Perugini, Colli Martani, Colli di Orvieto, Colli Amerini, Colli Appenninici). Lacking a dairy industry, the cooking of Umbria remains as distinct from the cream-based cooking of Emilia-Romagna, not far to the north, as it does from the marked spiciness of southern Italian food.

The long-standing agricultural traditions of the region should not delude the visitor into the belief that the food on offer is itself 'traditional' in any long-standing sense. Rural poverty was so widespread in Umbria for centuries that the average diet was extremely and sometimes dangerously restricted. Few Umbrians ate meat regularly until this century, and when they did that meat might be badger, hedgehog or porcupine (this last is still eaten by country people in the north of the region, despite official discouragement). In the last decades of the nineteenth century, the widespread dependence on maize flour led to a high incidence of pellagra, a disease marked not only by disfiguration of the skin but also by nervous and psychic disorders. With increased prosperity, a much higher proportion of Umbrians have been able to enjoy what their region can provide, and those in the country take great pride in what they themselves produce: the gifts most frequently offered to anyone who does a favour to their country neighbours are eggs, chickens, and rabbits from the farmyard, home-grown fruit and vegetables, extending perhaps to freshly picked mushrooms or chestnuts in autumn, wild boar in winter and the gift of a goose at Christmas or a lamb at Easter. Many of the genuinely simple country dishes of the past can also still be found in the region and are frequently delicious – so long, of course, as they do not constitute the only food available.

The pattern of Umbrian eating still tends to differ from that of northern Europe. Breakfast is taken very early in the country and frequently consists of nothing more than a cup of coffee. In the city, the meal will most likely be eaten standing up in a bar, when a brioche, croissant or sweet pastry may accompany a black coffee or cappuccino. In the country – and for school-children whose day begins early – a mid-morning snack (*merenda*) is common. Here – as at other odd times during the day – Umbrians may eat one of their most characteristic foods, the *torta al testo*. This flat bread, usually salted and variously made of white or maize flour, cooked on a griddle and often served with raw ham or sausage, is widely available and no one should believe they are familiar with Umbrian, especially Perugian, cooking without having tried it at least once.

The principal meal for most Umbrians today, which consists of a *primo piatto* or first course (usually pasta), and a second (meat) course, possibly preceded by an *antipasto*, and finishing with dessert (often fresh fruit), is largely a middle-class creation of the late nineteenth century which has gradually achieved a wider social diffusion with the recent increase in regional prosperity. This substantial meal, served in the middle of the day, is known in Umbria as *'pranzo'* (though called *'colazione'* in many other parts of Italy) and is eaten more widely than visitors from northern Europe might expect. For the most part, Umbria still shuts down for several hours in the middle of the day (with shops closing between 1 p.m. and 4 or 4.30 p.m. in winter and between 1 p.m. and 4.30 or 5 p.m. in summer). Even today, when so many younger women work outside the home, the extended Umbrian family – with grandmothers and even great-grandmothers frequently living under the same roof – mostly ensures that some female hand is available to prepare the family lunch. A simpler – sometimes very simple – meal, perhaps of a *piatto unico* or single dish, is usually served in the evening.

The conservatism of Umbrians as regards their food can be seen in the almost total lack of familiarity with any other kinds of eating, so that many (and most outside the towns) will never have tasted other Italian regional dishes, let alone other national cuisines. Umbrian supermarkets simply do not stock the variety of international foodstuffs now commonly available in Britain or in much of the United States, and international eating out is restricted to a small handful of Chinese restaurants, mostly in Perugia. When Umbrians go out to eat, they like to eat familiar food, so that the menus of restaurants throughout the region are marked by a much greater uniformity than is often the case elsewhere. Even the meals marking great family celebrations – christenings, first communions, and weddings – so beloved by Umbrians of even modest means, who invest their savings in extending invitations to dozens and sometimes hundreds of guests, stick to the same familiar pattern, simply adding a greater number of dishes to each course. There are, in fact, exceptions to these general rules at either end of the culinary spectrum. Strangely, even aberrantly, Umbria is home to one of Italy's finest and most innovative chefs, Gianfranco Vissani, whose recipes appear in the Friday colour supplement of the leading newspaper, *La Repubblica*, and whose restaurant at Civitella del Lago, on the road from Todi to Orvieto, is a regular, if controversial, winner of culinary honours. (In the autumn of 1994, it was named the best in all Italy by two leading restaurant critics, Edoardo Raspelli, of *La Stampa*, and Federico Umberto d'Amato, of the *Espresso* restaurant guide.) At a less ex-alted (and less expensive) level, fast-food is represented in Umbria not only by the ubiquitous *pizza al taglio* or take-away pizza shops but, since 1994, by a branch of McDonald's in Perugia.

What then do Umbrians eat? *Antipasti* – the Italian hors d'oeuvre – are almost uniformly good. They include *bruschetta* and *crostini* – bread respectively toasted in the oven and served with the tasty local olive oil, and untoasted and topped with chicken liver pâté, mushrooms or truffles. If *bruschetta* and *crostini* have now become – and perhaps, with that rapid change of culinary fashion so alien to Italy, ceased to be – staples in numerous restaurants in London and New York, they are rarely as good there as in Umbria, for reasons that are not hard to understand. For a start, the most usual kind of Umbrian bread is notably different from other Italian breads. Characteristically, it is a close-textured bread made without salt, the feature – reput-edly a response to the hated imposition of a papal salt tax on Perugia in the sixteenth century – which leads to a division between those who find the bread insipid and those who think it delicious. (Few people fail to enjoy such Umbrian specialities as *pan nociato*, small bread rolls with pecorino and walnuts or pine kernels added.) *Bruschetta* demands the finest-quality olive oil and that Umbria offers in abundance, and with all the individual variations characteristic of locally or home-produced oil. The widespread use of chicken as a principal dish also ensures that the chicken livers used for *crostini* are fresh and not frozen. If

Umbria is far from unique in its use of mushrooms – Italians love and creatively exploit the full range of mushrooms available wherever they grow – its wooded hills are especially abundant in prized varieties like *porcini* and *ovuli*. So far as truffles are concerned, Umbria is renowned throughout Italy. The white truffle – also much prized in Piedmontese cooking – is characteristic of the area around Gubbio (top prices for the 1994 harvest reached a staggering L 3,000,000 a kilo!). More characteristic still is the black truffle, or *tartufo nero*, with its distinctively pungent smell and delicate flavour, found above all in the mountainous areas around Norcia, Cascia and Spoleto. There truffle hounds search out one of Umbria's most valued products, variously eaten grated on to pasta or risotto, as part of made dishes, or to flavour mayonnaise for *crostini*. (Some truffles are also used to make one of Umbria's least appealing products, liqueurs *al tartufo* which, to the surprise of no one except the locals, have made little progress beyond the region.)

If Norcia is the source of the region's finest truffles, it is also the most celebrated source of another much-used ingredient in Umbrian *antipasti*: raw hams, sausages and salami. Indeed, so famous is Norcia for these products that, in a very wide area of central Italy, extending south of Rome and beyond, the shops that sell these products are known are *norcinerie*. In fact, no one visiting Norcia itself will miss the importance of these delicacies, for squeezed between St Benedict's birthplace and the sixteenth-century papal fortress in the town's main square and extending to all the surrounding streets are numerous *norcinerie*, mostly marked by the stuffed heads of wild boar (*cinghiali*) that succeed in maintaining a ferocious appearance even in death (hams and small salami made from the meat of *cinghiali* are highly prized here, as elsewhere in the region). Umbria is, in fact, a significant pig-rearing area, and if Umbrian hams are stronger and more rustic than those of Parma or San Daniele, they are excellent nonetheless. Besides its range of hams, salami and *salamini*, Umbria also offers *capocollo* – a dried ham cut from above the shoulder, rolled and covered with pepper before being hung – which is called *coppa* elsewhere in central Italy. Confusingly – and the naming of Italian foods and dishes is nothing if not confusing – *coppa* in Umbria refers to a distinctive and excellent brawn flavoured with fennel seeds and orange peel.

Alongside such pork products, Umbria offers a number of other dishes which may be served as *antipasti* or even as a first course. Especially refreshing in summer – and considerably more delicious than its main ingredient may suggest – is *panzanella*, made by soaking stale bread in water for a quarter of an hour or so, squeezing it as dry as possible, seasoning it with olive oil, salt, pepper, vinegar and crushed basil leaves, and mixing it with diced tomatoes and onions and whatever other fresh vegetables are available, preferably red or green peppers. *Panzanella* is, in fact, a tastier variant of a dish much eaten by the poor in Umbria and elsewhere – *pancotto*, stale bread, covered with water and seasoned with a little salt and garlic, and cooked for around half an hour before being served with a little olive oil; though still eaten, especially by those who recall it as a dish from childhood, it is one of those acquired tastes that are perhaps not altogether worth acquiring.

What are worth searching out are the first courses of the Umbrian countryside. Contrary to popular belief abroad, pasta (at least in its myriad modern forms) is a relatively recent innovation in large areas of Italy. Certainly, a form of pasta was widely made in farmhouses in the last century, either from wheat flour alone or mixed with maize flour; this was then cut in thick ribbons (*tagliatelle* or, in local dialect, *tajatelle*) or roughly and unevenly cut (*maltagliati*). Other forms of pasta are of more recent derivation: the large international firm of Buitoni – based partly in Perugia – traces its origins back to 1827 when Giobatta Buitoni and his wife Giovanna Boninsegna opened a small pasta shop in the Tuscan town of Borgo San Sepolcro; in the 1850s, the family opened another shop just across the border in Città di Castello, the business expanding from there over the course of the next century. The first machine-made pasta, however, did not appear in Perugia until around 1870, when a small factory opened in Via dell'Oratorio; known as *pasta da Napoli*, it was considered a great luxury. Though most pasta eaten in Umbria today is commercially produced or bought as fresh pasta from specialist shops or supermarkets, many cooks still prefer to make their own and few would not make the effort at least for festive occasions. Especially characteristic of Umbria are the thick, square spaghetti known as *umbricelli*, or sometimes *ciriole* (as at Terni, where they are served *alla Ternana*, with a sauce made of tomatoes, garlic, olive oil, parsley, salt, pepper and the local sheep's cheese, pecorino). Among the sauces the visitor might hope to find in local restaurants – perhaps in the *agriturismi* which dedicate themselves to offering local dishes – *sugo alle rigaglie*, made with chicken innards, parsley, onion and herbs, is especially tasty; the mixture is sometimes served on *crostini* also. Pasta (often the short tubular *penne*) *alla Norcina* is a speciality of Norcia, now found widely throughout the region: the rich sauce is made of sausage, cream and grated truffle. Though by no means exclusively Umbrian, dishes such as *pasta e fagioli* (pasta and beans) or *pasta e ceci* (pasta and chickpeas) are made with local produce and widely eaten.

Among pulses, the most characteristically Umbrian are lentils. Those grown on the vast upland plain of Castelluccio, in the mountains above Norcia, are the most celebrated in all Italy – and priced accordingly. Unlike most pulses, these do not need soaking prior to use, but are cooked slowly in water, with garlic and celery. At the last moment, salt and the region's rich olive oil are added. The lentils may then be served on *bruschetta*. Eaten along with the rich *cotechino* sausage, lentils form the dish most typically eaten in Umbria – as throughout most of Italy – at midnight on New Year's Eve, to bring good luck in the coming year.

Polenta, too, is popular in the region. It may come as a first course, served with a tomato-based sauce or, occasionally, as an accompaniment to a main course. This habit almost certainly derives from the past when polenta – made from maize flour and hence more accessible to the poor – was served as a *piatto unico*. Spread out on a *spianatoia* – one of the huge pastry boards found throughout Italy – and marked roughly into individual portions, it would form the entire meal of the family who would consume it sitting around the kitchen table; if the sauce was made of sausage, a whole sausage might be placed in the middle, constituting a prize for the first to finish the polenta itself.

Such rough country dishes – made from inexpensive materials for a hard-working family – are perhaps the category of food that is fastest disappearing in the region. At their poorest, the passing of these dishes is perhaps not greatly to be lamented. *Sbobba*, for instance, was made of boiled and well-chopped cabbage, heated in a pan with olive oil, salt and bits of maize bread, while the same dish, made with cauliflower in place of cabbage, is *smulicato*. *Mpastojata* was made with a sauce of tomatoes, chopped herbs, and beans or chickpeas to which water was added, preparatory to the gradual addition of maize flour, the whole being eaten by the family from a single pot; any leftovers were served for breakfast the following day. Other *piatti unici*, however, were by no means poor fare, especially those connected with the annual killing of the pig, usually in January. Then, the family might eat *mijaccio*, made with salted pig's blood, to which was added pinenuts, sultanas, orange peel, fat, sugar and breadcrumbs, the whole being placed in a large earthenware dish and cooked for an hour or so. Around Gubbio, a dish made with pig's blood cooked with water, wine, orange peel, cheese, and beaten egg goes by the name of *miacetto*. None of these dishes is likely to feature on any menu a tourist sees and neither are many of the other ways in which Umbrians made use of every part of the pig which – if they were lucky enough to have one – would be their principal source of protein throughout the year. Neither *sanguinaccio* nor *budellucci affumicati* are any longer common; the former is a blood pudding, the second, pig's innards, seasoned with fennel seeds, salt and pepper, and left to smoke in the farmhouse chimney for a week. *Mazzafegati* (sometimes *mezzafegati*), a sausage made from pig's liver, with a little salt, orange or lemon peel and pine kernels, are still widely available from butchers' shops and occasionally feature on restaurant menus.

In comparison to these dishes, Umbrian main courses are both more conventional and widely available. Pork again features prominently throughout the region. The most famous dish is, surprisingly, found neither in restaurants nor at home but is sold from mobile vans which ply their trade in local markets and along the sides of Umbria's roads. This is *porchetta* – a young pig, roasted whole in a wood oven, with herbs and spices including fennel and black pepper. Served, sliced, in a crusty round roll, a *panino*, it is delicious. Otherwise, pork appears mostly in simple forms – pork chops, less fatty than those in England, are usually grilled very simply and often served with a sausage or two. Sausages may also be served as a main course in themselves, sometimes accompanied by beans as in Tuscany, or cooked on top of the oven in an earthenware pot with grapes – a truly Umbrian speciality seemingly unknown elsewhere (*faraona*, or guinea fowl, is also frequently cooked with grapes in this manner). Sheep-rearing is also an important activity in the region and lamb consequently makes frequent appearances on menus, although it is less often eaten at home. *Agnello alla scottadito* (a dish which, as 'finger-burning lamb', loses something in translation) consists of a generous portion of small chops, usually accompanied by lemon. Less frequently seen, though by no means uncommon, are *trecce* – the intestines – of lamb spiced and served in the plaits from which they take their name, and *coratella* or *coratina*, innards similarly spiced and served cut into small pieces. Either dish is well worth tasting and non-Italian speakers (even those who are certain they do not like offal) have been known to order and enjoy both. Veal – not factory-reared – is now seen frequently on menus though it could not be considered a typically Umbrian dish. Beef, however, is rarely offered and steaks are virtually unknown – surprisingly, perhaps, since northern Umbria borders on the Val di Chiana, source of the famous steaks sold in Florence as *bistecche alla fiorentina*.

Game, by contrast, is abundant in season and generally available, though frozen, at other times in tourist areas. Wild boar (*cinghiali*) are present in substantial numbers in the thick woods found throughout most of Umbria, where, between October and January – the dates vary – they are hunted, often with more noise and enthusiasm than success, by squads of hunters and their dogs. Umbrians are such keen hunters that while the region stands only in sixteenth place among Italy's twenty regions in terms of population, it is fourth in the number of hunting permits issued. Strangely, not all of those who invest such time, energy and expense in hunting the boar much care for its taste, so that there is usually plenty to be found in restaurants in the region. There, as in private homes, it is usually marinated in red wine and herbs (often for twelve or more hours) before being stewed with tomatoes, olive oil, lard, pepper and salt; the result is a dish at once rich and satisfying, especially in winter. The other principal game of Umbria are doves and hares. The former are hunted especially during the autumn migration in October and are frequently served with black olives; a recipe involving olives, raw ham, capers, garlic, onion, sage, red wine, oil, salt and pepper, sometimes known as *palombacce alla Todina* (i.e. from Todi), is found throughout the region. Hare are usually cooked using a very similar recipe.

If these meat dishes appear throughout the region, however, main dishes of fish are much more limited geographically, not least because of Umbria's lack of a sea coast, so that fresh fish is eaten principally in the area immediately around Lake Trasimeno and in some mountain areas, where river trout are caught. Lake Trasimeno has long been prized for its fish (it was much fought over in the twelfth and thirteenth centuries for that reason) but today little of the much-diminished catch is seen, except in local restaurants such as Da Settimio in San Feliciano, and Sauro, on one of the lake-islands, the Isola Maggiore. Today there are still 180 registered professional fishermen around the lake, but a survey in 1994 showed that just over half were aged sixty or more, and hence officially retired, while a further quarter would reach retirement age within three years; since only two registered fishermen are aged thirty or under, lake fish may soon become a thing of the past. At present, though, it is still possible to find a variety of fish, of which tench, carp and, especially, eel are the most prized. The most characteristic carp dish is *regina alla porchetta*, which involves placing a finely chopped blend of garlic, wild fennel, lard and seasonings inside a carp weighing two or three kilos, covering the fish with branches of rosemary and binding it together with reeds from the lake, after which the fish is cooked on a spit over an open fire. The lake eels may be served cut in pieces either as *tegamaccio*, a rich blend of tomatoes, chili peppers, onion, parsley, salt and pepper, or as a fish of around two kilos – called *capitone* – when it is covered in beaten egg yolk and breadcrumbs and cooked with tomatoes, garlic, white wine, parsley and seasoning. *Capitone* remains the traditional dish eaten in the area around the lake on Christmas Eve.

The association of particular dishes with different feast-days remains, in fact, much stronger in Umbria than in many other parts of Europe. This is particularly so where cakes, biscuits and other sweetmeats are concerned. Umbrians generally make few desserts for everyday meals, preferring fresh fruit (strawberries, melons, water-melons, apples, pears, apricots, and figs are all locally produced and seasonally available, alongside oranges, peaches and persimmons from elsewhere). Nor does cheese often form part of a meal at home, though Umbrian sheep's cheese (*pecorino*), available in different stages of maturation from the soft, young variety to the harder, nuttier older cheese, is excellent. (First-time visitors to the region may be disconcerted to find *pecorino sardo locale* on offer and should know that this 'local Sardinian pecorino' refers to the cheese made by Sardinian shepherds who migrated to Umbria to pasture their flocks in the 1960s, after native Umbrians had abandoned the land.) For special occasions, however, Umbria offers a remarkable range of characteristic breads and cakes, some of which are now available from cake-shops (*pasticcerie*) all year round, though often only in localized parts of the region. A typical autumn example from Perugia is *brustengolo*, based on maize flour combined with water to produce a kind of polenta which is then mixed with a little olive oil and sweetened with sliced apples, nuts, sultanas, and sugar, and cooked in the oven. For All Saints' and All Souls' Day (1 and 2 November and a big national holiday), *fave* and *stinchi dei morti* are popular. *Fave* are biscuits named for their shape, the word simply meaning 'broad beans', though they are allegedly late descendants of the sacral beans the Romans offered to their dead. In fact, most attempts to make connections between the eating habits of contemporary Umbrians and those of their Roman or Etruscan forebears are best taken with a pinch of salt. Virtually all that can be confidently said is that many of the Umbrian foodstuffs eaten today – such as truffles – were also enjoyed by the Romans, as we know from such works as Apicius's *De Re Coquinaria* – a work composed by various hands between the first and fourth centuries AD. *Stinchi dei morti*, made of peeled and crushed sweet and bitter almonds, diced candied fruit, a small glass of liqueur, powdered chocolate and egg white, are moulded into the shape of the dead men's shin-bones from which they take their gruesome name, and glazed with beaten and stiffened egg white and flour.

Christmas predictably has its traditions in Umbria, although in cooking as in other things – the use of the Christmas tree rather than the crib and Father Christmas rather than the Befana – some are of relatively recent appearance. Following the traditional *capitone* for Christmas Eve, Christmas dinner formerly included *cappelletti in brodo*, capon and *torciglione*. The *cappelletti* (meat-stuffed home-made pasta in a meat broth) remain, and though capon has now largely given way to other birds, including turkey as well as goose, the chosen bird will be served with another Umbrian speciality, *gobbi alla parmigiana* – cardoons, called *cardi* in Italian but always known as *gobbi* in Umbria, cooked in the oven with tomatoes and cheese. In some, but not all, parts of the region *maccheroni dolci* (sweet macaroni) are eaten at Christmas; extremely rich, they are made with pasta, honey, dark cocoa powder, breadcrumbs, lemon rind, hazelnuts, almonds, walnuts, nutmeg, cinnamon, rum and alkermes. Around Perugia, *torciglione* – based on flour and ground almonds and cooked in the oven – remains indispensable. What gives *torciglione* its real distinctiveness is its coiled shape – representing, by different accounts, a snake or the eels of Lake Trasimeno (this is emphasized by the provision of a head and eyes by the use of glacé cherries and silvered confectionery balls). These can be bought in almost any pastry-shop in the area – Perugia's leading *pasticceria*, Sandri, in the Corso Vannucci has an enticing display for much of the year – but many Perugians still make their own and for them Christmas without a *torciglione* would be as unthinkable as a Christmas without a Christmas pudding for many English people.

Another specifically Perugian creation is the *torcolo di San Costanzo*. The word *torcolo* itself is often used throughout the region to refer to any cake in the shape of a ring, so that *torcoli* are frequently made of sponge cake. The *torcolo di San Costanzo*, however, is quite distinct, being made of a sweet bread dough with sultanas and candied fruit. It is found only in Perugia, where it is made in honour of the city's patron saint, whose day falls on 29 January; again, despite ready availability around that date, many people continue to make their own at home. Carnival is no longer the great feast it used to be, but if you would be hard-pushed to find anyone eating *minestra con testa di maiale* – a soup with pig's head once eaten on Shrove Tuesday or Thursday – the Perugian taste for the Carnival treat of *strufoli*, made of yeast dough, deep-fried and covered with honey, remains strong. This typical sweet is found at no other time and nor are the *fritelle di San Giuseppe*, cinnamon-flavoured rice doughnuts, another speciality of Perugia and made only for the feast-day of St Joseph on 19 March. If Carnival has all but gone as a popular festival, so too has Lent ceased to be observed with the rigour of former days, and certainly gone for ever are the days when Umbrians might settle in, as they did in the last century, for forty days of *agoni fritti*: marinaded sardine-like fish, accompanied by *pancotto*.

Along with Christmas, Easter remains the other great Umbrian feast, and the one which suffers from fewer commercial pressures, though Easter eggs – including those of the Perugina chocolate firm – are familiar enough. Most distinctive among Easter culinary traditions is a breakfast consisting of *torta al formaggio*, *capocollo*, and hard-boiled eggs. The *torta al formaggio* (literally a cheese cake, but actually a bread, baked in a high conical shape with a mushroom-like cap, and studded with small pieces of cheese) is now also widely available in shops throughout the year, but traditional Umbrians, of whom there are many, continue to prefer to devote hours in the days preceding Easter to baking their own. Despite their hearty breakfast, Umbrians will be at the table again by one o'clock for another meal, this time consisting for most of *tortellini in brodo di castrato* and roast lamb. The meat-filled *tortellini* may differ little if at all from the Christmas *cappelletti*, but Umbrians will insist on the broth in which they are served being made from *castrato* – castrated year-old lambs – while the roast that follows will be new season lamb. The lucky visitor will finish his or her meal with *colomba*, the sweet, sugar-covered bread in the shape of a dove that originates from Milan and, though mostly made commercially, is excellent; the less fortunate may be given an Umbrian cake called *ciaramicola*, a sponge ring, coloured an alarming pink by the use of alkermes, smothered in royal icing and topped with hundreds and thousands.

Though *ciaramicola* has its admirers, it is perhaps best left to those still in the nursery. Even so, it is a rare failure among Umbrian cakes. Other cakes, less bound to a season, include local specialities like *rocciata*, a formidably rich rock-bun from Assisi, the *torta di Orvieto*, the dark *pampepato*, packed with candied fruit, from Terni, and the widely available *tozzetti*, made with flour, eggs, sugar, lard, peeled almonds, aniseed, grated lemon peel, and dried fruit, rolled, cooked in the oven and cut diagonally into bite-sized biscuits – a distinctive Umbrian variant, softer and always freshly produced, on the more familiar *cantucci* but like them intended to be served with a glass of sweet *vin santo*.

Wine, of course, is the most traditional accompaniment to the region's food. Red (*rosso*), white (*bianco*), and pink (*rosato*) are all produced locally. Umbria, in fact, has a very long tradition of wine production, for the vine was introduced by Greeks from Magna Graecia and one grape variety widely grown in Umbria is named '*greco*' – though whether this is really a survival from more than 2,500 years ago is much less certain. Wine undoubtedly thrived under the Etruscans. Unusually for the classical world, women as well as men drank wine at their banquets and the Etruscans had their own bibulous divinity, Fuflans, the counterpart of the Roman Bacchus. Archaeological finds in the region – especially in still important wine-producing areas such as Orvieto or Torgiano – have included amphoras and many other wine-related vessels of a kind which the Etruscans also introduced to Celtic northern Europe as early as the seventh century BC. Equally certainly, the Romans followed their Etruscan predecessors in cultivating the grape throughout the region. None of the most prized Roman wines were Umbrian – they mostly came from further south – but Pliny the Younger described enthusiastically how the vineyards 'spreading down

every slope weave their uniform pattern far and wide' around
his villa near Città di Castello. Pliny's account also suggests an
ordered cultivation of the vine which, if it was Roman practice
here, was certainly lost sight of for centuries after the fall of
Rome. Then, vines were allowed to grow promiscuously, strung
between trees, with other crops growing between the rows.
This practice, possible because of the natural fertility of the
Umbrian soil, survived until this century and, though dying
fast, can still be seen in parts of the countryside. Yet though we
know from medieval statutes that wine producing was taken
very seriously in the Middle Ages, with harsh penalties stipulated
for those who damaged vineyards, the lack of specialized care
inevitably prevented the production of really high-quality wines.
Cyrus Redding described this situation succinctly in his *A
History and Description of Modern Wines*, published in 1833: 'In
the Roman States the vines producing every quality of wine
grow together, without assortment of any kind. They are conducted from tree to tree, generally of the elm species, along the
boundaries of inclosures, and even by the high roads, where
they run in wild luxuriance, and waste their vitality, not in the
fruit, but in leaves and branches. Even where the vine is raised
on trellis-work or on poles, it is rarely pruned or trained.' Only
one wine grown in Umbria was really prized outside the
immediate locality: Orvieto, which was highly valued in Rome
and even in Florence. Both the dry and the more usual *abboccato*
(or semi-sweet) wines of Orvieto were well known, and the area
also produced what Redding described as 'excellent durable red
wines'; in recent years, fine red wine has again been made in
Orvieto by such producers as Decugnano dei Barbi. Redding
also ascribed 'good' wine to Terni – the only other location in
Umbria mentioned – though this area no longer has much of a
reputation for wine-production. Not without justice, Redding
laid the blame for the generally poor state of viniculture in
central Italy at the door of the papacy, which had allowed
agriculture generally to decline due to a lack of capital investment. Even the agricultural renewal which to some extent
followed on national unification after 1860 did not entirely
eradicate the problems which led Italian wines to be generally

looked down upon until very recently. While some imported grape varieties – such as merlot and gamay – were added to those of long-standing use in the region in the nineteenth century, they did not always survive the attentions of farmers who valued quantity over quality and uprooted the newcomers in favour of better-cropping varieties such as sangiovese or trebbiano. Even today, when varietal wines are so popular throughout Europe and America, only a few small proprietors offer such wines, though those who do often produce extremely good, and good-value, wines such as the gamay made by Miscio Solismo at Gioiella or Ruggero Veneri's merlot from Spello.

Many smallholders do still produce wine from tiny plots of vines for their own consumption at home and these are always worth tasting once (though less frequently twice). The general tendency in the region, however, is for reduced production of higher-quality wines, made either by private firms or by cooperatives. Most, though not all, of these higher-quality wines are eligible for classification as being *Denominazione di Origine Controllata* (DOC) or – the highest nationally recognized accolade of all – *Denominazione di Origine Controllata e Garantita* (DOCG). In 1992, 21.14 per cent of Umbrian wine production was DOC or above, far below that of Tuscany's 41.27 per cent to be sure, but well above the 13.94 per cent of another neighbour, Lazio.

Of all modern Umbrian wines, those of Orvieto remain the best known outside the region, though not necessarily the most prized within it. The vineyards around the town constitute the better (Classico) area but the Orvieto area extends north along the river Paglia and south along the Tiber into Lazio. Orvieto – the DOC appellation refers only to white wines – is made from a mixture of grape varieties: procanico, also known as trebbiano toscano (50–65 per cent), verdello (15–25 per cent) and grechetto, drupeggio and/or malvasia (20–30 per cent). Most of today's production is dry (*secco*), in line with modern tastes, but these wines, while clean and fresh, are often neutral to a fault, though single vineyard wines, like Bigi's Torricella and Il Poggio, have more character. The *abboccato* wines for which Orvieto was formerly known are excellent for drinking by themselves, though less easy to marry to suitable foods, hence their relatively low contemporary standing. Some leading producers also make a much richer and sweeter wine characterized by *muffa nobile*, or noble rot – the botrytis mould characteristic of the best sauternes and barsac wines of Bordeaux.

Other DOC areas of Umbria reveal very varied characteristics. One of the most interesting is Torgiano, whose vineyards lie along the road from Perugia to Bevagna. Although a well-known wine area for centuries, Torgiano has founded its modern reputation on one man, Giorgio Lungarotti, and his family. The red Rubesco di Torgiano and the white Torre di Giano are perhaps the best-known Umbrian wines after Orvieto and, particularly in the case of the red, deservedly so; the red is made with a blend of sangiovese, canaiolo, montepulciano and ciliegiolo, while the white has a mix of trebbiano and grechetto. Sangiovese and canaiolo for red wine, trebbiano and grechetto for white are, in fact, the principal grape varieties used throughout much of the region, so that soil, microclimates, quality control and vinification techniques combine to account for the very different qualities of wines obtained. The Lungarotti family has shown a willingness to experiment with grape varieties, however, which has continued to keep them at the forefront of Umbrian wine-making and the firm now produces pinot grigio, pinot nero, riesling italico, chardonnay and cabernet sauvignon wines, as well as a sparkling wine based on chardonnay. Even so, and despite the current Italian obsession with single varietal wines, Lungarotti perhaps succeeds best in its creative blending, as in its San Giorgio – the basic rubesco blend with the addition of 20–25 per cent cabernet sauvignon – a full, well-structured wine which will still be drinking well a decade after the vintage.

Such wines do not come cheaply, of course, but Umbria still offers superb value in wines that are not yet as well known as they deserve to be. The wines of Montefalco, for instance, are excellent – particularly from the top makers, who include Adanti, Benincasa, Arnaldo Caprai, Decio Fongoli, Rocca di Fabbri and the Tenuta Val di Maggio. Adanti, in particular, offer a *rosso d'Arquata* which remains among the best value wine of the entire region, although by 1995 Adanti's marketing was fast catching up with their wine-making skills. The particular blend used in this wine is unique to Adanti, but most reds from Montefalco are a blend of the ubiquitous sangiovese with some sagrantino added to give body to the wines. Sagrantino di Montefalco itself has recently been elevated to the status of a DOCG wine and occurs both in a dry version and as a *passito* wine (i.e. made of semi-dried grapes); both are good, the former going well with, say, game dishes while the latter is excellent at the end of a meal. The white wines of Montefalco do not have DOC status but the *bianco d'Arquata* from Adanti is worth searching out.

The other principal DOC areas of Umbria cover large areas and produce wines that are sound, drinkable and of a generally high standard without having very pronounced characteristics enabling them to be distinguished immediately from each other. In the north, the Colli Altotiberini wines are produced in the hills of the upper Tiber valley, where Pliny described the vineyards around his villa in the first century AD. The red wines here are sangiovese and merlot mixes (a *rosato* is also made from this blend) and the white is trebbiano-based. The Colli del Trasimeno DOC wines are produced in an area which extends right around the shores of the lake. Often a little fuller than the wines from the Altotiberini hills, the reds here add ciliegiolo and gamay to sangiovese, and can take longer ageing, though even the more complex of them are perhaps at their best at two or three years, when their fruit is at its freshest; again, the whites are principally trebbiano though with some grechetto, verdicchio and/or malvasia added. One of the best-known producers of Colli del Trasimeno wines, until his death in 1993, was Ferruccio Lamborghini, maker of some of the world's most sought-after sports cars. The son of a farmer, Lamborghini began making tractors in 1949, before turning to sports cars in 1967. On retiring, he declared his intention to achieve the same success with his wines, made at Panicarola on the southern shores of Lake Trasimeno. If he never quite succeeded, the Lamborghini wines stand alŏngside those of a wide range of other successful producers.

Two newer DOC areas are also making headway in Umbria: the Colli Martani and the Colli Amerini. The former appellation, located in the hills between Todi and Foligno, offers some characterful whites based on grechetto (almost invariably a more interesting grape than trebbiano) and some light sangiovese reds, ideal for summer drinking but with sufficient body to serve well in winter too; those reds aged for two years before release on to the market qualify as '*riserva*'. Further south, around Amelia, the Colli Amerini DOC wines are red, white, *rosato*, malvasia and *rosso novello*. Having apparently ignored the fashion for beaujolais nouveau for many years, the Italians of Tuscany and Umbria seem to have caught on to the idea just as everyone else seemed to be easing up on it, and these *novello* wines have nothing particular to offer. Otherwise, the area is well worth considering, especially since its wines are virtually unknown outside the region, a fact reflected in their prices. The white is based on trebbiano and grechetto but it is perhaps the red – a sangiovese-based blend to which a maximum of 35 per cent of montepulciano, canaìolo, ciliegiolo, barbera and merlot are permitted additions; the *rosso* of the local cooperative, the Cantina Sociale dei Colli Amerini, is excellent value. The remaining DOC area, the Colli Perugini, produces a considerable amount of red, white and pink wines, mostly consumed locally and, of all these DOC areas, the least interesting.

It would be a mistake, however, to think that only DOC wines are worth drinking. Here, as in many other wine-producing areas of Italy, the labyrinthine regulations and sometimes dubious decisions made by the authorities in awarding DOC or DOCG status have either resulted in the exclusion of excellent wines or led producers both large and small to exclude their products. To producers already mentioned like Miscio Solismo or Ruggero Veneri might be added many more names; these include Gisberto Goretti, the Fratelli Sportoletti, and Pietro Tili, but there are doubtless many others worth searching out. One very local curiosity is Vernaccia di Cannara; although 'vernaccia' usually refers to a grape producing white wine, in the area around Cannara it indicates a sweet red wine, of considerable character, drunk after a meal, like *vin santo*.

Vin santo, however, remains a case apart. As in so many areas where improvements in wine-making take place, there can be losses as well. Small growers did not always produce good table wine, but they often knew how to make an excellent *vin santo* – a wine remarkably hard to find today. For it, they gathered bunches of grapes – usually a mixture of trebbiano, malvasia and greco – which were hung from the rafters near the kitchen hearth until they were semi-dried; the wine made from these grapes was then put in barrel to age. The result was a strong wine (14 per cent or more), a rich golden-brown in colour, deeply perfumed and naturally sweet. Today, most *vin santo* is made with the addition of spirits to give it the characteristic blend of strength and sugar. Other producers make a dry *vin santo* that can be good in itself but which lacks the unctuousness of traditional wines. Virtually alone among Umbrian wines today, *vin santo* is likely to be found near its best when a glass is offered by the producer himself in his own home, or perhaps in a country restaurant which has been lucky enough to obtain a small supply from a neighbour. Fortunately, some good sweet *vin santo* is still available from commercial producers – notably Adanti and Miscio Solismo. With *tozzetti* at the end of a meal, a glass of *vin santo* can seem like the perfect marriage of Umbrian food and wine.

Lest this seem too idyllic a note on which to end, however, it should be noted that fewer and fewer Umbrians seem to be drinking wine at all. The average per capita intake of wine puts Umbria close to the bottom of the list of Italian regions. Mineral water is widely drunk at home – and Umbria produces some of Italy's best-known waters, including San Faustino, Sangemini, Nocera Umbra and Amerino. Beer is also widely drunk now. Since heavy drinking has never had a place in Italian youth culture, most young people eating out prefer to drink water, soft drinks, or beer. It is a tendency likely to ensure that, for the foreseeable future, Umbria will continue to produce less but better wine.

No one interested will find it hard to locate Umbrian wines in the region, but local patriotism does mean that while, say, Orvieto or Città di Castello will offer a splendid range of Orvietan wines and bottles from the Colli Altotiberini respectively, neither will offer much more. A good idea for oenophiles is to visit the wineries themselves; these are indicted by '*vendita diretta*' signs. A simple way of discovering what is on offer, however, even for the merely curious, is the Enoteca Regionale, or Regional Wineshop. Situated on one of Perugia's most attractive medieval streets – Via Ulisse Rocchi, which leads down from the cathedral to the Etruscan Porta Augusta – it shows a very extensive range of wines (as well as some local sparkling wines and spirits) selected from the entire region. Offering, as it does, a small selection of local foodstuffs, and with everything well displayed and on sale at very reasonable prices, the Enoteca provides a useful introduction to the wine and food of Umbria.

Gazetteer

✳

Abbey (Abbazia, Badia)

San Benedetto al Subasio (729 m.): Situated on the slopes of Monte Subasio, about six kilometres from **Assisi**, this tenth-century Benedictine abbey is one of the most important religious sites in the area to predate the birth of St Francis. Partly destroyed by the people of Assisi in 1399 for harbouring enemies of the town, the Romanesque church retains an interesting eleventh-century crypt, whose columns have finely decorated capitals; a second crypt is of even earlier date.

Sant'Eutizio (678 m.): The rugged mountains of the Castoriana valley (Valcastoriana) were extensively populated by hermits from an early date and Sant'Eutizio supposedly owes its foundation to the Syrian monk Eutizio in the late fifth century. By the year 1000, the abbey – under Benedictine rule – had become an important centre of power, controlling no fewer than 100 dependent churches and castles, and known for its library and important medical school (see **Preci**). The present church was built in 1190 by a Master Petrus whose name is recorded on a tablet on the façade (1236), which has a Romanesque doorway and rose-window with symbols of the evangelists. The imposing aisle-less interior has a very high raised presbytery over a crypt and, behind the altar, a funeral monument to St Eutizio (1514), attributed to Rocco di Tommaso. The situation of the abbey – hugging the thickly wooded mountainside – is particularly appealing, with the bell-tower set on a rock high above an attractive cloister.

San Felice (440 m.): In a fine position amid the Martani hills, not far from the town of **Giano dell'Umbria**, the impressive abbey church of San Felice stands in a location supposedly marking the burial place of the martyred Bishop of Martana. A community of cenobitic monks occupied the site before Benedictines settled here in the eighth century; it was these last who built the church and monastery complex. The church itself is twelfth-century – partly altered in the sixteenth century and recently restored – and Romanesque in style, showing some affinity with churches in **Spoleto**, such as San Gregorio Maggiore (see page 386). The façade has a large portal surmounted by a three-light window, while the high central apse, with gallery, at the rear is extremely imposing; the interior has a raised presbytery over a crypt and a barrel-vaulted central aisle of a kind rare in Umbria.

Santi Fidenzio e Terenzio (413 m.): Set in lovely countryside close to **Massa Martana**, this attractive eleventh-century abbey church is dedicated to the saints who brought Christianity to the region. They were martyred under the Emperor Diocletian and their remains are interred in the crypt here. The square bell-tower to the left of the church stands on a twelve-sided base of huge tufa blocks, probably taken from the former Roman station of Vicus ad Martis, along the Via Flaminia. The church's Romanesque façade, in pink and white stone, shows a simple door with a two-light window above, while the interior has a raised presbytery over an unusually constructed crypt. Among the materials used in the church are a Roman burial tablet and decorative reliefs of Longobard design; there is also a decorated thirteenth-century marble pulpit.

San Pietro in Valle (364 m.): Even in a region rich in abbeys, San Pietro in Valle is exceptional, both for its fine position on the slopes of Monte Solenne, above the Nera valley, and for its immense cultural value. Founded by the Longobard Duke of Spoleto, Faroaldo II, who retired there after being deposed by his son around 720, the present abbey church dates from the tenth to eleventh centuries. The imposing and finely decorated twelfth-century campanile is of a kind unusual in Umbria, being more commonly found in Rome and throughout Lazio.

The triple-apsed church has a broad nave extensively decorated in the twelfth century with one of the most significant fresco cycles of the period to be found anywhere in Italy (they were restored in 1995; see page 213). Besides these biblical scenes, there are also important frescoes in the central and left apses. The church also holds a number of sarcophagi, variously decorated with geometrical patterns, portraits, banqueting, hunting and Dionysiac scenes, including a particularly fine one from the third century, reputed to have held the remains of Faroaldo. The barrel vault of the crossing – immediately in front of the central apse – is the only example of its kind in Italy, although similar examples are widely found in France and Germany. A door in the right wall of the nave leads to an especially attractive twelfth-century cloister; the door is flanked on the cloister side by two splendid statues of Sts Peter and Paul from the eleventh and twelfth centuries. The remainder of the monastery complex, from a later date, is now given over to a restaurant.

San Salvatore di Monte Corona (239 m.): Lying just over three kilometres south of **Umbèrtide**, this abbey was founded by St Romuald and Camaldolesian monks in 1008. The Romanesque abbey church was remodelled in the eighteenth century but has been partly restored to its earlier state with a raised presbytery and remains of fourteenth-century frescoes; there is a particularly fine eighth-century ciborium, brought here from a nearby church.

Santi Severo e Martirio (325 m.): Two and a half kilometres south of Orvieto are the remains of an important monastery founded by the Benedictines in the early twelfth century and later given to the Premonstratensians. Besides the church, there are a refectory, a medieval factory, and the abbot's palace (now a hotel), as well as a twelve-sided bell-tower related to that of the church of Sant'Andrea in **Orvieto**.

Sassovivo (520 m.): This Benedictine foundation is situated some six kilometres from **Foligno**, on a hilly road winding through olive groves on its way to Colfiorito and the Marches. Originally dating from around the year 1000, the abbey flourished until the fifteenth century. The present church is modern but the abbey's jewel is the magnificent Romanesque cloister, the finest in Umbria. Similar in style to contemporary cloisters in Rome, it was designed in 1229 by a Roman craftsman, Pietro di Maria, as an inscription on the south side testifies. It consists of 128 twinned columns, sculpted with extraordinarily imaginative variety, supporting fifty-eight arches, and a classical frieze, decorated with cosmatesque mosaics; remarkably, each piece was separately carved in Rome, brought by river and road, and assembled on site.

Acquasparta (320 m.): Located in an area known since Roman times for its mineral waters (now exploited commercially: Amerino, Furapane), this pleasant hill-town formed part of the territory of the Arnolfi in the tenth century, passing into the jurisdiction of the Abbey of Farfa in 1118, the bishops of Todi in 1278, and the Papal State in 1517. Today, the centre of Acquasparta is dominated by the imposing Palazzo Cesi built in 1565, after contemporary Roman models. It was there in 1609 that the scholar Prince Federico Cesi reformed the Accademia dei Lincei, the most important of the Italian scientific academies, founded six years previously in Rome, and there, too, that he entertained Galileo in 1624. Cesi is buried in a late-sixteenth-century chapel in the church of Santa Cecilia. Just outside the walls is the small church of San Francesco (1294), a transitional Romanesque–Gothic construction with an interesting altar. A Rassegna del Lied Tedesco, dedicated to the study of German art-song by young singers, is held here each summer. See also **Carsulae, Massa Martana, San Gémini**.

Alviano (251 m.): On a summit above the Tiber valley, close to the border with Lazio, the medieval village of Alviano is dominated, as it has been for 500 years, by the imposing bulk of its late-fifteenth-century castle. Like the surrounding area, this belonged to the Liviani family, whose most famous member, the *condottiere* Bartolomeo d'Alviano, fought in the service of the Republic of Venice, being rewarded with the lordship of the northern town of Pordenone. Despite the formidable appearance of the castle, with square plan and massive cylindrical towers, the comparative lateness of its construction is seen in the elegant forms of its Renaissance courtyard. There are several reminders in the village that it was close to here, by tradition, that St Francis quieted the swallows whose noise was disturbing his preaching. Appropriately enough, the nearby Oasi d'Alviano – a small lake created by the damming of the Tiber for hydro-electric purposes – is a wildlife reserve; it is a peaceful place, and well-situated hides allow the possibility for sightings of birds otherwise rare in these parts, including grey and purple herons, bitterns, stilts, redshanks, godwits, several species of duck and goose, marsh harriers and even osprey. See also **Amelia, Baschi, Giove, Lugnano in Teverina**.

Amelia (370 m.): From a distance, Amelia presents an impressive sight, rising up from its ancient walls to the cathedral at the very top of the conical peak on which the town is situated, in the hills dividing the Tiber and Nera valleys. From early times, the site encouraged the development of settlements here: the town was an Umbrian stronghold and then a Roman *municipium*, known as Ameria. It was this town, indeed, that gave its name to the important Roman artery the Via Amerina, which linked southern Etruria with Todi and Perugia. Almost razed by the Goths in 548, the town became a free commune in the Middle Ages before being nominally incorporated into the papal territories in 1307 – though it long harboured Ghibelline sympathies and participated in rebellions against the Church. The hostility was long-lived: in 1571, all the surrounding villages were excommunicated for refusing to pay extra taxes needed to fund the papal wars against the Turks. Nor did the Synod of 1596, which condemned the celebration of Carnival, improve relations between the town and the Church.

Any visit to Amelia begins with the town's most remarkable monument – its walls. These date back to the time of the Umbrian settlement in the fifth century BC and still dominate Amelia's entire urban plan. Composed of huge irregular stone blocks – perfectly fitted together without mortar – the walls reach a maximum height of over eight metres and are almost four metres thick. The town itself can only be entered at a single point – the Porta Romana (1703) – which leads into the Via della Repubblica, flanked for the most part by dark medieval stone buildings. Shortly past the gate, a turning to the right leads to the church of San Francesco, also known as Santi Filippo e Giacomo (1287). Behind the Gothic façade – with ogival door and double rose-window – of the original building, the interior reveals a near-total eighteenth-century remodelling. However, a recently restored chapel to the right of the nave contains no fewer than six tombs, from the fifteenth and six-teenth centuries, of the Geraldini family, whose most famous member, Alessandro Geraldini (1455–1525), was the first bishop appointed to the New World after Columbus's voyages of discovery. Finest among the tombs is the monument to Matteo and Elisabetta Geraldini (1477) by Agostino di Duccio which – though poorly reconstructed – reveals, in such characteristic touches as the mourning angels, Duccio's delicate and elegant art. Next to the church is an attractive sixteenth-century cloister.

Further up the Via della Repubblica, a turning to the left leads down steeply to the mid-sixteenth-century Palazzo Farrat-tini by Antonio da Sangallo the Younger; besides some contem-porary frescoes, the palace also contains two mosaics from an earlier Roman building on the site. The Via della Repubblica now begins to rise even more steeply; there are other smaller Renaissance *palazzi* to be seen to the left and, beyond the narrow, curving Via Cavour to the right, the Vico Lancia is a tiny, covered stepped passageway, characteristic of much of the old town. From here, the Via della Repubblica swings to the right and up to the so-called Arco di Piazza, a medieval arched passageway – incorporating part of a Roman frieze – which leads into the Piazza Marconi. This rectangular piazza contains, to the left of the arch, the Loggia dei Banditori, where town proclamations were once read out, and, to the right, two substan-tial palaces, on either side of the stepped Via del Duomo. The larger of these palaces is the sixteenth-century Palazzo Petrignani, while the smaller Palazzo Nacci dates from the previous century.

Taking the Via del Duomo and turning left into the Via Pellegrino Carleni, the rear of the Palazzo Nacci reveals an elegant Renaissance doorway leading into a small arcaded courtyard. Climbing yet still more steeply through a medieval quarter of town, the road leads to Amelia's cathedral, dominating the town at the top of the hill. To the left of the façade is an isolated twelve-sided Romanesque bell-tower dating from 1050; among the large stone blocks employed in its construction are to be seen many Roman fragments, including part of an elegant frieze. The cathedral itself, originally built in the eleventh and twelfth centuries, today presents a largely seventeenth-century appearance, both in its pleasing brick façade and its interior. Among notable monuments here is, to the right of the entrance, a Romanesque column at which, by tradition, the patron of Amelia, Santa Fermina, was bound and flagellated. There are also a reconstructed funerary monument (1476) with a relief by Agostino di Duccio and pupils, another monument (1564) by Ippolito Scalza, and a number of worthwhile paintings, including those by Niccolò Pomarancio and a *Virgin and Child* attributed to Antoniazzo Romano. The balcony in front of the cathedral offers a splendid panorama over the surrounding hills.

Just below the cathedral, the road divides in two: one direction is that followed in the ascent, the other – to the right – leads down to the Romanesque–Gothic church of Sant'Agostino, also known as San Pancrazio or St Pancras. The church has a fine flat-screen façade – reconstructed in 1477 – boasting a single, large and magnificently decorated ogival doorway, in the lower half, and a rose-window above. After the façade, the interior comes as something of a shock, for it was impressively remodelled in late Baroque style between 1747 and 1762; the frescoing of the dome and vaulting is by Francesco Appiani and there is a *Madonna in Glory* by Antonio Pomarancio on the first altar to the right. Continuing along the Via Cavour, and swinging to the left, notice the maze of tiny medieval alleys and courtyards on either side, before the Piazza Matteotti is reached. Here, to the right, is the Palazzo Comunale, whose small courtyard contains a variety of archaeological fragments; inside are to be seen a number of paintings, including a *Madonna and Child, with St John the Baptist and St Francis* and a *St Anthony Abbot* by Pier Matteo d'Amelia (active 1467–1508), the painter born in the town and now identified with the so-called Master of the

Gardner Annunciation. Beneath this piazza lies a vast second-century Roman cistern, divided into ten vaulted chambers; used, like the similar though smaller cisterns uncovered in **Narni**, to gather rainwater for the city, the cisterns are to be restored and opened to the public. The Via Garibaldi soon leads to the Piazza Marconi and, by way of the Via della Repubblica, to the Porta Romana. See also **Giove, Lugnano in Teverina, Narni**.

Arrone (239 m.): This small village, founded in the ninth century, is situated on a rocky outcrop strategically sited above the river Nera, some fourteen kilometres from **Terni**. A modern development is situated beneath the hill but the old medieval centre, with houses clustered around the castle, remains virtually intact behind the medieval walls. A very steep climb to the summit gives access to splendid views along the rugged Valnerina, towards Rieti, and along the steep-sided blind valley terminated on the Umbrian border by Monte la Pelosa. Just outside the old walls, the parish church, Santa Maria, with its fifteenth-century doorway, holds some attractive works of art, including a fresco in the apse by Vincenzo Tamagni and Giovanni da Spoleto, modelled on Lippo Lippi's work in Spoleto, some votive frescoes of the plague saints, Roch and Sebastian, a *Betrothal of the Virgin* derived from Perugino, and a painted terracotta statue of a languidly elegant Renaissance Madonna suckling her child. See also **Terni**.

Assisi (424 m.): How Assisi appeared to pilgrims in the late Middle Ages we can only imagine, yet even today the small pink and white stone-built town, strung out along the north-western edge of Monte Subasio, watched over by its sombre fortress and visually dominated by the imposing basilica of St Francis, retains the power to impress, even from a distance. Visited on a special occasion – such as Good Friday, when the evening procession of hooded, barefoot penitents through the town takes place by the light of flaming torches – Assisi can be as atmospheric as anywhere in the region. Most importantly, the town continues to draw pilgrims – both religious and cultural – attracted by the many sites associated with, or built and decorated in honour of, St Francis.

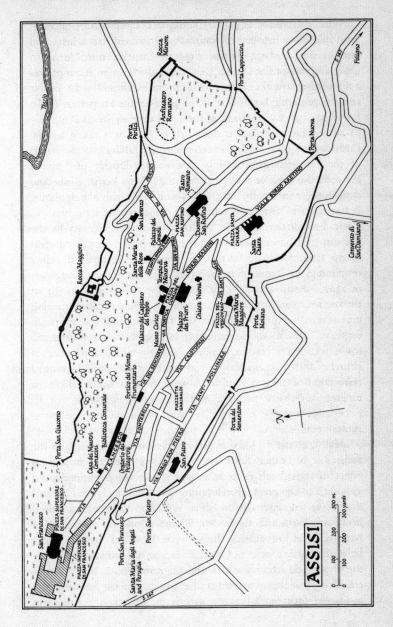

ASSISI

Although indissolubly linked today in the popular imagination with this most beloved of saints, Assisi already had a long and distinguished history by the time of Francis's birth in 1182. Once a centre of the ancient Umbrians, the Roman Asisium was a flourishing town, as its surviving monuments and walls testify, and the probable birthplace of the poet Sextus Propertius (*c.* 50 BC–*c.* AD 14). Evangelized in the third century by St Rufino – to whom the cathedral is dedicated – Assisi was taken by the Ostrogoths under Totila, before eventually falling into the hands of the Longobards, forming part of the Duchy of Spoleto between the sixth and twelfth centuries. A powerful Ghibelline commune, continually in conflict with its Guelph neighbour, Perugia, Assisi famously rebelled in 1198 against its governor, Conrad of Lutzen, Duke of Spoleto, imposed on the city by the emperor, Barbarossa. Although the town passed into the control of the Church in the fourteenth century – Cardinal Albornoz rebuilding the larger of its two fortresses, the Rocca Maggiore, in 1367 – Assisi was held by a succession of *signori* throughout the late fourteenth and fifteenth centuries before finally returning under direct papal control at the beginning of the sixteenth century. Even in the seventeenth and eighteenth centuries the town retained a certain importance – to which a number of churches and *palazzi* testify – and if the early-twentieth-century restoration of the town did not always improve on the effects of nineteenth-century neglect, Assisi remains remarkable for its essentially medieval character, as well as for the richness of its monuments.

Ideally, a visit to Assisi might reserve the essential visit to the basilica of St Francis until last – if only to avoid the offputting effect of coachloads of tourists and a horribly commercialized approach to the great church (anyone wanting a plaster figure of a friar in an Inter Milan shirt will find it here). Starting, however, from the Porta San Pietro – one of several large parking areas just outside the town walls – and walking away from the basilica, it is not hard to escape the crowds and enjoy the silence and serenity which are still, remarkably, to be experienced in various quarters of the town. Almost immediately inside the fourteenth-century gate is the church of San Pietro, originally built in 970 and rebuilt at the beginning of the thirteenth century in Romanesque–Gothic style. The rectangular façade has three doors (the central one is especially noteworthy) and as many rose-windows; the spacious interior is divided into three aisles and contains the remains of frescoes from the eleventh to the fourteenth centuries, as well as a number of fourteenth-century funerary monuments. From the church, the Via Borgo San Pietro and Via Sant'Apollinare lead up through a fourteenth-century district as far as the Romanesque church of Santa Maria Maggiore, which served as Assisi's cathedral until the early eleventh century. The present tripartite façade dates from the twelfth century and incorporates, above the main door, part of the basin of a Roman fountain; there is an attractive Romanesque–Gothic bell-tower. The three-aisled interior is built on the basilical plan with a semicircular apse and contains frescoes from the fourteenth and fifteenth centuries; beneath the presbytery is a crypt which has survived from the original tenth-century church. In a neighbouring garden, part of the Roman city walls is still visible. The Vescovado or episcopal palace next to Santa Maria Maggiore was where St Francis renounced his inheritance and where he was cared for, while gravely ill, until he asked to be carried down to the Portiuncula – now in Santa Maria degli Angeli (see below), shortly before his death. From the Piazza del Vescovado a road to the right – the Via Sant'Agnese – leads up to the Piazza di Santa Chiara, at the opposite end.

There, on the edge of the city, stands the church of Santa Chiara, or St Clare, St Francis's first female follower and founder of the order of the Poor Clares. In contrast to the three enormous and dramatic flying buttresses on its left flank, the façade of the church is simple, consisting of alternating horizontal bands of delicate pink and white local stone, adorned with a fine rose-window. Built in Gothic style between 1257 and 1265, the church follows the pattern established by the basilica of St Francis, having a single huge nave, divided into four bays, with a gallery running around the walls. The interior – and particularly the vaulting of the presbytery and transepts – was richly decorated in the late twelfth and early thirteenth century, with scenes from the Bible and from the life of St Clare. The saint's body now lies in the nineteenth-century crypt. In a large chapel in the middle of the right wall of the nave is to be seen the twelfth-century crucifix which, by tradition, spoke to St Francis in San Damiano (see below); opposite, in a display case, are a number of relics of St Francis and St Clare, including a friar's habit, belt, and cloak. Higher up the nave, the Cappella del Sacramento is decorated with frescoes – including a *Madonna and Child* attributed to the local artist Puccio Capanna – by thirteenth-century Umbrian followers of Giotto. The thirteenth-century painted crucifix in the apse is attributed to another painter from Assisi, the so-called Master of Santa Chiara. From the piazza in front of the church there are views of the adjoining convent and the lower town. The road along the left flank of the church leads past the flying buttresses – the recently restored fountains are of Roman origin – to the polygonal apse and tall, square bell-tower. Passing beneath the archway known as the Porta Pucci, the road leads into the Via Borgo Aretino; just before the Porta Nuova is reached, a small stepped alley to the right leads down to the twelfth-century gate known as the Porta di Moiano. Returning instead back into town, the Corso Mazzini leads from Santa Chiara to the heart of Assisi.

The Piazza del Comune, an elongated medieval piazza, with a road leading into it at each of its four corners, owes its unusual shape to the contours of the spur on which Assisi stands. The site was once thought to have been that of the Roman forum but is now believed to have been occupied by a balcony in front of the Temple of Minerva, overlooking the Vale of Umbria. Although much transformed in the course of the centuries, the piazza offers a remarkable conspectus of more than 2,000 years of Assisi's history. Most important among its buildings is the Temple of Minerva itself, built in the first century BC, transformed into a church in the sixteenth century, and given a Baroque interior in 1634. This was the building – the first classical work he had ever seen – which so aroused Goethe's enthusiasm when he visited Assisi in 1786, though he fled from the 'dreary' basilica of San Francesco, without a second glance. The temple's six fluted columns, with Corinthian capitals, rest most unusually on plinths located on the steps leading up to the entrance, a solution imposed on the builders by a lack of space. Part of the terrace on to which the temple once faced can today be seen in the Civic Museum which is to be found in the eleventh-century crypt of the church of San Nicolò (now demolished and replaced by a post-office built in 1927).

Also in the Piazza del Comune is the thirteenth-century Palazzo del Capitano del Popolo, poorly restored in 1927, as was the adjacent medieval tower, originally built between 1212 and 1305. On the southern side of the square, the Palazzo dei Priori (now the Palazzo del Comune) dates from 1337. Today it holds the town's art collection, which includes detached frescoes by local followers of Giotto, including the Master of Santa Chiara and Puccio Capanna, together with fifteenth- and sixteenth-century works by Andrea d'Assisi, called L'Ingegno, Tiberio d'Assisi, and Dono Doni, all from Assisi, and paintings by Ottaviano Nelli from Gubbio and Nicolò Alunno from Foligno. Just behind the Palazzo dei Priori, to the left, is the elegant Renaissance Chiesa Nuova or New Church, built in 1615, after the model of Sant'Eligio degli Orafi in Rome, at the expense of King Philip III of Spain, on the site of the family home of St Francis.

From the Piazza del Comune, the Via San Rufino leads steeply up to the Piazza San Rufino and the cathedral, dedicated to the martyr-bishop who evangelized the area. The present church was built between 1134 and 1228 by Giovanni da Gubbio on the site of the earlier eleventh-century cathedral, whose crypt survives beneath the piazza. San Rufino's regular Romanesque façade is simple enough in form – a screen divided into three vertically by pilasters and into two horizontally by a blind arcade, surmounted by a pediment added in the late thirteenth century – but boasts exceptionally rich decoration. The lower part of the façade, divided into squares in the manner of churches, notably San Pietro, in the Spoleto area, has three doorways, finely ornamented and with varied biblical and animal reliefs. The arcade above rests on a cornice abundantly decorated with animal motifs, while the superb central rose-window, made up of three concentric circles, variously embellished, is surrounded by the symbols of the evangelists and held up by three telamones standing on as many fabulous beasts. To the left of the façade is a robust but elegant eleventh-century campanile.

After the strong impression made by the façade, the interior of the cathedral comes as a severe disappointment, having been entirely remodelled in 1571 by the Perugian architect Galeazzo Alessi. The most interesting feature, in fact, dates back to long before the building of the cathedral, for immediately inside the left doorway is a large cistern, rectangular in plan and barrel-vaulted, which also serves as foundations for the bell-tower; a faint inscription above the entrance gives the names of the *marones*, the ancient Umbrian magistrates of Assisi, responsible for the construction of the cistern. Elsewhere in the cathedral are to be seen a number of pictures by Dono Doni, some fine intarsia work choir-stalls (1520) and the font where St Francis, St Clare and Frederick II were baptized.

Some steps to the right of the cathedral façade lead down to a small museum where the crypt of the former cathedral can be seen, along with some eleventh- and twelfth-century frescoes. A Roman sarcophagus, decorated with the myth of Diana and Endymion, once held the remains of St Rufino. From the piazza in front of the cathedral there is a good view of the Rocca Maggiore, the fortress built by direction of Cardinal Albornoz. It is possible to reach this by taking the steep Via di Porta Perlici which leads through the medieval Perlici district, although it is also worth taking a detour as far as the twelfth-century Perlici gate itself, built close to the elliptical Roman amphitheatre, and offering a good view of the so-called Rocca Minore, another part of the city's medieval defences. From the massive Rocca Maggiore, which recalls, in its total domination of the city, the contemporary fortresses of **Spoleto**, **Narni** and **Gualdo Tadino**, there is a magnificent view of Assisi and the surrounding countryside.

Leaving the Rocca, return as far as the deconsecrated fourteenth-century church of San Lorenzo and turn right at the bottom of a flight of steps to the right of the church as far as Santa Maria delle Rose, another deconsecrated church, whose thirteenth-century façade incorporates elements from earlier buildings; the Via Santa Maria delle Rose now leads past the so-called Palazzo dei Consoli, built in the early thirteenth century, to the left, back to the Via San Rufino and to the Piazza del Comune. From the piazza take the Via Portica, to the left of the Museo Civico, noting the aedicule with a frescoed *Madonna del Popolo* by a follower of Simone Martini. Between them, the Via Portica, later the Via del Seminario, and finally the Via San Francesco form one of the principal arteries of the modern as well as of the medieval city, leading directly from the Piazza del Comune to the basilica of St Francis, and usually thronged in consequence.

The route begins by passing between buildings of the thirteenth and fourteenth centuries before passing under a thirteenth-century archway at the end of the Via del Seminario. Immediately afterwards, to the left, is a sixteenth-century fountain and then the Portico del Monte Frumentario, built as part of a hospital in 1267; it retains fragmentary frescoes from the fourteenth century. Further along the street, the Oratorio dei Pellegrini is another former hospital, this time dating from 1431. The fresco on the façade, *Christ in Glory, with St James and St Anthony Abbot and Angels* (1486), is by Matteo da Gualdo; in the interior are another fine fresco by Matteo da Gualdo and works by Mezzastris and others. Some distance ahead, on the opposite side of the street, the Palazzo Giacobetti holds the Civic Library, among whose rich collection of older books and manuscripts is the oldest surviving text of the writings of St Francis, including the *Cantico del Sole*. The street continues with many medieval houses and *palazzi* – including the Casa dei Maestri Comacini, once owned by builders from Lombardy, who worked in the region in the fifteenth century. Eventually, the street ends with a view across a grassy square of the splendid façade of the basilica itself.

However inappropriate so magnificent a church may seem to be for the apostle of poverty and humility, it is hard not to be impressed both by the structure itself and by the extent of the devotion St Francis inspired in his lifetime, which led to construction work beginning just two years after the saint's death. The building of the basilica – comprising two churches, one over the other – was willed by Brother Elias, the Vicar General of the Franciscans; work commenced on the day after the saint's canonization in 1228, the first stone being laid by Pope Gregory IX. The saint's body was interred here from 1230, the great bell-tower was completed by 1239, and Pope Innocent IV consecrated the church in 1253. It remains one of the finest buildings in Umbria and arguably the greatest repository of medieval art in the whole of Italy. The basilica is also Umbria's principal religious site, drawing pilgrims from all over the world.

The flat-screen façade of the Upper Church is divided horizontally into three by cornices. On the lowest level, a large ogival portal encloses twin doors; above, there is a single, large and richly decorated rose-window, while the façade is completed by a simple pediment with an oculum. To the left, between the church and the huge monastery, whose massive escarpments give the complex the appearance of a fortress from a distance, is the tall, robust yet elegant campanile. Entered through one of the twin doors, the Upper Church presents a remarkable appearance – its aisle-less interior vast yet simple, full of light and wholly frescoed throughout, both along the walls and on the cross-vaulted roof, with paintings of exceptional richness and quality. So profuse, in fact, is the decoration that no brief account can do more than indicate some of the principal works of interest. The most immediately striking frescoes – if only because their position, low down on the walls of the nave, makes them especially easy to see – are those representing scenes from the *Life of St Francis* (*c.* 1290–95), traditionally attributed to Giotto, but certainly the work of several hands. Intended as visual aids to reinforce the preaching of the Franciscans, the individual scenes retell the story of the saint's conversion, evangelizing, miracles and death, in images which are the single most important source for later Franciscan iconography and the model for other painted lives of St Francis, in Umbria and elsewhere. These frescoes – twenty-eight scenes in all – run along the length of the entire nave on both sides and on the inner façade, being integrated with the architecture of the church, both by their symmetrical placing between the clustered columns which divide the nave into four bays and by an extremely deceptive painted cornice. A passageway runs around the nave walls above this cycle and further frescoes fill the space around the windows in the upper part of the nave wall.

These frescoes consist of an Old Testament cycle on the left wall and a New Testament cycle on the right. Once attributed to Cimabue, the paintings are now generally thought to be by Roman artists including Jacopo Torriti and Filippo Rusuti. The scenes of Isaac and Jacob and Isaac and Esau, on the upper right wall, and the paintings of the Doctors of the Church in the vault of the first bay of the nave are attributed to the same, exceptional artist, believed by some to have been Giotto, and known to others as the Isaac Master. The overwhelming sense of unity the nave presents, on entering the church, derives in large part from the need for clear sight lines. This was pre-eminently a preaching church, and while the eye is led to the altar and the stained-glass windows of the apse, the transepts are virtually invisible until the head of the nave is reached. Here, though, is another great cycle of frescoes, painted by Cimabue from around 1277. Despite the fact that the work has taken on the appearance of a photographic negative, the great *Crucifixion*, in the left transept, retains considerable dramatic power. In the right transept are scenes from the *Life of St Peter* and, in the apse, a Marian cycle. The thirteenth-century altar is made of marble with cosmatesque decoration, while the stained glass, with stories from the Bible and lives of the saints, is the work of German, and some early Italian, masters, dating in part from as early as 1260.

The Lower Church can be reached by means of a doorway at the rear of the left transept, but it is better, perhaps, to exit by the principal door of the Upper Church and descend the large staircase to the head of the fifteenth-century arcaded piazza known as the Piazza Inferiore di San Francesco. To the left, a doorway set in a simple façade gives access to the fifteenth-century Oratory of St Bernardino of Siena, while the large double doorway to the right, surmounted by a rose-window, leads into the Lower Church. The contrast with the church above is striking. In place of the Upper Church's simple, luminous interior, the Lower Church presents a dark and, at first, confusing appearance, its low-roofed single aisle, built between

1228 and 1239, transformed on both flanks by the addition of deep chapels in the fourteenth century. The difference between the two churches was, in part, foreseen from the beginning, for while the Upper Church was intended to serve for preaching, the Lower Church was designed, first and foremost, to house the body of St Francis. This, indeed, it still does, although the body was lost from the fifteenth century until 1818, after it was moved to thwart Assisi's traditional enemy, Perugia, which had long threatened to loot the saint's remains; today the body lies directly beneath the main altar, in a small crypt (1925–32) which, rather remarkably, given the vast throng of tourists, retains a devotional air.

The profuseness of the decoration of the Lower Church does little to dispel the initial sense of confusion but it is well worth persevering, for the frescoes here include works as varied as they are magnificent. Almost immediately to the left of the entrance, beyond the Chapel of St Sebastian, with seventeenth-century decoration, is the *Madonna della Salute*, painted in International Gothic style by the fifteenth-century artist Ceccolo di Giovanni, whose only known work this is. At the far end of the entrance transept, opposite the door, the polygonal Cappella di Santa Caterina, or St Catherine's Chapel, built by the great architect Matteo Gattapone by order of Cardinal Albornoz, has a series on the saint's life (1368) by Andrea da Bologna; Albornoz himself, who is represented on the left wall kneeling before three saints, was buried here at his death in 1367, prior to the removal of his body to Toledo in his native Spain. The frescoes in the nave itself include scenes from the *Life of St Francis* (to the left) and from Christ's Passion (to the right), painted about 1260 by the so-called Master of St Francis; their importance resides not only in their artistic merits, though they are the most important frescoes before Cimabue began painting here, but in their presentation of St Francis as a *type* of Christ. On the left wall, at the head of the nave, is a Gothic pulpit, decorated in coloured marbles and mosaics, above which is a *Coronation of the Virgin*, attributed to Puccio Capanna.

Of the several chapels in the nave, the first to the left, the Cappella di San Martino, is one of the finest of all, and not simply for the sumptuous yet graceful cycle on the life of St Martin by the Siennese painter Simone Martini but for the stained glass and marble inlay floor that Martini also designed, making the chapel an unspoiled masterpiece of Gothic decoration, unsurpassed anywhere in Italy. The chapel at the head of the right wall of the nave – the Cappella della Maddalena or Magdalene Chapel – contains scenes from the Life of St Mary Magdalene; these have been attributed to Giotto himself (and there are resemblances to his work in Padua) but are more likely by his pupils. The figure represented on the west wall of the chapel, on whom St Rufino is placing a mitre – and also, perhaps, the kneeling figure in a cloak, whose hand reaches out to Mary Magdalene, on the east wall – is Tebaldo Pontano da Todi, Bishop of Assisi between 1296 and 1329, who commissioned the chapel. In the adjoining Cappella di San Valentino is the pavement tomb of an early English Franciscan, Brother Hugh of Hartlepool, who died in 1302.

The barrel-vaulted transept of the Lower Church is, if anything, even more dazzlingly decorated than the nave and chapels. Here, in the vaults above the crossing, are allegorical frescoes attributed to the so-called Maestro delle Vele, or Master of the Vaults, a painter influenced by Giotto; they represent Poverty, Chastity, and Obedience, together with the Apotheosis of St Francis. Especially noteworthy among the paintings in the right transept are the *Enthroned Madonna and Child, with St Francis* (*c.* 1280), by Cimabue, which – though much restored – includes what is perhaps the single most famous representation of the saint; the cycles on the *Childhood of Christ* (1315–20) and on the posthumous miracles of St Francis (*c.* 1320) are attributable to the school of Giotto, as is the *Crucifixion* (*c.* 1320), while the *Madonna and Child, with Two of the Wise Men* (1321–6) is by Simone Martini. The polygonal chapel beyond the right transept, the Cappella di San Nicola, contains scenes from the life of St Nicholas by pupils of Giotto, and the tomb of Giovanni Orsini (1292). The left transept contains a masterly fresco cycle on the *Passion of Christ*, by Pietro Lorenzetti, probably painted between 1320 and 1330. Lorenzetti exhibits an extraordinary range, from the colourful crowd scenes and cityscapes in the *Entry into*

Jerusalem or *The Road to Calvary*, through the architectural and decorative schemes of the *Last Supper, Washing of the Disciples' Feet* or *The Flagellation of Christ*, to the domestic and human detail (a cat sleeping by the fire, a dog licking clean a plate in the *Last Supper* or the child with a monkey on a leash in the *Flagellation*). Yet Lorenzetti's is not merely a decorative art, and if his *Crucifixion* exhibits dramatic vigour, then it is difficult to know what most to admire in his *Deposition of Christ*: the composition, the sombre handling of colour or the pathos with which the entire scene is suffused. Lorenzetti also painted a tender *Madonna and Child with St Francis and St John the Evangelist* on the south wall of the transept and a notably different, triptych-like, treatment of the same subject (with St John the Baptist replacing his namesake) in the adjoining chapel. From either transept, it is possible to gain access to the large cloister of the monastery, where the Museo del Tesoro, or Treasury, is located; the rich contents, incorporating the F. M. Perkins collection, include works by Lorenzetti, the Beato Angelico, Bicci di Lorenzo, Bartolo di Fredi, Nicolò Alunno, Tiberio d'Assisi, Lo Spagna, and Signorelli, as well as church plate, manuscripts, reliquaries and a Flemish tapestry of St Francis presented by Pope Sixtus IV in 1471.

Once outside the church, the road from the Piazza Inferiore di San Francesco leads back to the starting point of the Piazza San Pietro. Even a superficial visit to Assisi requires time and stamina, but it would be a pity not to stray occasionally from the route outlined, in order to find the tranquillity offered by the small stepped passageways which connect the town's principal thoroughfares. It is also desirable to visit one or more of the nearby Franciscan sites – the convent of San Damiano, a short walk from the town, the Eremo delle Carceri, buried in the greenery of dense ilex woods, four kilometres away, or the basilica of Santa Maria degli Angeli, on the plain below the town.

Closest to Assisi is the convent of San Damiano, one of the spots most closely linked to St Francis and to St Clare. At the beginning of the thirteenth century, San Damiano was a tiny oratory where, by tradition, St Francis was addressed by the Christ depicted on the crucifix now in the church of Santa

Chiara: '*Vade Francisce, et repara domum meam*' ('Go Francis, and repair my house'). The young merchant's son hurried home and sold a packhorse and cloth belonging to his father, bringing the money he acquired by the sale to the priest of San Damiano; when the latter refused the offering, Francis flung it from a window of the church, later restoring the building with his own hands. More reliably, St Francis is known to have composed the *Canticle of the Sun* at San Damiano, in the winter of 1224–5. By then, the oratory had been transformed into a convent occupied by St Clare and her first followers and it was from the small door in the upper part of the church façade that St Clare is supposed to have appeared to face the Saracen troops sent by Frederick II to seize Assisi from the Guelph faction and put them to flight.

Since much of the surviving fabric of the tiny convent dates from the thirteenth century, San Damiano is one of the most appealing of the Franciscan sites, especially if visited outside the main tourist season. In the small square in front of the church is a niche with a popular fifteenth-century fresco of the Virgin and Child; there is a further fresco under a portico to the right of the church. Today the monastery complex is entered through a door, to the right of the façade, which leads into the chapel of San Girolamo (St Jerome), where there is a good fresco of the *Virgin and Child, with St Francis, St Clare, St Bernardino and St Jerome* (1517) by Tiberio d'Assisi, and two votive frescoes of *St Sebastian and St Roch* by a pupil of the same artist. A tiny sixteenth-century chapel beyond is dominated by a large wooden crucifix (1637) by Fra Innocenzo da Palermo. The convent church beyond retains substantial portions of a fourteenth-century frescoed account of St Francis offering money for the restoration of San Damiano to the priest, while pursued by his irate father; the fresco surrounds the small window from which Francis is supposed to have thrown his rejected offering. There are also some backward-looking fourteenth-century frescoes in the apse and wooden choir-stalls (1504); the crucifix above the altar is a copy of that which supposedly spoke to the saint and is today held in Santa Chiara. Along the prescribed route through the convent are to be seen a frescoed *Crucifixion* (1482) by Pier

Antonio Mezzastris and, on the floor above, a tiny terraced garden and the Oratory of St Clare, with fourteenth-century frescoes and sinopia sketches. In the simple adjoining room, a cross marks the spot where St Clare died in 1253. A stairway leads down to the tiny cloister, off which is the plain, roughly vaulted refectory, with two rather weak frescoes by Dono Doni. In the cloister itself, however, are two much better works – *St Francis Receiving the Stigmata* and an *Annunciation* (1507) by Eusebio da San Giorgio. A doorway returns the visitor to the small piazza in front of the church.

The Eremo delle Carceri (literally, the Prison Hermitage) is today a small, picturesque convent – enlarged in the fifteenth century by St Bernardino of Siena – in a tranquil setting of great natural beauty. The wild site, however, located on the edge of a ravine, was originally chosen by St Francis and his first followers in their search for a return to the more primitive monastic life characteristic of many remote areas in Umbria during the first centuries of Christianity. From the gates, a path leads down to a triangular courtyard and a fifteenth-century church which includes an earlier chapel, Santa Maria delle Carceri, where there is a fresco of the *Virgin and Child, with St Francis* by Tiberio d'Assisi. The Grotta di San Francesco – a cave once lived in by the saint and containing one of the region's many 'beds' of St Francis (a stone slab) – can be visited, and walks among the lovely woods reveal other small caverns once occupied by hermits. The site offers splendid views of the wooded slopes of Monte Subasio and of the Vale of Umbria below. From here, a spectacular but untarmacked road over the mountain, practicable only in summer, leads to **Spello.**

If the Eremo delle Carceri offers a reminder of the original Franciscan simplicity, the same can hardly be said of the basilica of Santa Maria degli Angeli, which dominates the plain below Assisi. Erected on the site where the Franciscan order was founded, and where St Francis himself died, the great church – the eighth largest in the world – was designed to hold the tiny rustic oratory known as the Portiuncula, which now stands beneath the cupola. Santa Maria degli Angeli was begun in 1569 to a design by Galeazzo Alessi and completed just over a century later in 1679; after being damaged by an earthquake in 1832, it was restored and a grandiose new façade was added in 1928. Visible from miles around, the basilica has for long been one of the most important pilgrimage sites in Italy; the large fountain, with twenty-six spouts, to be seen on the left flank of the church, and built in 1610 at the expense of the Medici family, is known as the Pilgrims' Fountain. Despite a jarring discrepancy of scale between the new church and the Franciscan oratory it encloses, Santa Maria degli Angeli has a fine three-aisled interior, with side-chapels containing notable works of art from the sixteenth to the nineteenth centuries by such painters as Niccolò Pomarancio, Cesare Sermei and Franceso Appiani. The Portiuncula itself dates from the tenth or eleventh century and, ironically enough, was favoured by St Francis for its solitary situation. Today it bears the marks of more than seven centuries of devotion to the saint: the statue of the Madonna and Child on the façade, and the altarpiece (1393), with scenes from the life of St Francis, by Ilario da Viterbo are fourteenth-century, the frescoes on the right flank, and the Calvary scene on the rear wall by Andrea d'Assisi, known as L'Ingegno, date from the fifteenth, while the frescoes on the façade were painted by the German artist Friedrich Overbeck in 1829. To the right of the presbytery, the Cappella del Transito marks the spot where St Francis died, laid out on bare earth, dressed in a borrowed tunic, as an outward sign of the poverty he espoused. Today, the interior of the chapel reveals frescoes (c. 1520) by Lo Spagna and a majolica statue of St Francis by Andrea della Robbia, while the frescoes (1889) on the outer wall are by Domenico Bruschi. From the head of the right aisle, a corridor leads to the Roseto, or Rose Garden, whose thornless roses are said to derive from a miracle of the saint's; it is also possible to visit the crypt, which contains a majolica altarpiece by Andrea della Robbia, as well as the remains of the earliest Franciscan convent. The Chapel of the Rose Garden is in two main parts: the first, built by St Bernardino of Siena, and the second, added by St Bonaventure, have frescoes by Tiberio d'Assisi, dating from 1518 and 1506 respectively; among the former frescoes is a scene of St Francis casting himself naked into the rose bushes, causing them to lose their thorns in order not to harm him. In the adjoining museum are to be seen a Crucifix (1236–40) by Giunta Pisano, a celebrated panel portraying St Francis, by the so-called Master of St Francis, another portrait of the saint, very similar to that by Cimabue in the Lower Church in Assisi (and also attributed to the Tuscan artist), and works by L'Alunno and Mezzastris. See also **Bastia Umbra**, **Spello**.

Baschi (165 m.): Approached along the road from **Alviano** or **Lugnano**, this small hill village presents a bizarre appearance, for it is situated immediately above the main Rome–Florence motorway, the Autostrada del Sole. Once inside, however, it is surprisingly easy to forget Baschi's unique location, and if there is little otherwise to distinguish the village from many other pleasant settlements in the region, the parish church of San Nicolò – rebuilt by Ippolito Scalza from neighbouring **Orvieto** between 1575 and 1584 – has a fine triptych (*c.* 1440) by the Siennese artist Giovanni di Paolo, hung under an elegant eighteenth-century Murano glass chandelier. Not far from Baschi, a twisting panoramic road runs through vineyards and alongside the Lake of Corbara and the Tiber valley to **Todi**. See also **Alviano**, **Lugnano in Teverina**, **Orvieto**, **Todi**.

Bastia Umbra (300 m.): Few visitors make it to this busy town at the head of the Vale of Umbria, since its industrious appearance does little to attract those understandably bent on reaching nearby **Assisi**. Despite its evident modern prosperity – it is one of very few towns in Umbria to show a steady increase in population throughout the past century – Bastia has ancient origins, however, being known to the Romans as Insula Romana, from the time when it was indeed an island, surrounded by the waters which long filled the valley. An important fortified settlement in the Middle Ages – fought over by Perugia and Assisi – Bastia retains traces of its walls, and some fifteenth-century houses. The fourteenth-century church of Santa Croce, built in pink and white stone from Monte Subasio, has a single-naved interior and preserves a large triptych (1499) by Nicolò Alunno, a sixteenth-century processional standard by Bernardino di Mariotto, and frescoes by Tiberio d'Assisi (1515) and followers of Bartolomeo Caporali. See also **Assisi**.

Bettona (353 m.): A quiet agricultural town, situated on one of the most northerly outcrops of the Martani hills, Bettona occupies a classic Etruscan position, despite being on the 'wrong' (i.e. left) bank of the Tiber, which marked the division between the Etruscan and Umbrian worlds. Evidence of Bettona's Etruscan past – it was formerly Vettona – can be seen half-way up the hill from the direction of Perugia, in the form of a small, barrel-vaulted tomb by the roadside, and in the huge blocks of sandstone from the fourth century BC still incorporated within the medieval city walls. The town itself retains a predominantly medieval appearance, especially in the main square where the church of Santa Maria Maggiore and the Palazzo del Podestà recall Bettona's period of independence as a free commune in the late thirteenth and early fourteenth centuries. See also **Bevagna**, **Cannara**, **Foligno**, **Torgiano**.

Bevagna (210 m.): A small walled town situated on the plain of Foligno at the foot of the Martani hills, Bevagna was an ancient Umbrian settlement and later a Roman *municipium* on the Via Flaminia, known as Mevania. Destroyed on more than one occasion in the Middle Ages, the town passed into the control of the Church in 1439. Some Roman remains are still to be seen, notably parts of the theatre (now incorporated into medieval houses), a temple, and baths – these last include an extensive second-century mosaic of mythological marine scenes – and an amphitheatre outside the town. The present medieval walls (1249–1377) are likewise erected on the line of the preceding Roman walls. Bevagna's main attraction, however, is the Piazza Silvestri, one of the finest surviving medieval squares in Umbria – with the Palazzo dei Consoli and two exceptional Romanesque churches.

The Palazzo dei Consoli, erected around 1270 by the master-builder also responsible for the Palazzo Comunale in **Spello**, consists of a first-floor chamber over a ground-floor arcade, with a broad external stairway; the upper storey is now a delightful small theatre, restored and reopened at the end of 1994. To the right of the palace is the church of San Silvestro (1195) by the master Binello, who signed his name on a stone set at the side of the finely decorated doorway; the plain, three-aisled interior has a raised presbytery over a crypt, and retains some early frescoes. Across the piazza is a very similar church, San Michele Arcangelo, built, at the end of the twelfth century or the beginning of the thirteenth, by Binello and Rodolfo (also responsible for the magnificent secondary façade of the cathedral at Foligno), whose names are inscribed on a stone set in the façade. The beautiful central doorway has a Roman cornice and coloured cosmatesque mosaic decoration, while the spacious interior has a high, raised presbytery over a large crypt. The church contains a large, wooden outline Crucifixion group and a large eighteenth-century silver statue of the town's patron, St Vincent. Other churches in the town include the thirteenth-century San Francesco and Santi Domenico e Giacomo, both of which have frescoes by the local artist, Ascensidonio Spacco, known as Il Fantino, and the fourteenth-century Sant'Agostino. The characteristic Corso Matteotti, leading into the main piazza, has a number of interesting buildings, including the Palazzo Municipale which holds a small museum and art gallery (in much need of restoration). See also **Bettona**, **Cannara**, **Foligno**.

Calvi dell'Umbria (401 m.): The most southerly commune in Umbria, Calvi stands on a hill just across the border from Lazio, amid lovely countryside. Ancient in origin, and medieval in appearance, it has a somewhat forlorn air today. Formerly in the possession of the Abbey of Farfa and later part of the Church territories, Calvi knew a period of affluence in the late Middle Ages but suffered badly from plague in 1527 and was sacked by the French in 1798. Among the surviving monuments are a Franciscan church, built on a site given to St Francis by Bernardo da Calvi, later martyred in Morocco, Santa Maria (1394) and twin churches with a single façade, the left of which, Sant'Antonio, has a sixteenth-century crib with more than thirty large figures, in partly-glazed terracotta. See also **Narni**, **Otrícoli**.

Campello sul Clitunno (290 m.): Campello itself is today a modest village, distinguished principally by the sixteenth-century church della Bianca, on the main square, whose interior was decorated by Valadier and which has frescoes by Lo Spagna and Fabio Angelucci. Close by, however, are to be found both the fortified village of Campello Alto and two of Umbria's most celebrated sites, the Fonti del Clitunno and the Tempietto del Clitunno.

Campello Alto (514 m.) is reached by means of a serpentine road which winds for some six kilometres up a hillside entirely covered by terraced olive groves. The tiny village, dating back as far as 925, retains a complete circle of medieval walls and a single gate, together with a church and a small number of houses, huddled closely together. Both the village and the road leading to it afford extraordinary views of the surrounding countryside: thickly wooded hills to the east and, beyond the Vale of Umbria, which appears, quite vertiginously, below, the Martani hills; among the towns clearly visible in the distance are Spoleto and Montefalco.

The Fonti del Clitunno, or Springs of Clitumnus, almost inevitably risk disappointing the visitor today, sited as they are close to a busy road and usually crowded by coachloads of tourists. Yet, visited early in the morning or at dusk, this famously green space, its clear waters emerging from the rock and spreading out in shallow pools among weeping willows and poplars, can still evoke something of the spell it cast on generations of travellers. In Roman times, the site was sacred to the god Clitumnus, and its waters used to purify the white cattle intended for sacrifice; among others, both Propertius and Virgil described it in their poetry. It was Pliny the Younger, however, who gave the fullest account (*Letters*, VIII, 8), of which this is a short extract:

There is a fair-sized hill which is densely wooded with ancient cypresses; at the foot of this the spring rises and gushes out through several channels of different size, and when its eddies have subsided it broadens out into a pool as clear as glass. You can count the coins which have been thrown in and the pebbles shining at the bottom ... The banks are clothed with ash trees and poplars, whose green reflections can be counted in the clear stream as if they were planted there. The water is as cold and as sparkling as snow. Close by is a holy temple of great antiquity in which is a standing image of the god Clitumnus himself clad in a magistrate's bordered robe.

Such was the fame of the springs in antiquity that many generations of classically minded travellers visited this site, even as they ignored every vestige of medieval Umbria; among them were Joseph Addison, Tobias Smollett, and Byron, who described the springs in *Childe Harold's Pilgimage* (IV, 66–8), beginning:

> But thou, Clitumnus! in thy sweetest wave
> Of the most living crystal that was e'er
> The haunt of river nymph, to gaze and lave
> Her limbs where nothing hid them, thou dost rear
> Thy grassy banks whereon the milk-white steer
> Grazes; the purest god of gentle waters!
> And most serene of aspect, and most clear;
> Surely that stream was unprofaned by slaughters –
> A mirror and a bath for Beauty's youngest daughters!

The reason for the coachloads of tourists who visit the site today, however, is neither Pliny nor Byron but one of Italy's most famous nineteenth-century poets, Giosuè Carducci, whose 'Alle Fonti del Clitumno' was for long a classic school text, known to generations of pupils; it was in this fine poem that Carducci famously hailed 'Green Umbria':

> Salve, Umbria verde, e tu del puro fonte
> nume Clitumno! Sento in cuor l'antica
> patria e aleggiarmi su l'accesa fronte
> gl'ital iddii.

> [Hail, green Umbria, and you, Clitum-
> nus, genius of the pure spring! I feel the
> ancient fatherland in my heart and the
> Italic gods alight upon my fevered
> brow.]

A few hundred metres from the Fonti del Clitunno stands yet

14a. (*Above*) Assisi, showing the basilica of St Francis and the Rocca Maggiore above the town

14b. (*Left*) Assisi, with the cathedral of San Rufino (1134–1228)

15. Basilica of St Francis, Assisi (1228–53)

16. The interior of the basilica, Assisi, showing the *Life of St Francis* cycle (*c.* 1290–95), attributed to Giotto

17. Gubbio, with the Palazzo dei Consoli (1332–7), with Monte Ingino behind

18. Spoleto, with the Rocca Albornoz and the Ponte delle Torri (14th century)

19. The cathedral, Spoleto (late 12th century)

20. The cathedral, Orvieto (late 13th–early 14th century)

21. The Rocca Paolina, built to ensure papal supremacy over Perugia (1540–43); the fortress was destroyed by the Perugians in 1860

22. Pietro Vannucci, Il Perugino; self-portrait (*c.* 1500) in the Collegio del Cambio, Perugia

23. Oratory of San Bernardino
da Siena, Perugia (1457–61)

24. Santa Maria della Consolazione, Todi (1508–1607)

25. The Cascata delle Marmore, Terni; the falls were created by the Romans in 271 BC, admired by centuries of travellers, and served as the basis of the industrial revolution in Umbria in the nineteenth century

another celebrated monument, whose proximity to the springs was once the source of much confusion. This is the Tempietto del Clitunno, once wrongly identified with the numerous small temples dedicated to minor deities that Pliny described as characteristic of the area but now known to be a palaeo-Christian church – one of the most important in the region – constructed using classical materials (perhaps from those same temples). The exact dating of the church – also known as San Salvatore or the Holy Saviour – is still not entirely certain but it was probably built in two stages, beginning in the late fourteenth century with the single barrel-vaulted chamber, later embellished with a temple-like tetrastyle front, with four columns and two semi-pilasters supporting the entablature and pediment. An inscription on the architrave dedicates the church to the 'SCS DEVS ANGELORVM QVI FECIT RESVRRECTIONEM' or 'Holy God of the Angels who made the Resurrection'; the pediment is finely decorated with a cross, flanked by bunches of grapes, vines and flowers. The small, rectangular *cella* terminates in an apse, fronted by an aedicule, with frescoes depicting Christ the Redeemer with St Peter and St Paul and angels; these frescoes, now in poor condition, have been dated to the eighth century, and are very similar to others in Santa Maria Antiqua in Rome.

Between the Tempietto and the Fonti del Clitunno lies the village of Pissignano (280 m.). The modern development, situated alongside the Foligno–Spoleto road, holds nothing of interest but a narrow road rises steeply up the hillside to the old fortified village, similar in appearance to Campello Alto, which retains a remarkable number of well-preserved tower-houses within its walls; once more the site offers splendid views, including a particularly spectacular one of neighbouring **Trevi**.

Cannara (191 m.): This tiny agricultural centre was founded on the plain of Foligno by the neighbouring, and once important, Roman town of Urbinum Hortense, whose remains are still being excavated. Today the quiet streets invite a leisurely stroll, and there are a number of worthwhile churches, including San Francesco with a large circular tower and the nearby San Giovanni, with a good *Virgin and Child, with Saints Francis and*

Sebastian by Nicolò Alunno. The large church of San Matteo (1786) also has a fine work by Alunno – *Virgin and Child, with Saints Francis and Matthew* – and a *Madonna of the Rosary*, by a late follower of Alfani. The town is also known for the sweet red Vernaccia di Cannara wine, found nowhere else. See also **Bettona, Bevagna, Foligno**.

Carsulae (450 m.): Situated on a large plain below thickly wooded hills to the east, and offering a vast panorama in other directions, the abandoned Roman *municipium* of Carsulae occupies one of the loveliest sites in Umbria. Long known for its waters (see **San Gémini**) and wine production, the city grew up in the first to third centuries as an important centre on the Via Flaminia – a long section of which is still clearly visible. Even today – after centuries of looting, quarrying, and earthquake – enough of the Roman city remains to make it easy to envisage its former appearance. To the right of the Via Flaminia (heading north) are the basilica, raised above street level, an amphitheatre – unusually, this was erected within the city walls, probably to make use of a natural declivity – and a large theatre; there is also a Roman cistern and a second-century building transformed 900 years later into the small church of St Damian. To the left of the Roman road are raised twin temples from the first century, perhaps dedicated to the Dioscuri, and the *curia* (council house). From there, it is possible to walk along the Via Flaminia as far as the north gate of the city (the Porta San Damiano, also known as Trajan's Gate), whose central arch still spans the road; just beyond are two huge tombs, each composed of a raised drum on a square. See also **Acquasparta, San Gémini, Terni**.

Cascia (653 m.): The town is dominated today, physically and economically, by the modern basilica of Santa Rita – built in honour of the fifteenth-century Augustinian nun, born in nearby Roccaporena, who was canonized in 1900 – an internationally important and much-visited site of popular devotion to the patron saint of impossibilities. Once a Roman settlement, later destroyed by an earthquake, Cascia has known more than its fair share of natural and human destruction, even by Umbrian

standards. Sacked by the Longobards and Saracens in the High
Middle Ages, it was later fiercely contested by Spoleto, the
Church, and the Holy Roman Empire as well as coming under
the sway of the Trinci family of Foligno. Subsequently, it
fought cities as far away as L'Aquila in the Abruzzo, but
especially Spoleto, before coming under papal control in 1490,
against which it still attempted, unsuccessfully, to rebel in 1516.
Cascia has also been destroyed or badly damaged by earthquakes
in 1300, 1599, 1703 and 1979.

Unless visited for devotional reasons, the basilica of St Rita,
built between 1937 and 1947, is unlikely to give much satisfaction, except to connoisseurs of kitsch, for its ugly exterior –
Byzantine and Romanesque pastiche by a number of architects
apparently at odds with each other – is only surpassed in
tastelessness by the lurid interior decoration (somewhat redeemed
of late by the new high altar trappings by Giacomo Manzù).
Despite this – and the inevitable drawbacks associated with mass
religious tourism – Cascia has a good deal to offer the visitor, in
the form of monuments to previous periods of prosperity in the
late Middle Ages and in the seventeenth century. The large
Gothic church of San Francesco in the Piazza Garibaldi, for
instance, has an extremely fine carved doorway, surmounted by
a rose-window, and a spacious, remodelled interior whose varied
highlights include fifteenth- and sixteenth-century frescoes, a
large, carved wooden pulpit placed high on the nave wall,
fourteenth-century choir-stalls, and a monumental altar to the
left of the crossing holding Niccolò Pomarancio's *Ascension*
(1596), his last work. Across the road from the church, a road
descending steeply to the medieval east gate of the town (half-
way down there is a vaulted passageway to the left) leads down
to the church of Sant'Antonio Abate. An exceedingly plain
exterior does nothing to prepare the visitor for the well-
preserved and recently restored frescoes within. Behind a large
Renaissance altar, the apse holds an early-fourteenth-century
Life of St Anthony Abbot, attributed to the Maestro del Dormitio
di Terni, while in the former nuns' choir behind is another
extensive fresco cycle – this time a *Life of Christ* (1461) – by
Nicola da Siena, including a large crucifixion scene and a

depiction of Christ on the ceiling with four female saints at the angles. The church now forms part of a museum spread throughout the town – including the recently restored Palazzo Carli and Palazzo Santi – holding, among other items, a beautiful painted wooden sculpture of Tobias and the Angel by the workshop of Antonio Rizzo. Midway up the hill, between Sant'Antonio Abate and the basilica of St Rita, is the large collegiate church of Santa Maria, founded in the ninth century but much altered subsequently. In the piazza in front of the church, and to the right of the façade, are two Romanesque lions; to the side of the left of the two late Renaissance doors is a niche with a frescoed St Sebastian. Inside, there are numerous paintings from different periods, including an attractive fourteenth-century *Virgin and Child*, on a pillar near the entrance, and the remains of frescoes by Nicola da Siena. At the very top of Cascia's hill is the large pink and white stone church of Sant'Agostino and what little remains of the fortress, destroyed by papal troops after Cascia rebelled in 1516. From here, as from down in the town itself, the lovely views of the mountains surrounding Cascia are somewhat spoiled by apparently unplanned suburban sprawl. See also **Monteleone di Spoleto**.

Castelluccio (1,452 m.): This tiny village on the border with the Marches is, at 1,452 metres, the highest in the region and is much frequented in winter by skiers using the nearby slopes. Castelluccio is especially noteworthy for its magnificent position overlooking the great plain (Piano Grande) of Castelluccio – an eight-kilometre-long amphitheatre, above which Umbria's highest peak, Monte Argentella (2,201 m.), rises to the north-east. The plain is especially renowned for its extraordinarily colourful display of spring flowers but, blanketed by snow in winter, or with its grazing flocks of sheep and herds of semi-wild horses in summer, is worth visiting at any time of the year. Even today, however, heavy snows can cut off the village for days at a time, harking back to the days when the papal government forbade travellers to attempt to cross the plain between November and March. The tiny lentils grown on the Piano Grande are the most prized in all of Italy. Climbers use Castelluccio as a base for the ascent of neighbouring peaks; from the summit of Monte Vettore (2,476 m.) – which can be reached with the aid of a guide in three and a half hours – it is possible on a clear day to see both the Adriatic and Tyrrhenian coasts of Italy. See also **Norcia**.

Castel Rigone (653 m.): Even by Umbrian standards, this hilltop village overlooking Lake Trasimeno enjoys stupendous views, taking in not only the lake but the Tuscan hill-towns of Montepulciano and Chianciano Terme and extending beyond Monte Cetona (1,148 m.) to include the characteristic outline of the extinct volcano, Monte Amiata (1,738 m.), the highest peak in peninsular Italy west of the Apennines; on clear days, the view of the Apennine peaks, as far south as Monte Vettore (2,476 m.), is equally fine. Not surprisingly, the village – which retains a small working population – is an increasingly popular holiday spot. It can be approached from several directions: from **Perugia** (via **Magione**), **Umbèrtide**, or the lakeside town of **Passignano**. From this last, it is worth following the old road via the tiny hamlet of San Vito, with its unusual detached Romanesque bell-tower. Castel Rigone itself retains part of the old defensive walls and towers as well as its steep medieval streets and an attractive square.

Just beyond the walls lies a superb early Renaissance temple, the Santuario della Madonna dei Miracoli, built in 1494 at the instigation of Perugia to commemorate the miracles attributed to a small image of the Virgin on the site. Recently restored, the church has an elegant façade decorated by Domenico Bertini da Settignano, called Topolino; the bell-tower is a nineteenth-century replacement. The restoration has shown up the clean lines of the interior which has much fine artwork, including a *Coronation of the Virgin* attributed to G. B. Caporali and the *Madonna del Rosario* by the Florentine Bernardo di Girolamo Rosselli, which includes a depiction of the sanctuary itself. The original image of the Virgin and Child is now to be seen in the Cappella della Madonna with its fine wrought-iron screen. On the superb altar (1528), by the Perugian Bernardino di Lazzaro, is a seventeenth-century copy of the *Adoration of the Magi* painted by Domenico Alfani between 1527 and 1534 from a cartoon by Rosso Fiorentino (the original was looted by the troops of

Ferdinand II, Grand Duke of Tuscany, in 1643); the accompanying lunette and tondos are by Alfani himself. See also **Passignano sul Trasimeno**, **Magione**.

Castel Ritaldi (297 m.): A small farming town of Roman origin, Castel Ritaldi retains part of its thirteenth-century fortifications and a parish church with frescoes by Lattanzio di Nicolò (1509) and Tiberio d'Assisi (1512). Just north of the town is the twelfth-century Romanesque church of San Gregorio, whose noteworthy façade, with a doorway from 1141, has unusual decoration interweaving vegetal designs with monstrous figures. See also **Campello sul Clitunno**, **Giano dell'Umbria**, **San Giacomo di Spoleto**, **Spoleto**.

Castel San Felice (334 m.): On a small outcrop on the right bank of the river Nera, across the river from **Sant'Anatolia di Narco**, just a kilometre away, this fortified village retains its medieval appearance almost intact. Beyond the walls, at the foot of the village, is the twelfth-century Romanesque church of San Felice di Narco, whose beautiful façade has recently been restored. Above the door are an intricately carved rose-window, surrounded by the symbols of the evangelists, and two small *bifore*, with finely sculpted columns and capitals, beneath an arched frontal with cosmatesque mosaic decoration; in the tympanum above is a sculptured Agnus Dei. Beneath the rose-window there are relief scenes from the life of San Felice. The high interior has a raised presbytery over a crypt with two apses, and a number of frescoes. See also **Sant'Anatolia di Narco**, **Vallo di Nera**.

Castiglione del Lago (304 m.): Now a predominantly modern town on Lake Trasimeno with an economy based on tourism, Castiglione was settled by the Etruscans and fought over throughout the Middle Ages before quirkily becoming an independent duchy for almost a century, between 1550 and 1643. The old quarter – very quiet outside the peak holiday season – is picturesquely situated between strong defensive walls on a promontory projecting into the lake (once Trasimeno's fourth island). At the centre is the large Palazzo Ducale of the ruling Della Corgna family, transformed in Renaissance style in the mid sixteenth century and retaining the greater part of its contemporary frescoed decoration – including a representation of the Battle of Lepanto in 1571, at which Ascanio della Corgna fought. A covered fortified pathway close by leads to the impressive castle sited above the lake; there is a tall triangular keep and a chain of sturdy defensive walls offering fine views of the surrounding area. The town churches include the mid-seventeenth-century San Domenico and the Maddalena, remod-elled in the nineteenth century, but retaining one of Eusebio da San Giorgio's finest works, a *Virgin and Child, with Saints Anthony Abbot and Mary Magdalene* (1500). See also **Città della Pieve**, **Paciano**, **Panicale**.

Cerreto di Spoleto (557 m.): Isolated on a strategically impor-tant spur above a spot where two side valleys meet the valley of the Nera, Cerreto offers a magnificent prospect over the sur-rounding countryside, and the large number of surviving *palazzi* provide reminders of the small town's former importance. Bit-terly fought over through the centuries by Spoleto and Norcia, Cerreto retains the recently restored former Benedictine monas-tery of San Giacomo, with sixteenth-century frescoes, at the extreme edge of town, and a number of other churches, includ-ing Santa Maria Annunziata, with a good Renaissance font (1546). The town's inhabitants – known as *cerretani* – were famous in the Middle Ages as itinerant spice sellers, and their wandering habits led to the corruption of their name into *ciarlatani*, in English 'charlatans'. Anything but a charlatan, Cer-reto's most famous son was the celebrated Renaissance humanist Giovanni Pontano (see p. 139). Cerreto's former outpost, Borgo Cerreto – with its tiny late-thirteenth-century Franciscan church of San Lorenzo – is also worth visiting. See also **Ponte**.

Cesi (437 m.): This small town clings somewhat grimly to the lower slopes of Monte Torre Maggiore (1,121 m.), the last peak of the Monti Martani, some nine kilometres north-west of **Terni**. In response to the difficulties of the site, the once-important settlement – overhung by the craggy and densely wooded mountain – developed along a single, elongated axis, whose ends are marked by the Porta Tudertina and Porta Ternana. Given the modern road around the town – and parking restrictions – the visitor will enter the town at the former Terni gate, where immediately to the right the confused façade of the Sant'Angelo church betrays various stages of construction between the eleventh and eighteenth centuries. A steep and winding route leads through the medieval fabric of the town as far as the convent of St Agnes, at Cesi's eastern edge; the convent itself is almost hidden from view but its church dominates the tiny piazza revealing an unexpected but attractive Baroque façade (1613). In the heart of the town stands the parish church of Santa Maria Assunta, built between 1515 and 1525, on the site of an earlier, Franciscan, church dedicated to St Anthony Abbot. In a small museum in the sacristy are to be found an important *Virgin and Child* (1308) by the so-called Master of Cesi and a thirteenth-century wooden sculpture, also of the Virgin and Child, once in the local church of Santa Maria di Fuori; beneath the sacristy, in a cross-vaulted room that once formed part of the church of St Anthony Abbot, is a large, frescoed *Crucifixion* (1425) by Giovanni di Giovannello, a backward-looking painter from Narni. Just before the Porta Tudertina – or Todi Gate – is reached, a small piazza opens out, marked on one side by the small church of Sant'Andrea (1160), which still clearly reveals the many interesting Roman fragments, taken from nearby **Carsulae**, employed in its construction; across the piazza is the imposing sixteenth-century Palazzo Cesi, built for the Cesi family of Acquasparta.

While the period between the twelfth and sixteenth centuries represented the apogee of the modern village's fortunes, Cesi is built close to a much older settlement whose remains can be reached by means of a narrow, serpentine road leading up, through ilex woods, to Monte Eolo (or Monte Erasmo). There, at the height of 790 metres, on a small plain offering extensive views of the entire Terni basin, are to be seen the remains – comprising some large polygonal blocks of stone – of a fortified Umbrian settlement dating back to the sixth century BC and still occupied as late as the first century BC. Close by stands the small Romanesque church of Sant'Erasmo – its simple façade relieved by an unusual window – and some traces of a twelfth-century fortress. From here, a panoramic but untarmacked road leads virtually to the summit of Monte Torre Maggiore. See also **Carsulae, San Gémini, Terni**.

Citerna (480 m.): An attractively sleepy village perched on a steep hill overlooking the Tiber valley, Citerna was inhabited by the Romans, destroyed by northern invaders, and rebuilt between the seventh and eighth centuries. Its exceptional position gave Citerna strategic importance and it changed hands many times, belonging to the Vitelli family of Città di Castello, the Malatestas of Rimini, and the Bourbons of Monte Santa Maria Tiberina, among others. More recently it was occupied by the Germans, who blew up its fortress before leaving in the face of the Allied armies in 1944. Today the ruined fort offers a splendid panorama over the Tiber valley and the Apennines beyond, as well as good views over the surrounding hills towards Monte Santa Maria and into Tuscany. Just below the fortress is the somewhat gloomy church of San Michele Arcangelo, which holds a *Crucifixion* by Niccolò Pomarancio, an attractive glazed terracotta *Madonna, Child and Angels* by followers of della Robbia, and a bell – signed by its maker and dated 1269 – from a local church, destroyed by earthquake in 1917. Lower down are the church of San Francesco – with a fresco attributed to Signorelli and one by Raffaellino del Colle, a *Deposition* by Pomarancio, together with more della Robbian work – and a small Casa Prosperi-Vitelli, which has a superbly carved sixteenth-century fireplace. A narrow alley leads down to a covered medieval pathway which circles part of the town. From Citerna it is only a short trip across the border with Tuscany to Monterchi, which clings appealingly to a small hill and is famous for holding one of Piero della Francesca's best-known frescoes, the *Madonna del Parto*, showing two angels drawing back drapes to reveal a heavily pregnant Mary. See also **Città di Castello, Cospaia, Monte Santa Maria Tiberina**.

Città della Pieve (509 m.): A small agricultural town built, unusually for Umbria, of red brick, Città della Pieve once enjoyed considerable importance for its strategic position dominating the Chiana valley, close to the border with Tuscany. Occupied by the Etruscans and Romans, it was known in the Middle Ages as Castrum Plebis and later Castel della Pieve. Subject to a series of *signori*, but for long an outpost of Perugia, the town eventually fell into the control of the Church, and in 1601 Pope Clement VIII made it a bishopric, changing its name to Città della Pieve. Its greatest boast is to have been the birthplace of the painter Pietro Vannucci, Il Perugino. Clustered together at the top of the hill on which it is built are the city's principal religious and civic monuments: the cathedral, the Palazzo dei Priori, the Palazzo Bandini, the civic tower and the Palazzo della Corgna. The present cathedral stands on the site formerly occupied by the old church, or *pieve* (hence the town's original name), dedicated to Sts Gervasio and Protasio. Although the sixteenth- and seventeenth-century remodelling of the interior is undistinguished, the cathedral does contain a number of worthwhile paintings, including the frescoes in the apse and two panels by Niccolò Pomarancio, a *Virgin, Child and Saints* (1521) by Domenico Alfani, a *Virgin and Saints* by Giannicola di Paolo (also born in the town), and two paintings by Perugino – a *Baptism of Christ* (1510) on the first altar to the left and a *Madonna and Child, with Saints* (1514) in the apse. Just to the side of the cathedral stands the twelfth-century Torre del Pubblico, begun in stone and raised in brick to its present height of thirty-eight metres in 1471. Across from the tower, the Palazzo dei Priori dates from the early thirteenth century but has been much altered. On the opposite side of the square is the sixteenth-century Palazzo della Corgna, built for the city's governor, Ascanio della Corgna, and decorated by Salvio Savini with mythological scenes in 1580.

From the piazza, the Via Pietro Vannucci runs downhill to the eighteenth-century church of Santa Maria dei Bianchi, just inside the city walls. Despite its unprepossessing external appearance, the church holds one of Perugino's finest works: a magnificently composed and richly detailed *Epiphany* (1504). Just beyond the walls is the large church of Sant'Agostino, originally founded in the thirteenth century but remodelled in late Baroque style at the end of the eighteenth century; it contains a number of works by sixteenth- and seventeenth-century artists including Salvio Savini. Continuing past the right flank of the church, it is possible to walk around the city walls as far as the church of San Francesco, another thirteenth-century foundation, completely transformed in the eighteenth century and now a popular place of devotion as a Sanctuary of Our Lady of Fatima. While the church itself has two good pictures – a *Virgin and Saints* (*c.* 1520) by Domenico Alfani and a later-sixteenth-century *Pentecost* by Pomarancio – a more interesting fresco is to be seen in the adjacent Oratory of San Bartolomeo, to the right of the church, which has a large and characteristically Siennese *Crucifixion* (1342–3) by Jacopo di Mino del Pellicciaio, in which the sky around Christ is filled with weeping angels. Directly opposite San Francesco is the Rocca, the square town fortress with imposing towers built in the 1320s by Perugia to ensure control of the western edge of its territory; it was here in 1503 that Cesare Borgia, who had sacked the town, had the Duke of Gravina and Piero Orsini strangled for having conspired against him. From the Rocca, the Via Vittorio Veneto leads rapidly back to the centre of town, though it is worth turning left down the Via Roma, of medieval appearance, passing on the right the large brick-built Palazzo Bandini (originally fourteenth-century but remodelled in the sixteenth by Galeazzo Alessi), as far as the late-thirteenth-century church of Santa Maria dei Servi; this was unhappily restructured in the seventeenth century with the loss of much decoration by Perugino, only a partly damaged *Deposition* being left. Among the most picturesque corners of the medieval town is the Vicolo Bacciadonne, or 'Kiss-the-Women Lane', considered (at least in Città della Pieve) to be the narrowest street in Italy. See also **Castiglione del Lago**, **Monteleone d'Orvieto**, **Panicale**.

Città di Castello (288 m.): With almost 40,000 inhabitants, Città di Castello is the largest town of northern Umbria. It lies on a plateau overlooking the river in the upper Tiber valley and is the principal centre for the area's important tobacco-growing industry, as well as being known for furniture, printing and high-quality textile manufacture. Close to the border with Tuscany, Città di Castello has a character quite distinct from that of most Umbrian towns, due both to the materials, styles and colours of the buildings and to the extensive presence of Tuscan artists – among them the Arezzo-born Giorgio Vasari – who worked there extensively in the sixteenth century. Raphael also produced some of his finest early work here though, sadly, his pictures have been dispersed. Despite this loss – and heavy bombing and artillery bombardment in 1944 – the town retains sufficient evidence of its long and diverse history to make it a particularly varied as well as rewarding town to visit. As a Roman settlement, the town was known as Tifernum Tiberinum (the source of the present name of its inhabitants, *tifernati*); Pliny the Younger, who had a villa at nearby San Giustino, built a temple here at his own expense. The Tiber no longer runs directly below the thirteenth-century city walls, but its present course can be seen from the public gardens close to the cathedral. Anyone prepared for the steep climb up the nearby civic tower (Torre Civica) will enjoy a still better view of the town and the Tiber valley as far north as Monte La Verna, in Tuscany, where St Francis received the stigmata; the large church visible on a hill to the north-east is the Santuario della Madonna del Belvedere, whose construction was dragged out over two centuries from 1669 to 1884. The tower stands on the triangular Piazza Gabriotti, where a lively market takes place on Thursdays and Saturdays.

Across the piazza is the city's cathedral, with its distinctive, thirteenth-century circular campanile. Like the bell-tower, the cathedral is Romanesque in origin but was substantially rebuilt in 1356 and again between 1494 and 1529; the Baroque façade was never completed. The aisle-less interior has an attractive panelled wood ceiling and frescoes (*c.* 1573) by Niccolò Pomarancio, though the finest painting is Rosso Fiorentino's dramatic *Transfiguration* (1530) in a side-chapel. The small museum which adjoins the cathedral should not be missed. Among the items on display are the sixth-century 'treasure of Canoscio', found near the sanctuary of that name by chance in 1935 – a collection of beautifully worked palaeo-Christian plate used for celebrating Mass. There are also a superb silver-gilt narrative altar front from the twelfth century, a fourteenth-century crozier attributed to the Siennese Goro di Gregorio, and, among the paintings, two attractive *putti* attributed to Giulio Romano and a delicate *Virgin and Child with a Young John the Baptist* attributed to Pinturicchio. Close to the cathedral stands the Palazzo Comunale, designed by the architect Angelo da Orvieto and one of the most important examples of its kind in central Italy. The long flank of the former Palazzo del Podestà – also attributed to Angelo da Orvieto – can be seen in the Corso Cavour, which leads into the Piazza Matteotti. This always crowded square – the heart of the city – contains a mix of buildings built between the fourteenth and nineteenth centuries, including the short side of the Palazzo del Podestà, which was bizarrely reworked in Baroque style in 1697. Among the buildings in the piazza is one of the five *palazzi* built in the town by the Vitelli family, who were lords of the city in the fifteenth and sixteenth centuries; this one is in sixteenth-century Tuscan Renaissance style. Along the Via Angeloni, which leads off the Piazza Matteotti, is the large church of San Francesco, built in the early fourteenth century. The interior underwent a largely uninspired remodelling in the eighteenth century but the Vitelli chapel (immediately to the left inside the main door) is a good example of Giorgio Vasari's work as an architect; he also painted the altarpiece and the chapel has a particularly fine wrought-iron screen (1566) by Pietro di Ercolano. Further up the nave is a good majolica depiction of St Francis receiving the stigmata, by the School of della Robbia. The fourth altar to the left of the nave once held Raphael's celebrated *Betrothal of the Virgin*, painted for the church in 1504 but looted by the French in 1798 and now in the Brera in Milan; the present picture is a copy. To the right of the presbytery is a German, polychromed wooden *Pietà* from the fifteenth century.

From San Francesco it is a short walk along the Via degli Albizzini to the Piazza Garibaldi, dominated by the long façade of the largest of the Vitelli palaces, the Palazzo Vitelli a Porta

Sant'Egidio, built in 1540 for Paolo Vitelli, at the site of one of the former city gates. Designed by Giorgio Vasari, the *palazzo* has rich decoration in the vaulting of the entrance by Cristoforo Gherardi, and frescoes celebrating the achievements of the Vitelli family by Prospero Fontana in the large first-floor salon. The stylish interior façade gives on to a large garden, terminated by an elaborately decorated *palazzina*. Just across from the Vitelli palace stands the late-fifteenth-century Palazzo Albizzini, one of two sites now occupied by the uniquely important collection of his work donated to his home-town by Alberto Burri (1915-95), a painter of international stature; the second site, in former tobacco-drying sheds in Via Francesco Pierucci, just outside the city centre, holds larger paintings, as well as sculptures, by the artist (see pp. 233-4).

The city's municipal gallery can be reached either by cutting back through the busy town centre or by following the line of the old city walls along the Viale Antonio Gramsci, which ends at the church of Santa Maria Maggiore, and then continuing just inside the walls along the Via Borgo Farinario. The recently restructured gallery is the second most important collection in Umbria, after the Galleria Nazionale in **Perugia**. It is housed in yet another Vitelli palace, the Palazzo Vitelli alla Cannoniera, built for Alessandro Vitelli between 1521 and 1532 by Antonio da Sangallo the Younger and Pier Francesco da Viterbo. The façade giving on to the once famous gardens is lavishly decorated with graffiti to a design by Vasari, while the interior frescoes include scenes by Cola dell'Amatrice (1537), celebrating the exploits of the Vitelli family. Among the highlights of the collection by native (or adoptive) Umbrian artists are a fourteenth-century *Maestà* by the local Master of Città di Castello, a range of paintings by Luca Signorelli, including an especially powerful *St Sebastian*, with an elaborate cityscape in the background, and a double-sided *stendardo* by the young Raphael. There are also important works by the Florentine Neri di Bicci, the Siennese Giorgio di Andrea di Bartolo, a fine head of Christ attributed to Giusto di Gand, the Flemish painter in the service of Federico da Montefeltro, and a *Coronation of the Virgin* by Ghirlandaio. A small loggia looking on to the garden holds a selection of

majolica pictures by Giovanni, Andrea and Luca della Robbia –
artists whose work is otherwise almost entirely absent from
Umbria outside Città di Castello (apart from the exceptional
terracotta *dossale*, or altar-frontal, by Andrea della Robbia in the
apse of the basilica of Santa Maria degli Angeli, near **Assisi**).
There is also an early-fifteenth-century Florentine enamelled
silver reliquary. On exiting from the museum, retrace your steps
along the Via Borgo Farinario as far as the Largo Mons. Muzi,
which leads to the massive preaching church of San Domenico,
built in 1424; the façade is incomplete but there is a good ogival
doorway on the left flank and the somewhat dark interior has
some interesting fifteenth-century frescoes, as well as a copy of a
Crucifixion by Raphael, now in the National Gallery of London.
Continue along the Largo Mons. Muzi, turn left on to the Via
Marconi, and you will soon arrive at the rear of the cathedral,
which offers the best view of the circular bell-tower.

Two kilometres outside the town, on the road to Perugia, is
the Centro delle Tradizioni Popolari, a local folk museum. It
specializes in recreating the domestic and working environment
of country people of the upper Tiber valley in past centuries.
See also **Citerna**, **Cospaia**, **Monte Santa Maria Tiberina**, **Montone**, **Morra**.

Collazzone (469 m.): Perched on its hill above the middle
Tiber valley, Collazzone retains a predominantly medieval
appearance and a nearly complete ring of defensive walls, a
reminder of the days when the village was a defensive outpost of
Perugia, close to the territory of Todi. The great Franciscan
ascetic and poet Jacopone da Todi (*c.* 1236–1306) spent the last
years of his life in the convent of San Lorenzo here, after being
released from the papal dungeons at Palestrina, where he had
been confined by Pope Boniface VIII, whom he had savagely
attacked in his verse. See also **Deruta**, **Gualdo Cattaneo**.

Collemancio (507 m.): A tiny hilltop village at the northern
limits of the Monti Martani, Collemancio retains a generally
medieval appearance, along with a ring of walls. It grew up in
the Middle Ages around the Romanesque church of Santo Stefano

and has a noteworthy Palazzo del Podestà, built in the thirteenth century. A little to the north of the village are to be seen the remains of Urbinum Hortense, a Roman *municipium* mentioned by Pliny the Elder; these include a temple, a basilica, and baths (though the polychrome mosaic found here is now in the Museo Nazionale Romano, in Rome). See also **Bettona**, **Bevagna**, **Cannara**.

Collescìpoli (238 m.): As Terni expands, this hilltop village is beginning to seem almost a suburb, but it long enjoyed importance as a defensive outpost of the city. The regular late-medieval town plan gives Collescìpoli a distinctive appearance, and the village contains many substantial houses from the sixteenth and seventeenth centuries, as well as a number of worthwhile churches. The latter includes San Nicola da Bari, Romanesque in origin but much altered, with a *Coronation of the Virgin* (1507), in poor condition, by the Roman painter Evangelista Aquili, some interesting popular frescoes, and some truly awful modern works. The fifteenth-century Santa Marìa Maggiore has a fine sixteenth-century doorway and a very fine Baroque interior, with some rich and extremely accomplished Baroque stucco-work (quite exceptional in Umbria), as well as a number of good paintings. Just outside the village, at the cemetery, is the Romanesque church of Santo Stefano, with a long inscription on the façade dating from 1093, and an unusual bell-tower. See also **Stroncone**, **Terni**.

Corciano (408 m.): In many respects, Corciano appears the epitome of the small Umbrian hill-town, almost perfectly re-stored within its ring of thirteenth-century defensive walls. Its obvious appeal to tourists is indicated by the proliferation of small ceramic plaques indicating the former use, or historical importance, of the town's buildings – useful guides but running the (not entirely avoided) risk of turning Corciano into a museum. The former importance of the town derives from its strategic importance at the gates of Perugia on the road from the city to Tuscany; indeed, it belonged to Perugia from the eleventh to fifteenth centuries before passing into the hands of the Della

Corgna family of Castiglione del Lago and eventually into the possession of the Church. Among surviving buildings testifying to Corciano's former importance are the fifteenth-century Palazzo del Capitano del Popolo, and the Palazzo dei Priori and Palazzo Comunale from the following century.

Of the several churches in the town, the thirteenth-century Santa Maria was given an indifferent interior remodelling in the nineteenth century but it possesses both a *gonfalone* by Bonfigli in the first chapel to the left and, on the altar, an attractive late *Assumption* by Perugino, with *Annunciation* and *Nativity* scenes in the predella. A medieval defensive tower adjoining the church was used to create a bell-tower in the nineteenth century. The building materials used for the sixteenth-century San Cristoforo include blocks of stone from a pre-existing Etruscan sanctuary; the church today holds a small museum of religious art. At the top of the hill is the monastery of Sant'Agostino, which dates from 1334, making it one of the first Augustinian sites in Umbria. The church of San Francesco, just outside the walls, was founded in the lifetime of the saint – who stayed in Corciano in 1211 – and employs the pink and white stone bands characteristic of Assisi; some fourteenth- and fifteenth-century frescoes survive inside. A small piazza on the edge of town – guarded by two stone lions variously alleged to be Etruscan or Romanesque – offers a fine view of the valley leading from Perugia to Lake Trasimeno. At Christmas the town becomes most museum-like of all but charmingly so, for the contents of the Museo della Casa Contadina (visitable at other times), representing agricultural life in the area in the past, are taken out and arranged throughout the town streets, leading to the crib, placed in a real stable.

To the north of Corciano is the Pieve del Vescovo, a fourteenth-century castle, remodelled in the sixteenth century by Alessi, which was the summer residence of Gioacchino Pecci, bishop of Perugia, and the future Pope Leo XIII. See also **Magione**, **Perugia**.

Cospaia (376 m.): The few undistinguished houses and a church on a small rise over the upper Tiber valley amount to very little today, yet – due to an oversight by surveyors carving up the territory in the mid fifteenth century – Cospaia remained a tiny independent republic between Tuscany and the Church State for almost 400 years, from 1440 until 1826, when its nuisance value as a centre for contrabanders led its larger neighbours to suppress the minuscule state. See also **Città di Castello**.

Deruta (218 m.): No one driving along the *superstrada*, or dual-carriageway, from Perugia to Terni can fail to notice Deruta or to remain ignorant for long of its principal product. In fact, the small hill-town has been known for its majolica since at least the thirteenth century, and the modern part of the town below the hill contains dozens of small factories, with shops attached, producing some of Umbria's most attractive ceramic ware, much still decorated by hand in traditional styles. Of ancient, probably Roman, origin, Deruta formed part of the territory of Perugia from as early as the eleventh century, but as a fortified outpost of the city from the thirteenth century it suffered at the hands of Perugia's enemies, being sacked by Braccio Fortebraccio in 1408, Cesare Borgia in 1500 and Braccio Baglioni in 1534. The town flourished in the sixteenth century, thanks to its superb majolica production, known throughout Europe, examples of which can be seen in the town's art gallery and ceramics museum, as well as in many collections world-wide.

Situated in the fourteenth-century Palazzo Comunale in the old town, the gallery has some good works, including a double-sided *gonfalone* (1468) by Nicolò Alunno and a fresco by Fiorenzo di Lorenzo, depicting St Roch and St Romanus (1477–8) and including a view of Deruta. The ceramics collection includes work by local artists from the sixteenth to twentieth centuries. Opposite the Palazzo Comunale is the fourteenth-century church of San Francesco, which has two ogival doorways, a good rose-window and an attractive brick bell-tower: the church retains its original aisle-less interior, with a polygonal apse. There are a number of frescoes from the fourteenth century onwards, including a *Life of St Anthony of Padua* by a local artist of the fifteenth century, a *Madonna with Saints* (1520) by Domenico Alfani, and fifteenth-century depictions of St Jerome and St Anthony attributed to Gian Battista Caporali.

About three kilometres away, and clearly signposted from the *superstrada*, is the small church of Madonna dei Bagni, which has a unique collection of more than 500 Deruta-ware votive tablets, dating from the seventeenth to the twentieth centuries. Though sadly diminished by theft during the present century, the collection still presents a remarkably colourful account of popular life in the region during the period, seen through the eyes of those who, in the best way they knew how, offered thanks to the Virgin for deliverance from assorted travails – including sickness, injury by animals, near-drowning and eviction. See also **Collazzone**, **Torgiano**.

Ferentillo (260 m.): Even in Umbria, it would be hard to find a mountain settlement with a general aspect more evocative of the Middle Ages than this magnificently sited small town, which is divided into two quite distinct settlements – Matterella and Precetto – on either side of the steep and rugged valley of the river Nera. Founded in the eighth century and linked to the nearby **Abbey** of San Pietro in Valle, both are circled by defensive walls and retain the remains of their respective fortresses; the more impressive is that of Matterella, with a large keep. Matterella has a large church, Santa Maria, dating from the thirteenth century but much altered, while Precetto's Santo Stefano, divided into an upper and lower church, conserves a number of rather sad mummies, accidentally preserved by local soil conditions. See also **Arrone**, **Terni**.

Ficulle (437 m.): The remains of its medieval walls and thirteenth-century towers serve to indicate Ficulle's former importance as a much fought-over settlement on the road from **Città della Pieve** to **Orvieto**. Today, an active terracotta industry gives the small town a busier appearance than some of its neighbours in the area. The local Collegiata, within the walls, was designed by Ippolito Scalza, and the church of Santa Maria Vecchia, a little way outside, has a good Gothic doorway, some fifteenth-century frescoes, a large, polychrome wooden *Assumption* and, in the shallow apse to the left, an ancient *cippus* testifying to a Mithraic cult in the area. About six kilometres to the south is the imposing Castello della Sala, built by the Monaldeschi family of Orvieto in the fourteenth century and now owned by the Antinori family, who make a well-known Orvieto wine here. The castle itself is square, with an enormous cylindrical defensive tower joined to the remainder of the building only by a high covered gallery; just inside the main entrance is a tiny chapel with a frescoed *Adoration of the Magi* and, beyond, an attractive inner courtyard. See also **Monteleone di Spoleto**.

Foligno (234 m.): Few centres in Umbria reveal such varied cultural influences as the region's third largest city (with a population of just over 50,000). That Foligno is not better known to visitors must be attributed to a combination of several factors – its position on the plain, the industrial sprawl of its suburbs, and its proximity to so many other notable towns, including **Montefalco**, **Spello** and **Trevi** – drawing tourists away. If Foligno is not among the region's best-known towns, however, the varied attractions of its compact centre give it a particularly distinctive character. Once known as Fulginium, the city was an important Roman *municipium*, sited close to the river Topino, at the point where the two branches of the Via Flaminia met, and its geographical location ensured that it retained an importance as a node of road – and, from the 1860s, rail – communications that continues today. An early centre of Christianity in Umbria – through its third-century martyr-bishop, St Felicianus – Foligno survived the fall of the Roman Empire and absorbed the inhabitants of another Roman city near by, Forum Flaminii, after this had been destroyed by the Longobards in the first half of the eighth century. Despite suffering at the hands of Magyar and Saracen invaders, Foligno thrived in the Middle Ages, becoming a free commune before passing into the hands of, by turns, the Church and the Empire. St Francis is supposed to have begun his evangelical work in the city, and the celebrated Franciscan mystic the Blessed Angela (1248–1309) was a native of Foligno. Between 1310 and 1439, Foligno was a powerful *signoria* under the Trinci family, rivalling Perugia in wealth and prestige and controlling an area which included

Assisi, Spello, Nocera, Montefalco, Bevagna and Trevi. In 1439 the city was captured by papal forces under Cardinal Vitelleschi (from another local family) and remained part of the Church State thereafter. Initially influenced by the art of Gubbio and later by that of the Marches, Foligno developed its own tradition within the Umbrian School of painting of the fifteenth century, through such artists as Bartolomeo di Tommaso, Nicolò Alunno and Pier Antonio Mezzastris; it was for the cathedral that Raphael painted one of his most celebrated works – the *Madonna di Foligno* – now in the Vatican. Foligno was also one of the first centres of printing in Italy and seemingly the very first to print a book – Dante's *Divina Commedia* – in Italian, in 1472.

Today a visit might most profitably begin in the always thronged Piazza della Repubblica, the very centre of the walled town as it developed in the thirteenth century, and the best indication of the modern city's prosperity and vitality. Here are Foligno's principal religious and civic monuments, including the cathedral, the Palazzo Comunale and the palace of the Trinci family. From the outside, the Duomo, or cathedral, built of pink and white stone, retains a good deal of its original twelfth-century appearance, though it has undergone much external as well as internal remodelling. The principal façade (1133), just off the piazza, for instance, retains many Romanesque elements but was reconstructed at the beginning of this century, when the mosaic was added. Fortunately the secondary façade (1201), on the piazza itself, survives, and constitutes one of the greatest masterpieces of Romanesque decoration in Umbria. The work of Rodolfo and Binello (who also worked in Bevagna), the decoration of the ornate doorway includes cosmatesque mosaics, the symbols of the evangelists and the signs of the zodiac, as well as relief representations of the Emperor Barbarossa and the bishop Anselm; the wooden doors date from 1620. Above the portal, the façade boasts a classical-style frieze embellished with animal protomas, and a fine arcade.

The cathedral was enlarged in the fifteenth, and again in the sixteenth, century – when the dome was added – and completely remodelled internally in the eighteenth century by Giuseppe Piermarini, after a design by Luigi Vanvitelli. Today the spacious interior contains some good Baroque frescoes by Sebastiano Cipriani in the apse, besides some painted figures by L'Alunno serving as background to a wooden crucifix in the sacristy; the baldachin over the high altar is an exact replica of that by Bernini in St Peter's in Rome. Across the piazza from the cathedral lies the Palazzo Comunale, thirteenth-century in origin but significantly altered between 1546 and 1620 and given a new façade in the nineteenth century; the turreted bell-tower is fifteenth-century. Just to the right of the Palazzo Comunale, and in need of repair, is a very fine Renaissance palace, the Palazzetto Orfini, supposed site of the printing press operated in the 1470s by Emiliano Orfini with the German Johann Numeister. On the short side of the piazza to the north-west stands the brick-built Palazzo Trinci, built between 1389 and 1407 but damaged by an earthquake in 1832 and subsequently given a new façade. The palace was also bombed – as was much of Foligno – during the last war and subsequently rebuilt. The interior courtyard, with its fine Gothic stairway, remains impressive. The entire *palazzo* has recently been restored in order to house the city's art gallery and museum; among the works on display will be numerous frescoes from the original decoration, including a series on the *Life of the Virgin* (1424) by Ottaviano Nelli in the chapel, representations of heroes of Ancient Rome in the Sala dei Giganti, by followers of Nelli, and works by the local artists Bartolomeo di Tommaso, L'Alunno, and Mezzastris.

From the right corner of the Palazzo Trinci, turn down the Via XX Settembre which leads to one of the bridges crossing the Topino, from where there is a good view of the remains of the city walls and a defensive tower. Turn back along the Via Corso Nuovo, where, immediately to the left, is the unfinished façade of the large convent church of San Giacomo (1402), its lower half in pink and white stone dominated by a large ogival door; the interior, remodelled in the eighteenth century, holds a number of works from the fifteenth century onwards, including a fine intarsia-work lectern. Follow the Via Corso Nuovo to its end and turn left along the Via Garibaldi; continue along this street but note, among several turnings to the right, leading into a largely medieval quarter, the particularly characteristic arcaded alley called the Via Servoli. Along the Via Garibaldi, two churches face each other. To the left is the fourteenth-century San Salvatore, with a flat-screen façade in pink and white stone and heavy bell-tower; the interior, remodelled by Vanvitelli, contains some early frescoes and an important triptych of the *Virgin and Child, with Saints* (1437) by Bartolomeo di Tommaso. To the right, Sant'Agostino – also fourteenth-century in origin with a large bell-tower – was more radically remodelled in the eighteenth century, revealing an attractive Baroque interior with a particularly fine high altar. Still further along the Via Garibaldi lies the unfinished neo-classical church of the Santissima Annunziata (1760) and, just beyond, the eastern limit of the medieval city.

Return along the Via Garibaldi as far as the small eighteenth-century church of Santa Maria del Suffragio, at the beginning of the Via Mazzini. A few metres past the church, and a little off the street, is the flank of the Nunziatella, a small church built in 1494. Recently restored, it is notable for a fresco by Perugino of the *Baptism of Christ* (1507). Back on the Via Mazzini, note the small Palazzetto di Gentile da Foligno, a small Gothic palace with a ground-floor portico and ogival windows. Now continue along the same long street, past a number of private *palazzi* from the sixteenth and seventeenth centuries, as far as the Piazza San Domenico, close to the western edge of the old town. On the far side of the piazza stands Santa Maria Infraportas, with an imposing bell-tower. It is one of Foligno's most interesting churches and certainly that which maintains most fully its medi-eval appearance. Built in the eleventh and twelfth centuries, the church is preceded by a portico including four columns with Romanesque capitals. The interior, divided into three aisles, retains a fascinating collection of frescoes from different periods in the church's history. On the right wall are three different *Crucifixion* scenes: the first is by Mezzastris, the second – dated 1525 – is a copy of the first, though by a painter influenced by L'Alunno, while the third is by a local painter of the early fifteenth century who looked back to earlier Siennese models. Mezzastris's work is particularly well represented here. The *St Jerome* at the head of the right aisle is his, and so too is the *St Roch* on the third pilaster to the left of the central aisle (itself painted directly opposite an earlier votive fresco dedicated to the same saint). Among much else, there is an attractive, if old-fashioned, fresco of the *Virgin and Child, with St John the Evangelist* (1500), by the Foligno-born Ugolino di Gisberto, in the left aisle, as well as a painted stucco *Virgin and Child* in Florentine style, on the third pilaster in that aisle, and an elegant Renaissance tabernacle on the left wall of the presbytery. Of greatest interest is the walled-off chapel, the Cappella della Assunta, at the beginning of the left aisle, which dates from the second half of the twelfth century. It has two fine small windows with sculpted columns and a number of early frescoes in Byzantine style. Chief among these is a large depiction of Christ and Sts Peter and Paul, over a splendid painted oriental tapestry decorated with lions, which is contemporary with the chapel.

The large pink and white stone Dominican church (1251), on the north side of the piazza, has a tall bell-tower and a façade with a large ogival door; the spacious hall interior has recently been converted into an auditorium. Pass along the right flank of San Domenico into the Via Frezzi, where immediately to the left is the very impressive Palazzo Bruno-Candiotti, built in brick on an enormous scale in the eighteenth century. Shortly afterwards, the Via della Scuola delle Arti e Mestieri leads into a quiet quarter of mainly medieval houses, passing the tiny pink and white church, San Tommaso 'De Cippischis', built in 1190 – as two tablets on the façade indicate – and on to the church of San Nicolò. This large convent church, built in the fourteenth century and remodelled between the sixteenth and eighteenth centuries, has a once fine but worn Renaissance doorway; it retains a number of works of art, including good paintings by L'Alunno. Note the sinuous Via del Liceo opposite the church's left flank, and return along the Via delle Arti e Mestieri. From here, turn left into what now becomes the Via Gramsci. This street contains a remarkable number of private *palazzi*, dating from the sixteenth to the eighteenth centuries. They include the relatively simple Palazzo Vitelleschi (seventeenth-century), the Palazzo Vallati-Guidicci (sixteenth-century) – opposite which is a medieval house incorporating large stone blocks and an acanthus frieze from a first-century mausoleum – and the Palazzo

Alleori-Ubaldi (seventeenth- to eighteenth-century), with particularly fine windows and cornice. The splendid Renaissance Palazzo Nuti-Deli, with a fine portal and sixteenth-century carved doors, incorporates a tall medieval tower-house. Immediately beyond, the street returns you to the Piazza della Repubblica. See also **Abbey of Sassovivo**, **Montefalco**, **Nocera Umbra**, **Spello**, **Trevi**.

Fossato di Vico (584 m.): A former Roman settlement close to one of the Apennine passes, Fossato is now divided into a lower modern town and the medieval village, Fossato Alto, on a steep hill above. Its position led Fossato to change hands many times during the thirteenth to fifteenth centuries, especially in the conflicts between Gubbio and Perugia. Today, the covered pathways around the village and the steep, narrow streets twisting up the hill give this silent village an appearance little different from that of the Middle Ages. There are a number of interesting churches, including the eleventh-century San Pietro, the tiny Santa Maria della Piaggiola, frescoed by a follower of Ottaviano Nelli, and – outside the walls – San Benedetto, with a portrait of Pope Urban V by Matteo da Gualdo. Fossato is a mere three kilometres from the border with the Marches, which can be reached either by a modern tunnel or via the old pass (733 m.). A road running north-west passes along the Chiascio valley at the foot of Monte Cucco (1,566 m.), passing in the space of fifteen kilometres through the villages of Sigillo (490 m.), Scirca (505 m.), Costacciaro (567 m.) and Schéggia (580 m.), each of which repays attention; twelve kilometres from Schéggia is the Romanesque abbey of Santa Maria di Sitria, founded by St Romuald. The road to the abbey runs through the beautiful scenery of the Monte Cucco Regional Park, which includes one of Italy's largest caves; the park can be explored by car or on foot. See also **Gualdo Tadino**.

Giano dell'Umbria (546 m.): Like several neighbouring settlements in the Martani hills, Giano was much fought over in the Middle Ages by its larger neighbours, Todi and Spoleto. Unusually, however, Giano – along with Castel Ritaldi and a few small villages – maintained at least a nominal independence for 200 years, between the twelfth and fourteenth centuries, as part of a territory called Normandia, or Normandy (the name supposedly deriving from Normans who settled in the area after fighting for Pope Gregory VII in the late eleventh century). The small town's Roman origins are indicated by some traces of its Roman walls, but the present appearance is predominantly medieval. Giano's principal ring of walls and its unusual town plan – deriving from its origins in what were once two distinct fortified villages – date from the Middle Ages. There is a Palazzo Pubblico and two thirteenth-century churches, the Pieve and San Michele. Just outside the walls is a much altered Franciscan preaching church, San Francesco, with a number of fourteenth-century frescoes, including a cycle in the Cappella del Crocifisso, attributed to Giovanni di Corraduccio. Some two kilometres outside the town is the Romanesque **Abbey of San Felice**. See also **Gualdo Cattaneo**, **Massa Martana**, **Montefalco**.

Giove (292 m.): This small village overlooking the Tiber valley, close to the border with Lazio, retains much of its medieval appearance. Fiercely contested for centuries by Todi and Amelia, Giove lost its walls and most of its fortifications in 1503 when they were destroyed by the troops of Cesare Borgia, in his efforts to bring the area securely under papal control. In the seventeenth century, what remained of the fortress was employed to create the Palazzo Ducale, notable for a spiral ramp leading to the first floor, designed to permit the passage of coaches. The parish church dell'Assunta has a panel of the *Assumption* by a follower of L'Alunno. See also **Amelia**, **Lugnano in Teverina**.

Gualdo Cattaneo (446 m.): Of ancient origin, Gualdo Cattaneo takes its name from the time of the Longobard presence in the region, 'Gualdo' deriving from the German *Wald*, or wood. Situated on a hill, in the heart of the Monti Martani, the small town was much fought over by Foligno, Spoleto, and Todi. It still retains its medieval walls and defensive towers, as well as an enormous cylindrical tower, built in 1494 at the direction of

Pope Alexander VI, who was intent on securing control of the area. The parish church was rebuilt in 1804 but retains some sculptural elements from the previous, thirteenth-century, church on its façade, as well as a thirteenth-century crypt. A road down from the Palazzo Comunale leads to the church of Sant'Agostino, also remodelled, which retains a Gothic doorway and a number of frescoes, including a *Crucifixion* by followers of Nicolò Alunno. See also **Bevagna**, **Collazzone**, **Giano dell'Umbria**, **Montefalco**.

Gualdo Tadino (536 m.): On a steep hill in the shadow of Monte Serra Santa (1,421 m.) and dominated by its ancient fortress, Gualdo can seem a forbidding place, especially in winter. The town's position on an important route across the Apennines, however, has ensured its continued settlement throughout many centuries and also long made it a site of contention between warring factions. Once the Tarsinater cursed in the Eugubine Tablets as the inveterate enemy of the people of Gubbio, the town was refounded by the Romans as Tadinum in a position on the plain, close to the Via Flaminia. Destroyed by the Goths, whose leader, Totila, was defeated and killed near by in 552, Gualdo was repeatedly devastated by northern invaders until its inhabitants returned to the present hill site, in search of the protection of the local Benedictine abbey, leading the town's bishopric (established in the fifth century) to be transferred to neighbouring **Nocera Umbra**. The town, then known as Gualdo di Nocera – its name deriving from the Longobard *Wald*, or wood – was eventually refounded in the late twelfth century. After a brief period as a free commune in the thirteenth century, it passed under the control of Perugia and, eventually, in the sixteenth century, of the Church. A major earthquake in 1751 caused the loss of Gualdo's principal civic buildings from the Middle Ages, but the town has a number of worthwhile churches, grouped closely together, within its still largely medieval fabric.

The two principal churches – San Benedetto and San Francesco – stand on opposite sides of Gualdo's main piazza, the Piazza dei Martiri della Libertà (named for a number of the town's civilian inhabitants massacred by the Germans during the last war). San Benedetto, once the church of the Benedictine abbey, is now also the town's cathedral, a status accorded it as late as 1915. The façade has three doors – that in the centre being particularly fine – and a notable rose-window; a legend in the upper part of the façade recalls the restoration of the church after the earthquake. Unfortunately, San Benedetto's interior was entirely remodelled in the late nineteenth century in a sumptuous but otherwise unremarkable manner. On the outer right wall of the cathedral is an attractive sixteenth-century fountain attributed to Antonio da Sangallo the Elder. Across the piazza, which also holds the Palazzo Comunale, is the flank of the large thirteenth-century San Francesco, whose simple façade has an ogival doorway. The spacious aisle-less interior, with encircling wall-passage, is one of a number of Franciscan churches in Umbria to be directly modelled after the basilica of St Francis in Assisi; it retains a number of fifteenth-century frescoes, including some by the local artist Matteo da Gualdo (c. 1435–c. 1503). Until recently San Francesco also held the local picture gallery – a notable collection containing important works by artists from Umbria, Tuscany and the Marches, including Matteo da Gualdo, Nicolò Alunno, Sano di Pietro and Antonio da Fabriano. (The gallery has been closed but is due to reopen in the Palazzo del Podestà.) The nearby church of Santa Maria dei Raccomandati, along the Corso Italia, in Piazza XX Settembre, holds another significant work by Matteo da Gualdo, the triptych *Virgin and Child, with St Sebastian and St Roch* (1480).

A steep walk to the top of the town leads to Gualdo's ancient fortress, the Rocca Flea. This compact building, with massive angle towers, was strengthened in the thirteenth century by the Emperor Frederick II and, in 1394, by the powerful lord of Perugia, Bordo Michelotti; it has been undergoing restoration for the past two decades but should soon serve to house a museum of the ceramic work for which Gualdo has long been famous, and which is readily on sale throughout the town. See also **Fossato di Vico, Nocera Umbra**.

Gubbio (522 m.): One of the most rewarding cities in Umbria for the visitor, Gubbio is notable both for its monuments and for its fine geographical position, hugging the lower slopes of Monte Ingino. Already inhabited in prehistoric times, the city was an important settlement of the early Umbrians, and the town museum today holds the most important surviving record of these Umbri: a series of seven bronze tablets from the third to first centuries BC, engraved in Etruscan and Roman characters with texts concerning the religious practices of the '*Tota* [city] *Ikuvina*'. The Romans knew the city as Iguvium – and the inhabitants are still known as *eugubini* today. Just beyond the city walls are the well-preserved remains of the first-century theatre – one of the largest of the Roman world – where classical plays are performed during the summer. The old city suffered greatly during the decline of the empire at the hands of northern invaders and, after total destruction by Totila in 552, was rebuilt higher up the mountain. Subsequently a Byzantine and then Longobard stronghold, the city passed nominally into the hands of the papacy before emerging as a free commune in the eleventh century. In 1151, led by its bishop, Ubaldo, Gubbio withstood an attempt by a league of eleven cities, headed by Perugia, to control its expansionist tendencies, and a combination of military and diplomatic skills led to the recognition of its independence by Barbarossa in the 1160s. Gubbio was now a flourishing city-state of 50,000 inhabitants (today the entire commune – which, at more than 500 square kilometres, is one of the largest in Italy – has only 30,000).

Even two centuries of intermittent warfare with Perugia – during which time part of its territory, including **Nocera**, changed hands – did nothing to prevent Gubbio from entering the fourteenth century as a wealthy and powerful commune, as many buildings of the time still testify. Towards the end of the century, the local Gabrielli family made repeated attempts to establish a *signoria* there until, in 1384, the city voluntarily gave itself up to the control of the Montefeltro family of Urbino, under whose control it remained until 1508. After just over a century of rule by the Della Rovere family, Gubbio was presented in 1624 to the Church – against which it rebelled in 1831, having its own provisional government for forty days. It was considered as part of the Marches until being joined to the new region of Umbria at Italian unification in 1860. During 1944, the mountains east of Gubbio saw heavy partisan activity to which the occupying Germans responded savagely, most notably in the infamous massacre of forty randomly selected citizens, machine-gunned to death close to the church of the Madonna del Prato; there is a monument to them on the site and the vast Piazza dei Quaranta Martiri is named for them. The town also suffered heavy bombardment by German artillery throughout most of July 1944, as Allied troops strove to capture it.

An austere medieval city with grey, limestone buildings, its steep, narrow streets giving suddenly on to extensive mountain views, Gubbio is an excellent city to explore at leisure on a fine and not-too-hot day. The following route takes in the principal sights. A good starting point is the Piazza dei Quaranta Martiri, which offers a promising view of the town above. The square's northern side is given over to the Ospedale della Misericordia (1326), preceded by a portico where a small market still takes place; the Loggiato dei Tiratori dell'Arte della Lana above was erected in the seventeenth century by the powerful woollen guild. The small adjoining church, Santa Maria dei Laici, dates from the early fourteenth century and contains a number of Baroque works, including the last canvas by Federico Barocci. On the opposite side of the piazza, the enormous preaching church of San Francesco was built in the mid thirteenth century in honour of the saint, who stayed in Gubbio in 1206–7. The church's simple, unfinished façade has a Romanesque doorway, while the left flank has another doorway with a rose-window above; there are three polygonal apses, from the earliest building stage, and an octagonal fifteenth-century bell-tower. The interior, divided by columns into three aisles, was substantially remodelled in the early eighteenth century. Fortunately, much of the original decoration survived the remodelling. Particularly noteworthy among frescoes from the thirteenth to fifteenth centuries are *Scenes from the Life of Mary* (1408–13), one of the finest works of the Gubbio-born Ottaviano Nelli. A doorway at the side of the apse leads, via the sacristy, into the convent cloister.

Exit from San Francesco and take the Via Cavour, which begins at the far end of the square past the town hospital. This makes a sharp right-hand turn leading to the other great preaching church, San Domenico, whose Gothic interior was also transformed in line with eighteenth-century taste; it retains a number of poorly preserved fourteenth- and fifteenth-century frescoes, including ones by Nelli and Raffaellino del Colle, as well as a fine late-sixteenth-century choir and lectern. Continue on up the intact medieval streets of Via Vantaggi and Via Gabrielli to the Palazzo del Capitano del Popolo, built just inside the Porta Metauro, one of the city gates, at the end of the thirteenth century. Beyond the walls is a small church, Santa Croce della Foce, where a representation of the Passion and Death of Christ, accompanied by singing and the playing of wooden instruments called *battistrangoli*, has been held every Good Friday without interruption since the Middle Ages. Back inside the walls, turn left and along the Camignano torrent – there is a good view of one of the town's surviving defensive towers to the right – as far as the Via dei Consoli. Here there are more defensive towers and a large number of shops selling the ceramics for which Gubbio has been famous for centuries. Almost immediately, to the right, is the simple Palazzo del Bargello, built in 1302. In front of it is a sixteenth-century fountain, the Fontana dei Matti. Visitors who run around the fountain three times are – understandably – permitted to claim the title of *matto* (Madman). The Via dei Consoli proceeds between lines of well-preserved medieval stone houses to reach one of the finest sites in Umbria.

The Piazza della Signoria is a huge balcony which offers a magnificent panorama over the lower town and surrounding countryside. On one of the short sides of the piazza is the Palazzo dei Consoli, one of the finest medieval buildings in Italy, built by Angelo da Orvieto between 1332 and 1337. In a fine piece of medieval town planning, it is complemented across the piazza by the Palazzo Pretorio (1349), designed by the Gubbio-born architect Matteo Gattapone. Today the Palazzo dei Consoli holds the city museum and art gallery. Though not large, the collections are sufficiently varied to give a good sense of Gubbio's long history and cultural independence. At the top of the exterior staircase is the palace's vast barrel-vaulted principal chamber. Today it holds a number of Roman remains, including a sarcophagus, and a large fresco by Guido Palmerucci. A room, reached by an inside stairway, holds the beautifully engraved Gubbian tables, written in the Umbrian language, using either Etruscan or Roman characters (Table 5 employs both). On the second floor, a collection of ceramics includes a finely painted work by the local master, Giorgio Andreoli, purchased at auction in London by public subscription in 1991. Among the painters represented in the gallery on the top floor are the Maestro della Croce di Gubbio, Mello da Gubbio, Guido Palmerucci, and Ottaviano, Tommaso and Martino Nelli. An early-seventeenth-century fresco by Felice Damiani represents the legend of St Francis and the (most amiable-looking) wolf that had been terrorizing Gubbio. A short passage leads from the gallery on to a small loggia offering magnificent views of the town and hills beyond.

On leaving the Palazzo dei Consoli, follow the steps of the Via Galeotti up to the steep Via Ducale, which leads to the Palazzo Ducale and the cathedral. In marked contrast to the medieval *palazzi* just below, the Ducal Palace – built for Federico da Montefeltro, Duke of Urbino – was designed in advanced Renaissance style after 1476, probably by the Siennese architect Francesco di Giorgio Martini. The palace boasts a magnificent courtyard and has finely proportioned rooms with some good fireplaces and one splendid wooden ceiling. There is an archaeological site below the palace, with remains dating back to the tenth century, and a small museum including paintings and some inlaid wood doors (the only surviving reminiscence of the palace's superb intarsia work which culminated in the Duke of Montefeltro's study, now in the Metropolitan Museum in New York). Opposite the palace is the fourteenth-century Gothic cathedral whose façade includes Romanesque symbols of Christ and the evangelists from an earlier church. The impressive interior consists of a vast nave with ten enormous transverse Gothic arches supporting the roof. The cathedral contains work by local artists and those from elsewhere, as well as fine choir-stalls painted to resemble intarsia work, by

Benedetto Nucci, and a carved episcopal throne by Girolamo Maffei, both from 1557. From the cathedral it is possible to make the long haul up to the sanctuary of Sant'Ubaldo (see below), but this can also be reached by road or, more dizzyingly, by cable-car, from just beyond the Porta Romana.

Returning down the Via Ducale, turn left on to the Via XX Settembre, which leads to the Porta Romana and, just beyond the city gate, to the monastery of Sant'Agostino. The large early-thirteenth-century church shows the ogival transverse arches so characteristic of medieval architecture in the Gubbio region; the surviving frescoes include an accomplished if some-what sombre *Life of St Augustine* cycle by Ottaviano Nelli and his followers. Back inside the city gate, turn right for a short distance and then left on to Via Savelli della Porta; almost immediately on the left is the fourteenth-century church of Santa Maria Nuova, whose seventeenth-century interior (badly in need of restoration) includes one of Ottaviano Nelli's finest works, the *Madonna del Belvedere* (1408 or 1413), in which a delicate Virgin and Child are depicted surrounded by angel musicians, saints and donors. From here, the Via Nelli and Via Vincenzo Armanni lead down to San Pietro. Originally an eleventh-century foundation, the church has undergone several remodellings; the present interior dates from the sixteenth and eighteenth centuries and contains numerous works of art, includ-ing a *Visitation* attributed to Giannicola di Paolo and a *Nativity* by Raffaellino del Colle. A detour through the nearby Porta Vittoria soon leads to Santa Maria della Piaggiola, with a frescoed *Madonna and Child* by Ottaviano Nelli and works by Tommaso Nelli and Domenico di Cecco. Otherwise, the Via Reposati leads back to the Piazza dei Quaranta Martiri.

The Sanctuary of Sant'Ubaldo stands at 827 metres and offers fine views. The church – dedicated to Gubbio's patron, whose remains rest here – was greatly enlarged in 1514 by the Della Rovere family, in often splendid Renaissance style. In the first aisle to the right are the three extremely tall and heavy wooden machines composed of two octagonal prisms, one on top of the other, called *ceri*, or candles, used in the town's celebrated race, which takes place every 15 May. In a

region increasingly given over to 'medieval' pageants of often
dubious provenance the Corsa dei Ceri stands out for its genuine
antiquity – it may even antedate the bishop the eve of whose
feast it nominally celebrates – and is perhaps the finest such
event in central Italy apart from Siena's famous bareback horse
race, the Palio. First, the *ceri* are brought down from the
sanctuary to the town on 1 May. At midday on the 15th, three
teams dressed in striking, vividly coloured costumes each display
one of the *ceri* – St Ubaldus for the builders, St George for
traders, and St Anthony Abbot for the agricultural labourers –
up, down and around this very steep town. At six in the
evening, after the *ceri* have been blessed, they are raced at
extraordinary speed from the Piazza della Signoria up the mountain to Sant'Ubaldo, where they remain until the following
year. The Corsa attracts thousands of spectators each year,
including many emigrants who return home for the event. On
the last Sunday in May, a crossbow competition, first held in or
before 1461, takes place between Gubbio and the Tuscan town
of Borgo San Sepolcro; a return match takes place in San
Sepolcro on the first Sunday in September. See also **Fossato di
Vico, Gualdo Tadino, Umbèrtide**.

Isola Maggiore (309 m.): This is the second largest, and only
inhabited, island in Lake Trasimeno. Covered with a mixture of
pines, cypresses and olive trees, it today supports a small population of fishermen and lace-makers who live in the single, tiny
village. According to the Franciscan legend as recounted in the
Fioretti, St Francis spent Lent here in 1211, eating only half of
one of the two loaves of bread he brought with him. The
island's association with the saint led to the founding of a
Franciscan convent – converted to private use in the nineteenth
century – where visitors included St Bernardino of Siena. Besides
the former convent, the island has a small Romanesque church,
San Salvatore, and the mid-fourteenth-century Gothic church of
San Michele Arcangelo, which stands on the island's highest
point and contains a *Crucifixion* by Bartolomeo Caporali. The
island, which offers splendid views of the lake and surrounding
hills, forms part of the commune of Tuoro and can be reached

by ferry services from there, or from **Castiglione del Lago** or **Passignano**.

Lugnano in Teverina (419 m.): Built on an isolated hilltop position overlooking the Tiber valley, Lugnano was fiercely contested in the Middle Ages by Todi, Amelia and Orvieto, and was sacked in 1503 by the forces of Cesare Borgia. Nevertheless, this now tranquil village preserves a generally medieval appearance, besides boasting one of the finest Romanesque churches in the region. Originally dating from the second half of the twelfth century, Santa Maria Assunta underwent some alteration in both the fourteenth and eighteenth centuries, and was subject to interior restoration this century. Approached across the small piazza on to which it faces, the church makes a magnificent impression, its façade preceded by a portico which brings to mind those of Santa Maria in Pensole, in **Narni**, and Santa Pudenziana, near Visciano. The portico is supported by two L-shaped corner pillars and four columns, two of them spiral, taken from earlier buildings; between these pillars and columns, above the trabeation, are five very shallow arches, with reliefs of the symbols of the Evangelists and the remains of once-rich cosmatesque decoration. Above the portico, two small circular windows give light to the side aisles, and between them a large rose-window, in the form of a double-wheel, illuminates the central aisle. This rose-window is itself placed within a square, whose decoration repeats the symbols of the Evangelists, and is flanked by two two-light windows, after a model derived from the church of San Pietro at Tuscania, in Lazio; a much smaller rose-window above shows the remains of what were once seven polychrome ceramic dishes. On the external wall to the left of the portico, a three-faced figure symbolizes the Trinity.

The interior has a high barrel-vaulted central aisle, two lower cross-vaulted flanking aisles, and a presbytery raised over a small crypt. Despite considerable criticism of the remodelling of the interior – which has been considered arbitrary – there is much to admire in the separate elements of the architecture and decoration. There are finely carved and very varied capitals to the columns of the nave, for instance. The third to the left is of particular interest, depicting the celebration of the Eucharist according to the Byzantine rite (recognized from the position of the celebrant's hands) and a symbolic representation of evil, in the figure of a man with a serpent issuing from his mouth. The reconstruction of the choir at the head of the central aisle has been particularly criticized but, again, the individual elements are of high quality; these include two decorated pulpits, and two finely carved relief sculptures, depicting *The Archangel Michael and the Dragon* and what has been read as two men, in thirteenth-century dress, exchanging the kiss of peace. The rich cosmatesque floor decoration is largely a modern restoration (1969). Behind the ciborium in the elevated presbytery there is a good triptych by L'Alunno, the central panel of which depicts the *Assumption*, while those at the side show *St Francis* and *St Sebastian*. A small chapel to the right of the presbytery has an unexpected but accomplished *Beheading of John the Baptist* (1571) by Livio Agresti, the Mannerist painter from Forlì who worked in southern Umbria during the 1560s and 1570s.

From its elevated position above the Tiber valley, Lugnano also offers a matchless panorama of this part of central Italy; the view westward across the river, framed by Monte Cimino (1,053 m.) in Lazio and Monte Amiata (1,738 m.) in Tuscany, takes in parts of three regions. Just below Lugnano, on the east bank of the Tiber, the village of **Alviano**, dominated by its castle, is clearly visible, close to the lake of Alviano; the hill-town of Montefiascone, in Lazio, is to be seen in the distance to the west. From Lugnano, a panoramic road winds its way along the side of the hills, by the way of Guardea (387 m.), with the fifteenth-century Castello di Poggio, to **Baschi**. See also **Alviano**, **Amelia**, **Baschi**.

Magione (299 m.): This industrious small town is now particularly known for brass and copper ware. Its position on the road from Perugia to Siena and Florence once gave it a strategically significant position, as can be seen from the remains of the thirteenth-century defensive tower, known as the Torre dei Lambardi, which dominates the hill overlooking the town. The fine, square castle on the edge of town was built for the crusading Knights of Malta by the Bolognese architect Fieravante Fieravanti, around 1420; it has an attractive balconied interior courtyard, where concerts are sometimes held during the town's August festival. The tiny thirteenth-century church of the Madonna delle Grazie has a fresco (1371) attributed to Andrea di Giovanni da Orvieto, while the undistinguished parish church has a surprisingly conventional fresco cycle (1947) by the Futurist painter Gerardo Dottori. The town was the birthplace of the Franciscan Fra Giovanni da Pian di Carpine – the plain below the town was once covered with *carpine*, or hornbeam – who, during St Francis's own lifetime, led missions to Germany, Hungary, Poland and Spain. In 1245, Pope Innocent IV sent him on a mission to the east which took him as far as Karakorum in Mongolia; when he returned, over two years later, he wrote a *Historia Mongolorum*, the most important source of western knowledge of the area before Marco Polo. The renowned and bloody *condottiere* Niccolò Piccinino (1386–1444) was born near by. See also **Castel Rigone**, **Montecolognola**.

Massa Martana (351 m.): The town has a long history, going back to the time when it was a station, Vicus ad Martis, along the Via Flaminia. In the Middle Ages it was vigorously contested by Spoleto, Todi and the Church. All the same, Massa Martana is something of a disappointment today – despite the promise of its tenth-century gate and thirteenth-century walls, and the elegant octagonal Renaissance church, the Madonna della Pace, built just outside the town as a Marian sanctuary. In compensation, the town is set among lovely countryside, on the south-west slopes of Monte Martano (1,094 m.), with one of Umbria's earliest churches near by. This is Santa Maria in Pantano, built in the seventh or eighth century by adapting an existing Roman building on the Via Flaminia; there is an adjoining medieval tower, with bell-gable. The apse is the earliest part of the church, while the interior – divided into three aisles by columns in the twelfth century – shows traces of the earlier Roman building as well as some medieval frescoes; the façade dates from the fourteenth century. Massa Martana is known for Villa San

Faustino mineral water. See also **Abbey of Santi Fidenzio e Terenzio**.

Mongiovino (318 m.): Though attractive, the tiny medieval walled village of Mongiovino Vecchio (490 m.), close to Tavernelle, in the commune of **Panicale**, has little to distinguish it from countless similar settlements in Umbria. Below the village, however, is the interesting Renaissance sanctuary of the Madonna di Mongiovino, erected to a design variously attributed to Bramante and to Michelangelo. It was begun in 1513 by Rocco di Tommaso, on the site of an apparition of the Virgin, as were many other contemporary Marian sanctuaries in the region (see, for example, **Castel Rigone**, **Todi**). The centrally planned church, with an octagonal cupola, has finely decorated doorways by Rocco di Tommaso and others, and the interior is extensively decorated by some of the major artists working in Umbria in the sixteenth century, including the Dutch painter Heinrich van den Broek, known as Arrigo Fiammingo, the Pisan Niccolò Pomarancio, and Mattia Battini from Città di Castello. In the nearby village of Fontignano (294 m.) is the tiny church of the Annunziata, which has a late (and weak) fresco by Perugino, who died here of the plague in 1523. See also **Panicale**.

Montecastrilli (391 m.): This small town, long an outpost of Todi, retains its ring of medieval walls and a large, circular defensive tower. The parish church, with a good bell-tower, has a noteworthy fifteenth-century wooden crucifix and some later paintings, while the Convent of the Clarisse, or Poor Clares, dates from 1500. Montecastrilli is ringed by a number of Romanesque churches, including those of San Lorenzo in Nifili, San Martino, Santa Maria in Ciciliano and Canto. Just outside the neighbouring village of Dunarobba lies the *foresta fossile*, or fossil forest, consisting of some forty trunks of sequoia that once grew on the shores of the vast Tiber Lake, which extended through much of the region. These were buried between 1.5 and 3.5 million years ago, in a peculiar combination of clay and silt which preserved them; some, quite exceptionally, are still in an upright position. Unfortunately, vandalism has meant that the trees are now protected by shelters and fenced off, making the forest difficult to see properly, at least for the time being. See also **Acquasparta, Amelia, San Gémini, Todi**.

Montecolognola (410 m.): Perched on a steep, olive-covered hill on the eastern shore of Lake Trasimeno, Montecolognola offers exceptional views of the lake and surrounding area, extending across Umbria's borders into neighbouring Tuscany. The perfectly preserved ring of medieval walls of this attractively tranquil village dates back to 1293. The strategic importance of the site – on the road from Perugia to Florence – led to it being occupied by Braccio Fortebraccio in 1416, by the Florentines in 1479 following the Pazzi conspiracy, and again in 1643 by the troops of the Tuscan Archduke Ferdinand II, who looted the bells, subsequently given to Bibbiena (between Arezzo and Florence). The fourteenth-century parish church retains some frescoes from the fourteenth to sixteenth centuries. See also **Magione, Passignano, San Feliciano**.

Montefalco (472 m.): Due to its exceptional position, commanding extensive views around 360 degrees, this small hill-town in the Martani hills is known as the Balcony of Umbria. On a clear day, it is possible to take in almost the entire Vale of Umbria from Perugia to Spoleto – a view which includes Assisi, Spello, Foligno, Trevi, Bettona, Bevagna, and Pissignano. As the home-town of no fewer than eight saints, Montefalco has been more fancifully called 'a piece of heaven on earth'. Having replaced celestial by an earthier fame, it is now one of Umbria's leading wine towns. Montefalco's strong defensive position and its fertile hills have led it to be a highly regarded place of settlement for many centuries. A free commune in the twelfth century, and subsequently an imperial city, it was destroyed by the armies of Frederick II in the mid 1300s, only for Pope John XXII to choose it as the residence for the papal governor of Spoleto in the first half of the fourteenth century. Later it belonged to Foligno, then to the Church, and was sacked in the troubled year of 1527. Today Montefalco has a prosperous appearance and retains considerable evidence of its former cultural importance, including one of Umbria's most attractive museums.

It is a good idea to enter the town by way of the Porta Sant'Agostino, the principal gate. Once inside the well-preserved fourteenth-century walls, follow the Corso G. Mameli uphill to the church of Sant'Agostino on the left. The Augustinian foundation was built in Gothic style between 1279 and 1285, and enlarged in the following century; its somewhat dark single-aisled interior preserves many notable frescoes from the fourteenth to sixteenth centuries. At the top of the hill sits the main square, the Piazza del Comune, around which gather the Palazzo Comunale (dating from 1270 but greatly altered), the church of Santa Maria di Piazza, and a number of fine fifteenth- and sixteenth-century buildings.

The Via Ringhiera dell'Umbria leads down away from the square and to the deconsecrated church of San Francesco, now the town museum, which holds one of the region's most important collections of art. The church itself was built by the Franciscans between 1336 and 1338, the façade being altered in the sixteenth century. The large preaching church was originally undivided, though a small aisle was subsequently added to the right flank. Here, Benozzo Gozzoli frescoed the small chapel of St Jerome (San Girolamo) between 1450 and 1452. Among a wealth of fine decoration in the nave by painters of the Umbrian School are works by Perugino (including a characteristic *Nativity*), Mezzastris, Tiberio d'Assisi, and Francesco Melanzio, who was born in the town. The principal attraction of the church, however – and one of the most influential works in Umbria – is Gozzoli's decorative fresco cycle, the *Life of St Francis* (1452), in the polygonal central apse. The power and influence the Franciscan movement had acquired by the mid fifteenth century is indicated by the depiction, at the base of the frescoes, of twenty-three of its leading members – including saints, popes, philosophers and doctors of the church. The two smaller flanking apses contain works of art by Umbrian artists of the late thirteenth and fourteenth centuries. Notable among works displayed in the small museum incorporated in the church are a thirteenth-century painted crucifix, a late-fifteenth-century panel with scenes from the life of Christ, and a *gonfalone* (1498) by Melanzio. This artist was also responsible for the *Madonna del Soccorso* (1510) – a vigorous treatment of a theme particularly popular in Umbria, in which the Virgin drives away a diabolic figure inadvertently summoned by a mother's exasperated cry to her naughty child, 'May the Devil take you.' Among pieces by artists from elsewhere, there is a beautifully composed and executed painting of Sts Vincent, Illuminata and Nicholas of Tolentino, by Antoniazzo Romano. The museum also contains an archaeological section, comprising Roman, palaeo-Christian and medieval materials from the area.

From San Francesco, the Via Ringhiera dell'Umbria goes down to a viewing point just outside the walls. A road running clockwise around the town soon arrives at the Porta di Federico II, dating back to 1244; the imperial eagle and Swabian cross commemorate the Emperor's stay in Montefalco – which also, though not always voluntarily, was host to Barbarossa and several popes. Just inside the gate is the particularly lovely eleventh-century Romanesque apse of the church of San Bartolomeo, set in a well-preserved medieval quarter of town. From outside the gate, the road leads to the large church of Santa Chiara, dedicated not to the famous follower of St Francis but to the mystic, St Clare of Montefalco. (It is much disputed whether Montefalco's Clare was a Franciscan or an Augustinian, a dispute which reached its nadir in 1478, when the convent named for her split – fourteen nuns leaving to follow the Franciscan rule and just three remaining Augustinians, in line with the bishop's direction.) There are still nuns in Santa Chiara today, and it is possible to visit not only the church but also the adjoining Cappella di Santa Croce – which has frescoes commissioned in 1333 from Umbrian painters evidently familiar with Lorenzetti's work in the Lower Church at **Assisi**. Beyond Santa Chiara, along the Via Verdi, is the Renaissance church of Santa Illuminata, with a *Madonna della Misericordia* (1500) by Melanzio in the lunette above the door, and frescoes in the interior by the same artist, as well as others by Mezzastris. Just under a kilometre further on stands the fifteenth-century church of San Fortunato

– named for the bishop of Todi who is credited with evangelizing Montefalco. It merits a visit for its attractive porticoed courtyard, frescoed in 1512 by Tiberio d'Assisi and, later, by Gozzoli, who executed here a lovely *Virgin and Child, with Saints Francis and Bernardino, and Angels*; Gozzoli also painted a *San Fortunato* and other frescoes inside the church.

The excellent wines of Montefalco – Montefalco Rosso and the more complex Sagrantino – are widely available in the town, which also hosts a Settimana Enologica, or Wine Week, around Easter each year. See also **Bevagna**, **Foligno**, **Gualdo Cattaneo**, **Trevi**.

Montelabate (387 m.): A small village in the hills above the upper Tiber valley, Montelabate is dominated by the large church of Santa Maria in Val di Ponte, which once belonged to the former Benedictine abbey of Montelabate. At the height of its power in the twelfth century, this abbey possessed extensive lands, including twenty *castelli* and thirty parish churches. Built in transitional Romanesque–Gothic style, the church has an ogival doorway and a large rose-window while its flanks are supported by powerful buttresses. The campanile, half as tall again until last century, dates from 1269. Though the political power of the abbey was lost early in the fifteenth century, the church continued to commission artists for another 100 years and, besides a thirteenth-century *Crucifixion* in the Chapter House, the interior reveals frescoes by Bartolomeo Caporali (1488) on the left wall, and a frescoed *Crucifixion* (1492) by Fiorenzo di Lorenzo on the right. The crypt derives from an earlier, eleventh-century, church, and there is also an attractive late-thirteenth-century cloister, with ogival arches. See also **Gubbio**, **Perugia**, **Umbèrtide**.

Monteleone d'Orvieto (500 m.): Occupying a high spur overlooking the Val di Chiana, on the twisting road from **Città della Pieve** to **Orvieto**, Monteleone once had a strategic importance greatly at odds with the village's present tranquillity. Founded in the mid eleventh century by Orvieto as an outpost on the city's borders with Perugia and Siena, it was fought over for centuries by Orvieto's warring families, as well as by different states, until its fortress was finally destroyed after fighting between the Grand Duchy of Tuscany and the Church State in 1643. Today, the village's situation and plan – it is built on three parallel roads running along the spur – make for a pleasant visit. The principal gate leads on to the central street, whose houses retain some impressive and curious doorways, and the Collegiata dei Santi Pietro e Paolo, which has two paintings by followers of Perugino and, in the crypt beneath the high altar, the rather grotesquely displayed body of San Teodoro, brought here in 1778. The belvedere at the very end of the town offers a magnificent panorama over the Val di Chiana, towards Monte Cetona, with Monte Amiata behind. See also **Ficulle**.

Monteleone di Spoleto (978 m.): With a population of just 666, according to the 1991 census, this remote hilltop village is one of the smallest communes in Umbria and, at 978 metres above sea-level, also the highest. Located in a mountain area populated for thousands of years, Monteleone occupies a picturesque and strategically significant site above the Corno valley. The oldest part of the village, now silent and mostly empty, stands at the top of the hill. Here are to be seen the remains of a fifteenth-century fortress, and the large fourteenth-century church of San Francesco, with a superbly decorated Gothic doorway, an arcaded cloister, and a frescoed lower church; there is also a small Renaissance church, San Nicola. Below San Francesco, a street running down to a fifteenth-century gate, which formed part of a later ring of walls, has a number of sixteenth- and seventeenth-century *palazzi*. Some distance outside the village, at Colle del Capitano, on the road to Poggiodomo, is the site (now a farmyard) of a late Bronze Age burial place, discovered in 1902. Here, one of the forty-four tombs, from the sixth century BC, unearthed disclosed the extraordinary *biga*, or two-horse parade chariot, exquisitely decorated with bronze relief scenes from the life of Achilles (now in the Metropolitan Museum in New York), a remarkable testimony to the level of the contemporary culture in this now isolated location. In fact, the whole area – where mules are still regularly used to gather wood as protection against the harsh winters – is full of surprises. Further along the road from Monteleone to the even smaller commune of Poggiodomo (just 220 inhabitants in 1991), with a couple of fourteenth-century churches, is the agricultural hamlet of Usigni (1,001 m.), graced, quite bizarrely, with a fine seventeenth-century church built, in Roman Baroque style, by direction of Fausto Poli, a cardinal at the court of Urban VIII, who was born here. See also **Ponte**, **Sant'Anatolia di Narco**.

Monte Santa Maria Tiberina (688 m.): One of the most spectacularly sited villages in the entire region, this tiny community of just 145 people has enjoyed a distinguished past and is still the *capoluogo* or administrative centre of its commune. The past importance of the village – it was in origin an Etruscan settlement – resides largely in the dominant position on the top of a high hill, to the right of the Tiber valley, close to the border with Tuscany. Today it offers extensive views over the entire surrounding area. Much fought over in the Middle Ages, it was elevated to the status of an independent marquisate by the Holy Roman Emperor, Charles IV, in 1355; the ruling Del Monte family were subsequently granted the right to call themselves Bourbon Del Monte by the ruling house of France. The most prominent reminder of Monte Santa Maria's past is the great mass of the Del Monte castle – medieval in origin but substantially remodelled in Renaissance style in the late sixteenth century. The parish church of Santa Maria contains an early Christian altar-frontal, an octagonal font from the late fifteenth or early sixteenth century, and some notable funeral monuments. See also **Citerna**, **Città di Castello**.

Montone (482) m.): This fortified village dates back to the ninth century, and was an independent commune by the mid twelfth century, although its commanding position above the Tiber valley, and on one of the trans-Apennine routes, meant that it was fought over for much of its history by Perugia, Città di Castello, and Gubbio. Historically, Montone is most celebrated as the stronghold of Andrea Braccio, called Braccio Fortebraccio (1368–1424), a great *condottiero* and lord of Perugia between 1416 and 1424. Today it is one of the most appealing of all such medieval villages in Umbria, its narrow streets winding steeply between silent houses to the summit of the hill. The most significant monument is the church of San Francesco, a large preaching church whose simple nave contains frescoes from the fourteenth and fifteenth centuries, including one depicting St Anthony of Padua (1491) by Bartolomeo Caporali. Caporali was probably also responsible for the important *gonfalone*, the *Madonna del Soccorso* (1482). The Collegiata di Santa Maria preserves the *Sacra Spina*, a thorn said to be from Christ's crown of thorns, which Carlo Fortebraccio gave to Montone in 1473 (it is shown every Easter Monday, when a commemorative pageant in medieval dress is also held). The church also contains a *Last Supper* by the Antwerp-born Denis Calvaert (*c.* 1545–1619). The remains of the fortress are also to be seen.

Nearby, to the north-east, is another massive fortress, the Rocca d'Aria (or Aries). See also **Città di Castello**, **Umbèrtide**.

Morra (306 m.): Along the valley of the Nestore torrent, and beneath the mountains which divide Umbria from neighbouring Tuscany, lie the scattered houses of this small and mostly undistinguished village. It is worth visiting, however, for the fifteenth- to sixteenth-century church of San Crescentino, which holds some excellent and surprisingly little-known frescoes by Cortona-born Luca Signorelli (1441/50–1523). These include a *Flagellation* closely related to the painting by the artist now in the Brera in Milan. See also **Città di Castello**, **Umbèrtide**.

Narni (240 m.): The town's rocky outcrop, overlooking the Nera at a point where the river flows through a gorge, at the south-western edge of the Terni basin, always possessed a strategic importance which led successive generations to build on the site. Narni was the birthplace of the Roman emperor Marcus Cocceius Nerva (*c.* 30–98), of John XIII, Pope between 965 and 972, and of the great *condottiero* Erasmo da Narni (1370–1443), known as Gattamelata, a captain of the Venetian Republic, commemorated in Padua by a great equestrian bronze by

Donatello. Once an Umbrian centre, Nequinum, the settlement was known as Narnia to the Romans, who established a colony there in 299 BC. The town became an important station on the Via Flaminia and – after the building, in 27 BC, of its famous bridge (see below) – the starting point for the new, and eventually more important, branch of the road which went to Foligno by way of Terni and Spoleto. Narni's position led successive waves of northern invaders to occupy the site, and it was later a centre of Longobard power in the area. In the twelfth century the town was a free commune, but though successfully defended on several occasions, it was sacked by one of Barbarossa's commanders in 1174 and successfully besieged by Frederick II in 1242. In 1353 Cardinal Albornoz seized Narni for the Church and built the great fortress which still dominates the town. Narni's long period of power and affluence eventually came to an end in 1527, when Charles V's notorious mercenaries, the *lanzichenecchi*, comprehensively looted the city on their return from the Sack of Rome. Only with the industrial development of the late nineteenth century did Narni find renewed prosperity, though the singularity of the site ensured that this development took place at the foot of the town rock in Narni Scalo, leading to an uneasy split between the old and new towns which still exists.

In the centre of the old town, on the winding road that goes between the two principal city gates – the Porta Ternana and the Porta Romana – lies the irregular Piazza Garibaldi, once the site of a large Roman cistern and now marked by a fifteenth-century bronze fountain. To one side of the piazza is the left flank of the cathedral, consecrated in 1145 by Pope Eugenius III. Originally Romanesque in style, the cathedral has undergone several partial remodellings and the plain façade, on the Piazza Cavour, now boasts an elegant Renaissance portico. Along the right flank, the heavy stone and brick-built bell-tower is decorated with coloured ceramic plates. The interior, designed on the basilical plan, originally had three aisles, divided by columns taken from pre-existing buildings, with interestingly varied capitals; a fourth aisle was added to the right in the fifteenth century. Immediately to the right on entering, on the inside wall of the façade, is an appealing frescoed *Virgin and Child*, by a

local artist of the early fifteenth century. The added right aisle
has both a good Renaissance tomb and a fine chapel (1499) by a
north Italian sculptor, Sebastiano Pellegrini. Immediately beyond
is the Sacello dei Santi Giovenale e Cassio, a funerary chapel
dedicated to both St Juvenal, the patron and first bishop of the
city, and St Cassius. The chapel took on its present form only in
the seventeenth century, but among the materials employed are
palaeo-Christian reliefs from the sixth century and Romanesque
decoration including cosmatesque mosaics; two niches on the
outer wall hold, to the left, a pleasing fifteenth-century statue of
St Juvenal and, to the right, a fifteenth-century German *Pietà*.
On an inner wall is a ninth-century mosaic of Christ giving a
blessing, along with twelfth-century frescoes; this inner chapel
was built using part of the old Roman city wall, which can also
be seen beyond the portico, immediately to the right of the
cathedral façade. A painting of St Juvenal, on the pilaster at the
head of the right aisle, is attributed to the Siennese artist Vecchietta (1412–80). The altar is surmounted by a canopy, and beneath
the apse, with some fifteenth-century frescoes, partly hidden by
the finely carved choir-stalls (1490), is a large crypt offering
glimpses of the impressive Nera gorge far below. The left aisle
has two good funerary monuments: one to Bishop Pietro Gomaz
with a *Madonna, Child and Angels* in the lunette, and another, to
Pietro Cesi, attributed to the Florentine Bernardo da Settignano,
which dates from 1477. The large polychromed wooden statue
of St Anthony Abbot (1474) is also by Vecchietta.

Across the Piazza Cavour from the cathedral, a small road to
the right leads to one of the former Roman gates, remodelled in
the Middle Ages. To the left of the piazza, the Via Garibaldi
(which later becomes the Via Mazzini) leads to many of the
town's principal civic and religious monuments. Clearly visible
up a short street to the left of the Via Garibaldi is the fourteenth-
century church of San Francesco, built on the site of an oratory
supposedly founded by St Francis, who visited Narni in 1213.
The façade has a fine doorway and an aedicule with a poorly
conserved sixteenth-century fresco, while the interior – which
would be more attractive without the gaudy modern stained
glass in the large Gothic window in the apse – has several

side-chapels added in the fourteenth and fifteenth centuries. The frescoed scenes from the life of St Francis by Pier Antonio Mezzastris, in the first chapel in the right aisle, are decidedly derivative. However, the columns dividing the nave are richly decorated with interesting votive frescoes, including a good *Virgin and Child with Donor* on the first column to the right, and a striking St Francis on the first to the left.

From here, return to the Via Garibaldi, which almost immediately opens out to form the long, narrow Piazza dei Priori – the centre of the medieval city, built on the site of the Roman forum. Here, two medieval public buildings face each other: the Palazzo dei Priori, to the right, and the Palazzo del Podestà, to the left. All that remains of the Palazzo dei Priori, following the Sack of Narni, is the loggia – built in the mid fourteenth century, apparently by Matteo Gattapone. Though now truncated, it still impresses by its huge dimensions. Adjacent to the Palazzo are a tall defensive tower, a pulpit from which civic decrees were once read, and the Casa Sacripanti, with three medieval low-reliefs inset in the wall. On the opposite side of the piazza is the thirteenth-century Palazzo del Podestà, uniquely created by joining together three separate tower-houses; the remodelling work, part of which dates from the fifteenth century, can still be clearly seen. To the right of the façade are some interesting Romanesque bas-reliefs, depicting a variety of subjects including a duel between two knights and the beheading of Holofernes. A small inner courtyard contains a fifteenth-century well and some archaeological materials, as well as an open staircase leading to the first floor (the building is still used for the administrative offices of the commune). In the council chamber is a large and much-imitated *Coronation of the Virgin*, splendidly painted by the Florentine artist Domenico Ghirlandaio. In the predella are three scenes – *St Francis Receiving the Stigmata*, a *Pietà*, and *St Jerome* – and the whole is contained in a fine frame, decorated with saints and angels. Opposite this is a large fresco of St Francis receiving the stigmata, attributed to Lo Spagna. (Until the opening of the new civic gallery in the Bishop's Palace – across the Piazza Cavour from the cathedral – a number of other works are also held in the Palazzo del Podestà and may be seen on request; they include a notable *Annunciation* by Benozzo Gozzoli, a fourteenth-century wooden statue of the *Virgin and Child*, and an Egyptian mummy and wooden sarcophagus from the fourth century BC.) Just beyond the Palazzo is the most important of Narni's several fountains; it was built in 1303 and is similar in form to the Fontana Maggiore in Perugia.

Immediately to the right at the beginning of the Via Mazzini which leads out of the piazza is the beautiful Romanesque church of Santa Maria in Pensole, built around 1175. The façade, preceded by a fine portico with columns taken from earlier buildings, has three exceptional doors with splendid, though worn, marble decoration. The small interior is divided into three aisles by columns also taken from elsewhere; all have fine capitals (the third to the right is especially noteworthy), and there are satisfying geometrical designs on the pilasters at the heads of the aisles. Beneath Santa Maria in Pensole are to be seen the interesting, and recently restored, remains of what was once thought to be a Temple of Bacchus but which modern scholarship – always capable of turning wine into water – now declares to be a Roman cistern. The Via Mazzini continues with buildings from different periods, notably the late-sixteenth-century Palazzo Scotti and two more tall medieval tower-houses. A little further on, to the left, is the large preaching church of San Domenico, originally built entirely in pink and white stone, though the façade, with its once fine doorway, has been very indifferently patched. In recent years the church has been clumsily adapted for use as a library and auditorium, making it difficult to make clear sense of the interior, remodelled in the fifteenth and sixteenth centuries. The adjacent Dominican convent, perched on the edge of town, was demolished as recently as the 1950s but recent excavations (carried out by the active local caving club) have brought to light some fascinating remains beneath the church. These include a large cistern used for collecting rainwater, a small cell covered with clearly legible graffiti by prisoners held there between the mid eighteenth century and the Napoleonic period, and – most interestingly of all – a small twelfth-century church below the apse of the upper church, which retains numerous frescoes, still awaiting full restoration.

From San Domenico the road continues down to Piazza Galeotto Marzio; from here, turn to the right and down the Via Marcellina and Via Gattamelata. Among the houses in this late-medieval quarter of town is one supposed to be the birthplace of the *condottiero* Gattamelata himself. The large church to the left is Sant'Agostino, built in the fifteenth century. To the right of the doorway, a niche holds a frescoed *Madonna, Child and Saints*, attributed to Antoniazzo Romano, while the richly decorated three-aisled interior contains a number of interesting works. These include a frescoed *Madonna and Saints* (1482) attributed to Pier Antonio d'Amelia, just inside the entrance, a *Crucifixion* by a follower of Antoniazzo Romano, a wooden crucifix from the sixteenth century, and a fourteenth-century altar in the apse. Set in the wooden ceiling of the church is a canvas celebrating St Augustine, by the sixteenth-century Narnese painter Carlo Federico Benincasa. A right turn shortly after Sant'Agostino returns you to the end of the Via Garibaldi, facing the cathedral.

Before leaving Narni, it is worth crossing the Piazza Garibaldi and following the steep Via del Monte, which rises through a particularly evocative medieval quarter of town, as far as the imposing fortress (322 m.). This Rocca, built on a square plan with powerful towers at the angles, was erected around 1370 by Ugolino di Montemarte, at the command of the papal legate, Cardinal Albornoz, and has recently been restored. From the top of the hill, as from many vantage points around the town, there are fine views of the Nera gorge and surrounding countryside. The small monastery clearly visible across the river, in the midst of an ilex wood, is San Cassiano, a Benedictine establishment from the twelfth century, recently restored; the Romanesque church has a good doorway and simple three-aisled interior and there is a fine Romanesque bell-tower. Rather harder to see is what, for centuries, was Narni's most famous monument, the so-called Bridge of Augustus, built, in 27 BC, at the beginning of the Emperor's reign, which crosses the Nera close to the modern road leading from Narni Scalo to the old town. The bridge, now reduced to a single arch, was once almost 130 metres long and thirty metres high. Sought out and admired by travellers for centuries, the bridge is the subject of a lovely painting, now in the Louvre, by Corot.

Though the industrialized area between Narni and Terni may not seem immediately attractive to the visitor, there are in fact a number of worthwhile excursions to be made. At Visciano (206 m.), to the south-west of the town – just off the road to **Otrícoli** – is the eleventh-century Romanesque church of Santa Pudenziana. Now isolated in the middle of the countryside, Santa Pudenziana makes a particularly strong first impression, due to the marked contrast between the small, squat church and its tall, slim bell-tower to the left. The simple façade, with a brick-built tympanum, is preceded by a portico supported by two Roman columns in stone, with attractive capitals, flanked by two brick pillars; other Roman remains are embedded in the church walls. The unusual polygonal apse has been linked to similar examples in Ravenna and Torcello. Santa Pudenziana's three-aisled interior, like its crypt, makes extensive use of materials taken from pre-existing buildings; there is a stone ciborium over the altar on the raised presbytery and an episcopal throne in the apse.

Further away, to the south-east, near the village of Vasciano, is the Sacro Speco di San Francesco (568 m.), one of Umbria's most characteristic Franciscan monasteries, recently reoccupied by monks living by the simple First Rule of St Francis. Hidden deep in a wood of ilex and chestnut trees, close to the border with Lazio, the monastery owes its origin to the saint himself, who lived in a nearby grotto in 1213. The buildings seen today were begun by St Bernardino of Siena, and include a small oratory with fourteenth-century frescoes. See also **Amelia**, **Calvi dell'Umbria**, **Collescìpoli**, **Otrícoli**, **Terni**.

Nocera Umbra (520 m.): Especially if approached from the direction of **Gualdo Tadino**, this small town reveals itself as one of the most magnificently sited in Umbria: clinging to a hill above the Topino valley, surrounded by mountains. Once settled by the ancient Umbrians as Noukria, the town – then probably at the foot of the hill – was later an important station on the Via

Flaminia, known to the Romans as Nuceria Camellaria. It was at Nocera, in fact, that a subsidiary road departed for Ancona; a Roman milestone (AD 76) relating to this route is to be seen in the city art museum (see below). Subsequently, Nocera became a notable Longobard centre on the borders of the Duchy of Spoleto, as the discovery in 1898 of an exceptionally important sixth- and seventh-century necropolis confirmed. Sacked by Frederick II in 1248, Nocera was long fought over by Perugia and Spoleto, and belonged to the Trinci family of Foligno for a while in the fifteenth century, before becoming part of the Church State in 1439.

The town is entered today by the Porta Vecchia, which lies beyond the modern Viale Matteotti, just to the side of the route of the Via Flaminia. From here, the lower part of the old town is dominated by the Via Vittorio Emanuele, which winds its way steeply up to the church of San Francesco in the Piazza Caprera. In Nocera, however, even more than elsewhere in Umbria, it is necessary to wander off the principal route in order to discover the most characteristic corners of the medieval town. Immediately to the right of the Porta Vecchia, in fact, is the Portico San Filippo, a covered medieval passage which runs around the edge of the town as far as the nineteenth-century church of San Filippo Neri. Further up the Via Vittorio Emanuele – with its mix of medieval and later dwellings – another covered way to the right leads into the characteristic Via Fossatello, while almost at the top of the street, the Via Sasso, to the left, has more thirteenth-century houses, including two clearly displaying the 'porta del morto'. (These 'dead men's doors' – especially characteristic of northern Umbria – are bricked-up doorways, raised above street level; their popular name derives from the story that they were opened only to permit the passage of coffins, but they have also been explained as defensive measures, and also as doors which merely gave access to the upper storeys of houses, while street-level doors led down to the cellar.)

The Piazza Caprera is dominated by the church of San Francesco, which was built in the fourteenth century but enlarged during the fifteenth, giving rise to its present far-from-unified appearance; the single aisle, with the large ogival arches characteristic of northern Umbria, retains a good deal of its fifteenth-century decoration. The church is now home to the city art collection, which includes some notable paintings, among them a *Crucifix* by a late-thirteenth-century Umbrian follower of Cimabue, some frescoes by Matteo da Gualdo and a panel by the same painter representing the meeting of St Anne and St Joachim, parents of the Virgin Mary, at the Golden Gate of Jerusalem (a popular medieval legend). There is also a magnificent polyptych by Nicolò Alunno, showing the *Nativity, the Coronation of the Virgin and Saints* (1483), in a splendidly carved gilt frame from the same period. From the Piazza Caprera the Via San Rinaldo leads on up to the very top of the town, where the cathedral appears quite unexpectedly, tucked away in a corner. A modest Romanesque doorway gives access to the church itself, which was entirely remodelled internally in the eighteenth century in undistinguished Baroque taste. Despite this disappointment, however, it is well worth persevering to the summit of the hill, since a narrow passage between the cathedral and the scant remains of the medieval fortress gives access to a tiny viewing point, offering a captivating panorama over the Topino valley and the surrounding mountains.

From Nocera, a road leading south-west across the hills to Colfiorito, close to Umbria's border with the Marches, passes through Bagni di Nocera, famous as a spa during the seventeenth and eighteenth centuries, and recently restored. See also **Foligno**, **Gualdo Tadino**.

Norcia (604 m.): One of Umbria's most distinctive towns, Norcia is situated at the edge of a large high plain (the Piano di Santa Scolastica), ringed entirely by high mountains, not far from the borders with the Marches and Lazio. Despite its harsh surroundings and susceptibility to earthquakes – the town was very badly damaged in 1328, 1567, 1703, 1730, 1859 and 1979 – Norcia has been continuously important since the fifth century BC, when it was one of the most northerly Sabine settlements. Known to the Romans as Nursia, the town was the birthplace of the founder of western monasticism, St Benedict, and his twin-sister, St Scholastica. Subject to attack by Goths, Longobards, and Saracens, it survived to become a flourishing commune in the Middle Ages, before finally becoming part of the Papal State. Being completely flat and still surrounded by a magnificent ring of medieval walls, Norcia invites leisurely – or, in winter, brisk – exploration on foot. The city's principal monuments are all gathered closely together around the main square, the Piazza San Benedetto. The fourteenth-century basilica of San Benedetto retains a fine doorway and rose-window, though the interior underwent a rather anonymous remodelling in the eighteenth century; it has some interesting pictures but is most noteworthy for its crypt, where some Roman remains are traditionally identified as the birthplace of Sts Benedict and Scholastica. The sixteenth-century cathedral was also transformed in the eighteenth century, following damage by earthquake, while the Palazzo Comunale shows evident signs of alterations at various periods. Dominating the piazza is the square papal fortress with angled towers called the Castellina, erected between 1554 and 1563 to a design by Vignola, at the desire of Pope Julius III. Elsewhere in town are the fourteenth-century church of San Francesco and the tiny Edicola, built by Vanni Tuzi in 1354, as well as many indications of Norcia's former prosperity in the shape of numerous *palazzi*. Among the most distinctive features of Norcia are the very large number of *norcinerie*, or pork butchers, immediately recognizable by the menacing heads of wild boar which adorn the shop-fronts (the long-standing fame of Norcia for its hams, salami and related products has led a pork-butcher's to be known as a *norcineria* throughout a large part of central and southern Italy). One of the pleasures of visiting Norcia is the splendid scenery all around. If at all possible, it is worth taking the steep, winding road – offering superb views of the town and surrounding mountains – that leads up to the attractive winter sports station of Forca Canapine, and across the Piano Grande to Umbria's highest settlement, **Castelluccio di Norcia** (1,452 m.)

Orvieto (325 m.): However it is approached, Orvieto is unmistakable. Situated on an enormous isolated tufa outcrop, high above the Paglia valley, this splendid medieval city is domi-

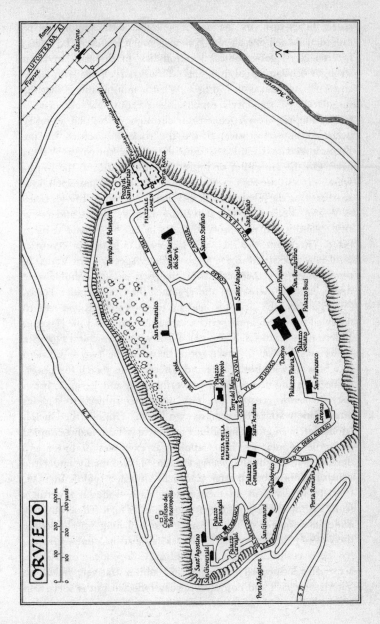

ORVIETO

0   100   200   300m.
0   100   200   300 yards

Autostrada A1
Roma
Firenze
Stazione
Funicolare railway (funivia)

Pozzo di San Patrizio
Porta Rocca
Tempio del Belvedere
PIAZZALE CAHEN
VIA ROMA
Santa Maria dei Servi
VIA CAVOUR
Santo Stefano
San Paolo
San Domenico
VIA DELLA PACE
CORSO
Sant'Angelo
VIA DELLA CAVA
Palazzo del Popolo
Torre del Moro
CORSO CAVOUR
Sant'Andrea
PIAZZA DELLA REPUBBLICA
Palazzo Comunale
San Ludovico
Palazzo Faina
Palazzo Soliano
Duomo
VIA DUOMO
San Bernardino
Palazzo Papale
Palazzo Buzi
San Francesco
San Lorenzo
VIA DEI MAGONI
VIA GARIBALDI
Porta Romana
S.71
Crocifisso del Tufo necropolis
Sant'Agostino
San Giovenale
Palazzo Petrangeli
Palazzo Carvaial
San Giovanni
Porta Maggiore
Rio Maranzo

nated, in its turn, by the imposing bulk of the region's finest cathedral. Much else about Orvieto is much less clear, however, for the city's geographical location has, in the past, given it stronger economic, cultural, and administrative links with Lazio and Tuscany than with Umbria. What is indisputable is that the singularity of the city's remarkable position has exercised a fascination for many generations throughout history. Already occupied in prehistorical times, the rock was settled by the Etruscans, who founded a flourishing city known as Velzna here. On the same site, or more probably a little to the south-west, was also the Fanum Voltumnae, the most famous religious sanctuary of the Etruscans. A city here, known to the Romans as Volsinii Veteres, was destroyed by them in 264 BC and a new city, Volsinii Noves – now Bolsena in Lazio – founded in its place. Thereafter, the rock was largely abandoned for centuries until it was resettled in the High Middle Ages as Urbs Vetus. In the sixth century the Goths took the rock as a stronghold, were dispossessed by Belisarius, and regained the citadel under Totila. Subsequently, the city was held by the Longobards and rose to renewed power and prosperity as a free commune in the eleventh and twelfth centuries. Variously allied with Rome and Florence – the city lies on a direct route between the two – Orvieto fought wars with both Siena and Viterbo in its search for a port, while suffering attack from powerful Todi and Perugia. From the thirteenth century the city was also subject to vicious internecine warfare between its two leading families, the Guelph Monaldeschi and the Ghibelline Filippeschi (whom Dante coupled with the Montagues and Capulets as examples of bitter and unending rivalry in *Purgatory*, vi, 106–8). Nominally under the control of the Church after Cardinal Albornoz took it in 1354, Orvieto survived as an independent state, under many rulers from within and beyond the city, until, in 1450, it fell definitively under the control of the papacy, who had long sought refuge there when Rome was under attack. At various times, Orvieto has been culturally Etruscan, politically dependent on Rome, artistically influenced by Siena, and administratively linked to Viterbo – a rich and complex history reflected in the social and artistic heritage of the modern city.

Since parking is difficult in the town centre, visitors arriving by car should use the car-park close to the railway station and take the funicular railway – constructed in 1888 and recently modernized – which goes from the station to the eastern edge of the city rock. This approach to Orvieto has the advantage not only of being unusual and offering good views of the Paglia valley but of leaving the visitor at a spot which immediately reveals a remarkable conjunction of monuments from different stages in Orvieto's history. A little distance to the right, on exiting from the funicular, lie the remains of the important Etruscan temple dating from the last decades of the fifth century BC. Built in travertine, the temple had three *cellae* fronted by a *pronaos*, or inner portico, with a double row of columns – a plan greatly resembling the Etruscan–Italic model described by the great Roman architect Vitruvius in his *De Architectura*. To the left of the funicular are the remains of the ROCCA – the medieval fortress Cardinal Albornoz ordered to be built in 1364, as a means of ensuring papal domination of the city. Destroyed by the townspeople in 1390, the fortress was rebuilt after 1450 and now serves as a pleasant town park, offering a splendid panorama over the surrounding countryside from its ramparts. From here, there is also a good view of the Porta Postierla, one of the city's medieval gates, with its two ogival arches, built prior even to the fortress. Last, in order of construction, is the Pozzo di San Patrizio, or St Patrick's Well, located between the funicular and the temple. This masterpiece of Renaissance engineering was erected between 1528 and 1537, to a design by Antonio da Sangallo the Younger, at the command of Pope Clement VII. Like so many of his predecessors, the Pope had taken refuge in Orvieto, on this occasion after the Sack of Rome in 1527, and was anxious to ensure the city's water supply in case of siege. The well itself is a cylinder sixty-two metres deep, around which two broad and shallow stairways (designed to allow the passage of mules) spiral in the form of a double helix – one stairway for the descent and one for returning to the surface; seventy-two windows allow just sufficient light to penetrate right to the bottom of the well where, in gloom, amid the cold and damp (dress warmly!), the visitor crosses a tiny bridge over the water to the ascending stairway.

From the large square in front of the funicular, the Piazzale Cahen, the visitor should turn left, past the fortress, and along the Via Postierla. Some distance along this road, on the left, lies the monastery of San Paolo, whose church has elaborately stuccoed altars and frescoes from the fifteenth and sixteenth centuries. Further along the Via Postierla and also on the left are the impressive sixteenth-century Palazzo Marsciano and the church of San Bernardino; the latter, built between 1657 and 1666, celebrates Franciscan simplicity in paradoxically elaborate Baroque style but has a good altarpiece, *Madonna and Child with Saints Francis and Bernardino*, and an attractive holy-water stoup. From here, the road passes between the imposing façade of the late-sixteenth-century Palazzo Buzi, by Ippolito Scalza, and the flank of the Palazzo Soliano, originally built for Pope Boniface VIII in 1297. Impressive as all this is, however, it does little to prepare the visitor for the cathedral square just beyond. It is best, perhaps, to cross the piazza immediately, to the stone benches on the walls of the palaces opposite the cathedral, and then turn to face the great façade, one of the finest sights in Umbria.

When the cathedral is lit by the rays of the sun, the first impression is of profuse colour from the polychrome mosaics that adorn large areas of the façade (they were included in the original conception but, after papal depredations, now date variously from the fourteenth to the nineteenth century). The initial impression past, the cathedral reveals its extraordinary fusion of architecture, sculpture and mosaics. The builder, Lorenzo Maitani, carefully balanced the great height of the façade (fifty-two metres) by horizontal features – a cornice below and gallery above – running across the forty-metre-wide front. He also combined the simplicity of the basic geometrical shapes – triangle, square and circle – that he employed in the construction with a breathtaking variety and profusion of decoration. This consists of reliefs, statues, and mosaic pictures, in stone, marble, bronze and coloured glass, marvellous in themselves, yet always subordinate to the overall design. The lower part of the façade is composed of four sturdy piers, topped by a cornice, on which sit the four symbols of the evangelists – the angel, lion, ox and eagle (this last especially dramatic) cast in bronze, perhaps by Maitani himself. Above the cornice, the piers are continued by slim pillars, offsetting the heaviness of the base, topped by elegant spires. Between the piers are three portals: the two flanking ones slim and ogival, their doors completed by tall windows, while the much larger central doorway terminates in a semicircular arch above the cornice, its lunette holding a marble sculpture of the *Madonna and Child*, attributed to Andrea Pisano (1347), beneath a bronze canopy with angels by Maitani. All three portals are surmounted by cusps which rise either to the base of the arcade, in the case of the outer doors, or to its top, as with the central doorway (the bronze doors themselves were added between 1964 and 1970, to designs by Emilio Greco). Above the gallery, the lower cusps are echoed directly over the flanking doorways, while the central section of the façade boasts a magnificent rose-window (1359–61) by the Florentine Andrea Orcàgna, surrounded by sixteenth-century statues of the apostles, and topped by a large cusp; this terminates at the same height as its flanking spires, and is decorated with a vast mosaic, depicting the enthronement of the Virgin. Seen from close up, it is the marble reliefs on the four pillars which catch, and detain, the eye. Each of the four piers making up the lower part of the façade is adorned with relief sculptures retelling different biblical stories. From left to right, these are: the Creation story, the expulsion from the Garden, and the story of Cain and Abel; the messianic prophecies of the Old Testament, culminating in a depiction of the Crucifixion; the prophets and episodes from the life of Christ; and, on the last pier, the Final Judgement. Astoundingly, given the extraordinary complexity of the reliefs, Maitani's project was conceived of as a whole from the very beginning, and the carving of the different stones was done on the ground; the piers were then assembled subsequently, leading to some almost unbelievably difficult joins, whose successful management is an indication of the extraordinary skill of the craftsmen who built the cathedral.

In contrast to the richness of the façade, the interior initially impresses by its spaciousness and comparative simplicity – an effect enhanced by the fact that the floor rises imperceptibly towards the apse, while the impressively carved capitals of the columns dividing the aisles fall in height. The horizontal black and white bands of travertine and basalt continue throughout the interior, both on the columns and on the side walls, with their elegant semicircular chapels. Just inside, and to the right of the central doorway, is a late-fifteenth-century stoup; a second stands close to the flanking doorway to the right. To the left there is an elaborate Gothic baptismal font (1390–1407), in white and red marble, supported by eight crouching lions and surmounted by a statue of John the Baptist. In the chapels along the right wall of the cathedral the remains of votive frescoes from the fourteenth and fifteenth centuries are still to be seen. At the end of the right aisle there is a notable wrought-iron screen and, beyond, the Cappella Nuova or Cappella della Madonna di San Brizio, flanked by two late-sixteenth-century statues of Adam and Eve by Fabiano Toti.

The San Brizio chapel itself is decorated throughout by some of the finest fresco work anywhere in the region. Begun in 1447 by the Beato Angelico, assisted by Benozzo Gozzoli and others, the decoration of the chapel was soon suspended, shortly after Angelico was called to Rome. Attempts later in the century to proceed with the frescoes were abortive (Perugino stopped work after a few days) until, in 1499, Luca Signorelli was employed to finish the decoration of the vaulting. Thereafter, he was commissioned to paint the walls, completing his great work in 1504. His choice of subjects – including the Preaching of the Antichrist, the Resurrection of the Dead, the Final Judgement, Heaven and Hell – was influenced by the career of the ascetic Dominican preacher Savonarola, burnt at the stake in Florence in 1498. The paintings – remarkable as much for their audacious use of colour as for their powerful figure-studies – are not only Signorelli's masterpiece, but also one of the most challenging cycles of Renaissance Italy, and a notable precursor of Michelangelo's *Last Judgement* in the Sistine Chapel, painted a quarter of a century later. The San Brizio chapel also contains, on the altar, a work known as the *Madonna di San Brizio*, by a fourteenth-century painter from Orvieto.

To the right, on exiting from the chapel, is a large marble relief of the *Epiphany*, from the sixteenth century, and beyond an *Ecce Homo*, the last work of the Orvietan sculptor and architect Ippolito Scalza, who completed it at the age of seventy-six. The apse was decorated by artists of varied background: the stained glass (1325–34) is the work of the Assisian Giovanni di Bonino, the intarsia choir-stalls (1331–40) are by the Siennese Giovanni Ammannati, and the frescoes were painted by the Orvietan Ugolino di Prete Ilario in the 1370s. To the left of the apse, a marble relief of the *Visitation* balances that of the *Epiphany* to the right. Close to the pilaster at the head of the left aisle is a monumental if rather cold *Pietà*, showing the Virgin and the dead Christ flanked by Mary Magdalene and Nicodemus; it was carved, from a single block of marble, by Ippolito Scalza in 1579. The chapel which terminates the left crossing is the chapel of the Holy Corporal – the linen cloth stained by blood which, dripping miraculously from the host, converted a doubting Bohemian priest to the doctrine of transubstantiation and led to the building of Orvieto cathedral itself. Erected between 1350 and 1361, the chapel was frescoed by Ugolino di Prete Ilario between 1357 and 1364, and today contains a beautiful large panel – the *Madonna dei Raccomandati* (1320) – by the Siennese Lippo Memmi. The fourteenth-century tabernacle on the altar holds one of the greatest achievements of Italian precious metalwork, a bejewelled gold reliquary (1338), adorned by twelve enamelled scenes from the life of Christ, by the Siennese goldsmith Ugolino di Vieri; its Gothic three-cusped form is especially notable for echoing the façade of the cathedral. In the side chapels along the left flank of the cathedral are to be seen the remains of more early votive frescoes, while just before the left doorway of the church is a lovely fresco (1425) of the Virgin, holding an engagingly lively Child, by Gentile da Fabriano.

On exiting from the cathedral, walk down the right flank, which has both a marble sibyl by Fabiano Toti and a superb Gothic doorway (this may be by Arnolfo di Cambio and perhaps formed part of the previous church on the site). The Papal Palace, at the rear of the cathedral, was originally built as the bishop's palace in the twelfth century. It was subsequently enlarged by popes Urban IV and Martin IV in the second half of the thirteenth century. Today the building holds the National

Archaeological Museum, principally given over to finds from the Etruscan necropolises around Orvieto. Among the most impressive items are the important detached frescoes, with banqueting scenes, from the two Golini tombs, discovered at the Settecamini necropolis. There are also many fine examples of Etruscan ceramics, and a complete set of armour, also from the Settecamini necropolis, unearthed in the nineteenth century. If visitors are lucky enough to find them open – and they have been in the process of rearrangement for many years now – the other museums close to the cathedral are even more significant. The imposing two-storey Palazzo Soliano, also to the right of the Duomo, with its broad external stairway, was begun in 1297 by Pope Boniface VIII (though it has been much restored through the centuries). Since 1991, the palace has held, on its ground floor, a museum devoted to the works of the Sicilian sculptor Emilio Greco, who designed the cathedral's bronze doors. The upper storey should hold the civic and cathedral museums, whose already fine collections may be extended by works removed for conservation purposes from the cathedral façade and replaced there by copies. The museum has some excellent paintings including a *Virgin and Child* (1260–70) by Coppo di Marcovaldo, an incomplete but glowing polyptych (1321) by Simone Martini, and a self-portrait (1500) by Luca Signorelli. Even finer, however, is the collection of sculpture, which includes works in wood and marble from the fourteenth century onwards by Umbrian and Tuscan artists, including Andrea Pisano; it culminates in some enormous late-sixteenth- and seventeenth-century statues of saints formerly in the nave of the cathedral, and the *Annunciating Angel* and the *Virgin*, two figures (1605–9) by Francesco Mochi, considered among the most important of early Baroque sculpture anywhere in Italy. The museum also has an important reliquary (for the head of St Savino) made around 1340 by Ugolino di Vieri and Viva di Lando, and a lovely sixteenth-century *Annunciating Angel* in glazed terracotta from the Della Robbia school. Opposite the façade of the cathedral in the Palazzo Faina is yet another archaeological museum, devoted to Etruscan finds from the city and the surrounding area. Here the holdings include Villanovan cinerary jars, some fine sixth-

and fifth-century BC black- and red-figure vases from Greece, a particularly rich collection of *bucchero* ware from the sixth to fifth centuries, and an Etruscan sarcophagus from the late fourth century, which retains traces of its original polychrome decoration.

From the cathedral, take the Via Maitani, directly opposite the façade, to the large preaching church of San Francesco (1240–70), where, in 1297, Pope Boniface VIII canonized King Louis IX of France; the interior has been radically altered but retains a wooden crucifix by a follower of Maitani. Turn to the left along the Via Scalza, where the small church of San Lorenzo de Arari soon appears on the right. The exterior shows a small bell-gable, a semicircular apse, and a fifteenth-century doorway. The three aisles of the church are divided by columns taken from Roman sites, while the present altar – adapted from an Etruscan altar stone – is now covered by a twelfth-century ciborium, which also holds a crucifix from the 1300s. The main interest of the church, however, resides in its fourteenth-century frescoes, especially those on the left wall of the central aisle – a *Life of St Laurence* (1330), including scenes showing his martyrdom and his rescue of souls from purgatory. Other frescoes include a very backward-looking *Christ in Glory* in the apse.

Continuing in the same direction into the Via degli Alberici, which later becomes the Via Garibaldi – with a number of Renaissance *palazzi* – turn left down to the Piazza de' Ranieri, where the neat Baroque church of San Lodovico makes an interesting juxtaposition with a massive medieval defensive tower. From here, a left turn leads down through one of the fascinating parts of the medieval town – built, like virtually all of Orvieto, of the local travertine stone – to the church of San Giovanni. A small piazza, situated on the very edge of the city rock, gives splendid views over the surrounding countryside and across the medieval city. A road which descends, only to climb back up, the western edge of the rock offers a great variety of views of the medieval town, before eventually reaching one of Orvieto's oldest churches, San Giovenale. The church was founded in 1004, and has a simple Romanesque façade set off by an imposing fortified bell-tower. The simple, three-aisled interior reveals the remains of votive frescoes, and some Romanesque carvings at the base of the twelfth-century altar. Near by, the great mid-thirteenth-century Augustinian church, Sant'Agostino, still impresses by its sheer bulk, and there is a fine thirteenth-century doorway (although seemingly haphazard conversion of the church and adjoining monastery makes it hard to predict the outcome of the wholesale restoration work being conducted in 1995).

From the rear of San Giovenale, take the Via Malabranca – a street whose predominantly medieval appearance is modified by some imposing Renaissance *palazzi*. These include – on the right – the Palazzo Carvajal, built by Ippolito Scalza for a Spanish nobleman, who had the legend '*Carvajal de Carvajal por comodidad de sus amigos padrón*' ('Carvajal de Carvajal owner of this house for the comfort of his friends') engraved across the façade. A little further on, to the left, is one of the most charming corners of the city. Concealed behind the heavy wooden door of the Palazzo Pietrangeli is a wonderfully elegant and evocatively faded fifteenth-century courtyard, with an airy portico more redolent of Renaissance Florence than of this medieval corner of Orvieto (it is now believed to be the work of the Florentine architect Bernardo Rossellino). The Via Malabranca now offers splendid views of the city's medieval rooftops to the right. Also to the right, the steep Via della Cava affords an opportunity to walk down into one of the oldest quarters of town, before returning to the Via Filippeschi (as the continuation of the Via Malabranca is named). This leads almost immediately into Orvieto's principal city square.

The Piazza della Repubblica was once the site of the Etruscan and Roman forums and the centre of medieval life. Today, however, it amounts to rather less than the sum of its parts. This may be due to the Renaissance remodelling of the medieval Palazzo Comunale, which dominates the piazza; the remodelling was never completed and the building now presents a merely jumbled appearance, especially given nineteenth-century additions. More interesting is the twelve-sided medieval bell-tower between the Palazzo Comunale and the large church of Sant'Andrea. The church itself has an attractive portico along the left flank, but its blandly reconstructed façade gives all too little indication that this is one of the most built-over, and historically important, sites in the whole of the city. Below the church there are traces of Villanovan and Etruscan cultures, along with the remains of the mosaic pavement of a sixth-century basilica; above, there are traces of building from the tenth to the twelfth centuries as well as more visible evidence of Gothic and Renaissance remodellings. The present interior – long under restoration – contains numerous remains of frescoes from the fourteenth and fifteenth centuries and a funerary monument by followers of Arnolfo di Cambio. It was in this church that Innocent III proclaimed the Fifth Crusade in 1216 and that Martin IV was crowned pope in 1281. From the left, arcaded, flank of Sant'Andrea, take Orvieto's principal shopping street, the Corso Cavour, as far as the Palazzo dei Sette, once occupied by magistrates chosen by the guilds to govern the city, and the Torre del Moro, a forty-two-metre-high tower, surmounted by a large bell made in 1316 for the Palazzo del Popolo. From here, a right turn along the Via del Duomo leads past some of the many shops in the city selling local ceramics, and back to the cathedral.

A left turn at the Torre del Moro leads along a narrow street to Orvieto's largest square, the Piazza del Popolo – dominated by the Palazzo del Popolo, one of the finest civic buildings in central Italy. Built in the second half of the thirteenth century, after the example of similar north Italian buildings, the Palazzo originally had just the large, vaulted lower storey and a large room above for meetings of the people; later, living quarters for the *capitano del popolo*, and a bell-tower, were added. The building is now characterized by a broad external stairway and balcony, and distinguished by fine three-light windows in the large first-floor meeting-room. Recently turned into a conference centre, the Palazzo preserves a number of interesting archaeological finds made during restoration work – an Etruscan temple area and a medieval aqueduct and cistern. A left turn along the rear of the Palazzo del Popolo, as far as the Piazza Corsica, and a right turn along the Via della Pace, soon leads to the church of San Domenico. This massive hall-church, consecrated by Pope Urban IV in 1264, has been sadly reduced in scale over the years but retains an attractive Renaissance chapel below the apse. Best of all, the church contains one of the finest works of the sculptor Arnolfo di Cambio – a funeral monument to the Cardinal de Braye (1285). Though badly mangled, and missing its original canopy, this elaborate monument – featuring a finely decorated base with richly carved columns and cosmatesque decoration – enacts a drama of death and faith in the resurrection. In the centre, two acolytes are caught in the act of pulling curtains across the body of the dead prelate, removing him from earthly view, while above St Mark and St Dominic present the cardinal to the enthroned Virgin and Child, who turn their heads – the infant's arms outstretched – to welcome him to eternity.

On exiting from San Domenico, walk across the road and a few metres to the right and take the Via Cavallotti down to the Corso Cavour. A left turn leads down past a number of medieval churches – Sant'Angelo and Santo Stefano to the right and Santa Maria dei Servi to the left – to the Piazzale Cahen and the funicular railway.

No one, however, should leave Orvieto altogether without visiting at least one of the Etruscan necropolises which surround the city rock. The most convenient is the necropolis of the Crocifisso del Tufo, to the north-west of the city, which dates back as far as the sixth century BC (unlike the Cannicella necropolis, this may be visited without appointment). Lying on a now isolated spot at the base of the city rock, the necropolis was rediscovered in 1830 and is still under excavation. It presents a fascinating glimpse of Etruscan planning, for the substantial square chamber tombs are arranged, like houses, on either side of straight streets. Virtually all the tombs in the excavated area are accessible, though their contents have long found their way into museums in the city and elsewhere. Constructed of often massive blocks of travertine, each tomb has a large architrave above the entrance engraved with the name of the person buried within – as in '*mi spuries achilenas*' (I am [the tomb of] Spurie Achilena). As a group, they offer a fascinating glimpse of the social composition of Orvieto in the sixth and fifth centuries BC, for alongside Etruscans, the necropolis contains the remains of Greeks ('*achilena*' is an Etruscanized form of Achilles), Umbrians, Oscans, and Latins. See also **Abbey of Santi Severo e Martirio**.

Otrícoli (209 m.): Few locations in the region have known such extremes of fortune as this hill-top village close to the border with Lazio. Once an important Umbrian settlement, later allied with Rome, it was destroyed by the Romans during the Social War in the first century, and rebuilt on the plain close to the Tiber, which was then still navigable at this point. For some centuries it flourished as the wealthy and fashionable city of Ocriculum, until, during the Middle Ages, flooding caused the inhabitants to move back up the hill. Lying on the Via Flaminia, Otrícoli was much frequented by later travellers but also much execrated by them for the poverty of its accommodations: Joseph Addison, who passed here at the beginning of the eighteenth century, spoke for many in calling it a 'very mean little village'. Today the village retains part of its medieval fortress and walls and also a number of porticoed houses on the main street, where travellers changed horses. The church of Santa Maria, at the top of the hill, dates back as far as the sixth century, but centuries of rebuilding have left few traces of its long past, beyond a notable number of architectural fragments displayed in the nave, where there is also an attractive Renaissance tabernacle. Below the village, in countryside more characteristic of northern Lazio than the rest of Umbria, lie the remains of Ocriculum, still largely unexcavated – though Pius VI had work carried out here in the second half of the eighteenth century, bringing to light some notable finds, now in Rome. Among the ruins visible are those of a large theatre, an amphitheatre, and the baths. See also **Calvi dell'Umbria**, **Narni**.

Paciano (391 m.): Of medieval appearance, this small village retains its ring of defensive walls intact, along with fourteenth-century towers and gates. From feudal origins, it became part of the Church State for centuries, cut off from most of the surrounding territory by the lack of a proper road, which was finally built only in 1810. The church of San Giuseppe contains a *gonfalone* (*c.* 1480) from the workshop of Benedetto Bonfigli, a reminder of the plague which hit the village at the time. The adjacent church of San Carlo has a fine seventeenth-century doorway, while the Confraternità del Santissimo Sacramento, next to the Palazzo Comunale, has a fifteenth-century frescoed *Crucifixion* by Francesco di Castel della Pieve, supposed teacher of Perugino. Just beyond the walls is the small church of Santi Sebastiano e Rocco – another reminder of the plague, being dedicated to the two most popular plague-saints – and the Renaissance Madonna della Stella (1572–9), with frescoes by Scilla Pecennini (1579); early-seventeenth-century frescoes in the sacristy recount the history of the sanctuary. Occupying a spur of Monte Petrarvella, Paciano offers a fine panorama over the southern shore of Lake Trasimeno and the Val di Chiana. See also **Panicale**.

Panicale (431 m.): Today, the usually sleepy agricultural town of Panicale is much frequented in summer by visitors who rightly value the splendid views it offers of Lake Trasimeno and the surrounding countryside. Formerly, the town's position on a hill above the lake's southern shores gave it great strategic importance. In 1037 it became one of the earliest free communes in Italy and succeeded in retaining a measure of independence for some centuries, despite being repeatedly fought over by Chiusi and Perugia, eventually becoming an outpost of the latter. Panicale also has the dubious distinction of having been the birthplace of one of the most ferocious *condottieri*, Boldrino da Panicale (1331–91), for a while *signore* of the town. Still medieval in appearance, the town retains a large part of its walls, towers, and gates. It also has an interesting series of squares, rising up the hill from the attractively irregular Piazza Umberto I – holding the Palazzo Pretorio, decorated with stone escutcheons, and a fifteenth-century fountain – by way of the Piazza San Michele, to the thirteenth-century Palazzo del Podestà, in what is still called the Piazza Masolino (though no one, except the town's inhabitants, still believes that the great Florentine artist, Masolino da Panicale, was actually born here). The town's principal church, the Collegiata, in the Piazza San Michele, is a late-seventeenth-century construction which has a good *Adoration of the Shepherds* by Gian Battista Caporali, recently restored. Attractive as the old town is, Panicale's finest monument lies just outside the walls. This is the church of San Sebastiano, which contains two frescoes by Perugino: a *Coronation of the Virgin*, brought here from the church of Sant'Agostino, and a beautiful and highly stylized *Martyrdom of St Sebastian* (1505), in which four archers prepare to aim at the saint, bound to a pillar before an imposing marble arcade; beyond the arcade lies one of the finest of Perugino's many evocative renderings of the local landscape. See also **Castiglione del Lago**, **Città della Pieve**, **Mongiovino**, **Paciano**.

Passignano sul Trasimeno (289 m.): Perhaps the most appealing of the lakeside towns, Passignano can be thronged, during the summer months, with visitors intent on enjoying its beaches, or simply the views from the promenade. If it gets too crowded, a respite can be found in the narrow streets of the old town, perched on a rocky promontory and still enclosed behind medieval walls. Even today, it is easy to grasp the town's former strategic importance – which led to its repeated sacking over the centuries – lying as it does on the main route from Perugia to Siena and Florence. Apart from the tall, triangular defensive tower, the old town has a number of medieval churches, although the best is to be found a little distance away, at the cemetery. This is the Pieve di San Cristoforo, from the tenth or eleventh century, whose fourteenth-century frescoes have recently been restored. The modern monument in the lake reminds visitors that Passignano was home to the Società Aeronautica Italiana – formerly the town's leading employer – which, in the 1920s and 1930s, produced record-breaking seaplanes (and later boats); a flying school was also based here in the inter-war years. This industrial activity led to the town being heavily bombed during the Second World War. Passignano is also one of the principal points of departure for the ferries which ply between the lakeside towns and the Isola Polvese and **Isola Maggiore**. About a kilometre outside the town is an elegant Renaissance church, the Madonna dell'Olivo, which has a fresco attributed to Bartolomeo Caporali as well as a fine high altar and holy-water stoup. See also **Castel Rigone**, **Magione**, **Montecolognola**.

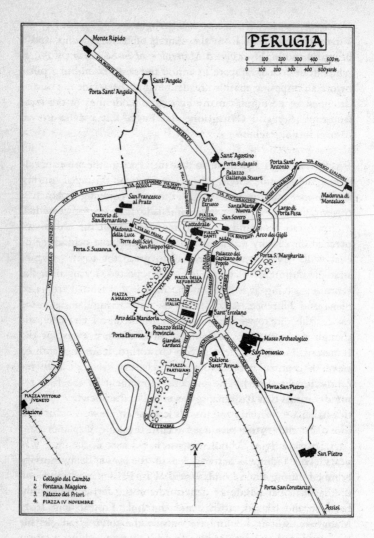

PERUGIA

0 100 200 300 400 500m
0 100 200 300 400 500 yards

Monte Ripido

Sant'Angelo

Porta Sant'Angelo

Sant'Agostino
Porta Bulagaio
Palazzo
Gallenga Stuart

Porta Sant'
Antonio

San Francesco
al Prato

Arco
Etrusco
Santa Maria
Nuova
San Severo

Madonna di
Monteluce

Oratorio di
San Bernardino

Largo di
Porta Pesa

Madonna
della Luce
Torre degli Sciri
San Filippo Neri

Cattedrale

Arco dei Gigli

Porta S. Susanna

Palazzo del
Capitano del
Popolo

Porta S. Margherita

PIAZZA DELLA
REPUBBLICA

PIAZZA
A. MARIOTTI

PIAZZA
ITALIA

Sant'Ercolano

Arco della Mandorla
Palazzo della
Provincia
Porta Eburnea
Giardini
Carducci

Museo Archeologico

San Domenico

PIAZZA
PARTIGIANI

Stazione
Sant'Anna

PIAZZA VITTORIO
VENETO

Porta San Pietro

Stazione

San Pietro

Porta San Constanzo

Assisi

1. Collegio del Cambio
2. Fontana Maggiore
3. Palazzo dei Priori
4. PIAZZA IV NOVEMBRE

Perugia (493 m.): With a population of almost 150,000, Perugia is Umbria's largest city, its most elegant, and that which, overall, offers the finest display of the region's rich and diverse cultural heritage. To the impatient, it can also prove an initial disappointment. The sprawling and still expanding suburbs can be discouraging, and the tortuous medieval town plan imposed on the city by its hilly site makes it all too easy for the first-time visitor to overlook major monuments as well as some of the city's most characteristic corners. Even so, the first sight of Perugia – built on a natural vantage point above the spot at which the Tiber valley meets the Vale of Umbria – can be exhilarating. The very skyline tells the story of a complex past. Here, we see a defensive tower belonging to the medieval walls, or the imposing outline of the huge fourteenth-century Dominican church; there, we observe the elegant fifteenth-century spire of the monastery of San Pietro rising into the sky, or the nineteenth-century *palazzo*, built on a spot where a great papal fortress once reminded a rebellious city who its rulers were. In fact, the city traces its origins back to a time long before the Middle Ages, and a closer look at the surviving walls shows clearly the imprint of the Etruscans and Romans who once lived here. Growing up, like Rome, from small hut-villages on adjacent hills, Perugia was an identifiably Etruscan city from the sixth century BC. The Etruscan walls, made of huge travertine blocks and incorporating a massive (and still-used) gate, go back to the third century BC, so that the plan of the modern city centre still follows that laid down more than 2,000 years ago.

A Roman city by the first century BC, Perugia was wilfully destroyed by fire when it opposed Octavius Caesar, only to be rebuilt by him when he became the Emperor Augustus. With the decline of the Roman Empire the city suffered destruction for a second time, on this occasion by the Goths, in 547. Its favoured position, close to Lake Trasimeno, and to good agricultural land, combined with the strategic importance of its position over the Tiber, on the route between Rome and Ravenna, ensured that the city soon flourished again. By the eleventh century Perugia was among the most powerful cities of the region, and by the second half of the thirteenth it boasted a cathedral, a great abbey church, and some of the most important public buildings in central Italy. For more than two centuries the city was a flourishing independent commune of real political, military and cultural distinction. Despite the claims of the Church – and the envious glances of powers as distant as Milan – Perugia retained its independence, under a series of lords such as the renowned *condottiero* Braccio Fortebraccio da Montone, who established a *signoria* there between 1416 and 1424. Shortly afterwards, the city fell under the control of the Baglioni family, whose rule lasted for a century, during which the city continued to grow commercially and artistically – despite internal feuding of a ferocity unparalleled anywhere in Italy. When, in 1540, Perugia was eventually conquered by papal troops, the Baglioni family houses on the Colle Landone (Landone hill) were either destroyed or incorporated into the powerful fortress which, for 300 years, was a hated symbol of papal rule. After six centuries of independence, the once great city was reduced to the status of a provincial town of the Church State. It was the beginning of an economic and cultural decline which would continue for three and a half centuries, to be arrested only by the belated introduction of modern industries in the early twentieth century. Since then, a mixture of manufacturing, commerce, and tourism has enabled Perugia to become one of the most flourishing towns of central Italy – and also one of the best at reconciling the often conflicting needs of a modern city with the desire to preserve its extraordinary cultural heritage.

Anyone arriving in Perugia by car, bus, or train can quickly see evidence of this blend of old and new by beginning their visit at Piazza Partigiani, which offers extensive underground parking beneath the bus terminal (with connections to the rail station). The piazza itself is unprepossessing, but an escalator opposite the bus station leads up to the Via L. Masi; follow this road as far as the sign indicating the '*scale mobili*' (escalators). The escalators rise steeply through covered passageways, to finish – in surreal fashion – in a maze of underground medieval streets. These narrow, ghostly alleys, with their houses, court-yards and defensive towers, once formed part of the Baglioni stronghold, saved from total destruction when the architect

Antonio da Sangallo the Younger used them as the foundations
for the papal fortress when it was built in the 1540s. Having
explored this medieval cityscape – and noting too the imposing
black metal sculpture by Alberto Burri which stands here – take
the final escalator upwards and emerge in the Piazza Italia. Here,
the balcony of the tiny Carducci Gardens offers one of the most
famous views in all of Italy. In one direction lies the plain
leading towards Lake Trasimeno and Tuscany, in another the
Tiber valley with the Martani hills behind, and in a third, the
Vale of Umbria watched over by Monte Subasio, where **Assisi**,
with its great basilica, churches and fortress, rises above the
plain. Across the Piazza Italia – on the other side of the
nineteenth-century Palazzo Provinciale – there is an urban view
as fine, in its way, as that offered by the Umbrian landscape.
From the piazza, Perugia's thronged main thoroughfare, the
pedestrianized Corso Vannucci – once the main artery of the
Etruscan and Roman cities – leads the eye past the subtle curve
of the Palazzo dei Priori to the Piazza IV Novembre, with its
famous fountain, and the pink and white flank of the cathedral,
which terminates the vista. This piazza, itself one of the city's
principal sights, also makes an ideal starting point for an exploration of this absorbing city.

The most symbolically significant space in the entire city, the
Piazza IV Novembre holds the principal civic and religious
monuments of the medieval commune. The fountain, superbly
decorated by Nicola and Giovanni Pisano between 1275 and
1278, is not only one of the most significant examples of
thirteenth-century sculpture anywhere in Italy but also a complex and richly nuanced emblem of the medieval city's political
independence and cultural aspirations, a fascinating blend of
historical, mythological, Christian and pagan motifs (see pp.
102–3). At the top of a short flight of shallow steps behind the
fountain stands the cathedral church of San Lorenzo (St Laurence).
An enlargement of an earlier, Romanesque, church (transformed
into the transept of the present cathedral), San Lorenzo was
rebuilt between the fourteenth and sixteenth centuries. The side
facing the piazza is most noteworthy for the attractive geometrical design of its fifteenth-century pink and white marble

facing, for the pulpit built by the city for the great Franciscan preacher St Bernardino of Siena, and for the bronze statue of Pope Julius III (1555). The cathedral façade was never completed and does little to prepare the visitor for the spaciousness of the vast interior, composed of three aisles of equal height. Among the many works of art in the nave are the *Madonna delle Grazie*, attributed to Giannicola di Paolo, on the third pillar to the right, and a bas-relief by Agostino di Duccio, which is to be found on the wall of the left aisle. The Cappella di San Bernardino, enclosed by a wrought-iron grille at the foot of the right aisle, contains a fine *Deposition* (1569) by Federico Barocci, and is being used for the moment to house the celebrated Sant'Onofrio panel, one of Luca Signorelli's earliest and finest works. The presbytery has magnificently carved inlaid wood choir-stalls by Giuliano da Maiano and Domenico del Tasso (1486–91), and a fine episcopal throne (1520–24). The chapel enclosed by a sixteenth-century wrought-iron grille at the foot of the left aisle is the Cappella del Sacro Anello, which holds the supposed wedding ring of the Virgin Mary – a sacred relic which Perugia looted from Chiusi in 1473; it is displayed once a year, on 30 July. It was for this chapel that Perugino painted his splendid *Betrothal of the Virgin*, now in Caen (the present picture is a copy by the nineteenth-century French artist, Jean-Baptiste Wicar). From the sacristy, a passage leads to a cloister and a canons' house which saw the election of no fewer than five popes, at conclaves held between 1216 and 1305. (The cathedral museum, with a fine collection, has been closed for many years.)

The door in the left aisle of the cathedral leads back to the Piazza IV Novembre where, immediately to the right, stands an elegant fifteenth-century loggia, erected during the lordship of Braccio Fortebraccio, as well as a small section of the Roman walls. Across the piazza is the short flank of the Palazzo dei Priori (1293–1443), one of Italy's finest medieval buildings. A fan-shaped stairway leads up to a large Gothic doorway, and balcony, on the first floor. Above the door are two large bronze statues which date from the late thirteenth century: the lion is the symbol of the Guelph party, the gryphon of Perugia itself. The stairway gives access to the Sala dei Notari, an enormous chamber with transverse ogival arches, decorated with thirteenth-century frescoes, and the painted coats-of-arms of the city's *podestà* and *capitani del popolo* from 1297 to 1499; the wooden benching along the walls dates from the sixteenth century. Returning once more to the piazza, walk back along the long flank of the Palazzo dei Priori, whose serendipitous curve results from the three separate stages in which the palace was built between 1293 and 1443. The principal door (1326) is distinguished both by its architecture and the superb and intricate carving; the three statues in the lunette represent St Louis of Toulouse, St Laurence and St Ercolanus, the patrons of the city.

Besides continuing to hold the council's administrative offices, the Palazzo dei Priori is also the seat of the recently renovated National Gallery of Umbria. This magnificent gallery has an unsurpassed collection of Umbrian art, much of it transferred here from churches and monasteries in the city and surrounding area, as well as a fine selection of works commissioned for the region by artists from elsewhere. Among other benefits of the recent renovation is the fact that the collection is now splendidly displayed and annotated (in Italian and English). The collection is far too extensive for any brief account to do more than gesture at its riches. However, among the early highlights must be accounted paintings by the thirteenth-century Master of San Francesco, Duccio, Meo da Siena, and the fourteenth-century Master of the Perugia Madonna. International Gothic is represented both by a lovely work by Gentile da Fabriano, and by others by the Gubbio-born Ottaviano Nelli. Among fifteenth-century works, two polyptychs by the Beato Angelico and Piero della Francesca would be outstanding anywhere. Predictably, the 'Umbrian School' is especially well documented. There are works by the early painters of the school, Benedetto Bonfigli and Bartolomeo Caporali, by its greatest figure, Perugino, and by Perugino's pupils and followers – a long list, including Pinturicchio, Lo Spagna, Fiorenzo Lorenzo, Nicolò Liberatore, called L'Alunno, Eusebio da San Giorgio, and Giannicola di Paolo. Later Umbrian painters, who followed different artistic currents, are also well represented. Apart from paintings hung in the usual manner, the National Gallery also includes the original

Priors' Chapel, from the Palazzo dei Priori. Here are to be found two important fresco cycles by Benedetto Bonfigli – one of which is notable for including detailed depictions of Perugia in the second half of the fifteenth century, giving us an unparalleled insight into its appearance at the end of the Middle Ages. The gallery also includes a splendid collection of sculpture (including works from many of the city's monuments, where they have been substituted by copies); among the artists represented here are Arnolfo di Cambio, Nicola and Giovanni Pisano, and Lorenzo Maitani. There is also a small but rewarding display of regional ceramics, especially Deruta ware.

A little way down the Corso Vannucci from the main door of the Priors' Palace is the insufficiently appreciated Collegio del Cambio – former seat of the city's money-changers – which survives intact and offers one of the finest examples of Renaissance decoration in the whole of Italy. Designed to a humanist scheme devised by Francesco Maturanzio, the principal chamber boasts a supremely confident fusion of Christian and classical values, in outstanding frescoes painted by Perugino and his assistants, around 1500. The chamber also has fine carved wooden seating by artists including Domenico del Tasso, and a fine representation of *Justice* in terracotta, by another Florentine, Benedetto da Maiano. The chapel in the adjoining room is dedicated to St John the Baptist and was richly decorated, in warm reds and blues, with scenes from the Baptist's life by Perugino's pupil, Giannicola di Paolo, between 1515 and 1518; the altarpiece (1512–13) is by Mariano di Ser Austerio. Close by the Collegio del Cambio is another guild chamber – the Sala dell'Udienza della Mercanzia, belonging to the powerful merchants; it was decorated in the course of the fifteenth century with inlaid wood, by artists from (or influenced by) northern Europe.

The large archway in the Palazzo dei Priori leads on to the steep Via dei Priori, one of the most interesting, crowded, and characteristic streets in the city. To the left is the tiny church of Sant'Agata (1290–1314), with numerous remains of fourteenth-century frescoes. Further down to the right, the Baroque church of San Filippo Neri (1627–34) makes an unexpected addition to its almost wholly medieval surroundings. The imposing façade

(1647–63) can best be seen from the far side of the small square opposite; the ornate interior contains many seventeenth- and eighteenth-century paintings, including an altarpiece by Pietro da Cortona (1596–1669) and an impressive fresco of the *Coronation of the Virgin* by Francesco Appiani (1704–92) in the cupola. Leaving the church by the principal door, cut across Via dei Priori and down the Via della Cupa – which has medieval houses and churches, as well as a stretch of Etruscan wall – as far as the Etruscan gate, known as the Porta della Mandorla. Returning to the Via dei Priori, continue downhill to another small church on the right. This is Santi Stefano e Valentino, with its tiny bell-tower and some fourteenth- and fifteenth-century frescoes inside. Close by is another Baroque church, Santa Teresa (1622–1718), and then a high tower-house – the twelfth-century Torre degli Sciri (forty-six metres high) – sole survivor of the many which once crowded within the city walls (as Bonfigli's fresco in the Priors' Chapel clearly shows). Just beyond the tower, the street forks: straight ahead is another Etruscan city gate (the Porta Trasimena), much altered in the Middle Ages, while to the right are two sixteenth-century churches. The first of these, the Madonna della Luce, contains work by Tiberio d'Assisi and G. B. Caporali; the second, San Luca, belongs to the Knights of Malta. The street now opens up completely, giving on to one of Perugia's loveliest spaces, the meadow where the Franciscans built their church in 1230 and which now contains, alongside it, the exquisite Oratorio di San Bernardino (1457–61) by Agostino di Duccio. The broad-naved preaching church of San Francesco is now closed (though due for restoration), but its reconstructed façade, in the pink and white stone of Assisi, can be admired. Even so, the adjoining oratory overshadows it in all but size. Here, to the harmony and elegance of construction of the polychromed façade, is added the beauty of Agostino di Duccio's delicate low-reliefs of the saint and angels, beneath a depiction of *Christ in Glory* in the tympanum. It is a truly lovely building, the finest architecture and most important sculpture of the early Renaissance to be found anywhere in Umbria. The simple interior, too, merits a visit, if only for the superbly carved fourth-century Christian sarcophagus which held the body of St Francis's follower, Brother Egidius, until the end of the nineteenth-century and now serves as an altar. Once back inside the old city walls, the Piazza IV Novembre can be regained either by way of Via dei Priori, or by striking off to the left and following a series of winding alleys back up the hill.

Starting again from the Piazza IV Novembre, take the short road opposite the corner of the Palazzo dei Priori down to the Piazza Matteotti, which has two splendid fifteenth-century buildings. To the left is the Palazzo del Capitano del Popolo, built between 1472 and 1481 in Renaissance style but with reference to the much earlier Palazzo dei Priori, as can be seen particularly in the fine doorway and the windows. Next to it, the Palazzo dell'Università Vecchia, built between 1490 and 1514, was the seat of the university until 1811. Although the remainder of the piazza – except for the church of the Gesù – is unremarkable, it is worth going through the large archway next to the Palazzo del Capitano del Popolo. Here, an animated covered market offers an exceptional range of local and imported produce – meat, fish, vegetables, cheeses, truffles, oil, and wine – while the balcony above affords a magnificent view of the city and the countryside around. From here, mists permitting, Assisi can be seen across the valley, and Spello is often visible at the far end of Monte Subasio, with Foligno on the plain below. Leaving the market, turn left along the piazza and left again down the Via Oberdan, which runs along the route of the old Etruscan walls. Where the street turns sharply left, keep straight on along the Via Porta Marzia as far as the massive Porta Marzia itself, a former Etruscan gate (second to first century BC) remodelled by the Romans and saved from destruction in the 1540s by Antonio da Sangallo, who moved it, stone by stone, four metres from its original position, to incorporate it in the papal fortress.

Retrace your steps and continue down Via Oberdan to the Porta di Sant'Ercolano, another Etruscan gate (though its present appearance is primarily medieval). Just beyond the gate is the church of Sant'Ercolano, built between 1297 and 1326 on the site of the martyrdom of the city's bishop and patron, St Ercolanus. Follow the narrow Corso Cavour down to the impressive bulk of San Domenico, which faces on to the irregularly shaped and provocatively named Piazza Giordano Bruno. (Bruno was an independently minded Dominican thinker, whose unwillingness to conform led to his execution in Rome in 1600.) San Domenico was originally built between 1304 and 1458, supposedly to a design by Giovanni Pisano. The vast three-aisled interior – remodelled by Carlo Maderno in the seventeenth century – can appear rather cold, though this impression is partly relieved by the cheerful, coloured marble altar designs. Among its notable works of art are an early-fourteenth-century funeral monument to Pope Benedict XI by a follower of Arnolfo di Cambio, a fine dossal (1459) by Agostino di Duccio, fifteenth-century stained glass in the apse, and superb Renaissance choir-stalls, as well as some early frescoes and a *gonfalone* (1494) by Giannicola di Paolo. To the left of the church is the former Dominican monastery, now given over to the State Archives – with important documents going back to the tenth century – and the Museo Archeologico Nazionale dell'Umbria (or National Archaeological Museum of Umbria). The museum has an extremely fine collection of materials from prehistoric Umbria (from the sixteenth to fourteenth centuries BC – including the important finds made at Abeto and the Tane del Diavolo di Parrano) as well as others from the Bronze and Iron Ages. The Etruscan section is exceptionally rich and varied, and includes the important *cippus* from the third or second century which has one of the longest surviving Etruscan texts, relating to a boundary dispute; there are also fine funeral urns and a range of ceramic and bronze work, from the Villanovan and Hellenistic periods. The equally strong Roman section includes sarcophagi, and a large head of the Emperor Claudius – one of several finds made at **Carsulae**.

From San Domenico, the Corso Cavour leads down to the medieval city gate of San Pietro, which is partly decorated, in a monumental Renaissance style derived from the Malatesta Temple in Rimini, by Agostino di Duccio and Polidoro di Stefano (1475–80). Just inside the fifteenth-century walls is the monastery of San Pietro, whose large church retains part of its tenth-century structure though it was substantially remodelled and enlarged at a later date. The prominent bell-tower has a twelve-sided base dating from the thirteenth century, while the upper part was added between 1463 and 1468. The frescoes on the church façade include, to the right of the door, an unusual representation of the Trinity, as a three-headed female figure (one of only three such representations in Italy). The three-aisled interior of the church is basilical in plan and has much fine art-work, especially from the sixteenth and seventeenth centuries. The central aisle was decorated by the Greek painter Aliense – a follower of Veronese – and the church also contains pictures by Perugino (four paintings in the sacristy), Eusebio da San Giorgio, Sassoferrato, Guercino and Reni – as well as a charming stoup, close to the first pillar on the left. The sixteenth-century choir-stalls – begun by the Perugian Bernardino Antonibi, with the Bolognese Nicola di Stefano, and finished by Stefano Zambelli from Bergamo – have been described as the finest in the whole of Italy. A door at the back of the presbytery (ask the sacristan) opens on to a small balcony. There, above the olive-covered slopes of the city, is another magnificent view of Monte Subasio, taking in Assisi and Spello, Montefalco and the Martani hills. From San Pietro, follow the Corso Cavour back to the centre of town.

Starting once more in the Piazza IV Novembre, take the Via Maestà delle Volte which, from the cathedral, leads down under huge arches into one of the most characteristic parts of the medieval city. Turn immediately to the right in the Piazza Cavallotti and go a little way down the Via Baldeschi, from where, to the left, there is a good view of the Via dell'Acque-dotto – the medieval aqueduct which once brought water to the Fontana Maggiore and is now a pedestrian pathway. Continue along the Via Baldeschi and turn left into the Via Ulisse Rocchi, which descends steeply to the Arco Etrusco (or Arco di Augusto), the great gate which is one of the symbols of Perugia. This massive structure – built by the Etruscans in the third century BC as the city's principal gate – was embellished by the Romans, and given a small loggia in the Renaissance; the huge blocks of stone at the base of the city walls at this point are also Etruscan. Just beyond the Etruscan arch is the Baroque Palazzo Gallenga Stuart (1748–58), the most important eighteenth-century building in Perugia, with a fine façade (note the elegant solution to the corners of the building) and a good interior. The building now holds the Università Italiana per Stranieri, founded in 1926 to help the diffusion of Italian culture among foreigners; its students today help lend Perugia a cosmopolitan air throughout the year, something which is otherwise rare in Umbria. Across the road, take the Corso Garibaldi, which runs through the heart of another characteristic medieval quarter of the city. To the right, the thirteenth-century church of Sant'Agostino – remodelled in the early nineteenth century – contains works of art going back as far as the fourteenth century. Further along, a turning to the left leads almost immediately to the convent of Sant'Agnese, where there is a frescoed *Madonna and Saints* by Perugino. Back on the Corso Garibaldi, the route leads past the former thirteenth-century charity hospital (at No. 84), the sixteenth-century convent of Santa Caterina, and the convent of the Beata Colomba (with a fresco by Lo Spagna), to one of the city's most beautiful and important churches, Sant'Angelo, in an attractively secluded and shaded setting just inside the medieval walls. The palaeo-Christian church, built in the fifth or sixth century, has a circular interior plan with a ring of sixteen columns, taken from pre-existing Roman buildings, around a raised central section with an altar formed from more Roman remains; the walls retain fragments of frescoes going back to the fourteenth century. The Corso Garibaldi ends at the large city gate of Sant'Angelo, a fifteenth-century addition to the thirteenth-century city walls. Beyond the gate, a short road leads past the thirteenth-century church of San Matteo degli Armeni, to the Franciscan monastery of Monte Ripido, with an important eighteenth-century library.

Having followed the Corso Garibaldi back to the Arco Etrusco turn left along the Via Pinturicchio, which shortly arrives at the church of Santa Maria Nuova, much altered from its original thirteenth-century state but graced with fine carved choir-stalls and an especially interesting plague *gonfalone* by Bonfigli, which includes a detailed representation of Perugia in the third quarter of the fifteenth century. A route through the fourteenth-century city gate (the Porta Pesa or Arco dei Tei) leads, by way of the Corso Bersaglieri, to the church of Sant'Antonio, where a frescoed *Crucifixion* (1499) has, since 1990, been attributed to the young Raphael. Beyond the Sant'Antonio gate, the Via Enrico Cialdini leads to the thirteenth-century Santa Maria di Monteluce – a former convent and now the principal city hospital. The convent church has a fine mid-fifteenth-century façade, with a pink and white geometrical design; its aisle-less interior has a number of frescoes and a good fifteenth-century marble tabernacle. Having retraced your steps to Santa Maria Nuova, take the Via del Roscetto (immediately to the left of the church) which leads to another Etruscan gate (now the Arco dei Gigli), and, along the Via Bontempi, through a predominantly medieval quarter to the Piazza Piccinino. Turn past the tiny sixteenth-century church by Bino Sozi and up the steps leading to the small chapel of San Severo, which holds a fresco of the *Trinity and Saints* (1505) by Raphael, which was completed, years later, by his teacher Perugino. Continue up as far as the piazza in front of the church of Sant'Angelo della Pace, from where there are beautiful views over the northern part of the town and the surrounding hills. A short walk down the hill leads to the Piazza Danti, next to the cathedral, and the Pozzo Etrusco, or Etruscan well – a huge stone water reservoir (over five and a half metres in diameter and thirty-seven metres deep) from the third century BC. On leaving, it is well worth turning right as far as the adjacent Piazza Piccinino and immediately right again, into a covered alleyway leading to one of the most characteristic medieval corners of the entire city, the covered alley running down to the Piazza Matteotti, a few paces from the Piazza IV Novembre.

Exhausting as they may sound, these skeletal itineraries do no more than give a sense of the range of monuments Perugia offers from its varied past. Though some steep climbs are involved, however, it should be quite possible comfortably to follow each of the routes on foot. Of the many monuments in the surrounding area which merit a visit but demand transport, the most worthwhile is the Ipogeo dei Volumni. It is not the easiest place to find, though it can be reached by the road leaving the Porta San Pietro (about seven kilometres), or by taking the signposts on the *superstrada* (dual-carriageway) in the direction of Rome. The hypogeum is located in one of the most important Etruscan necropolises in Umbria; the elaborate Volumni tomb, belonging to the Velimna family, was in use for 200 years until the first century BC, and contains a number of fine funerary urns, and the sarcophagus of the patriarch, Arnth.

To get to know Perugia undoubtedly requires time and several visits, and it would be a pity simply to concentrate on its artistic heritage, for the city is a charming and lively place in which to wander. The Corso Vannucci, with its elegant shops and open-air cafés, is tremendously animated not just during the tourist season but throughout the year. This is where the Perugians themselves make their morning and evening *passeggiata* – the place in Perugia to see and be seen. As such, it makes for as enjoyable a stroll on a cold winter morning as on a warm summer evening – as irresistible a place of commerce and resort today as it has been for more than 2,000 years.

Piediluco (375 m.): Now a popular resort in summer, this attractive medieval village stands on the shores of the Lago di Piediluco, an irregularly shaped lake on Umbria's south-eastern boundary with Lazio. Taking its name from the sacred wood (in Latin *lucus*) which covers the conical hill above the town, Piediluco was much contested in the Middle Ages by Terni, Rieti, Spoleto and Foligno. The hill is now topped by the remains of the fortress built in 1364 by order of Cardinal Albornoz, as part of his mission to reclaim the region for the papacy. It was here, the following year, that Albornoz's nephew was murdered, along with his son; the cardinal had the village razed four years later. Today the principal evidence of Piediluco's past is the late-thirteenth-century Gothic church of San Francesco, which has a number of sixteenth-century frescoes, including a *Madonna and Two Saints* (1514) by Marcantonio di Antoniazzo; there are also a stoup adapted from a Roman capital and a Roman female statue, as well as a fifteenth-century wooden crucifix. See also **Terni**.

Ponte (441 m.): The exceptional position of this tiny village, on a high conical hill overlooking the point where the Tissino joins the Nera, makes it easy to see why it enjoyed a former strategic significance. Even so, it is hard to believe that, as a ninth-century Longobard stronghold, it was once the most important settlement in the entire area, controlling the surrounding territory as far as **Norcia** and **Cascia**. Today, Ponte is worth visiting for its early-thirteenth-century Romanesque church, the Pieve di Santa Maria, and the remains of the fortress, as well as the lovely views of the neighbouring villages and surrounding mountains. The church has a flat-screen façade and a beautifully carved rose-window with the symbols of the evangelists and a pleasing telamon; the exterior of the apse is also decorated with hanging arches and carved heads. Inside the church, which once held the beautiful sculpture of the Virgin and Child by the Master of Cesi, now in the Diocesan Museum in Spoleto, are some fifteenth- and sixteenth-century frescoes. From the church it is a long and steep, but rewarding, climb up to what is left of the medieval fortress. See also **Cerreto di Spoleto**.

Preci (596 m.): The small fortified village stands on a hill overlooking the Castoriana valley (Valcastoriana), on the road leading from **Norcia** to Visso in the Marches. Though severely depopulated today (the 1991 census showed the population to be less than half that forty years previously), Preci still shows signs of its former prosperity, not least in the large number of *palazzi* built in 1534, when the town was rebuilt following its destruction by Norcia six years previously. For centuries the town was celebrated for its surgeons, whose skills – particularly in eye surgery and lithotomy – were renowned throughout Europe. The surgical tradition of Preci derived from the nearby Benedictine **Abbey** of Sant'Eutizio after the Church banned monks from performing surgery in the early thirteenth century. Thereafter the art was handed down from father to son among a group of thirty or so families, who also produced notable surgical textbooks. In 1588, Cesare Scacchi travelled to London to treat Elizabeth I for cataract, and other local surgeons operated on European monarchs from the fifteenth to eighteenth centuries.

Preci also became a centre for the manufacture of surgical implements. Today, the church of Santa Maria retains its Romanesque and Gothic doors, a stone *Pietà* and a carved and gilded font (1521), while Santa Caterina has a Gothic portal and small bell-tower. On either side of the Valcastoriana can be found a number of small mountain villages which repay a visit, including the finely positioned Sant'Angelo, and Campi Vecchio – with three good churches, the Madonna di Piazza, Sant'Andrea, and San Salvatore, with a beautiful façade and particularly interesting frescoes (1464) by Giovanni and Antonio Sparapane. A small road leading south-west from Preci climbs up to three more remote villages: Roccanolfi, Poggio di Croce, and Montebufo (1,012 m.). See also **Abbey of Sant'Eutizio, Norcia**.

San Feliciano (279 m.): Situated on the eastern shore of Lake Trasimeno, this tiny fishing village is a convenient place to pick up the ferry for the Isola Polvese, the largest of the lake's islands, long abandoned by the fishermen and monks who once lived there. San Feliciano also has an interesting Museo della Pesca, a museum offering a fascinating overview of fishing in the lake, both past and present. Not far away is the Castello di Zocco, a castle dating back to the late thirteenth century; it is remembered in a poem by Vittoria Aganoor Pompili (1855–1910), a considerable poet whose work is still anthologized and who lived near by, following her marriage to the politician Guido Pompili. See also **Magione, San Savino**.

San Gémini (337 m.): Famous for centuries for its mineral water and the spa in neighbouring San Gémini Fonte, this small and prosperous town is today a popular haunt of wealthy holidaymakers from the Italian capital. Formerly an ancient Roman settlement on the old branch of the Via Flaminia, it was destroyed by Saracens in 882 and, once rebuilt, continually contested between the Church and Narni. Enclosed behind its ring of walls, San Gémini retains much of its former medieval appearance, and many indications – some elaborate doorways, for instance – of later periods of prosperity. On the Piazza Palazzo Vecchio, at the heart of town, stands the twelfth-century

Palazzo Pubblico or Pretorio, incorporating a medieval defensive tower transformed into a campanile in the eighteenth century; opposite is the thirteenth-century former Cappella dei Priori (now the Oratorio), which has an unusual ciborium, elaborately frescoed by a follower of the painter Giovanni di Piermatteo, known as Boccati, from the Marches. The former twelfth-century parish church, San Giovanni Battista, has a fine Romanesque doorway with cosmatesque decoration and two stone lions, and an inscription, dated 1199, naming Nicola, Simone and Bernardo as architects; this doorway is to be found on the left flank of the church in relation to the usual present entrance on a small square. Originally built on an octagonal plan but now peculiarly transformed into an irregular hexagon, the church retains traces of fourteenth- and fifteenth-century frescoes and some elaborate Baroque altars. A narrow passageway to the right of the square gives on to a balcony at the edge of town offering fine views of the surrounding countryside. Just beyond the walls, at the other end of town, is San Francesco (1291), a Franciscan church whose fourteenth-century wooden doors are some of the oldest to survive in Umbria. The church's aisle-less interior – with seven large ogival arches – contains frescoes from the fifteenth to the seventeenth century. The unusual placing of the cathedral, at the southern edge of town, reflects the fact that San Gémini was elevated to the status of a city by Pius VI only in 1781; the simple fourteenth-century Gothic façade gives way to a handsome early-nineteenth-century interior unhappily decked out in the taste of later-nineteenth-century pietism, with the exception of a fine fourteenth-century wooden crucifix. Just outside the town lies another early church, San Nicolò, now in private hands; dating from the eleventh century, it once belonged to the powerful Abbey of Farfa, near Rieti, in northern Lazio. The church's richly decorated marble portal is now in the Metropolitan Museum in New York and has been replaced here by a copy. The interior has three aisles, divided by columns with fine capitals, at least one of which was taken from neighbouring **Carsulae**; there are a number of detached frescoes including, in the apse, the only known work (1295) of Rogerino da Todi. See also **Amelia**, **Carsulae**, **Narni**, **Terni**.

San Giacomo di Spoleto (243 m.): Though little known even within Umbria, this small and mostly modern village, some seven kilometres from Spoleto, merits a visit for two reasons. The first is its curious castle, erected on a square plan, with angle towers, by order of Cardinal Albornoz in the four-teenth century; today, the grim dark-grey castle is entirely occupied by modest houses built of the same stone arranged along five tiny regular streets. In complete contrast is the church of San Giacomo, directly opposite the castle; originally built in the thirteenth century, the church now has a simple Renaissance façade and a splendidly carved stone doorway (1589). Inside the church there are a number of sixteenth-century frescoes, includ-ing some of Lo Spagna's finest work, notably a *Coronation of the Virgin*, and two scenes from the life of San Giacomo, or St James the Greater, telling the story of a miracle performed by the saint, who appeared at the gibbet to support an unjustly hanged youth until the young man's parents rushed to the judge to report that their son was still alive; when the judge, at table, declared the hanged man to be no more alive than the fowls he was eating, these too were miraculously revived on his plate. See also **Campello sul Clitunno**, **Spoleto**.

San Savino (314 m.): Situated on an outcrop above the eastern shore of Lake Trasimeno, this village was founded around the year 1000 and still retains its medieval walls and a triangular tower dating from the fourteenth century. Close by is the late-nineteenth-century outlet, used to help regulate the level of the lake, which replaced that built almost 500 years previously, in 1422, by Braccio Fortebraccio, lord of Perugia, on the site of a still earlier Roman emissary. See also **San Feliciano**, **Magione**.

Sant'Anatolia di Narco (328 m.): On the left bank of the river Nera, this small commune is situated in one of the longest continuously inhabited areas of the region; the necropolis of Naharci, discovered here in 1883, disclosing extensive remains now in the Archaeological Museum in Florence, dates from the eighth century BC. With just 550 residents, Sant'Anatolia has a deserted air today but it retains a number of interesting churches both within the village and in the surrounding area. Inside the village's fourteenth-century walls is the parish church of Sant'-Anatolia, whose fourteenth-century frescoes have suffered disastrous water damage in recent years; just outside the west gate, the attractive Renaissance church of Santa Maria delle Grazie (1572–5) has a number of popular votive frescoes and, in the heavily restored presbytery, a lovely *Virgin and Child, with Saints*, by the fifteenth-century Master of Eggi. A road leading south-east from Sant'Anatolia to **Monteleone di Spoleto** touches some dramatically located mountain hamlets on its way through some of Umbria's most spectacular and rugged scenery, with Monte di Civitella (1,565 m.) to the right, and Monte Coscerno (1,685 m.) to the left. At Caso (667 m.), there are sixteenth-century frescoes by the school of Lo Spagna in the church of Santa Maria delle Grazie and a sixteenth-century fresco by Pierino Cesarei in the parish church, while the tiny Romanesque church of Santa Cristina, located a little distance outside the village, has its side-walls entirely covered with interesting frescoes from the fourteenth to sixteenth centuries. From here the road rises steeply to Gavelli (1,153 m.), visible on a spur high above. There the fifteenth-century church of San Michele has numerous and notable frescoes by Lo Spagna, his pupils and other artists, including Bernardino di Nanni from Gubbio. Nine kilometres before Monteleone di Spoleto, a road to the left goes through mountain valley scenery, via Usigni and Poggiodomo, to **Ponte**. See also **Castel San Felice**, **Monteleone di Spoleto**, **Scheggino**, **Vallo di Nera**.

Scheggino (281 m.): A tiny village situated on either side of the river Nera, amid dramatic countryside, Scheggino retains its twelfth-century walls which protected it in 1522 from attack by Girolamo Brancaleoni, called Picozzo, one of the most notorious brigands of his day. The church of San Nicolò dates from the fourteenth century but was subjected to later remodelling; it retains some late frescoes (1526) in the apse by Lo Spagna and Giovanni di Girolamo, completed by Piermarino di Giacomo from nearby Castel San Felice (1533). There are also later works by Cesare Sermei (1595) and Guidobaldo Abbatini (1644). See also **Abbey of San Pietro in Valle, Castel San Felice, Sant'-Anatolia di Narco**.

Spello (280 m.): One of the loveliest towns of its size in Umbria, Spello occupies a low spur of the extreme southern end of Monte Subasio, just above Foligno and the Vale of Umbria. An important centre of the Umbri, the town was known to the Romans as Hispellum; under the empire it controlled territory from the Fonti del Clitunno almost as far as **Perugia**. Following the northern invasions, Spello became part of the Longobard Duchy of Spoleto and was a free commune in the thirteenth century. Subsequently it came under the predominant influence of Perugia, and from 1583 formed part of the Papal State. The characteristic appearance of Spello derives primarily from the pink and white stone used in its construction (as with **Assisi** at the opposite end of Monte Subasio), which gives the town a warm roseate glow, especially at evening. At the southern edge of the town is the first-century Roman gate (the Porta Consolare) incorporated into the town walls in the Middle Ages; it now adjoins a medieval tower. A short distance to the left lies another Roman gate, the Porta Urbica, and part of the Roman walls, while to the right the Via Consolare runs steeply up into the heart of the old town. On the left is the small fourteenth-century chapel of Sant'Anna, with some fine frescoes (1461) by Nicolò Alunno. Shortly afterwards, on the right, is the town's finest monument, Santa Maria Maggiore. Originally built between the twelfth and thirteenth centuries – and still retaining a Romanesque bell-tower – the church was remodelled in the sixteenth century; the present doorway uses materials from the earlier church, including an acanthus frieze. The undisputed highlight of the interior is the Baglioni chapel (1500), magnificently frescoed in the following year by Pinturicchio, who painted three principal scenes – an *Annunciation*, the *Adoration of the Shepherds and Arrival of the Magi*, and the *Dispute in the Temple* (which owes much to his teacher, Perugino). The chapel was given an attractive floor of Deruta majolica tiles in 1516. Amid the Baroque remodelling are a number of other features worth noting, including a splendid tabernacle (1515) by Rocco di Tommaso, inlaid wood choir-stalls (1515–20) by Pier Nicola da Spoleto, and a stone pulpit (1545) by Simone da Campione. The frescoes (1521) by Perugino on the pillars flanking the apse are poor late works, but the Cappella del Sacramento to the left of the crossing has two more lovely frescoes – a *Madonna and Child* and an *Angel* by Pinturicchio; there is also a fine High Renaissance tabernacle (1562) by Gian Domenico da Carrara. Adjoining the church is Spello's new and well-laid-out Pinacoteca Civica (art gallery), opened in 1994, whose collection is formed entirely of works from the town. Notable among the works on display are some excellent polychrome wood sculptures, including an Umbrian *Madonna and Child* of the late twelfth or early thirteenth century and a beautifully contrasted sixteenth-century treatment of the same theme, and a crucifix (1398) by the goldsmith Paolo Vanni, one of the finest of its kind in Umbria. The paintings include a diptych (1391) by Cola Petruccioli and a *Crucifixion* by Alunno, as well as works by Marcantonio Grecchi, including a *Madonna and Child, with St Felice Vescovo and the Blessed Andrea Caccioli* (c. 1610) which includes an interesting representation of Spello at the beginning of the seventeenth century.

A little further up the street (now the Via Garibaldi) on the right is the church of Sant'Andrea, a thirteenth-century foundation, which has a large fourteenth-century painted crucifix of the Umbrian school, frescoes from the fifteenth and sixteenth centuries, and a large *Madonna and Child with Saints* (1508) by Pinturicchio and Eusebio da San Giorgio. The nearby Piazza Repubblica is disappointingly anonymous, though the Palazzo Comunale retains some of its original thirteenth-century features, despite subsequent alterations. A little further up the hill, a right turn at the twelfth-century church of San Lorenzo leads up the Via Giulia through a largely intact medieval quarter to the monastery of Vallegloria, and by way of the Via Arco Romano to the highest part of town, formerly the Roman acropolis. The site, with its surviving Roman arch, is now occupied by the remains of the fortress built as a demonstration of papal power by Cardinal Albornoz in the fourteenth century, and offers extensive views over the surrounding countryside. From here, the Via Torre di Belvedere leads steeply down the west side of town to the impressive Porta Venere, from the reign of the Emperor Augustus, with its two twelve-sided towers, and back to the Via Cavour.

From Spello, it is possible to follow either of two scenically splendid routes across or around Monte Subasio, as far as Assisi. Both begin at the Porta Montanara, at the upper end of town; shortly beyond this gate, a road to the right winds through olive groves in the direction of Collepino (600 m.). This small fortified village, once an outpost of Spello, remains intact inside its ring of medieval walls; nearby is the small Romanesque church of San Silvestro and there are magnificent views over the surrounding countryside. From Collepino, an untarmacked road – only practicable in summer – leads high up beyond the woods of oak, ilex, hornbeam and beech to the pastures at the treeless summit of Monte Subasio (1,290 m.); the area is now a regional park, rich in animal, bird and plant life, which offers unrivalled views in all directions. Alternatively, it is possible to follow the narrow but tarmacked road through the wooded slopes of Subasio to the tiny fortified hamlet of Armenzano (759 m.) and on to Assisi; the route offers fine views of the quiet agricultural area lying below the mountain to the north. See also **Foligno**.

Spoleto (396 m.): In terms of the range and quality of its cultural heritage, Spoleto is one of the most significant and individual cities of Umbria. It is also, however, one of the most difficult to get to know, for several of its principal monuments lie some distance from the city centre while the steep, hilly site and tortuous medieval town plan do not allow for easy familiarity. Guarding one end of a long, broad and fertile valley and partly ringed by mountains, Spoleto occupies what has always been recognized as a strategically important position. Once a major centre of the ancient Umbri – their city walls, built in the fifth century BC, are still visible in part – the town became a Roman colony, Spoletium, in 241 BC, distinguishing itself by withstanding attack by Hannibal, fresh from his great victory over the Roman army at the Battle of Trasimeno in 217 BC. The city's importance continued up to and beyond the imperial

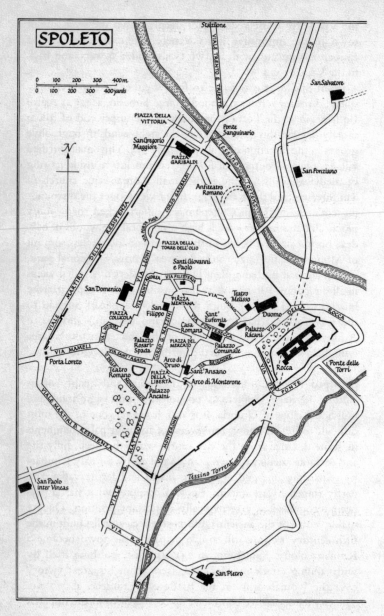

age, as numerous Roman remains testify. Totila's Goths occupied
the town in 545 and turned the Roman amphitheatre into a
fortress, but when the Longobards invaded Italy shortly afterwards, they chose Spoleto as the capital of an independent
duchy that flourished for the next 400 years and existed, at least
in name, until 1231. Thereafter, it became a valued possession of
the papacy, which ensured its control in the fourteenth century
by building an enormous fortress which dominates the city to
this day. Even as Umbria turned into a pontifical backwater
from the mid sixteenth century, Spoleto continued to attract
members of the papal nobility, who built impressive palaces in
the town, and when the Napoleonic army occupied the region,
Spoleto was elevated to the status of capital of a *département*
which included even Perugia. The economic decline of the late
nineteenth and early twentieth centuries has more recently been
partly reversed by the impetus given to tourism by the Italian-
American composer Giancarlo Menotti, who founded the
internationally known Festival dei Due Mondi, or Two Worlds
Festival, in the city in 1958. It is possible to see much of the city on
foot – though steep climbs up cobbled streets are involved – but
a number of monuments really require some form of transport.

Anyone arriving by car would do well to park at the foot of
the city, for long-term parking within it is impossible; a convenient and comparatively little-used parking area lies just outside
the Porta Loreto, to the west of the city centre. From the Porta
Loreto, the Via Mameli and the narrow Via Sant'Agata offer
both convenient access to the centre and a good introduction to
the city, climbing up as they do through an old medieval
quarter built in Spoleto's sober grey stone. Almost at the top of
the Via Sant'Agata is the monastery of Sant'Agata – now home
to an archaeological museum with an interesting collection of
mainly Roman remains. The street gives on to the Piazza della
Libertà, one of Spoleto's main squares. On the west side, the
remains of the first-century Roman theatre are visible (access via
the Archaeological Museum), while to the south is the
seventeenth-century palace of the Ancaiani family. Directly opposite the Via Sant'Agata, the Via Brignone leads up to the highest
part of town, formerly the heart of the Roman, Longobard, and

late-medieval cities. Immediately, Spoleto's characteristic – and confusing – jumble of remains from different historical periods becomes abundantly apparent. Just past the impressive sixteenth- to seventeenth-century Palazzo Mauri is the tiny Piazza Sant' Ansano, beyond which is the Arco di Monterone, the former south gate, set in a ring of city walls built in the third century BC. To the left of the piazza is the church of Sant'Ansano, flanked by the Arco di Druso – a first-century Roman arch erected to mark the entrance to the forum. The church of Sant'Ansano owes its present appearance to its late-eighteenth-century rebuilding, though it retains a cloister, and a frescoed *Madonna and Child* by Lo Spagna in the aisle-less interior, from the sixteenth century. Below the present church, however, is the Crypt of St Isaac the Hermit (Cripta di Sant'Isacco), which dates from the eleventh or twelfth century and was built on the site of a first-century Roman temple – one of whose columns can be seen on the outer left flank of the church, next to the Roman arch. The crypt itself – which is entered from the church by way of steps which belong to the Roman temple – has Roman columns with eighth- or ninth-century capitals, and some Byzantine-style frescoes – including scenes from the life of St Isaac, a fifth-century Syrian monk who settled near Spoleto, and an interesting *Last Supper* – from the eleventh or twelfth century. Exiting from the church pass under the Roman arch, noticing the different street levels (the arch remains partly under-ground), and into the Piazza del Mercato, the market-place built on part of the extensive space formerly occupied by the forum; the fountain which closes the square dates from 1746–8. To the right of the fountain the road leads up to the front of the Palazzo Comunale – dating in origin from the thirteenth century, though only part of its tower remains from that time. From there it is possible to take the steep road leading up to the Rocca or Papal Fortress, erected between 1359 and 1370 by Matteo Gattapone and the most imposing (or oppressive) of all the fortresses built by Cardinal Albornoz as part of his domination of the region for Innocent VI, after the papacy's long exile in Avignon. Employing materials quarried from the Roman amphi-theatre, the fortress is built on a rectangular plan, with two large courtyards and strong defensive towers at the angles. Besides its military use, the Rocca was for centuries the residence of papal governors, including Lucrezia Borgia, embellished by artists such as Lo Spagna (see below); eventually abandoned, it has been used as a barracks and, until very recently, a prison, since when restoration is bringing it back to its original condition.

Just around the corner from the Palazzo Comunale is the Casa Romana, or Roman house. Although only the floor plan has survived subsequent building on the site, the various areas of the first-century house – the atrium, with pluvium, triclinium, tablinum, and so on – are clearly recognizable and there are splendid black and white mosaic floors showing varied geometrical designs. Turn right on exiting from the house and around the corner is the rear entrance to the Palazzo Comunale, which holds Spoleto's Pinacoteca Comunale. Among the highlights of the gallery's interesting collection – covering the twelfth to nineteenth centuries – are a painted crucifix from the late thirteenth or early fourteenth century by the Maestro di Cesi, works by Jacopo Vincioli and L'Alunno, and a superb reliquary crucifix and panels and painted Christ in a bejewelled gold filigree frame by the Maestro di Sant'Alò, active in Spoleto in the late thirteenth and early fourteenth centuries. Three detached frescoes are also equally interesting. The earliest, by a Spoletine painter of the late twelfth century, depicting scenes from the lives of Sts Peter and Paul, comes from the church of Santi Giovanni e Paolo (see below). Two others, by Lo Spagna, were removed from the Papal Fortress. One is an allegorical rendering of Charity, Mercy, and Justice (1512–13) – painted in honour of Julius II but now adapted to frame a bust of the reactionary nineteenth-century Pope Leo XII, born in Spoleto. The other is Lo Spagna's masterpiece, a *Virgin, Child and Saints* (1514–16), in which the exquisite figures of the Madonna and her son, set among a group of saints arranged in a semicircle, show how much Lo Spagna had learned from Raphael. There are fine views of the cathedral and its piazza with the mountains behind to be had from the windows of the Palazzo.

Across the road from the Pinacoteca, a large doorway leads into the courtyard of the Archbishop's palace, which holds the magnificent church of Sant'Eufemia. Built in Romanesque style in the early twelfth century, the church was later incorporated into the surrounding buildings, only to be most fortunately rescued this century. Today, the imposing façade shows a simple doorway with a double window above, while the fine interior, built on the basilical plan, has three aisles divided by columns taken from earlier buildings, and spacious matroneums, for women to attend worship (it is the only church in Umbria so built); the altar, brought here from the earlier cathedral, has a particularly beautiful marble front showing the symbols of Christ and the Evangelists and decorated with cosmatesque work. To the left of the church stands the archiepiscopal palace, which holds a valuable collection of sacred art – well displayed and informatively annotated (though in Italian only) – drawn from churches and monasteries in the arch-diocese. As in the Pinacoteca Comunale, there are some fine early painted crucifixes by Spoletine masters, a lovely *Madonna and Child* (1315) attributed to the so-called First Master of Santa Chiara di Montefalco, a most accomplished *Madonna and Child with Saints* by the late fourteenth- and early-fifteenth-century Maestro della Madonna Straus and good works by Neri di Bicci, Filippo Lippi, Andrea da Cardarola and the sixteenth-century Siennese artist Domenico Beccafumi. There is also some excellent Umbrian sculpture from the thirteenth century onwards and a rich and touching collection of popular *ex-votos*, or votive tablets, from the sixteenth to nineteenth centuries.

From the gate of the Archbishop's palace it is only a brief distance to the Via dell'Arringo – the long flight of shallow steps leading down to the Piazza del Duomo – which offers a magnificent view of Spoleto's great Romanesque cathedral against a background of the hills around the town. The irregularly shaped piazza – used in the Middle Ages for public gatherings and now for concerts – is itself of considerable interest. To the right stands the sixteenth-century Palazzo Rácani, with (faded) graffiti traditionally attributed to Giulio Romano, a third-century Roman sarcophagus adapted to serve as a fountain, and a memorial tablet to the American conductor Thomas Schippers, closely connected with the Festival dei Due Mondi, whose ashes rest on the spot. High above, the massive fourteenth-century papal fortress overshadowing the town makes its oppressive presence strongly felt. To the left are the Casa dell'Opera del Duomo (1419), built in bands of pink and white stone, the small nineteenth-century Caio Melisso theatre (named for the dramatist who was the Emperor Augustus's librarian, born in Spoleto), and a pleasing octagonal Renaissance church, Santa Maria della Manna d'Oro. Dominating all of this, however, is the splendid façade of the Romanesque cathedral with its elegant, if unnecessary, portico (1491–1504), two pulpits, and a massive twelfth-century bell-tower, built of huge blocks of stone with the occasional aid of fragments taken from earlier buildings. Above the balustrade of the portico is a small blind arcade, with two telamones, a large rose-window surrounded by the symbols of the evangelists and four smaller rose-windows. The top area of the façade terminates in a triangular pediment with three rose-windows over three ogival arches, the middle and largest of which holds an enormous Byzantine-style mosaic, showing Christ with Mary and John the Baptist, executed in 1207 by an artist who signed his name, Solsternus. Beneath the portico, the main doorway of the cathedral dates from the twelfth century and is graced with fine, decorative carving on its pillars and architrave.

After the magnificence of the façade the Latin-cross interior of the cathedral comes, initially, as a disappointment, for virtually all trace of the original Romanesque form was removed by a radical transformation in the seventeenth century and the addition of unattractive altars in the nineteenth. Fortunately there are many compensations – not least the monumental frescoes by Fra Lippo Lippi in the central apse, which are considered the artist's masterpiece. The lovely mosaic floor of the central aisle is original. At the beginning of the right aisle is a chapel frescoed by Pinturicchio, while the Eroli chapel, which leads off from it, has good frescoes by unknown sixteenth-century artists. To the right of the presbytery is the fine Baroque Cappella della Santissima Icona by G. B. Mola, built to hold an image of the Virgin given to the city in 1185 by Frederick Barbarossa (by way of compensation for having burnt down Spoleto's earlier cathedral thirty years previously). Behind the high altar are Fra Lippo Lippi's frescoes, dedicated to a *Life of the Virgin*. However unexpected these very Florentine frescoes initially appear, they are splendidly adapted to their setting, both in terms of an impressive command of perspective (as in the *Annunciation* scene to the left) and in the use of architectural details taken from earlier buildings in Spoleto. The *Coronation of the Virgin*, which occupies all of the upper part of the apse, is quite magnificent, both in composition and in richness of colour. Lippi died in Spoleto while working on the frescoes (which were completed by assistants, including Pier Matteo d'Amelia) and was buried in the cathedral; a memorial tablet with bust, designed by his son, is to be seen in the transept. There is another fine chapel at the head of the left aisle, and at the foot a superb large crucifix – recently restored and now somewhat incongruously displayed – painted in 1187 by the earliest Umbrian artist whose name is known to us, Albertus Sotius. On the way out, notice (above the main doorway) a bronze bust of Urban VIII (1640) – who commissioned the remodelling of the cathedral – by the great Baroque sculptor Gian Lorenzo Bernini.

On exiting, take the Via del Duomo, which runs to the right of the long flight of steps leading down to the piazza. To the left, the Via della Spagna winds its way through one of the most characteristic parts of the medieval town and eventually up to the Piazza del Mercato and back under the Arch of Drusus to the Piazza della Libertà. From here, take the Corso Mazzini, facing the Palazzo Ancaiani, until, on the left, a short passageway leads to the Palazzo Rosari-Spada, now home to Spoleto's modern art museum, the Galleria d'Arte Moderna e Contemporanea (a single ticket permits entry to this gallery, the Roman House, and the Pinacoteca Comunale). The collection is not large but offers single works by modern Italian artists, including Giuseppe Capogrossi, Alberto Burri and Carla Accardi; there is also a fine sculpture by Arnaldo Pomodoro and the model for Alexander Calder's enormous black iron sculpture *Teodolapio* (1962), which dominates the piazza in front of Spoleto's railway station. The highlight of the museum, however, is the room dedicated to the art of Leoncillo Leonardi, called Leoncillo

(1915–68), born in Spoleto. From conventional enough beginnings, Leoncillo developed a highly distinctive art, using polychrome glazed terracotta, which lent itself to charming miniatures – a parrot and hoopoe in the first room, for instance – and portraiture – *Elsa* (1947) – as well as to some highly expressive art such as *Taglio grande bianco* (1959). One of Leoncillo's masterpieces, *San Sebastiano Nero* (1961), with its savagely gouged surface, mediates powerfully between traditional representation and modern abstraction.

A little further down the Corso Mazzini stands what is perhaps Umbria's finest Baroque church, San Filippo Neri (1640–71), by the Spoletine architect Loreto Scelli; the façade looks especially well after recent cleaning and the harmonious interior holds good paintings by Sebastiano Conca and Gaetano Lapis da Cagli, and a marble bust of the patron saint by Alessandro Algardi. A striking contrast is offered by the tiny twelfth-century church of Santi Giovanni e Paolo – reached by turning first left across the piazza from San Filippo Neri – the simple interior of which holds a number of frescoes whose interest outweighs their sometimes poor condition. Most notable of all is the scene immediately to the left of the entrance which portrays the murder of St Thomas à Becket in Canterbury Cathedral in 1170; the saint was canonized in 1173 and the fresco executed not long afterwards. An equally strong contrast is provided by following the Via Filitteria and Via Sant'Andrea down from Santi Giovanni e Paolo to the vast preaching church of San Domenico, begun in the second half of the thirteenth century. The church is built of bands of pink and white stone but its façade is quite plain and its right flank is relieved only by a single large Gothic doorway. The interior, which has been restored to its impressively simple medieval appearance, contains a large number of significant works of art. These include a large fresco, *Trionfo di San Tommaso d'Aquino*, representing the triumph of the Dominican theologian's scholastic philosophy in the fourteenth century, a chapel to the right of the presbytery, frescoed in the early fifteenth century with scenes from a *Life of St Mary Magdalene*, a lovely fifteenth-century *Madonna and Child*, behind the main altar, a fourteenth-century painted crucifix above it, a touching *Pietà*, and a fine representation of the Dominican St Peter Martyr by the fourteenth-century Maestro di Fossa.

On leaving, walk along the right flank of the church and down the Via Leoni, the Via Porta Fuga (with a thirteenth-century city gate) and the Corso Garibaldi to the modern Piazza Garibaldi. To one side of the piazza is the large church of San Gregorio Maggiore (1079–1146), whose bell-tower (partly reconstructed) was built with material taken from Roman sites. A portico – with a small frescoed chapel, containing an unusual Renaissance font, to the left – leads into the spacious Romanesque interior, with a raised presbytery over a crypt; there are numerous remains of early frescoes on the walls, including an interesting *Virgin and Child, with Eve* to the right, as well as a fifteenth-century Florentine *Madonna*, and a chapel with a fine Renaissance tabernacle, on the left wall. From the church, cross the piazza and descend a small flight of steps to the right of a statue of Garibaldi; below ground level are the impressive remains of the Ponte Sanguinario, built with massive tufa blocks in the first century BC, where the Via Flaminia crossed the Tessino torrent (whose course was altered in the Middle Ages). From the Piazza Garibaldi, it is possible to make short detours to see the remains of the Roman amphitheatre in the Via dell'Anfiteatro, or Calder's *Teodolapio* at the railway station. Alternatively, return along the Corso Garibaldi as far as the Via Porta Fuga – where a tablet commemorates Spoleto's feat of holding out against Hannibal – and continue up through this medieval part of town to the Piazza Torre dell'Olio, dominated by a twelfth-century defensive tower, on to the church of San Filippo Neri, and back to the Piazza della Libertà and, if necessary, from there to the Porta Loreto (which can also be reached by taking the Via Leoni at Porta Fuga and continuing past San Domenico, turning right down the Via L. Vittori and right again down the Via Mameli). A further detour beneath an unusual 300-metre-long Renaissance arcade – more reminiscent of towns in Emilia-Romagna than in Umbria – leads to the fine church of the Madonna del Loreto (1572).

Notwithstanding the wealth of monuments within the town

centre, it would be a mistake to leave Spoleto without visiting the several important sites outside the city. Of these, the most impressive – indeed one of the most historically significant buildings in Umbria – is San Salvatore, by the cemetery on the Cinciano hill to the north of town. Although expert opinion differs, this very large basilical church was probably a palaeo-Christian foundation of the fourth or fifth century – combining late-classical architecture with eastern influences attributable to the presence in the area of refugee Syrian monks – significantly remodelled during the period of Longobard rule during the eighth or ninth century. The façade – divided horizontally into two by a cornice, and once faced in marble – was originally completed by a tympanum and preceded by a portico; today, the lower part retains just its three marble doors, with finely decorated architraves, while the upper part has three large windows, the central one arched, the flanking windows with tympanum. The interior, which has three aisles, a square presbytery, a semicircular central apse and two square flanking apses, makes extensive use of classical materials taken from Roman sites in the area, some showing exceptionally fine decoration. There are also the remains of frescoes, most notably the ninth-century monogrammed cross in the central apse. Down the hill from San Salvatore is the Romanesque church of San Ponziano, built in the twelfth and thirteenth centuries. The façade, divided in two horizontally (and with a fourteenth-century tympanum), has a simple door with decorated architrave and a rose-window surrounded by the symbols of the evangelists. Giuseppe Valadier, who remodelled the Duomo, also entirely restructured the interior here in 1788, though fortunately the original – and extremely unusual – crypt, which makes extensive use of materials removed from other sites, remains.

To the south of the town are two other Romanesque churches meriting a visit. San Paolo inter Vineas was a palaeo-Christian foundation rebuilt in the tenth century and again in the thirteenth, being consecrated in 1234 by Pope Gregory IX as the church of a convent of Poor Clares. It has a fine façade with rose-window and simple doorway (with a late-fifteenth-century fresco added in the lunette) and an unusual interior – the unvaulted roof has disclosed beams throughout, a presbytery barely raised above the level of the nave, and no crypt. There is a simple but attractive altar and an early-twelfth-century fresco cycle of the *Creation*. Not far away, on a splendid site overlooking the Tessino and the Via Flaminia, is the late-twelfth-century church of San Pietro fuori le Mura (St Peter Without-the-Walls), originally a fifth-century foundation. Though the interior was remodelled in Baroque style in 1699, the church remains one of the most important Romanesque monuments in Umbria, principally for the relief sculptures which give the façade, divided into three levels, its unique appearance (these reliefs are generally considered the finest of their period in Umbria). On the lowest level, the central doorway is surrounded by an exceptionally elaborate frieze, composed of a meandering vegetal design, linked to a series of relief scenes and decorative pairs of miniature blind arcades, comprising an elaborate medieval allegory of the tree of life, the journey of the soul from sin to redemption. Above is a large lunette – oriental in appearance and perhaps originally part of a rose-window – flanked by two eagles and embellished with cosmatesque mosaics. On either side of the doorway are five large reliefs, drawing variously on the Bible and medieval bestiaries. Above the lunettes of the two flanking doors are reliefs of a bishop (right) and St Michael the Archangel killing the dragon (left). The middle level has three oculi, the large central one surrounded by the symbols of the evangelists and more cosmatesque work. The highest level (surmounted by a tympanum) has four reliefs showing Sts Peter and Andrew and two bulls.

From San Pietro a road leads up to the final great sight Spoleto has to offer: the Ponte delle Torri, a monumental aqueduct, composed of ten ogival arches, 230 metres long and standing eighty metres above a dizzying chasm where the Tessino flows between two neighbouring hills. Traditionally thought to be of Roman origin, the aqueduct was almost certainly erected in the twelfth century and restructured by Matteo Gattapone in the fourteenth in order to guarantee water supplies to the fortress he built for Cardinal Albornoz. In any case, it is a memorable sight when viewed from a distance (Turner made a notable painting of the bridge), while walking across it provides both a remarkable experience and exceptional views of the surrounding mountains, the Rocca, and the town below.

From Spoleto, a steep, winding road leads south-east to the important pilgrimage site of Monteluco (800 m.). Today, Monteluco is associated above all with St Francis, who founded a convent here in 1218. In fact, the mountain, densely covered with ilex-woods, was a holy spot long before the thirteenth century, taking its very name from *lucus* or 'sacred wood'. Pagan rites gave way to Christianity in the fifth century, when the Syrian monk Isaac of Antioch founded a cenobitic community here, and the mountain was later a Benedictine settlement. The present sanctuary occupies the site of the original Franciscan convent – from which a few small cells and an oratory survive – enlarged by, among others, St Bernardino of Siena, who spent time here in 1430. See also **San Giacomo di Spoleto**, **Vallo di Nera**.

Stroncone (451 m.): This attractive hill-top village, founded in the tenth century, once belonged to the important Benedictine abbey of Farfa, later becoming an outpost of Terni – just over eight kilometres to the north-west – in that city's struggles with its neighbour, Narni. It was sacked on two occasions; the first time in 1527 by troops marching on Rome and again in 1799. Stroncone still possesses part of its medieval walls, defensive towers and houses from the fifteenth century, and some noteworthy churches; it also offers good views of Narni and the surrounding countryside. In a square inside the town gate, the oratory of San Giovanni Battista is richly frescoed by Giuseppe Barbiani, who also painted the altarpiece representing the beheaded Baptist (1610). From the piazza, the Via del Mezzo leads to the Via dell'Arringo, and the Palazzo Comunale and the church of San Nicolò, whose Romanesque doorway, with relief decoration, dates from 1171; in the sacristy of the church there is a sixteenth-century altarpiece by Rinaldo da Calvi, depicting the *Coronation of the Virgin*, with scenes of the *Annunciation*, the *Birth of Christ* and the *Magi* in the predella. A little over a kilometre outside town, the church of San Francesco supposedly owes its foundation to St Francis himself; it is preceded by a Romanesque portico and retains a thirteenth-century doorway. Beneath the portico, a chapel to the left has a frescoed *Virgin and Saints* (1509) by Tiberio d'Assisi; inside the church are some earlier frescoes and a wooden statue of St Sebastian, by the school of Antonio Rizzo. See also **Collescìpoli**, **Terni**.

Terni (130 m.): There's no denying that Terni generally gets a pretty poor press as the least attractive town in Umbria, yet it is a reputation not wholly deserved. The real trouble is some dire unplanned suburban building and routes into the city centre which are not always easy to follow – a discouraging combination, given that the surrounding area offers a rich choice of more immediately appealing towns and villages, set amid impressive countryside. For those who make it, however, there are rewards. Though best known as the region's first industrial city, Terni has a long and varied history and, despite the recent unfavourable economic climate, has much more the feel of a city than most Umbrian towns. Known as Interamna ('between the rivers'), Terni has been continuously settled since the Bronze Age, and some extremely important archaeological finds were made in the late nineteenth century, during the building of the steelworks. An important Roman *municipium* on the Via Flaminia, the city was later subject to frequent destruction – by the Goths, the Byzantines, the Longobards and the troops of Barbarossa. After a period as a free commune and a *signoria*, the city became part of the Papal States around 1420. Aided by the easy availability of hydro-electric power, the city underwent such rapid industrial development in the late nineteenth century – with ordnance, steel, and chemical factories – that it became known as the 'Manchester of Italy' and a model for other cities in central Italy. The present appearance of the city owes a great deal to the intensive Allied bombing during the Second World War, which destroyed much of the city's fabric, and to the economic recession of the 1980s, which further damaged the city's already declining industries. Most recently, the city's industry has become somewhat unhappily known for producing the rifle that killed President Kennedy and for a murky connection with the alleged Iraqi supercannon.

A tour of the city centre might begin in the Piazza Europa, closed on one side by the imposing sixteenth-century Palazzo Spada – built on the model of Roman palaces, and now the town hall. Close by is the oldest surviving building in the city, the small circular palaeo-Christian church of San Salvatore, from the fifth century, enlarged in the twelfth century; the interior has some frescoes from the fifteenth and sixteenth centuries. Passing back through the courtyard of the Palazzo Spada, walk down the characteristic Via Roma, with its surviving defensive tower, and turn right to the remains of the Roman amphitheatre and the cathedral, medieval in origin (there is a fine Romanesque door) but almost wholly remodelled in the seventeenth century. Opposite the cathedral is the impressively elegant Palazzo Rosci or Bianchini-Riccardi. Continue along the Via XI Febbraio, making a slight detour to the small Romanesque church of Sant'Alò to the left, and on to the Palazzo Fabrizi. The palace was constructed from previously existing buildings, knocked together and given a handsome new façade in the eighteenth century; it has some interestingly decorated rooms. It is also the home of the city's art museum, a small but worthwhile collection whose highlights include a *Santa Caterina* by Gozzoli (showing the marked influence of his teacher, Angelico), a lovely *Madonna, Child and Saints* by the Master of the Gardner Annunciation (now generally identified with Pier Matteo d'Amelia), an interesting late work by Alunno, and a rather fine *Adoration of the Shepherds* by an unknown imitator of Barocci, in which the surface charm does not disguise disturbing premonitions of the fate of the infant Christ. There are also a number of naïf paintings by Orneore Metelli, showing Terni in the twenties and thirties, and a late Counter-Reformation scene of Franciscan martyrdom whose complacent brutality makes it a strong contender for the nastiest painting in Umbria. Exiting from the museum, turn left along Via Fratini and soon left again to the church of San Francesco, built in 1265, enlarged in the fifteenth and sixteenth centuries, with a large campanile from 1445; though badly damaged by bombing, it has some of Bartolomeo di Tommaso's best work, a recently restored fresco series on the *Last Judgement*, from the late fifteenth century.

From here, take the Via Lanzi and the Via Goldoni to the twelfth-century church of San Cristoforo (subsequently much enlarged), which has a number of fourteenth- and fifteenth-century frescoes. Turn left along the Via Angeloni to the Piazza Bruno Buozzi, which marks the edge of the old, pre-industrial city, and along the Corso Vecchio, which preserves remnants of Terni's medieval past, including the interesting complex of houses known as the Case dei Castelli, incorporating some adapted towers. Turn left to the seventeenth-century Palazzo Carrara, again developed from existing medieval dwellings, close to the large Augustinian church, San Pietro in Trivio, from the fourteenth century, with fifteenth-century frescoes. Opposite the church there are some houses by Mario Ridolfi – who contributed some important post-war architecture to Rome and also worked extensively in Terni – and Wolfgang Frankl. The Corso Vecchio now almost immediately ends in the Piazza della Repubblica, adjoining the Piazza Europa.

Among many places of interest in the general vicinity of Terni, one in particular stands out. This is the Cascata delle Marmore – or Marmore Falls – approximately seven kilometres outside the city at the end of the Nera valley or Valnerina. Set in the deep and narrow gorge of the Nera, surrounded by lush vegetation, the falls are – when seen in full flood – truly spectacular, the water cascading, with almost explosive force, in three stages, down over a 165-metre drop, sending up spray so thick as to create a permanent mist and, in sunlight, an ever-present rainbow. For centuries the falls were admired by travellers, few of whom failed to make the detour from the Via Flaminia in order to experience for themselves what Tobias Smollett, in the 1760s, called 'an object of tremendous sublimity' and which Byron, half a century later, celebrated in some famous stanzas in *Childe Harold's Pilgrimage* (IV, 69–71):

> The roar of waters! – from the headlong height
> Velino cleaves the wave-worn precipice;
> The fall of waters! rapid as the light
> The flashing mass foams shaking the abyss;
> The hell of waters! where they howl and hiss,

And boil in endless torture; while the sweat
Of their great agony, wrung out from this
Their Phlegethon, curls round the rocks of jet
That gird the gulf around, in pitiless horror set,

And mounts in spray the skies, and thence again
Returns in an unceasing shower, which round,
With its unemptied cloud of gentle rain,
Is an eternal April to the ground,
Making it all one emerald: – how profound
The gulf! and how the giant element
From rock to rock leaps with delirious bound,
Crushing the cliffs, which, downward worn and rent
With his fierce footsteps, yield in chasms a fearful vent

To the broad column which rolls on, and shows
More like the fountain of an infant sea
Torn from the womb of mountains by the throes
Of a new world, than only thus to be
Parent of rivers, which flow gushingly,
With many windings through the vale: – Look back!
Lo! where it comes like an eternity,
As if to sweep down all things in its track,
Charming the eye with dread, – a matchless cataract.

All of which makes it the more surprising to discover that the falls are no merely natural phenomenon. Instead, they were created, as long ago as 271 BC, by the Roman consul, Manlius Curtius Dentatus, who artificially channelled the waters of the Velino river, which was silting up and creating a vast swamp on the plain close to Rieti, so that they dropped into the Nera at this point. What was good for the inhabitants of Rieti, however, was bad for their neighbours, for the joint waters of the two rivers now periodically flooded Terni. The result was a conflict between the two cities, intermittently repeated from as early as the first century BC until the fifteenth century, after which the aggrieved parties turned their joint hostility against the papal authorities who now controlled the region. The problem was only satisfactorily resolved in 1787, but in the nineteenth century the possibility of harnessing the hydro-electric energy of the falls was triumphantly seized, resulting in the unprecedented industrial growth experienced by Terni in the century's final decades. While demonstrating that nature can certainly be improved on, however, these falls do have one considerable disadvantage for the casual visitor, since they are usually turned off (in order to provide hydro-electric energy). Nowadays they can only be seen at set hours, according to a horribly complicated schedule, best checked at the tourist information office in Terni. There are two principal viewing points: the Belvedere di Marmore at the top of the falls and the other to the side of the road at their foot; this latter probably affords the better view, though it is usually crowded.

Terni is also an excellent base for touring southern Umbria; see **Abbey of San Pietro in Valle**, **Amelia**, **Carsulae**, **Ferentillo**, **Narni**, **San Gémini**.

Todi (410 m.): Situated on a high hill overlooking the middle Tiber valley, Todi may not be as densely packed with monuments as some of its larger neighbours but in many respects it can seem the quintessential Umbrian town. Approached from the direction of Perugia, its medieval profile appears suddenly, as if by magic, from the mists below, amid some of the loveliest countryside in this part of the region. Once a centre of the ancient Umbrians, then colonized by the Etruscans, the town was conquered, around 340 BC, by the Romans, who dedicated it to Mars. Todi's strong defensive position and its Etruscan and Roman walls – part of which still survive – allowed it to escape the worst effects of the northern invasions. After it became a free commune in the twelfth century, the town knew a period of power and prosperity in the thirteenth and early fourteenth centuries which is still reflected in the public and religious buildings, as well as the ring of medieval walls, surviving from that time. After attempts by various pretenders to turn the town into a *signoria*, Todi was subjected to papal rule in the fourteenth century. Though it knew little real development thereafter, the town also boasts the finest Renaissance church in Umbria, Santa Maria della Consolazione.

With a single exception, Todi's principal monuments – the Palazzo del Popolo, the Palazzo dei Priori, the Palazzo del Capitano del Popolo, the cathedral, and the great Franciscan church of San Fortunato – are gathered closely together at the top of Todi's high hill, and allow the visitor to make comparatively easy initial acquaintance with the city; the exception is the church of the Consolazione, which lies outside the walls at the foot of the hill. A more thorough exploration of Todi, however, requires considerable climbing up extremely steep streets.

A visit might start at the Porta Romana, one of the city's medieval gates. Close by are three churches of interest: San Nicolò de Cryptis, an eleventh-century foundation on the site of the Roman amphitheatre, another San Nicolò built in Gothic style in the fourteenth century, and the attractive fifteenth-century church of San Filippo Benizi. From the gate, the Via Matteotti runs up through the medieval town. Opposite the church of San Silvestro, the Via Santa Maria in Camuccia leads to the church from which the street takes its name. A tiny Romanesque church, with a fine doorway, built in the thirteenth century above an earlier, eighth-century church, Santa Maria in Camuccia contains both a thirteenth-century wooden statue of the Virgin and Child and the remains of fifteenth-century frescoes. Returning to San Silvestro, carry on up the hill (now the Via Roma) through the Porta Marzia – a medieval arch erected with Roman materials – and up to the busy heart of the city, the Piazza del Popolo. Built on the site of the Roman forum, this piazza, with its cathedral and cluster of civic buildings, is one of the finest medieval squares anywhere in Italy. To the east, the Palazzo del Popolo (built between 1213 and 1267, and also called the Palazzo del Podestà) has a characteristic ground-floor loggia and two storeys marked by fine Gothic windows. A substantial outside staircase links the palace to the neighbouring Palazzo del Capitano del Popolo (1290), with distinctive gabled windows on the first floor. Together, the palaces give an illuminating insight into the gradual transition between Romanesque and Gothic building styles in the thirteenth century. (The Palazzo del Capitano del Popolo holds Todi's Etrusco-Roman museum and art gallery – including a *Coronation of the Virgin*, considered one of Lo Spagna's finest works – but these have been closed for many years.) To the south of the piazza is the much-altered Palazzo dei Priori, begun in 1293, completed between 1334 and 1337, with a façade remodelled in the early sixteenth century; the tall tower incorporated on the left dates from 1369–85. Directly opposite the Palazzo dei Priori, to the north, is the Duomo, preceded by a broad, high flight of steps. Begun in the twelfth century, the cathedral is mainly a thirteenth-century building, finished in the fourteenth century. The flat-screen façade is divided into three vertically by pillars and into three horizontally by simple cornices. On the lowest level are three doors: a large, magnificently decorated central doorway and two smaller flanking doors surmounted by small rose-windows. There is a narrow middle level and, above, a single large centrally placed rose-window dating from 1520. Given the extended period in which the façade was composed, the result is extraordinarily harmonious. The interior, restored to its original Romanesque forms, has three aisles divided by columns and pillars, with fine capitals; a fourth aisle to the right was added subsequently. Among the works of art are a fresco and panels by Lo Spagna and a *Last Judgement* by Ferraù da Faenza, inspired by Michelangelo's work in the Sistine Chapel. To the left of the cathedral stands the bishop's palace (1593) and, near by, in the Via Paolo Rolli, the house of the eighteenth-century poet from Todi, Paolo Rolli, who translated Milton into Italian. A road along the right flank of the cathedral allows a good view of the twelfth-century apse – the earliest surviving part of the building.

From the cathedral, the twisting Via Santa Prassede goes down to the fourteenth-century church named for the Roman virgin, Praxedes; the church is built in bands of pink and white stone and has a fine ogival doorway. From the church, a road leads through the Santa Prassede gate and steeply down through the medieval quarter of Borgo Nuovo, past the church of San Francesco in Borgo (remodelled but with a fourteenth-century fresco to the left of the altar) to the Porta Perugina, another city-gate, forming part of the medieval walls.

Having enjoyed the fine views of the surrounding countryside, return to the Piazza del Popolo; from the south-west corner, it is a short walk to the vast Franciscan church of San Fortunato, which stands atop a long flight of steps. One of the most important churches of its time in central Italy, San Fortunato was begun in 1292, while Todi was also building its palaces of the Capitano del Popolo and of the Priors. Though building work was well advanced by the end of the century, the (incomplete) façade – with a fine late-Gothic central door – dates only from the fifteenth century. What is immediately striking about the church is its immense breadth, and, in fact, the interior is quite different from the majority of Franciscan churches of its period in having three vaulted aisles of equal height, clustered columns, side-chapels and a polygonal apse – though the preaching requirements of the friars is respected in the church's extraordinarily clear sight-lines which allowed the pulpit to be placed high on the wall of the right-hand aisle. Besides the remains of frescoes dating from the time of the church's construction, there is also a frescoed *Madonna and Child with Angels* (1432) by Masolino – the great Florentine artist's only work in Umbria – two fine statues by a follower of Jacopo della Quercia, magnificent late-sixteenth-century choir-stalls by Antonio Maffei from Gubbio, and a stoup made from capitals probably taken from the preceding church. The crypt holds the remains of Todi's most famous son, the ascetic Franciscan Jacopone da Todi, one of the first great poets in the Italian language.

To the right of the church, a path leads into the quiet public gardens, built on the site of the now-ruined former fortress, from where the wonderful prospect over the city and surrounding countryside includes a particularly fine view of the Renaissance temple of the Consolazione at the foot of the town. Back at San Fortunato, take the steps of the Via San Fortunato, to the left of the church, which lead down to the Porta Marzia. Turn right down the hill, and then left into the Via Mercato Vecchio, which leads into a piazza – the site of the medieval market – containing the so-called Nicchioni (or large niches) with Doric frieze, monumental remains from the first century BC which may have formed part of the basilica. The church of Sant'Ilario (or San Carlo), with its characteristic bell-gable, situated just beyond the piazza, is Romanesque, and a little further on lies the

Scarnabecco fountain erected in 1241 at the direction of Scarnabecco dei Faisani of Bologna, then *podestà* of Todi. In the opposite direction from Sant'Ilario, the Via Cesia (or della Piana) leads to the church of San Silvestro, from where the Via Roma and Via Matteotti descend to the starting point of the Porta Romana.

Along the ring-road in the direction of Orvieto lies the great Renaissance church of Santa Maria della Consolazione, built between 1508 and 1607 on a Greek-cross plan with four apses (three polygonal and one semicircular), surmounted by a terrace with a high drum and dome. So fine is the church that the uncertainty as to its architect is the more mysterious. Once attributed to Bramante, and certainly influenced by his ideas, it seems to derive most closely from some architectural drawings by Leonardo da Vinci and to have been begun primarily by Cola da Caprarola and brought to conclusion by a series of architects including Peruzzi, Vignola and Sammicheli. To its vigorous and dynamic exterior – the irregularity of the design of the apses and variety of decoration encourage the viewer to walk around the church – the temple adds a luminous interior of great elegance centred on the high altar which holds the fifteenth-century image of the Virgin, whose miraculous properties prompted the building of the church. See also **Massa Martana**, **Orvieto**.

Torgiano (219 m.): Once a fortified village within the orbit of Perugia, Torgiano retains the imprint of a medieval past but owes its recent fame mainly to the work of Dr Giorgio Lungarotti, whose fine wines, from one of the smallest of all Italian areas entitled to the *Denominazione d'Origine Controllata* appellation, have found a place in markets throughout the world in the past two or three decades. The Lungarotti family also established the Museo del Vino, or Wine Museum, in the eighteenth-century Palazzo Baglioni – an exceptionally varied and well-ordered collection with appeal to anyone at all interested in wine. Beside wine-making equipment from the past, the museum has Etruscan, Roman and medieval wine containers and drinking vessels, a display relating the medicinal uses of wine, a valuable collection of majolica ware from the sixteenth to eighteenth centuries, and a wine library, including works from the Renaissance onwards. See also **Bettona**, **Deruta**, **Perugia**.

Trevi (412 m.): In an ideal world, Trevi might be approached at evening from the direction of Spoleto, when the rays of the setting sun give the small, ancient town a luminous quality that is quite magical. In fact, approached from almost any direction, at any time, Trevi's exceptional position on a conical hill above the Vale of Umbria places it among the finest hill-towns anywhere in Italy. Once located both on its present site and at the foot of the hill, close to the Via Flaminia, Trevi was known to the Romans as Trebiae. Subsequently restricted to the hilltop, the settlement formed part of the Longobard Duchy of Spoleto in the early Middle Ages, when it was razed on more than one occasion by invaders, including Saracens in the ninth century and Magyars in the tenth. Inevitably the town's strategically important position over the Via Flaminia led to its being fiercely contested throughout the late Middle Ages and, after a brief period as a free commune in the twelfth century, Trevi was variously incorporated in the territories of Perugia and Foligno, before passing, along with the latter town, into the Church State in 1439.

Today the town retains its essentially medieval appearance, both in the old centre and the Piaggia district, outside the original walls, on the town's south-west slopes. At the heart of Trevi is the Piazza Mazzini, entered from the modern Piazza Garibaldi through a vaulted passageway. There the fourteenth-century Palazzo Comunale gives varied evidence of its gradual transformation through the centuries, revealing a fifteenth-century portico, sixteenth-century windows, and nineteenth-century commemorative tablets; the powerful tower on the other side of the vaulted entrance to the square dates from the twelfth century. From the piazza, a stepped street – the Via Beato Placido Riccardi – leads up towards the cathedral; almost at the outset the gloomy and sinuous alleyway to the right is the appropriately named Vico Oscuro. The cathedral of Sant'Emiliano – named for the Armenian credited with evangelizing the area and martyred in 302 – has twelfth-century origins and retains a fifteenth-century doorway with an earlier relief of the patron saint between two lions; the remodelled interior is most notable for the large and finely carved stone altar (1522) by Rocco di Tommaso, in the left aisle. Just across from the cathedral entrance, the Renaissance Palazzo Lucarini has recently been restored to house the Trevi Flash Art Museum, a modern gallery which appears set to offer a virtually unique opportunity in the region to see contemporary trends in the visual arts, combining a permanent collection of works by artists from the region, the rest of Italy and elsewhere, with special exhibitions featuring leading artists from all over the world. Returning towards the Piazza Mazzini, a left turn leads to the church and convent of San Francesco and a quite different museum. The large hall church, which retains a largely unaltered interior, has a number of votive frescoes and, set into the right wall of the left apse, the red tombstone of the Blessed Ventura, who died in 1310; the convent has recently been restored to hold the town's art collection, which includes, among other Umbrian works of the fourteenth and fifteenth century, a fine *Coronation of the Virgin* (1522) by Lo Spagna, inspired by the important panel by Ghirlandaio held in the Council Chamber of the Palazzo del Podestà in **Narni**.

Among Trevi's many other churches – including San Giovanni Decollato, just off the Piazza Mazzini, and Santa Chiara and Santa Croce in Piaggia – the two most important lie a little way outside the town. From the Piazza Garibaldi, the panoramic Viale Ciuffelli leads to the fourteenth-century convent church of San Martino. In the lunette over the entrance is one of Tiberio d'Assisi's better works, representing the Virgin with a particularly charming Child and angels; in the small, aisle-less interior, the two paintings, just before the presbytery, are a *St Martin Giving His Cloak to the Beggar*, also by Tiberio, and a *Madonna and Child* by Pier Antonio Mezzastris. Far superior to any of these, however, is the fresco to be found in the tiny chapel situated to the left of the courtyard in front of the church. Here, Lo Spagna left one of his strongest works, an *Assumption, with Saints Jerome, John the Baptist, Francis and*

Anthony of Padua, with a view of Foligno in the background; the painting, showing Lo Spagna's technical accomplishment at its best, also fuses something of Perugino's sweetness – as in the mandorla of cherubs surrounding the Virgin – with an echo of Raphael's strength, notable especially in the depiction of the saints. Another fresco by Lo Spagna is to be found in the altogether grander church of the Madonna delle Lacrime (1487), set amid olive groves on the winding road which leads up to Trevi from the Via Flaminia. This is another of those Renaissance churches, so frequently found in Umbria, built on the site of a miracle associated with the Virgin – in this case, a weeping image, now displayed on the altar in the right transept of the church. The church façade is distinguished by a finely sculpted portal (1495) by the Venetian Giovanni di Gian Pietro, while the spacious Latin cross interior is notable both for a significant number of fine funerary monuments and for its many frescoes, chief among which are a *Deposition* by Lo Spagna, revealing how potent was the influence of Raphael on the painter, and a late *Epiphany* (1521) by Perugino, which repeats and simplifies other versions of this subject by the artist, notably the fresco in **Città della Pieve**. See also **Campello sul Clitunno**, **Foligno**, **Montefalco**.

Umbèrtide (247 m.): With a population of 15,000, Umbèrtide is the biggest town in the upper Tiber valley between **Città di Castello** and **Perugia**. Known as Fratta until it changed its name in 1863 in honour of Prince Umberto, son of the first king of the recently united Italy, the town was founded in the Middle Ages. Testifying to its importance as an outpost of Perugia – under whose control it soon fell – is the Rocca, or fortress, built between 1374 and 1390, with its massive circular towers and square keep. The *condottiero* Braccio Fortebraccio was imprisoned there in 1393, and was forced to give up his own castle of **Montone** in exchange for his freedom, though he returned in 1413 to sack the town. Umbèrtide suffered from heavy bombing during the Second World War, and it was just outside the town that King George VI reviewed the Allied troops pushing up the Tiber valley in July 1944. The town's central square, Piazza Matteotti, has an impressive seventeenth-century *palazzo* and there are a number of interesting churches, including the late-thirteenth-century San Francesco, the neighbouring church of Santa Croce (1651), with a *Deposition* by Signorelli, and Santa Maria della Pietà, a sixteenth-century church with frescoes attributed to Pinturicchio. Just outside the town walls is the graceful octagonal church of Santa Maria della Reggia (1559–1663), possibly by Galeazzo Alessi, which contains a fifteenth-century fresco of the *Madonna with Saints*.

A little under five kilometres to the north-east of Umbèrtide is the massive and splendidly maintained castle of Civitella Ranieri, remodelled in the fifteenth and sixteenth centuries (it is in private hands and only the exterior can be seen). At Niccone, just over three kilometres outside the town in the direction of the Città di Castello, a road to the left leads in the direction of Lisciano along the beautiful valley of the Niccone river, which marks the border between Umbria and Tuscany; tobacco is extensively cultivated here. After about ten kilometres, a small road winds up from the valley to Preggio (631 m.), which retains evidence of its medieval past and a church, Santa Maria delle Grazie, with a fresco attributed to Pinturicchio; a festival dedicated to the local chestnuts is held here each October. From Preggio, a road offering spectacular views of Lake Trasimeno and the hills of Tuscany beyond offers the possibility of returning to Umbèrtide or proceeding to **Castel Rigone**. See also **Abbey of San Salvatore di Monte Corona, Città di Castello, Montone**.

Vallo di Nera (467 m.): On a high outcrop on the left bank of the Nera, Vallo stands in close proximity to two earlier walled villages, **Castel San Felice** and **Sant'Anatolia di Narco**. Still encircled by its strong walls and their sturdy defensive towers, Vallo retains its medieval appearance intact – the cobbled streets winding steeply up the hill from one small piazza to another, flanked by houses of the characteristic, light-coloured stone. In the lower part of the village, the thirteenth-century Franciscan church of Santa Maria, with Gothic doorway and rose-window, has late fourteenth- and very early-fifteenth-century frescoes by

Cola di Pietro from Camerino and Francesco di Antonio. At the top of the hill, another small square holds the large parish church of San Giovanni Battista, built – like Santa Maria – of pink and white stone, with a rose-window and double bell-gable. Inside, the aisle-less interior culminates in an apse entirely frescoed with unexpectedly colourful and accomplished scenes – *Dormition*, *Assumption* and *Coronation* (1536) – from a *Life of the Virgin* by Jacopo Siculo, a Sicilian-born painter who worked extensively in the Spoleto and Norcia areas. See also **Castel San Felice**, **Sant'Anatolia di Narco**.

Further Reading

✳

The following list of titles for further reading should allow interested readers to follow up the principal themes dealt with in this book, chapter by chapter, either in English or in Italian. It is however, an extremely selective list. In particular, I have omitted reference to all of the very large number of books, principally in Italian, dedicated to the individual cities, towns or villages of the region. I would, however, wish to draw the attention of readers to the important work of Alberto Grohmann in *Assisi* (Rome and Bari: Laterza, 1989) and *Perugia* (Rome and Bari: Laterza, 1990).

General

Adams, Michael, *Umbria* (1964; repr. London: Bellew, 1988).

Attraverso Italia: Umbria (Milan: Touring Club Italiano, 1984).

Barzini, Luigi, *The Italians* (1964; repr. Harmondsworth: Penguin, 1987).

Conosci l'Italia, 12 vols. (Milan: Touring Club Italiano, 1957–68).

Guida d'Italia: Umbria (5th edn, Milan: Touring Club Italiano, 1978).

Guida d'Italia: Umbria (Milan: Touring Club Italiano, 1993).

Hearder, H., and Waley, D. P., *A Short History of Italy from Classical Times to the Present Day* (Cambridge: Cambridge University Press, 1963).

Keates, Jonathan, *Umbria* (London: George Philip, 1991).

Macadam, Alta, *Blue Guide: Umbria* (London and New York: A. & C. Black and W. W. Norton, 1993).

Morelli, Paola, *Geografia dei sistemi agricoli italiani: Umbria* (Rome: REDA, 1993).

Procacci, Giuliano, *History of the Italian People* (1968; repr. Harmondsworth: Penguin, 1973).

Tabarrini, Mario, *L'Umbria si racconta*, 3 vols. (Foligno: [Tabarrini], 1982).

Umbria (Milan: Electa, 1994).

Vetturini, Emilio, *Terre e acque in Valle Umbra* (Bastia Umbra: [Vetturini], 1995).

Ward, William, *Getting it Right in Italy* (London: Bloomsbury, 1990).

Whitfield, J. H., *A Short History of Italian Literature* (Harmondsworth: Penguin, 1960).

Zimmermanns, Klaus, *Umbria*, trans. Gabriella Morini (Milan: Idealibri, 1990).

CHAPTER ONE: *The Greening of Umbria*

Bracco, Fabrizio, and Irace, Erminia, 'La memoria e l'immagine. Aspetti della cultura umbra tra Otto e Novecento', in Renato Covino and Giampaolo Gallo (eds.), *Storia d'Italia: Le regioni dall'Unità a oggi. L'Umbria* (Turin: Einaudi, 1989), pp. 607–58.

Cesarini, Giuliano, and Lundborg, Gun, *Iconografia e sviluppo: il Trasimeno e il paesaggio umbro-toscano* (Perugia: Guerra, 1993).

Desplanques, Henri, *Campagnes ombriennes. Contribution à l'étude des paysages ruraux en Italie centrale* (Paris: Armand Colin, 1969).

Grohmann, Alberto, 'Caratteri ed equilibri tra centralità e marginalità', in Renato Covino and Giampaolo Gallo (eds.), *Storia d'Italia: Le regioni dall'Unità a oggi. L'Umbria* (Turin: Einaudi, 1989), pp. 3–72.

Hutton, Edward, *Cities of Umbria* (London: Methuen, 1905).

James, Henry, *Italian Hours* (1909; repr. London: Century, 1986).

Pater, Walter, 'Raphael' (1892), repr. in *The Renaissance: Studies in Art and Poetry*, ed. Kenneth Clark (1961; repr. London: Fontana, 1971).

Ricci, Corrado, *Umbria Santa*, trans. H. C. Stewart (London: Faber & Gwyer, 1927).

Sabatier, Paul, *Vie de S. François d'Assise* (Strasbourg, 1893).

St Aubin de Terán, Lisa, *A Valley in Italy* (1994; repr. Harmondsworth: Penguin, 1995).

CHAPTER TWO: *Umbrians and Etruscans*

Banti, Luisa, *Etruscan Cities and Their Culture*, trans. Erika Bizzarri (1968; repr. London: Batsford, 1973).

Dennis, George, *The Cities and Cemeteries of Etruria*, 2 vols. (London, 1848).

Giorgetti, Dario, *Umbria: itinerari archeologici* (Rome: Newton Compton, 1986).

Grant, Michael, *The Etruscans* (London: Weidenfeld & Nicolson, 1980).

Gray, Elizabeth Hamilton, *Tour to the Sepulchres of Etruria* (London, 1840).

Keller, Werner, *The Etruscans*, trans. Alexander and Elizabeth Henderson (1970; repr. London: Cape, 1975).

Les Étrusques en Europe (Paris: Éditions de la Réunion des Musées Nationaux, 1992).

Pallotino, Massimo, *The Etruscans*, trans. Joseph Cremona (1942; rev. and enlarged by David Ridgeway, London: Allen Lane, 1974).

Pianu, Giampiero, Stopponi, Simonetta, and Sensi, Luigi, *Itinerari etruschi*, 3 vols. (Milan: Electa, 1985).

Spivey, Nigel, and Stoddart, Simon, *Etruscan Italy* (London: Batsford, 1990).

CHAPTER THREE: *Roman Umbria*

Livy, *The Early History of Rome: Books I–V of 'The History of Rome from its Foundation'*, trans. Aubrey de Selincourt (1960; repr. Harmondsworth: Penguin, 1984).

Livy, *The Early History of Rome: Books VI–X of 'The History of Rome from its Foundation'*, trans. Betty Radice (Harmondsworth: Penguin, 1982).

Pliny the Younger, *The Letters of the Younger Pliny*, trans. Betty Radice (Harmondsworth: Penguin, 1963).

Propertius, Sextus, *The Poems*, trans. W. G. Shepherd (Harmondsworth: Penguin, 1985).

★

Boardman, John, Griffin, Jasper, and Murry, Oswyn, *The Oxford History of the Roman World* (Oxford: Oxford University Press, 1991).

Camporeale, Giovannangelo, 'La romanisation' (pp. 102–9) and [various authors], 'Les Étrusques et l'Europe: La médiation de Rome' (pp. 223–72) in *Les Étrusques en Europe* (Paris: Éditions de la Réunion des Musées Nationaux, 1992).

Cary, M., and Scullard, H. H., *A History of Rome down to the Reign of Constantine* (London: Macmillan, 1975).

Giorgetti, Dario, *Umbria: itinerari archeologici* (Rome: Newton Compton, 1986).

Harris, W. V., *Rome in Etruria and Umbria* (Oxford: Clarendon, 1971).

Highet, Gilbert, *Poets in a Landscape* (London: Hamish Hamilton, 1957), Ch. 3.

Scullard, Howard Hayes, *The Etruscan Cities and Rome* (London: Thames & Hudson, 1967).

CHAPTER FOUR: *From the Fall of Rome to the Longobard Supremacy*

Paul the Deacon [Paulus Diaconus], *History of the Longobards*, trans. William Dudley Foulke (Philadelphia: University of Pennsylvania, 1907).

Procopius, *History of the Wars*, trans. H. B. Dewing (1914; repr. London: Heinemann, 1979).

—, *Secret History*, trans. G. A. Williamson (Harmondsworth: Penguin, 1966).

★

Conant, Kenneth John, *Carolingian and Romanesque Architecture 800 to 1200* (1959; repr. New Haven: Yale University Press, 1993).

Decker, Heinrich, *Romanesque Art in Italy*, trans. James Cleugh (London: Thames & Hudson, 1958).

Gibbon, Edward, *The History of the Decline and Fall of the Roman Empire* (1776–88; repr. in 6 vols. London: David Campbell, 1993).

Llewellyn, Peter, *Rome in the Dark Ages* (London: Constable, 1993).

Menis, Gian Carlo (ed.), *I longobardi* (Milan: Electa, 1990).

Wickham, Chris, *Early Medieval Italy: Central Power and Local Society 400–1000* (London: Macmillan, 1981).

CHAPTER FIVE: *The Rise of the Communes*

Dante Alighieri, *The Divine Comedy*, trans. Mark Musa (1971–84; repr. Harmondsworth: Penguin, 1981–6).

★

Bloch, Marcel, *Feudal Society* (Chicago: University of Chicago Press, 1964).

Cavallucci, Francesco, *La Fontana Maggiore di Perugia* (Perugia: Quattroemme, 1993).

Cohn Jr, Samuel K., *The Cult of Remembrance and the Black Death: Six Renaissance Cities in Central Italy* (Baltimore and London: Johns Hopkins University Press, 1992).

Duby, Georges, *The Three Orders: Feudal Society Imagined*, trans. Arthur Goldhammer (1978; repr. University of Chicago Press, 1980).

Grohmann, Alberto, *Città e territorio tra Medioevo e età moderna: Perugia sec. XIII–XVI* (Perugia: Volumnia, 1981).

Henderson, G., *Gothic* (1967; repr. Harmondsworth: Penguin, 1972).

Howell, Martha C., *Women, Production, and Patriarchy in Late Medieval Cities* (Chicago: University of Chicago Press, 1986).

Hyde, J. K., *Society and Politics in Medieval Italy: the Evolution of the Civil Life, 1000–1350* (London: Macmillan, 1973).

Le Goff, Jacques, *Time, Work and Culture in the Middle Ages*, trans. Arthur Goldhammer (1977; repr. Chicago: University of Chicago Press, 1980).

—, (ed.), *The Medieval World*, trans. Lydia G. Cochrane (1987; repr. London: Collins & Brown, 1990).

Prandi, Adriano, et al., *Italia romanica 3: L'Umbria* (Milan: Jaca, 1979).

Shahar, Shulamith, *The Fourth Estate: A History of Women in the Middle Ages* (London: Methuen, 1983).

Southern, Richard William, *Western Society and the Church in the Middle Ages* (Harmondsworth: Penguin, 1970).

Waley, Daniel, *The Italian City-Republics* (1969; 3rd edn, London and New York: Longman, 1988).

White, John, *Art and Architecture in Italy 1250–1400* (1966; 3rd edn, New Haven: Yale University Press, 1993), esp. Chs. 2–7, 17 and 32.

CHAPTER SIX: *From Commune to* Signoria

Guicciardini, Francesco, *The History of Italy*, trans. Sidney Alexander (London: Collier Macmillan and New York: Macmillan, 1969).

Machiavelli, Nicolò, *The Prince*, trans. George Bull (Harmondsworth: Penguin, 1961).

Maturanzio, Francesco, *Chronicles of the City of Perugia 1492–1503*, trans. Edward S. Morgan (London: J. M. Dent, 1905).

★

Burckhardt, Jakob, *The Civilization of the Renaissance in Italy*, trans. S. G. C. Middlemore (1860; repr. London: Phaidon, 1951)

Burke, Peter, *The Italian Renaissance: Culture and Society in Italy* (1972; rev. Cambridge: Polity Press, 1987).

Hay, Denys (ed.), *The Age of the Renaissance* (London: Thames & Hudson, 1967).

Keen, Maurice, *Chivalry* (New Haven and London: Yale University Press, 1984).

McIntyre, Anthony, *Medieval Tuscany and Umbria* (London: Viking, 1992).

Murray, Peter, *The Architecture of the Italian Renaissance* (1963; 3rd edn, London: Thames & Hudson, 1986).

Plumb, J. H., *The Penguin Book of the Renaissance* (Harmondsworth: Penguin, 1964).

Symonds, John Addington, *History of the Renaissance in Italy*, 7 vols. (London, 1875–6).

Tabacco, Giovanni, *The Struggle for Power in Medieval Italy*, trans. Rosalind Brown Jensen (Cambridge: Cambridge University Press, 1989).

CHAPTER SEVEN: *St Francis and His Followers*

Bonaventure, St, *'The Soul's Journey into God'*, *'The Tree of Life'* [and] *'The Life of St Francis'*, trans. Ewert H. Cousins (London: SPCK and New York: Paulist Press, 1978).
The Little Flowers of St Francis [*I Fioretti*]: *The Acts of Saint Francis and his Companions*, trans. E. M. Blaiklock and A. C. Keys (London: Hodder & Stoughton, 1985).

★

Atanassiu, Gabriele, et al., *Francesco in Italia, nel Mondo* (Milan: Jaca, 1990).
Capitani, Ovidio (ed.), *Temi e problemi nella mistica femminile trecentesca* (Todi: Centri di studi sulla spiritualità medievale, 1983).
Cardini, Franco, *Francesco d'Assisi* (Milan: Mondadori, 1989).
Cohen, Jeremy, *The Friars and the Jews* (Ithaca: Cornell University Press, 1982).
Dozzini, Bruno, *Giotto: La leggenda francescana nella Basilica d'Assisi* (Assisi: Minerva, 1994).
Farmer, David Hugh, *The Oxford Dictionary of Saints* (Oxford: Clarendon, 1978).
Green, Julien, *God's Fool*, trans. Peter Hainegg (1985; repr. London: Hodder & Stoughton, 1986).
Origo, Iris, *The World of San Bernardino* (London: Cape, 1963).
Rusconi, Roberto (ed.), *Il Movimento religioso femminile in Umbria nei secoli XIII–XIV* (Perugia: Regione dell'Umbria e Scandicci: Nuova Italia, 1984).

CHAPTER EIGHT: *The Church State*

Addison, Joseph, *Remarks on Several Parts of Italy* (London, 1705).
Dickens, Charles, *Pictures from Italy* (London, 1848).
Goethe, Johann von, *Italian Journey*, trans. W. H. Auden and Elizabeth Mayer (1962; repr. Harmondsworth: Penguin, 1970).

Montaigne, Michel de, *Montaigne's Travel Journal*, trans. Donald M. Frame (1957; repr. San Francisco: North Point Press, 1983).

Morison, Fynes, *Itinerary* (London, 1617).

Owenson, Sydney (Lady Morgan), *Italy* (London, 1821).

Smollett, Tobias, *Travels through France and Italy*, ed. Frank Felsenstein (1766; repr. Oxford: Oxford University Press, 1979).

★

Fressoia, Luigi, *La Rocca Paolina di Perugia* (Perugia: Calzetti-Mariucci, 1993).

Grohmann, Alberto, *Vincenzo Pianciani e l'economia pontificia nell'età di Gregorio XVI* (Spoleto: Cassa di Risparmio di Spoleto, 1988).

Pemble, John, *The Mediterranean Passion: Victorians and Edwardians in the South* (Oxford and New York: Oxford University Press, 1987).

Sorbini, Alberto, *Perugia nei libri di viaggio dal Settecento all'Unità d'Italia* (Foligno: Editoriale Umbra, 1994).

Vecchi Ranieri, Marilena De, *Viaggiatori stranieri in Umbria 1500–1940* (2nd edn; Perugia: Volumnia, 1992).

Woolf, Stuart, *A History of Italy 1700–1860* (London: Methuen, 1979).

CHAPTER NINE: *The Kingdom of Italy and the First Republic*

Carocci, Giampiero, *Italian Fascism*, trans. Isabel Quigly (1972; repr. Harmondsworth: Penguin, 1975).

Catena, Stelvio, *Immagini di un cambiamento: fotografie di Perugia tra otto e novecento* (Perugia: Guerra, 1993).

—, *Immagini dell'Umbria tra '800 e '900: Le Campagne* (Perugia: Guerra, 1994).

Clarke, Martin, *Modern Italy 1871–1982* (London and New York: Longman, 1984).

Covino, Renato, and Gallo, Giampaolo (eds.), *Storia d'Italia: Le regioni dall'Unità a oggi. L'Umbria* (Turin: Einaudi, 1989).

Ginsborg, Paul, *A History of Contemporary Italy: Society and Politics 1943–68* (Harmondsworth: Penguin, 1990).

Giorgini, Michele, *Immagini dell'Umbria tra '800 e '900: Terni* (Perugia: Guerra, 1995).

Mack Smith, Denis, *Italy: a Modern History* (Ann Arbor: University of Michigan Press, 1959).

—, *Mussolini* (London: Weidenfeld & Nicolson, 1981).

Wolfson, Robert, *Benito Mussolini and Fascist Italy* (London: Edward Arnold, 1984).

CHAPTER TEN: *Umbrian Painting and Painting in Umbria*

Baxandall, Michael, *Painting and Experience in Fifteenth-Century Italy* (1982; repr. Oxford: Oxford University Press, 1982).

Beck, James, *Italian Renaissance Painting* (New York: Harper & Row, 1981).

Bertelli, Carlo, Briganti, Giuliano, and Giuliano, Antonio (eds.), *Storia dell'Arte Italiana*, 4 vols. (Milan: Electa, 1990).

Bertelli, Carlo, *Piero della Francesca*, trans. Edward Farrelly (1991; New Haven: Yale University Press, 1992).

Berti, Luciano, *Nel raggio di Piero: la pittura nell'Italia centrale nell'età di Piero della Francesca* (Venice: Marsilio, 1992).

Bonomi, Giorgio (ed.), *La Collezione Burri: arte contemporanea e scuola* (Perugia: GESP, 1995).

Ginzburg, Carlo, *The Enigma of Piero*, trans. Martin Ryle and Kate Soper (1981; repr. London: Verso, 1985).

Hale, J. R. (ed.), *Concise Encyclopaedia of the Italian Renaissance* (London: Thames & Hudson, 1981).

Hall, James, *Dictionary of Subjects and Symbols in Art* (1974; rev. edn, London: John Murray, 1979).

Hartt, Frederick, *History of Italian Renaissance Art* (London: Thames & Hudson, 1970).

Levey, Michael, *Early Renaissance* (Harmondsworth: Penguin, 1967).

Mancini, Francesco Federico, *Benedetto Bonfigli: l'opera completa* (Milan: Electa, 1992).

Murray, Peter, and Murray, Linda, *The Art of the Renaissance* (London: Thames & Hudson, 1963).

Scarpellini, Pietro, *Perugino: l'opera completa* (1984; 2nd edn, Milan: Electa, 1991).

Todini, Filippo, *La pittura umbra dal Duecento al primo Cinquecento* (Milan: Longanesi, 1989).

Vasari, Giorgio, *Lives of the Most Eminent Painters, Sculptors and Architects*, trans. G. du C. De Vere, 10 vols. (London, 1912–15).

—, *Lives of the Artists: A Selection*, trans. George Bull (1965; repr. Harmondsworth: Penguin, 1988).

White, John, *Art and Architecture in Italy 1250–1400* (1966; 3rd edn, New Haven: Yale University Press, 1993), esp. Chs. 12–13 and 25–27.

CHAPTER ELEVEN: *Food and Wine*

Apicius, *De Re Coquinaria/La cucina dell'antica Roma*, ed. Clotilde Vesco (1990; repr. Rome: Tascabili Economici Newton, 1994).

—, *Apicius: Cookery and Dining in Imperial Rome*, trans. Joseph Domners Vehling (New York: Dover and London: Constable, 1977).

★

Anderson, Burton, *Burton Anderson's Guide to the Wines of Italy* (London: Mitchell Beazley, 1992).

—, *Pleasures of the Italian Table* (London: Viking, 1994).

—, *Vino: The Wines and Winemakers of Italy* (London: Macmillan, 1980).

—, *The Wine Atlas of Italy* (London: Mitchell Beazley, 1990).

Boini, Rita, *La cucina umbra: sapori di un tempo* (Perugia: Calzetti-Mariucci, 1995).

Corsi, Guglielma, *Un secolo di cucina umbra* (4th edn; Santa Maria degli Angeli: Porziuncola, 1976).

Dallas, Philip, *Italian Wines* (3rd edn London: Faber, 1989).

David, Elizabeth, *Italian Food* (1963; repr. Harmondsworth: Penguin, 1977 and London: Barrie & Jenkins, 1987).

Grassetti, Carlo, and Breschi, Annalisa, *La cucina umbra* ([Perugia], [n.d.]).

Hazan, Victor, *Italian Wine* (1982; repr. Harmondsworth: Penguin, 1984).

Mariotti, Flavia Cerasa, *Cosa mangiavi nonna? tradizioni ed usi della cucina perugina* ([Perugia], [n.d.]).

Ray, Cyril, *The New Book of Italian Wines* (London: Sidgwick & Jackson, 1982).

Santolini, Antonella, *La cucina delle regioni d'Italia: Umbria* (Bologna: Mida, 1989) [with English translation].

Index

✳